Exploring the Illusion of Free Will and Moral Responsibility

Exploring the Illusion of Free Will and Moral Responsibility

Edited by Gregg D. Caruso

LEXINGTON BOOKS
Lanham • Boulder • New York • Toronto • Plymouth, UK

Published by Lexington Books
A wholly owned subsidiary of The Rowman & Littlefield Publishing Group, Inc.
4501 Forbes Boulevard, Suite 200, Lanham, Maryland 20706
www.rowman.com

10 Thornbury Road, Plymouth PL6 7PP, United Kingdom

Copyright © 2013 by Lexington Books

All rights reserved. No part of this book may be reproduced in any form or by any electronic or mechanical means, including information storage and retrieval systems, without written permission from the publisher, except by a reviewer who may quote passages in a review.

British Library Cataloguing in Publication Information Available

Library of Congress Cataloging-in-Publication Data
Caruso, Gregg D.
Exploring the illusion of free will and moral responsibility / Gregg D. Caruso.
p. cm.
Includes bibliographical references and index.
ISBN 978-0-7391-7731-0 (cloth : alk. paper) — ISBN 978-0-7391-7732-7 (electronic)
1. Free will and determinism. 2. Ethics. 3. Skepticism. I. Title.
BJ1461.C365 2013
123'.5—dc23
　　　　　　　　　　　　　　　　　　　　　　　　　　　　　　　　　2013010677
ISBN 978-1-4985-1621-1 (pbk:alk, paper)

∞™ The paper used in this publication meets the minimum requirements of American National Standard for Information Sciences Permanence of Paper for Printed Library Materials, ANSI/NISO Z39.48-1992.

Printed in the United States of America

Contents

Acknowledgments   vii

Introduction: Exploring the Illusion of Free Will and Moral Responsibility   1
Gregg D. Caruso

I: Philosophical Explorations: Free Will Skepticism and Its Implications   **17**

1. Skepticism about Free Will   19
   Derk Pereboom

2. The Impossibility of Ultimate Responsibility?   41
   Galen Strawson

3. Determinism, Incompatibilism and Compatibilism, Actual Consciousness and Subjective Physical Worlds, Humanity   53
   Ted Honderich

4. The Stubborn Illusion of Moral Responsibility   65
   Bruce Waller

5. Be a Skeptic, Not a Metaskeptic   87
   Neil Levy

6. Free Will as a Case of "Crazy Ethics"   103
   Saul Smilansky

7. The Potential Dark Side of Believing in Free Will (and Related Concepts): Some Preliminary Findings   121
   Thomas Nadelhoffer and Daniela Goya Tocchetto

8. The People Problem   141
   Benjamin Vilhauer

9 Living Without Free Will *Susan Blackmore*	161
10 If Free Will Doesn't Exist, Neither Does Water *Manuel Vargas*	177
11 Free Will and Error *Shaun Nichols*	203

II: Scientific Explorations: The Behavioral, Cognitive, and Neurosciences — **219**

12 The Complex Network of Intentions *John-Dylan Haynes and Michael Pauen*	221
13 Experience and Autonomy: Why Consciousness Does and Doesn't Matter *Thomas W. Clark*	239
14 What Does the Brain Know and When Does It Know It? *Mark Hallett*	255
15 If Free Will Did Not Exist, It Would Be Necessary to Invent It *Susan Pockett*	265
16 Free Will, an Illusion?: An Answer from a Pragmatic Sentimentalist Point of View *Maureen Sie*	273
References	291
Index	311
About the Contributors	321

Acknowledgments

This volume contains all original essays specially written for this collection with the exception of Galen Strawson's "The Impossibility of Ultimate Responsibility?" which was first published in *Free Will and Modern Science*, edited by Richard Swinburne (London: British Academy, 2011). It is reprinted here with the permission of the author and the British Academy. I would like to thank all of the contributors for their participation and hard work: Susan Blackmore, Thomas W. Clark, Mark Hallett, John-Dylan Haynes, Ted Honderich, Neil Levy, Thomas Nadelhoffer, Shaun Nichols, Michael Pauen, Derk Pereboom, Susan Pockett, Maureen Sie, Saul Smilansky, Galen Strawson, Daniela Goya Tocchetto, Manuel Vargas, Benjamin Vilhauer, and Bruce Waller. I would also like to thank Corning Community College for granting a sabbatical to work on this project as well as the encouragement I received from the following friends and family members: Liz Vlahos, Robert Talisse, Rob Tempio, David Rosenthal, Michael Levin, Josh Weisberg, Christine Atkins, Andrea Harris, James Cruz, John Celentano, the Hathaway family, Louis and Dolores Caruso, my brothers, brothers-in-law, their families, and George and Marina Kokkinos.

Lastly, I would like to thank my wife, Elaini, and my daughter, Maya, for their never ending supply of love and support—I cannot thank you enough!

Introduction

Exploring the Illusion of Free Will and Moral Responsibility

Gregg D. Caruso

This book is aimed at readers who wish to explore the philosophical and scientific arguments for free will skepticism and their implications.[1] Skepticism about free will and moral responsibility has been on the rise in recent years. In fact, a significant number of philosophers, psychologists, and neuroscientists now either doubt or outright deny the existence of free will and/or moral responsibility—and the list of prominent skeptics appears to grow by the day.[2] Given the profound importance that the concepts of free will and moral responsibility play in our lives—in understanding ourselves, society, and the law—it is important that we explore what is behind this new wave of skepticism. It is also important that we explore the potential consequences of skepticism for ourselves and society. That is what this volume attempts to do. It brings together an internationally recognized line-up of contributors, most of whom hold skeptical positions of some sort, to display and explore the leading arguments for free will skepticism and to debate their implications.

FREE WILL SKEPTICISM AND ITS IMPLICATIONS

Contemporary theories of free will tend to fall into one of two general categories, namely, those that insist on and those that are skeptical about the reality of human freedom and moral responsibility.[3] The former category includes *libertarian* and *compatibilist* accounts of free will, two general views that defend the reality of free will but disagree on its nature. The latter category includes a family of skeptical views that all take seriously the possibility that human beings do not have free will, and are therefore not morally responsible for their actions in a way that would make them *truly deserving* of blame and praise for them. The main dividing line between the two pro-free will positions, libertarianism and compatibilism, is best understood in terms of the traditional problem of free will and determinism. *Determinism*, as it is commonly understood, is roughly the thesis that every event or action, including human action, is the inevitable result of preceding events and actions and the laws of nature.[4] The problem of free will and determinism therefore comes in trying to reconcile our intuitive sense of free will with the idea that our choices and actions may be causally determined by impersonal forces over which we have no ultimate control.

Libertarians and compatibilists react to this problem in different ways. Libertarians acknowledge that if determinism is true, and all of our actions are causally necessitated by antecedent circumstances, we lack free will and moral responsibility. Yet they further maintain that at least some of our choices and actions must be free in the sense that they are not causally determined. Libertarians therefore reject determinism and defend a counter-causal conception of free will in order to save what they believe are necessary conditions for free will—i.e., the *ability to do otherwise* in exactly the same set of conditions and the idea that we remain, in some important sense, the *ultimate source/originator* of action. Compatibilists, on the other hand, set out to defend a less ambitious form of free will, one which can be reconciled with the acceptance of determinism. They hold that what is of utmost importance is not the falsity of determinism, nor that our actions are uncaused, but that our actions are voluntary, free from constraint and compulsion, and caused in the appropriate way. Different compatibilist accounts spell out the exact requirements for compatibilist freedom differently but popular theories tend to focus on such things as reasons-responsiveness, guidance control, hierarchical integration, and approval of one's motivational states.[5]

In contrast to these pro-free will positions are those views that either doubt or outright deny the existence of free will and/or moral responsibility. Such views are often referred to as skeptical views, or simply *free will skepticism*, and are the focus of this collection. In the past, the standard argument for skepticism was *hard determinism*: the view that determinism is true, and incompatible with free will and moral responsibility—either because it precludes the *ability to do otherwise* (leeway incompatibilism) or because it is inconsistent with one's being the "ultimate source" of action (source incompatibilism)—hence, no free will. For hard determinists, libertarian free will is an impossibility because human actions are part of a fully deterministic world and compatibilism is operating in bad faith.

Hard determinism had its classic statement in the time when Newtonian physics reigned (see, e.g., d'Holbach 1770), but it has very few defenders today—largely because the standard interpretation of quantum mechanics has been taken by many to undermine, or at least throw into doubt, the thesis of universal determinism. This is not to say that determinism has been refuted or falsified by modern physics, because it has not. Determinism still has its modern defenders, most notably Ted Honderich (1988, 2002), and the final interpretation of physics is not yet in. It is also important to keep in mind that even if we allow some indeterminacy to exist at the microlevel of our existence—the level studied by quantum mechanics—there would still likely remain *determinism-where-it-matters* (Honderich 2002, 5). As Honderich argues: "At the ordinary level of choices and actions, and even ordinary electrochemical activity in our brains, causal laws govern what happens. It's all cause and effect in what you might call real life" (2002, 5). Nonetheless, most contemporary skeptics defend positions that are best seen as successors to traditional hard determinism.

In recent years, for example, several contemporary philosophers have offered arguments for free will skepticism, and/or skepticism about moral responsibility, that are agnostic about determinism—e.g., Derk Pereboom (2001), Galen Strawson (1986/2010), Saul Smilansky (2000), Neil Levy (2011), Richard Double (1991), Bruce Waller (2011), and Gregg Caruso (2012).[6] Most maintain that while determinism is incompatible with free will and moral responsibility, so too is *indeterminism*, especially the variety posited by quantum mechanics. Others argue that regardless of the causal structure of the universe, we lack free will and moral responsibility because free will is incompatible with the pervasiveness of *luck* (Levy 2011). Others (still) argue that free will and ultimate moral responsibility are incoherent concepts, since to be free in the sense required for ultimate moral responsibly we would have to be *causa sui* (or "cause of oneself") and this is impossible (see Strawson ch.2). Here, for example, is Nietzsche on the *causa sui*:

> The *causa sui* is the best self-contradiction that has been conceived so far; it is a sort of rape and perversion of logic. But the extravagant pride of man has managed to entangle itself profoundly and frightfully with just this nonsense. The desire for "freedom of the will" in the superlative metaphysical sense, which still holds sway, unfortunately, in the minds of the half-educated; the desire to bear the entire and ultimate responsibility for one's actions oneself, and to absolve God, the world, ancestors, chance, and society involves nothing less than to be precisely this *causa sui* and, with more than Baron Munchhausen's audacity, to pull oneself up into existence by the hair, out of the swamps of nothingness. (1992, 218-19)[7]

What all these skeptical arguments have in common, and what they share with classical hard determinism, is the belief that what we do, and the way we are, is ultimately the result of factors beyond our control and because of this we are never morally responsible for our actions in the basic desert sense—the sense that would make us *truly deserving* of blame or praise.[8] This is not to say that there are not other conceptions of responsibility that can be reconciled with determinism, chance, or luck. Nor is it to deny that there may be good pragmatic reasons to maintain certain systems of punishment and reward. Rather, it is to insist that to hold people *truly* or *ultimately* morally responsible for their actions—i.e., to hold them responsible in a non-consequentialist desert-based sense—would be to hold them responsible for the results of the morally arbitrary, for what is ultimately beyond their control, which is (according to these views) fundamentally unfair and unjust.

In addition to these philosophical arguments, there have also been recent developments in the behavioral, cognitive, and neurosciences that have caused many to take free will skepticism seriously. Chief among them have been the neuroscientific discovery that unconscious brain activity causally initiates action prior to the conscious awareness of the intention to act (e.g., Benjamin Libet, John-Dylan Haynes), Daniel Wegner's work on the double disassociation of the experience of conscious will, and recent findings in psychology and social psychology on *automaticity, situationism,* and the *adaptive unconscious* (e.g., John Bargh, Timothy Wilson).[9] Viewed collectively, these developments indicate that much of what we do takes place at an automatic and unaware level and that our commonsense belief that we consciously initiate and control action may be mistaken. They also indicate that the causes that move us are often less transparent to ourselves than we might assume—diverging in many cases from the conscious reasons we provide to explain and/or justify our actions. These findings reveal that the higher mental processes that have traditionally served as quintessential examples of "free will"—such as goal pursuits, evaluation and judgment, reasoning and problem solving, interpersonal behavior, and action initiation and control—can and often do occur in the absence of conscious choice or guidance (Bargh and Ferguson 2000, 926). They also reveal just how wide open our internal psychological processes are to the influence of external stimuli and events in our immediate environment, without knowledge or awareness of such influence. For many these findings represent a serious threat to our everyday folk understanding of ourselves as conscious, rational, responsible agents, since they indicate that the conscious mind exercises less control over our behavior than we have traditionally assumed.

Even some compatibilists now admit that because of these behavioral, cognitive, and neuroscientific findings "free will is at best an occasional phenomenon" (Baumeister 2008b, 17; see also Nahmias forthcoming-a). This is an important concession because it acknowledges that the *threat of shrinking agency*—as Thomas Nadelhoffer (2011) calls it—remains a serious one independent of any traditional concerns over determinism. That is, *even if* one believes free will and causal determinism can be reconciled, the deflationary view of consciousness which emerges from these empirical findings must still be confronted, including the fact that we often lack transparent awareness of our true motivational states. Such a deflationary view of consciousness is potentially agency undermining (see, e.g., Nadelhoffer 2011; King and Carruthers 2012; Caruso 2012; Sie and Wouters 2010; and Davies 2009) and must be dealt with independent of, and in addition to, the traditional compatibilist/incompatibilist debate.

In addition to these specific concerns over conscious volition and the threat of shrinking agency there is also the more general insight, more threatening to libertarianism than compatibilism, that as the brain sciences progress and we better understand the mechanisms that undergird human behavior, the more it becomes obvious that we lack what Tom Clark (ch.13) calls "soul control." There is no longer any reason to believe in a non-physical self which controls action and is liberated from the deterministic laws of nature; a little *uncaused causer* capable of exercising counter-causal free will. While most naturalistically inclined philosophers, including most compatibilists, have long given up on the idea of soul control, eliminating such thinking from our folk psychological attitudes may not be so easy and may come at a cost for some. There is some evidence, for example, that we are "natural born" dualists (Bloom 2004) and that, at least in the United States, a majority of adults continue to believe in a non-physical soul that governs behavior (Nadelhoffer in press). To whatever extent, then, such dualistic thinking is present in our folk psychological attitudes about free will and moral responsibility, it is likely to come under pressure and require some revision as the brain sciences advance and this information reaches the general public.[10]

What, then, would be the consequence of accepting free will skepticism? What if we came to disbelieve in free will and moral responsibility? What would this mean for ourselves? Our interpersonal relationships? Society? Morality? The law? What would it do to our standing as human beings? Would it cause nihilism and despair as some maintain? Or perhaps increase anti-social behavior as some recent studies have suggested (Vohs and Schooler 2008; Baumeister, Masicampo, and DeWall 2009)? Or would it rather have a humanizing effect on our practices and policies, freeing us from the negative effects of free will belief? These questions are of profound pragmatic importance and should be of interest independent of the metaphysical debate over free will. As public proclamations of skepticism continue to rise, and as the mass media continues to run headlines announcing "Free will is an illusion" and "Scientists say free will probably doesn't exist…,"[11] we need to ask what effects this will have on the general public and what the responsibility is of professionals.

In recent years a small industry has actually grown up around precisely these questions. In the skeptical community, for example, a number of different positions have been developed and advanced—including Saul Smilansky's *illusionism* (2000), Thomas Nadelhoffer's *disillusionism* (2011), Shaun Nichols' *anti-revolution* (2007), and the *optimistic skepticism* of Derk Pereboom (2001, 2013a), Bruce Waller (2011), Tamler Sommers (2005, 2007b), and others.

Saul Smilansky, for example, maintains that our commonplace beliefs in libertarian free will and desert-entailing ultimate moral responsibility are illusions,[12] but he also maintains that if people were to accept this truth there would be wide-reaching negative intrapersonal and interpersonal consequences. According to Smilansky, "Most people not only believe in actual possibilities and the ability to transcend circumstances, but have distinct and strong beliefs that libertarian free will is a condition for moral responsibility, which is in turn a condition for just reward and punishment" (2000, 26-27). It would be devastating, he warns, if we were to destroy such beliefs: "the difficulties caused by the absence of ultimate-level grounding are likely to be great, generating acute psychological discomfort for many people and threatening morality—if, that is, we do not have illusion at our disposal" (2000, 166). To avoid any deleterious social and personal consequences, then, and to prevent the unraveling of our moral fabric, Smilansky recommends *free will illusionism*. According to illusionism, people should be allowed their positive illusion of libertarian free will and with it ultimate moral responsibility; we should not take these away from people, and those of us who have already been disenchanted ought to simply keep the truth to ourselves (see also ch.6).

In direct contrast to Smilansky's illusionism, Thomas Nadelhoffer defends *free will disillusionism*: "the view that to the extent that folk intuitions and beliefs about the nature of human cognition and moral responsibility are mistaken, philosophers and psychologists ought to do their part to educate the public—especially when their mistaken beliefs arguably fuel a number of unhealthy emotions and attitudes such as revenge, hatred, intolerance, lack of empathy, etc." (2011, 184). According to Nadelhoffer, "humanity must get beyond this maladaptive suit of emotions if we are to survive." And he adds, "To the extent that future developments in the sciences of the mind can bring us one step closer to that goal—by giving us a newfound appreciation for the limits of human cognition and agency—I welcome them with open arms" (2011, 184).

A policy of disillusionism is also present in the optimistic skepticisms of Derk Pereboom, Bruce Waller, Tamler Sommers, and Susan Blackmore. Derk Pereboom, for example, has defended the view that morality, meaning, and value remain intact even if we are not morally responsible, and furthermore, that adopting this perspective could provide significant benefits for our lives. In *Living Without Free Will* (2001), he argues that life without free will and desert-based moral responsibility would not be as destructive as many people believe. Prospects of finding meaning in life or of sustaining good interpersonal relationships, for example, would not be threatened (2001, ch.7). And although retributivism and severe punishment, such as the death penalty, would be ruled out, preventive detention and rehabilitation programs would be justified (2001, ch.6). He even argues that relinquishing our belief in free will might well improve our well-being and our relationships to others since it would tend to eradicate an often destructive form of "moral anger."

Bruce Waller has also made a strong case for the benefits of a world without moral responsibility. In his recent book, *Against Moral Responsibility* (2011), he cites many instances in which moral responsibility practices are counterproductive from a practical and humanitarian standpoint—notably in how they stifle personal development, encourage punitive excess in criminal justice, and perpetuate social and economic inequalities (see Clark 2012 review). Waller suggests that if we abandon moral responsibility "we can look more clearly at the causes and more deeply into the systems that shape individuals and their behavior" (2011, 287), and this will allow us to adopt more humane and effective interpersonal attitudes and approaches to education, criminal justice, and social policy. He maintains that in the absence of moral responsibility, "it is possible to look more deeply at the influences of social systems and situations" (2011, 286), to minimize the patent unfairness that luck deals out in life, and to "move beyond [the harmful effects of] blame and shame" (2011, 287).[13]

In contrast to all these views are those philosophers who argue that as a purely descriptive matter our lives would remain relatively unchanged, not getting better *or* worse, if we were to accept a skeptical or hard determinist perspective. Shaun Nichols, for example, has argued that "people will pretty much stick with the status quo" (2007, 406) when it comes to their everyday interactions and the *reactive attitudes* (P.F. Strawson 1962). He writes, for example: "If people come to accept determinism, what will happen? Opinions on this question differ radically. Some maintain that this would usher in a badly needed revolution in our practices. Others worry that the recognition of determinism would lead to catastrophe. I have a more humdrum guess—if people come to accept determinism, things will remain pretty much the same" (2007, 406). While this is not a defense of free will or compatibilism—for Nichols assumes incompatibilism is intuitive (2007, 405)—it is an interesting descriptive thesis, one which is at odds with the above positions.[14]

Who then is correct? What would the actual consequences of embracing skepticism be? What *should* they be? *Should* we reconsider our attitudes and policies in light of the philosophical and scientific arguments for free will skepticism? These remain important questions, as does the central question: Is skepticism about free will and moral responsibility justified on either philosophical and/or scientific grounds? Hopefully this collection will aid readers in thinking through these questions, as well as a variety of other issues surrounding free will skepticism and its implications.

CONTRIBUTIONS

The sixteen chapters to follow are divided into two main parts. Part I explores the philosophical arguments for free will skepticism and their implications (along with some related issues), while Part II explores recent developments in the behavioral, cognitive, and neurosciences and what they mean for human agency, free will, and moral responsibility.

In chapter 1, Derk Pereboom presents his argument for free will skepticism known as *hard incompatibilism*. Against the view that free will is compatible with the causal determination of our actions by natural factors beyond our control, he argues that there is no relevant difference between this prospect and our actions being causally determined by manipulators. Against event causal libertarianism, he advances the disappearing agent objection, according to which on this view the agent cannot settle whether a decision occurs, and hence cannot have the control required for moral responsibility. According to Pereboom, a non-causal libertarianism has no plausible proposal of the control in action required for responsibility. He goes on to argue that while agent causal libertarianism may supply this sort of control, it cannot be reconciled with our best physical theories. Since this exhausts the options for views on which we have the sort of free will at issue, he concludes that free will skepticism is the only remaining position. Finally, Pereboom defends the optimistic view that conceiving of life without free will would not be devastating to our conceptions of agency, morality, and meaning in life, and in certain respects it may even be beneficial.

In chapter 2, Galen Strawson recasts his now famous *Basic Argument* against the possibility of ultimate moral responsibility. He argues that we are not truly or ultimately morally responsible for our actions because we are not *causa sui*. The central idea behind the Basic Argument is that: (1) Nothing can be *causa sui*—nothing can be the cause of itself; (2) In order to be truly or ultimately morally responsible for one's actions one would have to be *causa sui*, at least in certain crucial mental respects; (3) Therefore no one can be truly or ultimately morally responsible. Strawson presents several restatements of the Basic Argument along the way, fleshing it out in more detail. He also argues that the Basic Argument cannot simply be dismissed because the idea that we are *causa sui* is a common one and is central to our understanding of ultimate moral responsibility. He concludes by considering possible compatibilist and libertarian responses to the Basic Argument.

In chapter 3, Ted Honderich defends the theory of determinism and explores its consequences. He argues that if we are good empiricists we should accept determinism as true or at least probable—"there ought not be any [reflective empiricists] who are not also determinists." He also argues that quantum mechanics has not falsified determinism. In fact, the standard interpretation of quantum mechanics, he argues, is a "logical mess" and contains "contradiction" in it. He goes on to explore the consequences of determinism for our lives and for free will. He argues that both compatibilist and incompatibilist approaches fail to adequately deal with the problem of determinism because they both share the mistaken assumption that there is only one conception of free will. Honderich instead argues that there are actually two conceptions of free will—free will as *voluntariness* and as *origination*. While the former is compatible with determinism, the latter is not. Honderich acknowledges, however, that the truth of determinism and the loss of origination create concerns for our "standing" as human beings. In an attempt to preserve some of what is lost when we give up the idea of origination and the responsibility attached to it, Honderich introduces his theory of *actual consciousness*. After briefly sketching how actual consciousness could leave us content despite the loss attendant on giving up origination, Honderich concludes with his "grand hope" for humanity which involves abandoning the "politics of desert" and embracing the Principle of Humanity.

In chapter 4, Bruce Waller explores "The Stubborn Illusion of Moral Responsibility." He begins by pointing out that there is a strange disconnect between the strength of philosophical arguments in support of moral responsibility and the strength of philosophical belief in moral responsibility. While the many arguments in favor of moral responsibility are inventive, subtle, and fascinating, Waller points out that even the most ardent supporters of moral responsibility acknowledge that the arguments in its favor are far from conclusive; and some of the least confident concerning the arguments for moral responsibility—such as Van Inwagen—are most confident of the truth of moral responsibility. Thus, argues Waller, whatever the verdict on the strength of philosophical arguments for moral responsibility, it is clear that belief in moral responsibility—whether among philosophers or the folk—is based on something other than philosophical reasons. He goes on to argue that there are several sources for the strong belief in moral responsibility, but three are particularly influential. First, moral responsibility is based in a powerful "strike back" emotion that we share with other animals. Second, there is a pervasive moral responsibility *system*—extending over criminal justice as well as "common sense"—that makes the truth of moral responsibility seem obvious, and makes challenges to moral responsibility seem incoherent. Finally, there is a deep-rooted "belief in a just world"—a belief that, according to Waller, most philosophers reject when they consciously consider it, but which has a deep nonconscious influence on what we regard as just treatment and which provides subtle (but mistaken) support for belief in moral responsibility.

In chapter 5, Neil Levy argues that we should be skeptics, not metaskeptics about moral responsibility. In the past, Levy has argued that agents are never morally responsible for their actions because free will and moral responsibility are undermined by luck (2011). In this chapter, he defends his skepticism from a recent challenge presented by Tamler Sommers' metaskepticism. Sommers (2012) denies that there are necessary and sufficient conditions of moral responsibility; instead, he claims, the conditions of moral responsibility vary from culture to culture. Levy admits that if this claim is correct, then no first-order view of moral responsibility, including responsibility skepticism, is true. But, he argues, there are moral reasons to favor skepticism over metaskepticism. Further, he argues that metaskepticism threatens either to collapse into normative nihilism or into first-order skepticism.

In chapter 6, Saul Smilansky introduces the term "crazy ethics" (or CE), which he uses in a semi-descriptive and non-pejorative way to refer to some views that we ourselves hold, or that we think might be true. He claims that some true ethical views are, in this interesting sense, crazy. An ethical view might be considered crazy if it clearly could not serve as a basis for social life. A society that tried to function in the light of such a view would quickly fail. Similarly, an ethical view might be considered crazy if it is self-defeating, so that attempting to implement it would make things worse, in terms of that very view. A view that would be considered far too demanding and thus would be overwhelmingly rejected would also earn the label "crazy"; as would a view that flies in the teeth of fundamental reflective moral beliefs. And an ethical view that needs to be kept apart from the vast majority of the people to whom it applies, an "esoteric morality," also involves craziness. After explicating what makes such views crazy, Smilansky explores the free will problem and attempts to show why viewing it as a case of CE is fruitful. He argues that many of the prevailing positions in the debate are "crazy" in this sense, as are the views he himself holds to be most plausible. He concludes by reflecting on what this means, particularly for morality, personal and social integrity, and the role of philosophy.

In chapter 7, Thomas Nadelhoffer and Daniela Goya Tocchetto explore the potential dark side of believing in free will. They survey some recent findings from moral and political psychology on the possible dark side of believing in free will (and related concepts), as well as report on two exploratory studies of their own, in order to shed some empirical light on the illusionism debate—i.e., the debate over whether we should counsel illusionism (e.g., Smilansky) or disillusionism (e.g., Nadelhoffer). They begin by briefly discussing two of the most recently developed psychometric tools for measuring people's agentic beliefs—namely, the Free Will and Determinism

Scale (FAD-Plus) (Paulhus and Carey 2011) and the Free Will Inventory (FWI) (Nadelhoffer et al. in prep.)—and they explore some of the interesting (and sometimes surprising) correlations that have been found between people's free will beliefs and their other moral, religious, and political beliefs. They then present and discuss the results of two exploratory studies they conducted to further explore the moral and political psychology of believing in free will. Finally, they attempt to lay the groundwork for future research. They conclude that there is a lot of psychological spadework and philosophical analysis that remains to be done before we can better understand the psychological and social consequences of widespread skepticism about free will.

In chapter 8, Benjamin Vilhauer tackles the "People Problem." He points out that one reason many philosophers are reluctant to seriously contemplate the possibility that we lack free will seems to be the view that we must believe we have free will if we are to regard each other as *persons* in the morally deep sense—the sense that involves deontological notions such as human rights. In the literature of the past few decades, this view is often informed by P.F. Strawson's view that to treat human beings as having free will is to respond to them with the reactive attitudes, and that if we suspend the reactive attitudes we can only regard human beings as objects to be manipulated in the service of social goals. This purported implication of suspending the reactive attitudes has persuaded many philosophers that we cannot truly treat human beings as persons without assuming that they have free will. Vilhauer argues that this line of thinking is misguided. He agrees with Strawson's worry that the consequentialism he sees as implicit in the objective attitude could undermine our ability to treat each other as persons, but he argues that it is a mistake to think that we must maintain the reactive attitudes, or any other attributions of free will or moral responsibility, to avoid a depersonalizing slide into consequentialism. He maintains that Kant's idea of treating people as autonomous ends in themselves, rather than as mere means to ends, provides a compelling analysis of what it means to treat humans as persons, and that there are ways of interpreting Kant's idea which do not involve reactive attitudes or any other attributions of free will or moral responsibility.

In chapter 9, Susan Blackmore defends optimistic skepticism and explores what it is like "Living Without Free Will." She explains how she came to view free will as an illusion and how she has learned to live without it. She expresses amazement at the many scientists and philosophers who do not believe there is free will but say they still have to live "as if" there is—including several she interviewed for her book *Conversations on Consciousness* (2005). Among the reasons for this contradictory attitude, she speculates, may be fear of letting go of control, fear of losing moral responsibility or acting badly, and fear that society would be impossible or law and order would break down if we all gave up the illusion. While she can appreciate these fears, she does not share them. She credits science and her thirty years of Zen practice with liberating her from the delusion of free will, and she concludes that living without free will is not only possible but preferable to sticking with the delusion.

In chapter 10, Manuel Vargas questions whether free will skepticism of the varieties usually embraced by scientists are hasty. He begins by arguing that there are three difficulties for such accounts. First, despite frequent appeals to determinism in the work of scientists, it is unclear that determinism is more than a theoretical aspiration in many scientific fields. Second, scientific skeptics too quickly dismiss compatibilist approaches as definitional gambits, rather than as serious accounts that have to be addressed before skepticism carries the day. Third, the powers that are at stake may be high-level, multiply realizable phenomena that resist reduction to the properties that figure in many forms of scientific skepticism. Yet while disputing many of the usual grounds for free will skepticism, Vargas also allows that there are a variety of conceptual and empirical reasons for doubt that we have the powers we ordinarily suppose. Nevertheless, he goes on to articulate an account of how such doubts do not entail the nonexistence of free will. It remains open, he argues, to adopt a revisionist position, where free will is not precisely what ordinary people (or free will skeptics) think it is. On such a view, scientific discoveries about the shape of our agency are not typically reasons for rejecting free will, but rather the basis for better understanding the diverse forms of our freedom and agency.

In the final chapter of Part I, Shaun Nichols explores the connection between free will and error. He maintains that like other eliminativist arguments in philosophy, arguments that free will is an illusion seem to depend on substantive assumptions about reference. According to free will eliminativists, people have deeply mistaken beliefs about free will and this entails that free will doesn't exist (e.g., Pereboom, Strawson). However, an alternative reaction is that free will does exist, we just have some deeply mistaken beliefs about it (e.g., Vargas). Here Nichols adopts the view that reference is systematically ambiguous. In some contexts, he argues, it is appropriate to take a restrictive view about whether a term embedded in a false theory refers; in other contexts, it's appropriate to take a liberal view about whether a token of the very same term refers. This affords the possibility of saying that the sentence "free will exists" is false in some contexts and true in others. This in turn affords a flexibility in whether we embrace the eliminativist claim. He concludes by arguing that in the case of free will there are practical considerations for and against eliminativism, and that the right conclusion might be a *discretionary* (in)compatibilism.

In Part II attention shifts to recent developments in the behavioral, cognitive, and neurosciences. It begins, in chapter 12, with neuroscientist John-

Dylan Haynes and philosopher Michael Pauen questioning whether intentionality is just an illusion. Intentionality is among those features that make humans special. According to many philosophers, intentions are of specific importance when it comes to the difference between mere behavior (stumbling, coughing) and goal-directed action (writing, problem-solving). Recent psychological and neuroscientific evidence, however, has been interpreted as putting the existence of intentions into question. Haynes and Pauen review this evidence and discuss the consequences that it has for our understanding of intentions. They conclude that intentions might well play a role in human action and decision making but that this role differs significantly from what commonsense as well as standard philosophical and folk psychological accounts of intentionality assume.

In chapter 13, Thomas Clark further explores the psychological and neuroscientific evidence and its relationship to consciousness, experience, and autonomy. He maintains that human freedom, responsibility, and autonomy have traditionally been linked to or even identified with conscious control of behavior, where consciousness is widely understood as possibly nonidentical with its neural correlates. But the rise of neuroscience strongly suggests that brain processes alone are sufficient for behavior control, and indeed nothing non-physical plays a role in scientific explanations of behavior. Clark addresses three worries that arise in response to investigations of consciousness: the philosophical worry about mental causation; the practical worry about the influence of unconscious processes; and the existential worry that, absent a contra-causal conscious controller, we lack freedom, responsibility, and autonomy. These worries can be defused, Clark argues, by: (1) acknowledging the causal powers of brain-based conscious capacities, those associated with (but perhaps not identical to) conscious experience; (2) expanding the reach of conscious capacities by understanding their limitations; and (3) naturalizing our conceptions of freedom and autonomy. On Clark's account, we need to move beyond the idea of "soul control" to a suitably naturalized understanding of autonomy, one that allows us to hold agents responsible—"at least in the consequentialist sense of being answerable to a moral community."

In chapter 14, neurologist and clinical neurophysiologist Mark Hallett asks "What does the brain know and when does it know it?" He begins his chapter with a brief review of what free will means, and he tries to eliminate any distinction between mind and brain which continues to muddle thinking about the subject. He then turns his attention toward the *qualia* that compose the sense of free will, that of *volition* itself and that of *agency*. The physiology of the qualia of volition and agency are then discussed with a focus on their timing. Hallett explains the neuroscientific findings of Libet et al. (1983), Soon et al. (2008), Lau et al. (2007), as well as findings of his own, and he questions whether volition can be a factor in movement decision or initiation. He concludes that "by timing arguments alone, it does not appear that the consciousness of willing has any influence, since it comes relatively late in the movement generation process." Hallett concludes his chapter by considering the implications of this physiology for responsibility.

In chapter 15, Susan Pockett argues that "If free will did not exist, it would be necessary to invent it." She launches her essay from the cosmologically narcissistic position that it would be a bad thing if the human race destroyed itself, an outcome which is increasingly possible in a technological sense. She argues that ideas matter, and that the concepts of free will and moral responsibility are the most useful tools we have for prevention of such a disaster. Thus, although it may be perfectly acceptable in an intellectual sense to conclude that free will and moral responsibility are merely illusions, teleologically such a conclusion is undesirable to the point of being dangerous. She then goes on to examine two major lines of evidence for the illusory nature of free will. The first line is that neuroscientific experiments show voluntary acts to be neither initiated nor controlled by consciousness. After a brief methodological discussion of the original and still most widely cited experiment of this group, she accepts the conclusion that actions are initiated unconsciously, but argues that free will does not have to involve the conscious initiation of actions. The second major argument for the illusory nature of at least incompatibilist free will is that the success of Western science proves the truth of determinism. She argues that this is not the case: determinism is not a proven fact and very possibly never can be. She therefore concludes that a version of incompatibilist free will which does not require conscious initiation of actions is not necessarily an illusion, and that reports of its death are greatly exaggerated.

In the final chapter, Maureen Sie investigates whether findings in the behavioral, cognitive, and neurosciences are relevant to the concept of free will when that concept is approached, not from a "metaphysical" perspective, but from a different angle—what she labels the *pragmatic sentimentalist* approach (PS-approach). Contrary to the metaphysical approach, the PS-approach does not understand free will as a concept that somehow precedes our moral practices. Rather it is assumed that everyday talk of free will naturally arises in a practice that is characterized by certain reactive attitudes that we take towards one another. First, she explains the social function of moral responsibility that is at the core of the PS-approach. Secondly, she explains how the exchange of reasons central to that social function give rise to a so-called space of reasons. Finally, she examines the scientific findings of recent decades, especially those in psychology and social psychology, that are most relevant to free will understood from the PS-approach. She concentrates on those findings that show that we (1) lack agential transparency, i.e., immediate and infallible introspective access to the motivational origin of our actions and that, as a result, (2) we are sometimes "mistaken" in our understanding of our own actions. She concludes that "this body of research should lead to serious reconsideration of the occasions on which we claim, e.g., 'to act on the basis of reasons and out of our own free will . . .'" She also concludes, however, that given the social function of moral responsibility ascriptions and the role of the concept of free will, the claim that it is an illusion makes no sense from the PS-approach.

NOTES

1. I am very grateful to Bruce Waller and Benjamin Vilhauer for helpful comments on earlier drafts of this introduction.

2. For an impressive list of scientists who have recently proclaimed skeptical positions, see Snyder (2012). Also helpful in tracking the rise of free will skepticism is the website run by George Ortega: www.causalconsciousness.com.

3. Most contemporary philosophers argue that *free will* and *moral responsibility* stand or fall together. Exceptions include John Martin Fischer (1994) and Bruce Waller (2011), but such views remain controversial. In fact, much of the philosophical tradition has simply defined "free will" as "a kind of power or ability to make decisions of the sort for which one can be morally responsible" (Fischer, Kane, Pereboom, and Vargas 2007, 1).

4. Traditional scientific determinism maintains that the state of the universe at any given time is wholly and unequivocally determined by the state of the universe at prior times and the laws of nature. Such determinism is sometimes illustrated by the thought experiment of *Laplace's demon*—an all-knowing intellect that given knowledge of all past and present facts, and the laws of nature, would be able to foresee the future down to the smallest detail. This idea was first given expression by the French mathematician and scientist Pierre Simon Laplace: "We may regard the present state of the universe as the effect of its past and the cause of its future. An intellect which at a certain moment would know all forces that set nature in motion, and all positions of all items of which nature is composed, if this intellect were also vast enough to submit these data to analysis, it would embrace in a single formula the movements of the greatest bodies of the universe and those of the tiniest atom; for such an intellect nothing would be uncertain and the future just like the past would be present before its eyes" (1814, 4). Although this conception of determinism represents the traditional way of understanding the contemporary problem of free will and determinism, there have been other related and historically important threats. For example, divine foreknowledge or theological determinism has, for many, posed as much a threat to free will as natural laws. As Robert Kane writes: "Many theologians through the centuries have believed that God's power, omniscience, and providence would be unacceptably compromised if one did not affirm that all events in the universe, including human choices and actions, were foreordained and foreknown by God. But many other theologians argued, with equal force, that if God did in fact foreordain or foreknow all human choices and actions, then no one could have chosen or acted differently, making it hard to see how humans could have ultimate control over their actions in a manner that would justify divine rewards and punishments. In such cases, the ultimate responsibility for good and evil deeds, and hence responsibility for evil, would devolve to God—an unacceptable consequence for traditional theists" (2002, 35).

5. Another position similar to compatibilism but not mentioned here is *semi-compatibilism*. Semi-compatibilists maintain that moral responsibility is compatible with determinism but remain agnostic about whether free will is (see, for example, Fischer 1994; Fischer and Ravizza 1998).

6. Bruce Waller maintains a skepticism of moral responsibility but not free will (see 2011 for details). Saul Smilansky's position is also hard to place. While Smilansky maintains a skepticism about our purportedly commonplace belief in libertarian free will, and endorses the difficult insights of a hard determinist perspective, he also maintains that compatibilism retains some truth (see 2000; fn.12 below; and ch.6). Other recent books that advance skeptical posi-

tions, but are mainly written for a general public, include Harris (2012), Oerton (2012), Evatt (2010), and Pearce (2010).

7. As quoted by Sommers (2007a, 61) and Strawson (ch.2).

8. Some skeptics, however, such as Benjamin Vilhauer (forthcoming), maintain an asymmetry in the justification of praising and blaming behavior according to which harmless praise can be justified in certain contexts but not blame.

9. See, for example, Libet et al. (1983); Libet (1985, 1999); Soon et al. (2008); Wegner (2002); Wegner and Wheatley (1999); Bargh (1997, 2008); Bargh and Chartrand (1999); Bargh and Ferguson (2000); Wilson (2002); Nisbett and Wilson (1977); Doris (2002). The literature on *Social Intuitionism* (e.g., Haidt 2001) is also sometimes cited in this regard—see Sie (ch.16) for a brief discussion of its possible relevance. And for those unfamiliar with Wegner's work, my reference here to the "double disassociation of the experience of conscious will" is to Wegner's finding that the feeling of having willed an action can be doubly dissociated from actually having caused an action—that is, someone can experience themselves as having caused an action that they actually have not caused (e.g., I-Spy experiment), just as someone can think they have not caused an action that they actually have caused (e.g., alien hand syndrome, automatisms) (see Wegner 2002; Wegner and Wheatley 1999).

10. Predicting what revisions will be made is difficult. It's possible that relinquishing the folk psychological idea of "soul control" will cause some to accept free will skepticism. But it's also possible that some might adopt a *free-will-either-way* strategy causing them to accept compatibilism on pragmatic grounds, fearing the alternative.

11. *The Chronicle Review* (March 23, 2012) and *Scientific American* (April 6, 2010) respectively.

12. Smilansky's *Fundamental Dualism*, however, also acknowledges that certain compatibilist insights are true. As Smilansky describes his position: "I agree with hard determinists that the absence of libertarian free will is a grave matter, which ought radically to change our understanding of ourselves, of morality, and of justice. But I also agree with the compatibilists that it makes sense to speak about ideas such as moral responsibility and desert, even without libertarian free will (and without recourse to a reductionist transformation of these notions along consequentialist lines). In a nutshell . . . 'forms of life' based on the compatibilist distinctions about control are possible and morally required, but are also superficial and deeply problematic in ethical and personal terms" (2000, 5; see also chapter 6).

13. According to Waller, "Blaming individuals and holding people morally responsible...is not an effective way of making either systems or people better; instead, it is a design for hiding small problems until they grow into larger ones and a design for concealing system shortcomings by blaming problems on individual failure. If we want to promote effective attention to the causes and correction of mistakes and the developments of more effective behavior and more reliable systems, then we must move away from the model of individual blame and instead encourage an open inquiry into mistakes and their causes and into how a system can be devised to prevent such mistakes and improve individual behavior" (2011, 291).

14. This descriptive thesis is only half of Nichols' overall argument. In the second half of his paper he turns to the prescriptive question, *should* the acceptance of determinism lead to major changes in our lives? Here he argues that "there are good reasons to resist the cries for a revolution in our everyday lives" (2007, 406). This is what I have above labeled Nichols' *anti-revolution* (see 2007 for details).

I

Philosophical Explorations: Free Will Skepticism and Its Implications

Chapter One

Skepticism about Free Will

Derk Pereboom

One of the core issues at stake in the historical free will debate is whether the sort of free will required for moral responsibility is compatible with the causal determination of our actions by factors beyond our control. Already from ancient times, but especially recently, the question has been extended to whether this sort of free will is compatible with indeterminacy in action. The position for which I argue is that free will, characterized in this way, is incompatible with this kind of causal determination, and with the type of indeterminacy of action that, for example, quantum physics specifies on one widespread interpretation. I contend that because our actions are likely either causally determined or indeterministic in this way, we need to take very seriously the prospect that we don't have the sort of free will at issue, and that the free will skeptic is right.[1]

It is important to recognize that the term 'moral responsibility' is used in a range of ways, and that the type of free will or control required for moral responsibility in several of these senses is uncontroversially compatible with the causal determination of action by factors beyond our control. But there is one particular sense of moral responsibility that has been at issue in the historical debate, and it is set apart by the notion of *basic desert* (Feinberg 1970; Pereboom 2001, 2007, forthcoming; G. Strawson 1986; Fischer 2006a, 82; Scanlon 2013). For an agent to be morally responsible for an action in this sense is for it to be hers in such a way that she would deserve to be blamed if she understood that it was morally wrong, and she would deserve to be praised if she understood that it was morally exemplary. The desert at issue here is basic in the sense that the agent would deserve to be blamed or praised just because she has performed the action, given an understanding of its moral statues, and not, for example, merely by virtue of consequentialist or contractualist considerations (Feinberg 1970). This characterization allows for an agent to be morally responsible for an action even if she does not deserve to be blamed or praised for it—if, for example, the action is morally indifferent. A belief that an agent is morally responsible in this sense at least typically accompanies expressions of reactive attitudes such as moral resentment and indignation, and is thus closely related to the notion of moral responsibility that P. F. Strawson develops (1962). But there are other notions of responsibility that are not at issue in the free will debate, and are not challenged by skeptical arguments about free will, and the legitimacy of some of them is an important feature of my position.

Baruch Spinoza (1677/1985) argued that due to very general facts about the nature of the universe we human beings lack the sort of free will required for moral responsibility in the sense at issue in the historical debate. About this I think he is right. More specifically, he contends that it is because of the truth of causal determinism that we lack this sort of free will; he is thus a hard determinist. By contrast, I am agnostic about the truth of causal determinism. I maintain, like Spinoza, that we would not be morally responsible in the basic desert sense if determinism were true, or, more exactly, if our actions are causally determined by factors beyond our control. But we would also lack this type of moral responsibility if the causal history of our actions was indeterministic and the causes of our actions were exclusively states or events. Such indeterministic causal histories would also preclude the control in action required for moral responsibility, although in a different way. However, it might be that if we were undetermined agent causes—if we as substances had the power to cause decisions without being causally determined to cause them—we would then have this kind of free will. But although indeterministic agent causality has not been ruled out as a coherent possibility, it is not credible that we have this power given our best physical theories. Accordingly, I do not claim that our having the sort of free will required for moral responsibility is impossible. Rather, I don't take a stand on whether it is possible. But because the only account on which we might have this kind of free will is not credible given our best physical theories, we must take seriously the prospect that we are in fact not free in the sense required for moral responsibility in the basic desert sense. I call the resulting variety of skepticism about free will 'hard incompatibilism' (Pereboom 2001). Naming it 'hard determinism' would be inaccurate, since I'm not committed to determinism, so a new term is needed. But I'll typically refer to the position with the more general term 'free will skepticism,' since many features of the particular skeptical view I advocate are also endorsed by skeptics who are hard determinists, or who, like Galen Strawson (1986), are impossibilists about the sort of free will at issue.

At the same time, I defend the optimistic view that conceiving of life without this type of free will would not be devastating to our conceptions of agency, morality, and meaning in life, and in certain respects it may even be beneficial. In particular, this conception is wholly compatible with rational deliberation, with practically viable notions of morality and moral responsibility, with a workable system for dealing with criminal behavior, and with a secure sense of meaning in life.

A MANIPULATION ARGUMENT AGAINST COMPATIBILISM

Defending the skeptical position requires facing up to compatibilism. I think that the most effective argument against the compatibilist begins with the intuition that if someone is causally determined to act by other agents, for example, by scientists who manipulate her brain, then she is not morally responsible for that action (Taylor 1966, 1974; cf. Ginet 1990; Kane 1996; Mele 2006). The argument continues by showing that there are no differences between cases like this and otherwise similar ordinary deterministic examples that can justify the claim that while an agent is not morally responsible when she is manipulated, she can nevertheless be responsible in the ordinary deterministic examples. The non-responsibility intuition remains strong even if when manipulated the agent satisfies the conditions on moral responsibility advocated by the prominent compatibilist theories. My multiple-case argument first of all develops examples of actions that involve such manipulation and in which these compatibilist conditions on moral responsibility are satisfied (Pereboom 1995, 2001, forthcoming). These cases, taken separately, indicate that it is possible for an agent not to be morally responsible even if the compatibilist conditions are satisfied, and that as a result these conditions are inadequate. But the argument has more force by virtue of setting out three such cases, each progressively more like a fourth, which the compatibilist might envision to be realistic, in which the action is causally determined in a natural way. An additional challenge for the compatibilist is to point out a relevant and principled difference between any two adjacent cases that would show why the agent might be morally responsible in the later example but not in the earlier one. I argue that this can't be done. I contend that the agent's non-responsibility generalizes from at least one of the manipulation examples to the ordinary case.

In the set-up, in each of the four cases Professor Plum decides to kill Ms. White for the sake of some personal advantage, and succeeds in doing so. The cases are designed so that his act of murder conforms to the prominent compatibilist conditions. This action meets certain conditions advocated by Hume: the action is not out of character, since for Plum it is generally true that selfish reasons typically weigh heavily—too heavily when considered from the moral point of view; while in addition the desire that motivates him to act is nevertheless not irresistible for him, and in this sense he is not constrained to act (Hume 1739/1978). The action fits the condition proposed by Harry Frankfurt (1971): Plum's effective desire (i.e., his will) to murder White conforms appropriately to his second-order desires for which effective desires he will have. That is, he wills to murder her, and he wants to will to do so, and he wills this act of murder because he wants to will to do so. The action also satisfies the reasons-responsiveness condition advocated by John Fischer and Mark Ravizza (1998): Plum's desires can be modified by, and some of them arise from, his rational consideration of the reasons he has, and if he knew that the bad consequences for himself that would result from killing White would be much more severe than they are actually likely to be, he would have refrained from killing her for that reason. Also, this action meets the condition advanced by Jay Wallace (1994): Plum has the general ability to grasp, apply, and regulate his actions by moral reasons. For instance, when egoistic reasons that count against acting morally are weak, he will typically regulate his behavior by moral reasons instead. This ability also provides him with the capacity to revise and develop his moral character over time, a condition that Al Mele emphasizes (1995). Now, supposing that causal determinism is true, is it plausible that Professor Plum is morally responsible for his action?

Each of the four cases I will now describe features different ways in which Plum's murder of White might be causally determined by factors beyond his control (Pereboom, forthcoming). In a first type of counterexample (Case 1) to these prominent compatibilist conditions, neuroscientists manipulate Plum in a way that directly affects him at the neural level, but so that his mental states and actions feature the psychological regularities and counterfactual dependencies that are compatible with ordinary agency (Pereboom 2001, 121; McKenna 2008b):

> Case 1: A team of neuroscientists is able to manipulate Plum's mental state at any moment through the use of radio-like technology. In this case, they do so by pressing a button just before he begins to reason about his situation, which produces in him a neural state that realizes a strongly egoistic reasoning process, which the neuroscientists know will deterministically result in his decision to kill White. He would not have killed White had the neuroscientists not intervened, since his reasoning would then not have been sufficiently egoistic. At the same time, Plum's effective first-order desire to kill White conforms to his second-order desires. In addition, the process of deliberation from which his action results is reasons-responsive; in particular, this type of process would have resulted in his refraining from deciding to kill White in some situations in which the reasons were different. His reasoning is consistent with his character since it is frequently egoistic and sometimes strongly so. Still, it is not in general exclusively egoistic, because he often regulates his behavior by moral reasons, especially when the egoistic reasons are relatively weak. Plum is also not constrained to act as he does, for he does not act because of an irresistible desire—the neuroscientists do not induce a desire of this kind, in fact they do not directly induce a desire at all.

In Case 1, Plum's action satisfies each of the compatibilist conditions just examined. But intuitively, he is not morally responsible for his decision. Thus it would appear that these compatibilist conditions are not sufficient for moral responsibility—even if all are taken together. An explanation for this intuition of non-responsibility is that Plum's action is causally determined by what the neuroscientists do, which is beyond his control, and he would not have decided to kill White had the intervention not occurred.

Next consider a scenario more like the ordinary situation than Case 1. On the traditional theological determinist conception, God creates us and our environments in such a way that our entire life-histories are intentionally deterministically programmed by him from the beginning of our lives. We might imagine Plum in a neuroscientific version of such a story:

> Case 2: Plum is like an ordinary human being, except that neuroscientists programmed him at the beginning of his life so that his reasoning is frequently but not always egoistic (as in Case 1), and sometimes strongly so, with the intended consequence that in the particular circumstances in which he now finds himself, he is causally determined to engage in the egoistic reasons-responsive process of deliberation and to have the set of first and second-order desires that result in his decision to kill White. Plum has the general ability to regulate his behavior by moral reasons, but in his circumstances, due to the strongly egoistic character of his reasoning he is causally determined to make his decision. The neural realization of his reasoning process and of the resulting decision is exactly the same as it is in Case 1 (although the external causes are different). At the same time, he does not decide as he does because of an irresistible desire.

Again, although Plum satisfies all the prominent compatibilist conditions, intuitively he is not morally responsible for his decision. So Case 2 also shows that these compatibilist conditions, either individually or in conjunction, are not sufficient for moral responsibility. Moreover, it would seem unprincipled to claim that here, by contrast with Case 1, Plum is morally responsible because the length of time between the programming and his decision is now great enough. Whether the programming occurs a few seconds before or forty years prior to the action seems irrelevant to the question of his moral responsibility. Causal determination by what the neuroscientists do, which is beyond his control, plausibly explains Plum's not being morally responsible in the first case, and I think we are forced to say that he is not morally responsible in the second case for the same reason.

Imagine next a scenario more similar yet to an ordinary situation. In various societies, many historical and some present-day, training and education results in different patterns of motivation, emotion, and action than we see in the sorts of cultural environments in which most of us were raised. We might suppose that Plum was brought up in an environment in which self-interest and violence are more strongly encouraged than they are in ours, even though morality also has a part. This sort of environment is not unusual in human history; it would seem, for instance, that fourteenth and fifteenth century European aristocratic households were often like this when it came to education of the male nobility.

> Case 3: Plum is an ordinary human being, except that he was causally determined by the training practices of his family and community so that his reasoning processes are often but not exclusively rationally egoistic (in this respect he is just like he is in Cases 1 and 2). His training took place when he was too young to have the ability to prevent or alter the practices that determined this aspect of his character. This training, together with his particular current circumstances, causally determines him to engage in the strongly egoistic reasons-responsive process of deliberation and to have the first and second-order desires that result in his decision to kill White. Plum has the general ability to regulate his behavior by moral reasons, but in his circumstances, due to the strongly egoistic nature of his reasoning processes, he is causally determined to make his decision. The neural realization of this reasoning process and of his decision is the same as it is in Cases 1 and 2. Here again he does not decide as he does due to an irresistible desire.

For the compatibilist to argue successfully that Plum is morally responsible in Case 3, he must adduce a feature of these circumstances that would explain why he is morally responsible here but not in Case 2. It seems there is no such feature. In all of these examples, Plum meets the prominent compatibilist conditions for morally responsible action, so a divergence in judgment about moral responsibility between these examples won't be supported by a difference in whether these conditions are satisfied. Causal determination by what the controlling agents do, which is beyond Plum's control, most plausibly explains the absence of moral responsibility in Case 2, and we should conclude that he is not morally responsible in Case 3 for the same reason.

Therefore it appears that Plum's exemption from responsibility in Cases 1 and 2 generalizes to the nearer-to-normal Case 3. Does it generalize to an ordinary deterministic case?

> Case 4: Physicalist determinism is true—everything in the universe is physical, and everything that happens is causally determined by virtue of the past states of the universe in conjunction with the laws of nature. Plum is an ordinary human being, raised in normal circumstances, and again his reasoning processes are frequently but not exclusively egoistic, and sometimes strongly so (as in Cases 1–3). His decision to kill White results from his strongly egoistic but reasons-responsive process of deliberation, and he has the specified first and second-order desires. The neural realization of his reasoning process and decision is just as it is in Cases 1–3. Again, he has the general ability to grasp, apply, and regulate his behavior by moral reasons, and it is not due to an irresistible desire that he kills White.

Given that we are constrained to deny moral responsibility in Case 3, could Plum be responsible in this ordinary deterministic situation? It appears that there are no differences between Case 3 and Case 4 that would justify the claim that Plum is not responsible in Case 3 but is in Case 4. In both of these cases Plum satisfies the prominent compatibilist conditions on moral responsibility. In each the neural realization of his reasoning process and decision is the same, although the causes differ. One distinguishing feature of Case 4 is that the causal determination of Plum's decision is not brought about by other agents (Lycan 1997). But the claim that this is a relevant difference is implausible. Imagine further cases that are exactly the same as Case 1 or Case 2, except that states at issue are instead produced by a spontaneously generated machine—a machine with no intelligent designer (Pereboom 2001) or a force field (Mele 2005). Here also Plum would lack moral responsibility.

From this we can conclude that causal determination by other agents was not essential to what was driving the intuition of non-responsibility in the earlier cases. I propose instead that we have the sense that Plum isn't responsible in these four cases because he is causally determined by factors beyond his control in each. Here's the reasoning: It's highly intuitive that Plum is not morally responsible in Case 1, and there are no differences between Cases 1 and 2, 2 and 3, and 3 and 4 that can explain in a principled way why he would not be responsible in the former of each pair but would be in the latter. We are thus driven to conclude that he is not responsible in Case 4. The salient factor that can plausibly explain why Plum is not responsible in all of the cases is that in each he is causally determined by factors beyond his control to decide as he does. This is therefore a sufficient, and I think also the best, explanation for his non-responsibility in all of the cases.

AGAINST LIBERTARIANISM

Defending hard incompatibilism also requires confronting libertarianism. Two contending versions of libertarianism are the event-causal and agent-causal types.[2] In event-causal libertarianism, actions are caused solely by *events*—such as *Anne's currently believing that she can help someone in trouble*. It is often claimed that all causation in the physical world is fundamentally by events, and not by things such as atoms, organisms, and agents, which we call *substances*. Although we might say, for example, that a missile—a substance—destroyed a weapons factory, when speaking more accurately, the idea is that we should say instead that *the missile's striking the factory at noon yesterday*—an event—caused the destruction. If we are more precise about what it is that causes effects, it turns out to be events, not substances. In accord with this position, event-causal libertarians contend that actions are caused solely by events, and further that indeterminacy in the production of actions by appropriate events is a highly significant requirement for moral responsibility (Kane 1996; Ekstrom 2000; Balaguer 2009, Franklin 2011).

According to agent-causal libertarianism, free will of the sort required for moral responsibility is accounted for by the existence of agents who possess a causal power to make choices without being determined to do so (Taylor 1966, 1974; Chisholm 1976; O'Connor 2000; Clarke 2003). On this proposal, it is crucial that the kind of causation involved in an agent's making a free choice is not reducible to causation among events involving the agent, but is rather irreducibly an instance of a substance causing a choice not by way of events. The agent, fundamentally as a substance, has the causal power to make choices without being determined to do so.

Critics of libertarianism have contended that if actions are undetermined, agents will lack the control in action required for moral responsibility. The classical presentation of this objection is found in Hume's *Treatise of Human Nature* (Hume 1739/1978, 411–12); there are several distinct versions of this objection (van Inwagen 1983; Mele 2006; cf. Franklin 2011). I believe that event-causal libertarianism is undermined by one in particular, but that agent-causal libertarianism might well evade it (cf. O'Connor 2000; Clarke 2003). The strongest challenge to the agent-causal position is rather one based on our best physical theories. Our choices produce physical events in the brain and in the rest of the body, and these events are, according to these theories, governed by physical laws. A libertarian view must make it credible that our choices could be free in the sense it advocates given the evidence we have about these physical laws. The concern is that agent-causal libertarianism does not meet this standard.

The objection that in my view reveals the deepest problem for event-causal libertarianism is what I call the *disappearing agent* (Pereboom 2001, 2004, forthcoming), which is a version of a more general objection to event-causal theories of action, (e.g., Hornsby 2004a, 2004b) but which targets basic desert moral responsibility rather than agency:

> *The disappearing agent objection*: Consider a decision made in a context in which moral reasons favor one action, prudential reasons favor a distinct and incompatible action, and the motivational strength of these sets of reasons are in close competition. On an event-causal libertarian picture, the relevant causal conditions antecedent the decision—agent-involving events—would leave it open whether the decision will occur, and the agent has no further causal role in determining whether it does. With the causal role of the antecedent events already given, whether the decision occurs is not settled by any causal factor involving the agent. In fact, given the causal role of all causally relevant antecedent events, *nothing settles* whether the decision occurs. Thus on the

event-causal libertarian picture agents lack the control required for moral responsibility.

The objection is not that agents will have no causal role in producing decisions, but that the causal role that is available to agents will be insufficient for the control moral responsibility demands. For on the event-causal libertarian view, the agent will disappear at the exact point at which moral responsibility for her decision requires her to exercise control.

To illustrate, consider Kane's example of a businesswoman—let's call her Anne—who has the option of deciding to stop to help an assault victim, whereupon she would be late for an important meeting at work, or not deciding to stop, which would allow her to make it to the meeting on time. For simplicity, suppose the relevant antecedent conditions are, against stopping, *Anne's desiring at t not to annoy her boss*, and *Anne's believing at t that if she is late for the meeting her boss will give her a difficult time*; and for stopping, *Anne's desiring at t to help people in trouble*, and *Anne's belief that she can be effective in helping the assault victim*. Suppose the motivational force of each of these pairs of conditions is for her about the same. In the event-causal libertarian conception, with the causal role of these antecedent conditions already given, both Anne's deciding to stop and her not deciding to stop are significantly probable outcomes. Suppose she in fact decides to stop. There is nothing else about Anne that can settle whether the decision to stop occurs, since in this conception her role in producing a decision is exhausted by antecedent states or events in which she has a part. If at this point nothing about Anne can settle whether the decision occurs, then, plausibly, she lacks the control required for basic desert moral responsibility for it. Thus it would appear that in an event-causal libertarian view there is no provision that allows the agent to have control over whether the decision occurs or not (in the crucial sorts of cases), and for this reason she lacks the control required for moral responsibility for it.

The agent-causal libertarian's solution is to specify a way in which the agent could have the requisite control, which involves the power to settle which of the antecedently possible decisions actually occurs. The suggested remedy is to reintroduce the agent as a cause, this time not solely as involved in events, but instead fundamentally as a substance. The agent-causal libertarian proposes that we possess a special causal power—a power for an agent, fundamentally as a substance, to cause a decision without being causally determined to cause it (Chisholm 1966; O'Connor 2000; Clarke 2003; Griffiths 2010).

I argue that the agent-causal position has not been shown to be incoherent (Pereboom 2004). But can agent-causal libertarianism be reconciled with what we would expect given our best physical theories? Consider first an agent-causal view supplemented by the claim that all events in the physical world are governed by deterministic laws. When an agent makes a free decision, she agent-causes the decision without being causally determined to do so. On the route to action that results from this undetermined decision, changes in the physical world, in particular in her brain or some other part of her body, are produced. At such points it seems that we would encounter divergences from the deterministic laws, since the physical changes that result from the undetermined decision would themselves not be causally determined, and they would thus not be governed by deterministic laws. One might object that it is possible that the physical changes that result from every free decision just happen to dovetail with what could in principle be predicted on the basis of the deterministic laws, and thus that nothing would actually occur that diverges from these laws. However, this proposal would seem to involve coincidences too wild to be credible. Consequently, agent-causal libertarianism is not plausibly reconcilable with the physical world's being governed by deterministic laws.

On one popular interpretation of quantum mechanics, the physical world is not in fact deterministic, but is instead governed by probabilistic statistical laws. But the same kind of problem arises for agent causation supposing physical laws of this sort. Consider the class of possible actions each of which has a physical component whose antecedent probability of occurring is approximately 0.32. It would not violate the statistical laws in the sense of being logically incompatible with them if, for a large number of instances, the physical components in this class were not actually realized close to 32 percent of the time. Rather, the consequence of the statistical law is that for a large number of instances it is correct to *expect* physical components in this class to be realized close to 32 percent of the time. Are free decisions on the agent-causal libertarian's view compatible with what the statistical law would have us expect about them? If they were, then for a large enough number of instances the possible actions in the specified class would almost certainly be freely chosen near to 32 percent of the time. But if the occurrence of these physical components were settled by the free choices of agent-causes, then their actually being selected close to 32 percent of the time would amount to a wild coincidence. The proposal that agent-caused free choices would not result in divergences from what the statistical laws predict for the physical components of our actions would be so sharply opposed to what we would be led to expect by these laws as to make it incredible.[3]

The libertarian agent-causalist might now propose that there are indeed divergences from the probabilities that we would expect absent agent-causes, and that these divergences would occur at the interface between the agent-cause and that part of the physical world that it directly affects—likely in the brain. But the worry for this proposal is that we have no evidence that such divergences occur. This difficulty yields a strong reason to reject this approach.

Thus the various kinds of libertarianism face significant problems. Because compatibilism is vulnerable to the argument from manipulation cases, the position that remains is free will skepticism, which denies that we have the sort of free will required for moral responsibility in the basic desert sense. The concern for this stance is not that there is considerable empirical evidence that it is false, or that there is a powerful argument that it is somehow incoherent, and false for that reason. Rather, the crucial questions it faces are practical: What would life be like if we believed it was true? Is this a sort of life that we can cope with?[4]

MORALITY, FORWARD-LOOKING RESPONSIBILITY, AND CRIMINAL BEHAVIOR

Accepting free will skepticism requires giving up our ordinary view of ourselves as blameworthy in the basic desert sense for immoral actions and praiseworthy in that sense for morally exemplary actions. At this point one might object that a skeptical conviction would have harmful consequences, perhaps so harmful that thinking and acting as if this skeptical view is true is not a feasible option. So even if the claim that we are morally responsible turns out to be false, there might yet be weighty practical reasons to believe that we are, or at least to treat people as if they were morally responsible in the sense at issue.

First of all, one might think that if we gave up the belief that people are blameworthy and praiseworthy, we could no longer legitimately judge any actions as morally bad or good. But this thought is mistaken. Even if we came to believe that some perpetrator of genocide was not blameworthy due to a degenerative brain disease, we could still affirm that it was morally extremely bad for him to act as he did. One might argue that if determinism precludes basic desert blameworthiness, it also undermines judgments of moral obligation. Because 'ought' implies 'can,' and if, for instance, because determinism is true one could not have avoided acting badly, it must be false that one ought to have acted otherwise. And given that an action is wrong for an agent just in case he is morally obligated not to perform it, determinism would also undercut judgments of moral wrongness (Haji 1998). All of this may be, but such reasoning does not also issue a challenge to judgments of moral goodness and badness (Haji 1998; Pereboom 2013b, forthcoming). So, in general, free will skepticism can accommodate judgments about moral badness and goodness, which are sufficient, in my view, for moral practice.

One might object that if we stopped treating people as if they were blameworthy in the basic desert sense, we might be left with inadequate leverage to reform immoral behavior (Nichols 2007; for a response see Pereboom 2009). But the free will skeptic can turn instead to other senses of moral responsibility that have not been a focus of the free will debate. Free will skeptics like Joseph Priestley (1788/1963), and their revisionary compatibilist cousins such as Moritz Schlick (1939) and J. J. C. Smart (1961), claim that given determinism a forward-looking kind of moral responsibility can be retained. On the version of this position I endorse (Pereboom 2013b), when we encounter apparently immoral behavior, it is legitimate to invite the agent to evaluate critically what his actions indicate about his intentions and character, to demand apology, or to request reform. Engaging in such interactions is reasonable in view of the right of those wronged or threatened by wrongdoing to protect themselves from immoral behavior and its consequences. We also have an interest in his moral formation, and the address described naturally functions as a stage in this process. In addition, we might have a stake in reconciliation with the wrongdoer, and calling him to account in this way might serve as a step toward realizing this aim. The main thread of the historical free will debate does not pose determinism as a challenge to moral responsibility conceived in this way, and free will skeptics can accept that we are morally responsible in this sense.

Does the skeptical view have resources adequate for contending with criminal behavior? According to retributivism, punishment of a criminal is justified for the reason that he deserves something bad to happen to him—pain, deprivation or death, for example just because he has done wrong (Kant 1797/1963; Moore 1987, 1998). This claim is typically subjected to qualifications such as that the agent had to have committed the wrong knowingly. The retribution theory does not appeal to a good such as the safety of society, or the moral improvement of the criminal in justifying punishment. Rather, the good by which retributivism justifies punishment, or the principle of right action that justifies punishment, is that an agent receive what he deserves only because of his having knowingly done wrong. This position would be undermined if the free will skeptic is right, since if agents do not deserve blame just because they have knowingly done wrong, neither do they deserve punishment just because they have knowingly done wrong. Retributivism justifies punishment solely on the grounds of basic desert, and the skeptical position is incompatible with retributivism because it claims this notion does not apply to us. The free will skeptic thus recommends that the retributivist justification for punishment be abandoned.

By contrast, a theory that justifies criminal punishment on the ground that punishment educates criminals morally is not jeopardized by free will skepticism per se. However, we lack strong empirical evidence that punishing criminals reliably results in moral education, and without such evidence, it would be immoral to punish them to achieve this aim. It is generally immoral to harm someone to realize some good without substantial evidence that the harm will produce the good. Moreover, even if we had impressive evidence that punishment is effective in morally educating criminals, non-punitive ways of achieving this aim would be morally preferable, whether or not criminals are morally responsible in the basic desert sense.

According to deterrence theories, punishing criminals is justified for the reason that doing so deters future crime. The two most-discussed deterrence theories, the utilitarian version and the one that grounds the right to punish on the right to self-defense and defense of others, are not threatened by the skeptical view *per se*. But they are questionable on other grounds. The utilitarian version, which claims that punishment is justified when and because it maximizes utility, faces well-known objections. It would counsel punishing the innocent when doing so would maximize utility; in certain situations it would recommend punishment that is unduly severe; and it would authorize harming people merely as means to the safety of others.

The type of deterrence theory that grounds the right to punish in the right we have to harm and threaten to harm aggressors in order to defend ourselves and others against immediate threats, advocated by Daniel Farrell, for example (1985, 38-60), is also independently objectionable. For a threat that one could justifiably make and carry out to protect against an aggressor in a situation in which law enforcement and criminal justice agencies have no role cannot legitimately be carried out in a context in which the aggressor is in custody. The minimum harm required to protect ourselves from someone who is immediately dangerous in the absence of law enforcement is typically much more severe than the minimum harm required for protection against a criminal in custody. If our justification is the right to harm in self-defense, what we can legitimately do to a criminal in custody to protect ourselves against him is determined by the minimum required to protect ourselves against him in his actual situation. If one proposes to harm him more severely, for instance to provide credibility for a system of threats, the right to harm in self-defense would not supply the requisite justification, and one would again be in danger of endorsing a position subject to the use objection.

What is the minimum harm required to protect ourselves from a violent and dangerous criminal in custody? It seems evident that nothing more severe would be required than isolating him from those to whom he poses a threat. Thus it would appear that Farrell's reasoning cannot justify *punishment* of criminals, exactly, supposing that punishment involves the intentional infliction of significant harm, such as death or severe physical or psychological suffering. Rather, in the case of violent and dangerous criminals it would at best justify only incapacitation by preventative detention. But this suggests an intuitively legitimate theory of crime prevention that is neither undercut by the skeptical view, nor threatened by other sorts of considerations. Ferdinand Schoeman (1979) argues that if we have the right to quarantine carriers of serious communicable diseases to protect people, then for the same reason we also have the right to incapacitate the criminally dangerous by preventatively detaining them. Note that quarantining someone can be justified when she is not morally responsible for being dangerous to others. If a child is infected with a deadly contagious virus that was transmitted to her before she was born, quarantine can still be justifiable. So even if a dangerous serial killer is not morally responsible for his crimes in the sense at issue, it would be as legitimate to incapacitate him by preventative detention as it is to quarantine a non-responsible carrier of a serious communicable disease.

It would be morally objectionable to harm carriers of communicable diseases more severely than is required to protect people from the resulting threat. Similarly, the free will skeptic would not advocate treating criminals more harshly than would be needed to protect society against the danger they posed. Moreover, just as moderately dangerous diseases may allow for only measures less intrusive than quarantine, so moderately serious criminal tendencies might only justify varieties of incapacitation less intrusive than preventative detention. In addition, an incapacitation theory supported by the analogy to quarantine would recommend a level of concern for the rehabilitation and well-being of the criminal that would alter much of current practice. Just as it's fair for us to try to cure the people we quarantine, it would be fair for us to attempt to rehabilitate those we preventatively detain. If a criminal cannot be rehabilitated, and if protection of society demands his indefinite detention, there would be no justification for making his life more miserable than required to guard against the danger he poses.

MEANING IN LIFE

Would it be difficult for us to cope without a conception of ourselves as credit- or praiseworthy for achieving what makes our lives fulfilled, happy, satisfactory, or worthwhile—for realizing what Honderich calls our *life-hopes* (1988, 382ff.)? He contends that there is an aspect of these life-hopes that is undercut by determinism, but that nevertheless determinism leaves them largely intact. I agree. First, it is not unreasonable to object that our life-hopes involve an aspiration for praiseworthiness in the basic desert sense, which on the skeptical view determinism would undermine. Life-hopes are aspirations for achievement, and it is natural to suppose that one cannot have an achievement for which one is not also praiseworthy in this sense, and thus giving up this kind of praiseworthiness would deprive us of our life-hopes. However, achievement and life-hopes are not as closely connected to basic desert praiseworthiness as this objection supposes. If someone hopes for a success in some project, and if she accomplishes what she hoped for, intuitively this outcome would be an achievement of hers even if she is not in this particular way praiseworthy for it, although the sense in which it is her achievement is diminished. For example, if someone hopes that her efforts as a teacher will result in well-educated children, and they do, then there is a clear respect in which she has achieved what she hoped for, even if because she is not in general morally responsible in the basic desert sense she is not praiseworthy in this way for her efforts.

One might think that free will skepticism would due to its conception of agency instill in us an attitude of resignation to whatever our behavioral dispositions together with environmental conditions hold in store (Honderich 1988, 382ff.). This isn't clearly right. Even if what we know about our dispositions and environment gives us reason to believe that our futures will turn out in a particular way, it can often be reasonable to hope that they will turn out differently. For this to be so, it may be important that we lack complete knowledge of our dispositions and environmental conditions. Imagine that someone reasonably believes that he has a disposition that might well be a hindrance to realizing a life-hope. But because he does not know whether this disposition will in fact have this effect, it remains open for him—that is, epistemically possible for him—that another disposition of his will allow him to transcend this impediment. For instance, imagine that someone aspires to become a successful politician, but he is concerned that his fear of public speaking will get in the way. He does not know whether this fear will in fact frustrate his ambition, since it is open for him that he will overcome this problem, perhaps due to a disposition for resolute self-discipline to transcend obstacles of this sort. As a result, he might reasonably hope that he will get over his fear and succeed in his ambition. Given skepticism about free will, if he in fact does overcome this difficulty and succeeds in his political ambitions, this will not be an achievement of his in quite as robust a sense as we might naturally suppose, but it will be an achievement in a substantial sense nonetheless.

How significant is the aspect of our life-hopes that we must relinquish given the skeptical view? Saul Smilansky argues that although determinism allows for a limited foundation for the sense of self-worth that derives from achievement or virtue, the hard determinist's (and also, more generally, the free will skeptic's) perspective can nevertheless be extremely damaging to our view of ourselves, to our sense of achievement, worth, and self-respect, especially when it comes to achievement in the formation of one's own moral character. Smilansky (1997, 94; 2000) thinks that in response it would be best for us to foster the illusion that we have free will in the sense at issue. I agree that there is a kind of self-respect that presupposes an incompatibilist foundation, and that it would be undercut if the free will skeptic is right. I question, however, whether Smilansky is accurate about how damaging it would be for us to give up this sort of self-respect, and whether the maintenance or cultivation of illusion is required.

First, note that our sense of self-worth—our sense that we have value and that our lives are worth living—is to a non-trivial extent due to features not produced by our volition, let alone by free will. People place great value on natural beauty, native athletic ability, and intelligence, none of which have their source in our volition. We also value voluntary efforts—in productive work and altruistic behavior, and in the formation of moral character. But does it matter very much to us that these voluntary efforts are also freely willed in the sense at issue in the historical debate? Perhaps Smilansky overestimates how much we do or should care.

Consider how good moral character comes to be. It is plausibly formed to a significant degree by upbringing, and the belief that this is so is widespread. Parents regard themselves as having failed in raising their children if they turn out with immoral dispositions, and they typically take great care to bring their children up to prevent such an outcome. Accordingly, people often come to believe that they have the good moral character they do largely because they were raised with love and skill. But those who believe this about themselves seldom experience dismay because of it. We tend not to become dispirited upon coming to understand that good moral character is not our own doing, and that we do not deserve a great deal of praise or credit for it. By contrast, we often feel fortunate and thankful. Suppose, however, that there are some who would be overcome with dismay. Would it be justified or even desirable for them to foster the illusion that they nevertheless deserve, in the basic sense, praise or credit for producing their moral character? I suspect that most would eventually be able to accept the truth without feeling much loss. All of this, I think, would also hold for those who come to believe that they do not deserve in the basic sense praise and respect for producing their moral character because they are not, in general, morally responsible in this way.

PERSONAL RELATIONSHIPS AND EMOTION

Is the assumption that we are morally responsible in the sense at issue in the free will debate required for meaningful and fulfilling human relationships? P. F. Strawson (1962) delivers a positive answer. In his view, moral responsibility has its foundation in the reactive attitudes, which are in turn required for the kinds of personal relationships that make our lives meaningful. Our justification for claims of blameworthiness and praiseworthiness is ultimately grounded in the system of human reactive attitudes, such as moral resentment, indignation, guilt, forgiveness, and gratitude, and since moral responsibility has this type of basis, the truth or falsity of causal determinism is not relevant to whether we legitimately hold agents morally responsible. If causal determinism was in fact true and did threaten these attitudes, we would face instead the prospect of a certain objectivity of attitude, a stance that in Strawson's view rules out the possibility of meaningful personal relationships.

I think that Strawson is right to believe that objectivity of attitude would seriously hinder our personal relationships, but that he is mistaken to hold that this stance would result or be appropriate if determinism did pose a genuine threat to the reactive attitudes (Pereboom 1995, 2001, forthcoming). First, some of our reactive attitudes, although they would be undermined by hard determinism, or more broadly by free will skepticism, are not required for good personal relationships. Resentment and indignation are undercut by the skeptical position, but I maintain that all things considered they are suboptimal relative to alternative attitudes available to us. Second, the attitudes that we would want to retain either are not threatened by a skeptical conviction, because they do not have presuppositions or attendant beliefs that conflict with this view, or else have analogues that would in this respect be in the clear. The attitudes and analogues that would survive do not amount to Strawson's objectivity of attitude, and are sufficient to sustain good personal relationships.

Of all the attitudes associated with moral responsibility, moral resentment, that is, anger directed toward someone due to a wrong he has done to oneself, and indignation, anger with an agent because of a wrong he has done to a third party, are particularly closely connected with it. It is telling that debates about moral responsibility most often focus not on how we react to morally exemplary agents, but rather on how we respond to those who have acted badly. The kinds of cases most often used to generate a strong conviction of moral responsibility in the basic desert sense involve especially malevolent harm. Perhaps, then, our attachment to moral responsibility in this sense derives partly from the role moral resentment and indignation have in our moral lives, and free will skepticism is especially threatening because it challenges their legitimacy.

Moral resentment and indignation often have a communicative function in personal relationships, and accordingly one might object that if we were to strive to modify or eliminate these attitudes, such relationships might well be damaged. But when we are targets of bad behavior in our relationships there are other emotional attitudes often present that are not challenged by the skeptical view, whose expression can also play the communicative role. These attitudes include feeling hurt or shocked or disappointed about what the other has done, and moral sadness or sorrow and concern for him. Often feigned disappointment or moral sadness is used to manipulate others, but what I have in mind are the genuine versions. It is thus not clear that anger is required for communication in personal relationships.

A case can be made that these alternatives are indeed preferable. Moral anger, of which resentment and indignation are subspecies, does have an important role in human relationships as they ordinarily function. It motivates resistance to oppression and abuse, and as a result it can make relationships better. But expression of moral anger frequently has harmful effects.

On many occasions, it fails to contribute to the well-being of those to whom it is directed. Expression of moral anger is often intended to cause physical or emotional pain, and it can give rise to destructive resistance instead of reconciliation. Moral anger also serves as a motivation to take harmful measures against the other. It thus also has a tendency to damage or destroy relationships.

Certain types and degrees of moral anger are likely to be beyond our power to affect, and thus even the committed skeptic might not be able to make the transformation her view recommends. So even if the best personal relationships do not require a disposition to moral anger, it may be that there is no mechanism generally available to us by which we might eradicate this disposition, or radically curtail its manifestations. Nichols (2007) cites the distinction between narrow-profile emotional responses, which are local or immediate emotional reactions to situations, and wide-profile responses, which are not immediate and can involve rational reflection. As free will skeptics we might expect that we will be unable to significantly reduce narrow-profile, immediate moral anger when we are seriously wronged in our most intimate personal relationships. But in wide-profile cases, we might well be able to diminish, or even eliminate moral anger, or at least disavow it in the sense of rejecting any force it might be thought to have in justifying harmful reactions to the wrong done. Such modification of moral anger and its typical presuppositions, aided by this conviction, might well be advantageous for our relationships.

Guilt and repentance are also threatened by free will skepticism, and one might argue that this consequence is more difficult to accommodate. There is much at stake here, the objector might contend, because these self-directed attitudes are required for good relationships for agents like us who can behave immorally. Without guilt and repentance, we would not be motivated to moral improvement after acting badly, we would be kept from restoring relationships impaired as a result, and we would be barred from reestablishing moral integrity. For absent guilt and repentance none of our psychological mechanisms can generate these effects. The skeptic's position would undercut guilt because it essentially involves a sense that one is blameworthy in the basic desert sense for an immoral action. If someone did not feel blameworthy in this way for the action he would also not feel guilty for it. Moreover, because feeling guilty is undermined by the skeptical view, repentance is also no longer an option, since feeling guilty is a prerequisite for a repentant attitude.

Suppose that you behave badly in the context of a relationship, but because you believe that free will skepticism is true, you reject the claim that you are blameworthy in the basic desert sense. However, you acknowledge that you have behaved badly, you feel deeply disappointed in yourself, and as Bruce Waller advocates, you feel deep sorrow and regret for what you have done (Waller 1990, 165–66; cf. Bok 1998). In addition, you resolve to do what you can to eradicate your disposition to behave this way, and you seek help to make this change. These responses arguably can realize the good that guilt is apt to achieve, and they are compatible with the skeptic's conviction.

On one conception of forgiveness, this attitude presupposes that the person being forgiven deserves blame in the basic desert sense, and is therefore an appropriate target of resentment or indignation. Wallace (1994, 72), for instance, contends that in forgiving people we express our acknowledgment that they have done something that would warrant resentment and blame, but we renounce the responses that we thus acknowledge to be appropriate. Given this conception, the skeptic's claims would put forgiveness at risk. In Wallace's view, forgiveness involves renouncing an attitude of resentment which is initially justified, but because on the skeptical position resentment never satisfies this constraint, forgiveness would lose its point. One might object that free will skeptics who renounce resentment generally thereby forgive every relevant offense, but this does not seem plausible. Forgiveness presupposes that some disavowed initial attitude on the part of the forgiver was legitimate prior to renunciation, and this core feature would be undercut.

But note that the skeptic's general disavowal does not deny acknowledgment of the other's making a commitment in a specific context to overcome a disposition to act badly, which forgiveness typically involves. It thus may be that forgiveness, or at least an important aspect of this attitude, survives without a role for renunciation of resentment (cf. Nelkin 2011, 44–50). Imagine a friend has wronged you a number of times by acting inconsiderately, and you find yourself resolved to end your relationship with him. You engage in a moral conversation with him, pointing out that his disposition to act this way is immoral and you challenge him to eradicate it—thereby, in Pamela Hieronymi's words, protesting the threat the disposition poses (Hieronymi 2001). He makes a serious effort to do so, assuming a firm disapproving stance toward the disposition, and committing himself to full elimination. You might now withdraw your protest to the threat the disposition poses, and agree to continue the relationship on a better footing. Even if forgiveness typically involves renunciation of resentment in addition, the attitude articulated in this description can have the role forgiveness has in many contexts, and it is not challenged by the skeptic's claims.

In another sort of case, independently of the offender's repentance one might just resolve to disregard his bad behavior as a reason to alter the character of the relationship. This attitude is also not called into question by the skeptic's view. We might also add that despite the skeptic's general disavowal of resentment, she may still actually feel resentment in a particular case, whereupon forgiveness could involve renunciation of this resentment (cf. Nelkin 2011, 44–50). Overall, my sense is that there are enough aspects of forgiveness not challenged by the skeptic's view for this attitude to remain in place, or at least for there to be an unchallenged related attitude that can play the role forgiveness typically has in relationships.

Gratitude might appear to presuppose that the agent to whom one is grateful is morally responsible in the basic desert sense for a beneficial act, whereupon a skeptical conviction would undermine this attitude (Honderich 1988, 518-19). But even if this is so, as in the case of forgiveness certain core aspects would remain unaffected, and these aspects can provide what is required for good personal relationships. Gratitude involves, first of all, being thankful toward someone who has acted beneficially. True, being thankful toward someone often involves the belief that she is praiseworthy in the basic desert sense for some action. Still, one can be thankful to a young child for some kindness without believing that she is praiseworthy in this way. This aspect of gratitude could be retained even without the supposition that the other is responsible in the basic desert sense. Gratitude typically also involves joy as a response to what someone has done. The skeptical view does not pose a threat to the legitimacy of being joyful and expressing joy when others are considerate or generous in one's behalf.

FINAL WORDS

Living without a conception of our actions as freely willed in the sense required for basic desert moral responsibility does not come naturally to us. Our natural reactions to good and bad actions presuppose that we are free in this sense. But as I have been arguing, there is a strong case to be made against this presupposition, and also, despite our initially apprehensive reaction to skepticism about this sort of free will, endorsing this perspective would not have unacceptable consequences for us. It would not seriously threaten meaning in life, because it is compatible with a veridical sense of accomplishment when we succeed in our projects. It would not hinder the possibility of the good personal relationships, but even holds out the promise of greater equanimity by reducing the moral anger that often impairs them. If we did in fact give up the assumption of the sort of free will at issue, then, perhaps surprisingly, we might well be better off as a result.

NOTES

1. Advocates of free will skepticism include Baruch Spinoza (1677/1985); Joseph Priestley (1788/1963); Galen Strawson (1986); Bruce Waller (1990, 2011); Derk Pereboom (1995, 2001, forthcoming); Daniel Wegner (2002); Shaun Nichols (2007); Stephen Morris (2009); Neil Levy (2011); Thomas Nadelhoffer (2011); Tammler Sommers (2012); Gregg Caruso (2012); and Benjamin Vilhauer (2012).

2. A third type is non-causal libertarianism, advocated by Carl Ginet (1990), Hugh McCann (1998), and Stewart Goetz (2008). See Clarke (2003) and Pereboom (forthcoming) for criticisms of this position.

3. For objections to this argument, see O'Connor (2003, 2008); Clarke (2003, 181 n.31); for replies see Pereboom (2005, forthcoming).

4. In responding to these questions, I have been inspired by others who have done excellent work in answering them, including Spinoza (1677/1985); Galen Strawson (1986); Ted Honderich (1988); Bruce Waller (1990), and Neil Levy (2011).

Chapter Two

The Impossibility of Ultimate Responsibility?

Galen Strawson

1. THE BASIC ARGUMENT

You set off for a shop on the evening of a national holiday, intending to buy a cake with your last five-pound note to supplement the preparations you've already made. There's one cake left in the shop and it costs five pounds; everything is closing down. On the steps of the shop someone is shaking a box, collecting money for Oxfam. You stop, and it seems clear to you that it is *entirely up to you* what you do next. It seems clear to you that you are truly, radically free to choose, in such a way that you will be ultimately morally responsible for whatever you do choose.

There is, however, an argument, which I will call the Basic Argument, which appears to show that we can never be truly or ultimately morally responsible for our actions. According to the Basic Argument, it makes no difference whether determinism is true or false.

The central idea can be quickly conveyed:

a. Nothing can be *causa sui*—nothing can be the cause of itself.
b. In order to be truly or ultimately morally responsible for one's actions one would have to be *causa sui*, at least in certain crucial mental respects.
c. Therefore no one can be truly or ultimately morally responsible.

We can expand the argument as follows:

1. Interested in free action, we're particularly interested in actions performed for a reason (as opposed to reflex actions or mindlessly habitual actions).
2. When one acts for a reason, what one does is a function of how one is, mentally speaking. (It's also a function of one's height, one's strength, one's place and time, and so on; but it's the mental factors that are crucial when moral responsibility is in question.)
3. So if one is to be truly responsible for how one acts, one must be truly responsible for how one is, mentally speaking—at least in certain respects.
4. But to be truly responsible for how one is, in any mental respect, one must have brought it about that one is the way one is, in that respect. And it's not merely that one must have caused oneself to be the way one is, in that respect. One must also have consciously and explicitly chosen to be the way one is, in that respect, and one must have succeeded in bringing it about that one is that way.
5. But one can't really be said to choose, in a conscious, reasoned, fashion, to be the way one is in any respect at all, unless one already exists, mentally speaking, already equipped with some principles of choice, "P1"—preferences, values, ideals—in the light of which one chooses how to be.
6. But then to be truly responsible, on account of having chosen to be the way one is, in certain mental respects, one must be truly responsible for one's having the principles of choice P1 in the light of which one chose how to be.
7. But for this to be so one must have chosen P1, in a reasoned, conscious, intentional fashion.
8. But for this to be so one must already have had some principles of choice P2, in the light of which one chose P1.
9. And so on. Here we are setting out on a regress that we cannot stop. True self-determination is impossible because it requires the actual completion of an infinite series of choices of principles of choice.
10. So true moral responsibility is impossible, because it requires true self-determination, as noted in (3).[1]

This may seem contrived, but essentially the same argument can be given in a more natural form.

1. It's undeniable that one is the way one is, initially, as a result of heredity and early experience, and it's undeniable that these are things for which one can't be held to be in any way responsible (morally or otherwise).

2. One can't at any later stage of life hope to accede to true or ultimate moral responsibility for the way one is by trying to change the way one already is as a result of one's genetic inheritance and previous experience.

For

3. Both the particular way in which one is moved to try to change oneself, and the degree of one's success in one's attempt to change, will be determined by how one already is as a result of one's genetic inheritance and previous experience.

And

4. Any further changes that one can bring about only after one has brought about certain initial changes will in turn be determined, via the initial changes, by one's genetic inheritance and previous experience.
5. This may not be the whole story, and there may be changes in the way one is that can't be traced to one's genetic inheritance and experience but rather to the influence of indeterministic factors. It is, however, absurd to suppose that indeterministic factors, for which one is obviously not responsible, can contribute in any way to one's being truly morally responsible for how one is.

2. ULTIMATE MORAL RESPONSIBILITY

But what is this supposed "true" or "ultimate" moral responsibility? An old story may be helpful. As I understand it, it's responsibility of such a kind that, if we have it, then it *makes sense* to suppose that it could be just to punish some of us with (eternal) torment in hell and reward others with (eternal) bliss in heaven. The stress on the words "makes sense" is important, because one certainly doesn't have to believe in any version of the story of heaven and hell in order to understand, or indeed believe in, the kind of true or ultimate moral responsibility that I'm using the story to illustrate. A less colorful way to convey the point, perhaps, is to say that true or ultimate responsibility exists if punishment and reward can be fair without having any sort of pragmatic justification whatever.

One certainly doesn't have to refer to religious faith in order to describe the sorts of everyday situation that give rise to our belief in such responsibility. Choices like the one with which I began (the cake or the collection box) arise all the time, and constantly refresh our conviction about our responsibility. Even if one believes that determinism is true, in such a situation, and that one will in five minutes' time be able to look back and say that what one did was determined, this doesn't seem to undermine one's sense of the absolute-ness and inescapability of one's freedom, and of one's moral responsibility for one's choice. Even if one accepts the validity of the Basic Argument, which concludes that one can't be in any way ultimately responsible for the way one is and decides, one's freedom and true moral responsibility seem, in the moment, as one stands there, obvious and absolute.

Large and small, morally significant or morally neutral, such situations of choice occur regularly in human life. I think they lie at the heart of the experience of freedom and moral responsibility. They're the fundamental source of our inability to give up belief in true or ultimate moral responsibility. We may wonder why human beings experience these situations of choice as they do; it's an interesting question whether any possible cognitively sophisticated, rational, self-conscious agent must experience situations of choice in this way.[2] But these situations of choice are the experiential rock on which the belief in ultimate moral responsibility is founded.

Most people who believe in ultimate moral responsibility take its existence for granted, and don't ever entertain the thought that one needs to be ultimately responsible for the way one is in order to be ultimately responsible for the way one *acts*. Some, however, reveal that they see its force. E. H. Carr states that "normal adult human beings are morally responsible for their own personality" (Carr 1961, 89). Sartre holds that "man is responsible for what he is" (Sartre 1946, 29) and seeks to give an account of how we "choose ourselves" (Sartre 1943, 440, 468, 503). In a later interview he judges his earlier assertions about freedom to be incautious—"When I read this, I said to myself: it's incredible, I actually believed that!"—but he still holds that "in the end one is always responsible for what is made of one" (Sartre 1970, 22). Kant puts it clearly when he claims that

> man *himself* must make or have made himself into whatever, in a moral sense, whether good or evil, he is to become. Either condition must be an effect of his free choice; for otherwise he could not be held responsible for it and could therefore be *morally* neither good nor evil. (Kant 1793, 40)

Since he is committed to belief in radical moral responsibility, Kant holds that such self-creation does indeed take place, and writes accordingly of "man's character, which he himself creates" (Kant 1788, 101), and of "knowledge of oneself as a person who . . . is his own originator" (Kant 1800, 213). John Patten, a former British Secretary of State for Education, claims that "it is . . . self-evident that as we grow up each individual chooses whether to be good or bad" (Patten 1992).[3] Robert Kane, an eloquent recent defender of this view, writes as follows:

> if . . . a choice issues from, and can be sufficiently explained by, an agent's character and motives (together with background conditions), then to be ultimately responsible for the choice, the agent must be at least in part responsible

by virtue of choices or actions voluntarily performed in the past for having the character and motives he or she now has. (Kane 2000, 317–18)

Christine Korsgaard agrees: "judgements of responsibility don't really make sense unless people create themselves" (Korsgaard 2009, 20).

Most of us, as remarked, never actually follow this line of thought. It seems, though, that we do tend, in some vague and unexamined fashion, to think of ourselves as responsible for—answerable for—how we are. The point is somewhat delicate, for we don't ordinarily suppose that we have gone through some sort of active process of self-determination at some past time. It seems nevertheless that we do unreflectively experience ourselves, in many respects, rather as we might experience ourselves if we did believe that we had engaged in some such activity of self-determination; and we may well also think of others in this way.

Sometimes a part of one's character—a desire or tendency—may strike one as foreign or alien. But it can do this only against a background of character traits that aren't experienced as foreign, but are rather "identified" with. (It's only relative to such a background that a character trait can stand out as alien.) Some feel tormented by impulses that they experience as alien, but in many a sense of general identification with their character predominates, and this identification seems to carry within itself an implicit sense that one is generally speaking in control of, or at least answerable for, how one is (even, perhaps, for aspects of one's character that one doesn't like). So it seems that we find, semi-dormant in common thought, an implicit recognition of the idea that true or ultimate moral responsibility for one's actions (for what one does) does somehow involve responsibility for how one is: it seems that ordinary thought is ready to move this way under pressure.

There are also many aspects of our ordinary sense of ourselves as morally responsible free agents that we don't feel to be threatened in any way by the fact that we can't be ultimately responsible for how we are. We readily accept that we are products of our heredity and environment without feeling that this poses any threat to our freedom and moral responsibility at the time of action. It's natural to feel that if one is fully consciously aware of oneself as able to choose in a situation of choice, then this is already entirely sufficient for one's radical freedom of choice—whatever else is or is not the case (see further the penultimate paragraph of this chapter). It seems, then, that our ordinary conception of moral responsibility may contain mutually inconsistent elements. If this is so, it is a profoundly important fact (it would explain a great deal about the character of the philosophical debate about free will). But these other elements in our ordinary notion of moral responsibility, important as they are, are not my present subject.[4]

3. RESTATEMENT OF THE BASIC ARGUMENT

I want now to restate the Basic Argument in very loose—as it were conversational—terms. New forms of words allow for new forms of objection, but they may be helpful nonetheless—or for that reason.

1. You do what you do, in any situation in which you find yourself, because of the way you are.

So

2. To be truly morally responsible for what you do you must be truly responsible for the way you are—at least in certain crucial mental respects.

Or:

1. When you act, what you do is a function of how you are (what you do won't count as an action at all unless it flows appropriately from your beliefs, preferences, and so on).

Hence

2. You have to get to have some responsibility for how you are in order to get to have some responsibility for what you intentionally do.

Once again I take the qualification about "certain mental respects" for granted. Obviously one isn't responsible for one's sex, basic body pattern, height, and so on. But if one weren't responsible for anything about oneself, how could one be responsible for what one did, given the truth of (1)? This is the fundamental question, and it seems clear that if one is going to be responsible for any aspect of oneself, it had better be some aspect of one's mental nature.

I take it that (1) is incontrovertible, and that it is (2) that must be resisted. For if (1) and (2) are conceded the case seems lost, because the full argument runs as follows:

1. You do what you do because of the way you are.[5]

So

2. To be truly morally responsible for what you do you must be truly responsible for the way you are—at least in certain crucial mental respects.

But

3. You can't be truly responsible for the way you are, so you can't be truly responsible for what you do.

Why can't you be truly responsible for the way you are? Because

> 4. To be truly responsible for the way you are, you must have intentionally brought it about that you are the way you are, and this is impossible.

Why is it impossible? Well, suppose it isn't. Suppose

> 5. You have somehow intentionally brought it about that you are the way you now are, and that you have brought this about in such a way that you can now be said to be truly responsible for being the way you are now.

For this to be true

> 6. You must already have had a certain nature N in the light of which you intentionally brought it about that you are as you now are.

But then

> 7. For it to be true that you are truly responsible for how you now are, you must be truly responsible for having had the nature N in the light of which you intentionally brought it about that you are the way you now are.

So

> 8. You must have intentionally brought it about that you had that nature N, in which case you must have existed already with a prior nature in the light of which you intentionally brought it about that you had the nature N in the light of which you intentionally brought it about that you are the way you now are . . .

Here one is setting off on the regress again. Nothing can be *causa sui* in the required way. Even if this attribute is allowed to belong (unintelligibly) to God, it can't plausibly be supposed to be possessed by ordinary finite human beings. "The *causa sui* is the best self-contradiction that has been conceived so far," as Nietzsche remarked in 1886:

> it is a sort of rape and perversion of logic. But the extravagant pride of man has managed to entangle itself profoundly and frightfully with just this nonsense. The desire for "freedom of the will" in the superlative metaphysical sense, which still holds sway, unfortunately, in the minds of the half-educated; the desire to bear the entire and ultimate responsibility for one's actions oneself, and to absolve God, the world, ancestors, chance, and society involves nothing less than to be precisely this *causa sui* and, with more than Baron Münchhausen's audacity, to pull oneself up into existence by the hair, out of the swamps of nothingness . . . (Nietzsche 1886, §21)

The rephrased argument is essentially exactly the same as before, although the first two steps are now more simply stated. Can the Basic Argument simply be dismissed? Is it really of no importance in the discussion of free will and moral responsibility, as some have claimed? (No and No.) Shouldn't any serious defense of free will and moral responsibility thoroughly acknowledge the respect in which the Basic Argument is valid before going on to try to give its own positive account of the nature of free will and moral responsibility? Doesn't the argument go to the heart of things if the heart of the free will debate is a concern about whether we can be truly morally responsible in the absolute way that we ordinarily suppose? (Yes and Yes.)

We are what we are, and we can't be thought to have made ourselves *in such a way* that we can be held to be free in our actions *in such a way* that we can be held to be morally responsible for our actions *in such a way* that any punishment or reward for our actions is ultimately just or fair. Punishments and rewards may seem deeply appropriate or intrinsically "fitting" to us; many of the various institutions of punishment and reward in human society appear to be practically indispensable in both their legal and non-legal forms. But if one takes the notion of justice that is central to our intellectual and cultural tradition seriously, then the consequence of the Basic Argument is that there is a fundamental sense in which no punishment or reward is ever just. It is exactly as just to punish or reward people for their actions as it is to punish or reward them for the (natural) color of their hair or the (natural) shape of their faces. The conclusion seems intolerable, but inescapable.

Darwin develops the point as follows in a notebook entry for 6 September 1838:

> The general delusion about free will obvious. . . . One must view a [wicked] man like a sickly one—We cannot help loathing a diseased offensive object, so we view wickedness.—it would however be more proper to pity than to hate & be disgusted. with them. Yet it is right to punish criminals; but solely to *deter* others. . . . This view should teach one profound humility, one deserves no credit for anything. (yet one takes it for beauty and good temper), nor ought one to blame others.—This view will do no harm, because no one can be really *fully* convinced of its truth. except man who has thought very much, & he will know his happiness lays in doing good & being perfect, & therefore will not be tempted, from knowing every thing he does is independent of himself[,] to do harm.[6]

4. RESPONSE TO THE BASIC ARGUMENT

I've suggested that it is step (2) of the restated Basic Argument that must be rejected, and of course it can be rejected, because the phrases "truly responsible" and "truly morally responsible" can be defined in many ways. I'll sketch three sorts of response.

(I) The first response is *compatibilist*. Compatibilists say that one can be a free and morally responsible agent even if determinism is true. They claim that one can correctly be said to be truly responsible for what one does, when one acts, just so long as one is in control of one's action in the way that we take an ordinary person to be in ordinary circumstances: one isn't, for example, caused to do what one does by any of a certain set of constraints (kleptomaniac impulses, obsessional neuroses, desires that are experienced as alien, post-hypnotic commands, threats, instances of *force majeure*, and so on). Compatibilists don't impose any requirement that one should be truly responsible for how one is, so step (2) of the Basic Argument comes out as false, on their view. They think one can be fully morally responsible even if the way one is is entirely determined by factors entirely outside one's control. They simply reject the Basic Argument. They know that the kind of responsibility ruled out by the Basic Argument is impossible, and conclude that it can't be the kind of responsibility that is really in question in human life, because (they insist) we are indeed genuinely morally responsible agents. No theory that concludes otherwise can possibly be right, on their view.

(II) The second response is *libertarian*. *Incompatibilists* believe that freedom and moral responsibility are incompatible with determinism, and some incompatibilists are libertarians, who believe that we are free and morally responsible agents, and that determinism is therefore false. Robert Kane, for example, allows that we may act responsibility from a will already formed, but argues that the will must in this case be

> "our own" free will by virtue of other past "self-forming" choices or other actions that were undetermined and by which we made ourselves into the kinds of persons we are . . . [T]hese undetermined self-forming actions (SFAs) occur at those difficult times of life when we are torn between competing visions of what we should do or become. (Kane 2000, 318–19)

They paradigmatically involve a conflict between moral duty and non-moral desire, and it is essential that they involve indeterminism, on Kane's view, for this "screens off complete determination by influences of the past" (Kane 2000, 319). He proposes that we are in such cases of "moral, prudential and practical struggle . . . truly 'making ourselves' in such a way that we are ultimately responsible for the outcome," and that this "making of ourselves" means that "we can be ultimately responsible for our present motives and character by virtue of past choices which helped to form them and for which we were ultimately responsible" (Kane 1989, 252).

Kane, then, accepts step (2) of the Basic Argument, and challenges step (3) instead. He accepts that we have to "make ourselves," and so be ultimately responsible for ourselves, in order to be morally responsible for what we do; and he thinks that this requires indeterminism. But the old, general objection to libertarianism recurs. How can indeterminism possibly help with moral responsibility? How can the occurrence of indeterministic or partly random events contribute to my being truly or ultimately morally responsible either for my actions or for my character? If my efforts of will shape my character in a positive way, and are in so doing essentially partly indeterministic in nature, while also being shaped (as Kane grants) by my already existing character, why am I not merely *lucky*?

This seems to be a very strong general objection to any libertarian account of free will. Suppose, in the light of this, that we put aside the Basic Argument for a moment, and take it as given that there is—that there must be—some respectable sense in which human beings are or can be genuinely morally responsible for their actions. If we then ask what sort of account of moral responsibility this will be, compatibilist or incompatibilist, I think we can safely reply that it will have to be compatibilist. This is because it seems so clear that nothing can ever be gained, in an attempt to defend moral responsibility, by assuming that determinism is false.

(III) The third response begins by accepting that one can't be held to be ultimately responsible for one's character or personality or motivational structure. It accepts that this is so whether determinism is true or false. It then directly challenges step (2) of the Basic Argument. It appeals to a certain picture of the *self* in order to argue that one can be truly free and morally responsible in spite of the fact that one can't be held to be ultimately responsible for one's character or personality or motivational structure.

It can be set out as follows. One is free and truly morally responsible because one's self is, in a crucial sense, independent of one's character or personality or motivational structure—one's CPM, for short. Suppose one is in a situation which one experiences as a difficult choice between A, doing one's duty, and B, following one's non-moral desires. Given one's CPM, one responds in a certain way. One's desires and beliefs develop and interact and constitute reasons in favor both of A and of B, and one's CPM makes one tend towards either A or B. So far, the problem is the same as ever: whatever one does, one will do what one does because of the way one's CPM is, and since one neither is nor can be ultimately responsible for the way one's CPM is, one can't be ultimately responsible for what one does.

Enter one's self, S. S is imagined to be in some way independent of one's CPM. S (i.e. one) considers the deliverances of one's CPM and decides in the light of them, but it—S—incorporates a power of decision that is independent of one's CPM in such a way that one can after all count as truly and ultimately morally responsible in one's decisions and actions, even though one isn't ultimately responsible for one's CPM. The idea is that step (2) of the Basic Argument is false because of the existence of S (for a development of this view see, for example, Campbell 1957).

The trouble with the picture is obvious. S (i.e., one) decides on the basis of the deliverances of one's CPM. But whatever S decides, it decides as it does because of the way it is (or because of the occurrence in the decision process of indeterministic factors for which it—i.e. one—can't be responsible, and which can't plausibly be thought to contribute to its ultimate moral responsibility). And this brings us back to where we started. To be a source of ultimate responsibility, S must be responsible for being the way it is. But this is impossible, for the reasons given in the Basic Argument. So while the story of S and CPM adds another layer to the description of the human decision process, it can't change the fact that human beings cannot be ultimately self-determining in such a way as to be ultimately morally responsible for how they are, and thus for how they decide and act.

In spite of all these difficulties, many of us (nearly all of us) continue to believe that we are truly morally responsible agents in the strongest possible sense. Many of us, for example, feel that our capacity for fully explicit self-conscious deliberation in a situation of choice suffices—all by itself—to constitute us as such. All that is needed for true or ultimate responsibility, on this view, is that one is in the moment of action *fully self-consciously aware of oneself as an agent facing choices*. The idea is that such full self-conscious awareness somehow renders irrelevant the fact that one neither is nor can be ultimately responsible for any aspect of one's mental nature: the mere fact of one's self-conscious presence in the situation of choice can confer true moral responsibility. It may be undeniable that one is, in the final analysis, wholly constituted as the sort of person one is by factors for which one cannot be in any way ultimately responsible, but the threat that this fact appears to pose to one's claim to true moral responsibility is, on this view, simply annihilated by one's self-conscious awareness of one's situation.

This is an extremely natural intuition; but the Basic Argument appears to show that it is a mistake. For however self-consciously aware we are as we deliberate and reason, every act and operation of our mind happens as it does as a result of features for which we are ultimately in no way responsible. And yet the conviction that self-conscious awareness of one's situation can be a sufficient foundation of strong free will is extremely powerful. It runs deeper than rational argument, and it survives untouched, in the everyday conduct of life, even after the validity of the Basic Argument has been admitted. Nor, probably, should we wish it otherwise.[7]

NOTES

1. Wouldn't it be enough if one simply endorsed the way one found oneself to be, mentally, in the relevant respects, without actually changing anything? Yes, if one were ultimately responsible for having the principles in the light of which one endorsed the way one found oneself to be. But how could this be?

2. See, e.g., MacKay (1960); Strawson (2010, 246–50; 1986, 281–86). When I cite a work I give the date of first publication, or occasionally the date of composition, while the page reference is to the edition listed in the bibliography.

3. Nussbaum has something much less dramatic in mind, I think, when she writes that "one's own character is one's own responsibility and not that of others" (Nussbaum 2004).

4. For some discussion of the deep ways in which we're naturally compatibilist in our thinking about free will or moral responsibility, and don't feel that it is threatened either by determinism or by our inability to be self-determining, see Strawson 1986, §6.4 ("Natural compatibilism"). Clarke and Fischer are prominent among those who misrepresent my position on free will to the extent that they focus only on the line of thought set out in the current paper. See, e.g., Clarke (2005), Fischer (2006b).

5. During the symposium on free will at the British Academy in July 2010, J. R. Lucas objected that this claim involved an equivocation. He suggested that it operated simultaneously as a conceptual claim and as a causal claim, in a way which vitiated it. I agree that it is both a conceptual claim and a causal claim, but not that this vitiates it. The following is a *conceptual* truth about the *causation* of intentional action: that with regard to the respect in which it is true to say that the action is intentional, it must be true to say that the agent does what he does—given, as always, the situation in which he finds himself or takes himself to be—because (this is a causal "because") of the way he is; and indeed because of the way he is in some mental respect; whatever else is true, and whatever else may be going on. The truth of this claim is wholly compatible with the fact that the way you are when you act is a function of many things, including of course your experience of your situation—which is part of the way you are mentally speaking. Certainly the way you are mentally speaking isn't just a matter of your overall character or personality, and the present argument has its full force even for those who question or reject the explanatory viability of the notion of character when it comes to the explanation of action (see, e.g., Harman (1999, 2000a); Doris (2002); see also Note 7 below).

6. Darwin (1838, 608). For "wicked" in the first line Darwin has "wrecked" (a characteristic slip).

7. On this last point, see, e.g., P. F. Strawson (1962); for a doubt, see Smilansky (1994). It will be interesting to see how the conviction of free will stands up to increasing public awareness of results in experimental and social psychology, which show that our actions are often strongly influenced by factors, situational or otherwise, of which we are completely unaware (see, e.g., Doris (2002), Wilson (2002), Nahmias (2007), Knobe and Nichols (2008)). The general effect of this "situationist" line of enquiry is to cast increasing doubt on our everyday picture of ordinary adult human agents as consciously aware of, and in control of, themselves and their motivations and subsequent actions in such a way that they are, generally speaking, fully morally responsible for what they do. Situationism finds a natural ally in Freudian theory, while considerably extending the range of factors that threaten to undermine our everyday picture of responsibility. It tells us that we are far more "puppets of circumstances" than we realize; it questions our conception of ordinary human beings as genuinely free agents in a way that is independent of any considerations about determinism or the impossibility of self-origination. At the same time (again in line with Freudian theory) it grounds a sense in which greater self-knowledge, a better understanding of what motivates one, can increase one's control of and responsibility for one's actions.

Chapter Three

Determinism, Incompatibilism and Compatibilism, Actual Consciousness and Subjective Physical Worlds, Humanity

Ted Honderich

DETERMINISM

Are there many determinists? It would be reassuring for the likes of me to think that there are an awful lot of empiricists, and so that there must be a good many determinists. But you will not be slow to ask, rightly, what I mean in speaking of empiricists. Empiricism can hardly be adequate if it is the practice of limiting oneself to propositions that are directly confirmed by sense experience—limiting oneself to perceptual consciousness. More has to get into inquiry and judgment. Few of us are attracted to the German and other tradition of philosophical Rationalism as opposed to English and other Empiricism. But most of us must be attracted to the idea that the hope of truth must lie in both experience and what you can call the three imperatives of the ordinary logic of intelligence—clarity, usually by analysis, and consistency and validity, and completeness, typically issuing in generalness (cf. Van Fraassen 1980).

Empiricism can indeed reasonably be taken as experience and ordinary logic. In another description, it is what includes a marriage or kind of cohabitation or visits back and forth of science and philosophy, the latter in its main tradition as a concentration on the ordinary logic of intelligence. Most of us will be content to embrace empiricism in this sense. It is distinct from Logical Empiricism or Logical Positivism (Ayer 1936; Carnap 1967). Maybe it is better called reflective empiricism.

One of its results in this present piece of informal thinking about determinism and its consequences, informal thinking that looks backward and forward, is that determinism is true or at least probable. There ought to be more determinists among us reflective empiricists. Indeed there ought not to be any of us reflective empiricists who are not also determinists.

My pretty standard conception of determinism (Honderich 1988, 71–258; 2002, 22–64) is as follows. Events, some of them long enough to be states, are things or entities having properties, and events are the only subject-matter of determinism. There is causal and other lawful connection between events, at bottom conditional connection, the existence of dependencies, connections stated in conditional statements. To speak only of causal connection, an event that is an effect is an event such that it would still have happened, if or since and after a causal circumstance happened, whatever else had happened consistently with a causal circumstance—such a circumstance being a set of conditions including what we may designate as the cause of the effect (1998, 13–70; 2002, 8–21).

It is important that lawfulness, for all its complexity, can in this way be made clear. This way does not rely, for a start, on what is too common, inexplicit reference to *law*. It does not include any speculative or theory-bound idea of causation, say that effects are no more than mere probabilities or are to be understood in terms of possible worlds. As we will be noticing, determinism is at least that essential first step nearer truth than its denial with respect to freedom and responsibility (cf. Hoefer 2010).

My life has been such that my reflective empiricism has never issued in doubt about the proposition that all events are effects—or anyway are lawful, the non-causal lawful pairs being correlates other than causal circumstances and effects. As noted in my previous and dogged thinking on determinism and freedom, there has been no chance event in my life, no event not lawful. No spoon has ever levitated at breakfast. No matter my inability to explain particular events, to arrive at one of its preceding sequence of full causal circumstances, there has been no event of which there has been reason to take it not to be the result of such a sequence.

I've never met anyone in ordinary thinking life, in all its parts and levels save one, who said that an ordinary event had no causal circumstance at all, nothing that made it happen, that it had no adequate explanation, whether or not found. No one thinks any car accident or even any falling out of love had no adequate causation. If you give any weight to overwhelming consensus in judgment and belief, a weighting most common in science, if you take some approximation to unanimity as being indicative of truth, that is a very large fact. The premise for an inductive inference, the kind of inference fundamental to most science, is the greatest premise there is.

You may not be slow to say, of course, that there is some science, some interpretation or application to the world of some mathematics, that is against me and other reflective empiricists. I am not slow to reply.

The interpretation of Quantum Mechanics, the application of that mathematics to the world, has long been allowed to be logically a mess, and it would be called so more often except for excessive deference to physics and to science. I mean that the indeterminist interpretation reported to us has *contradiction* in it, from the two-slit experiment onward (Honderich 1988, 304-36; 2002, 71-76; cf. Earman 1986; Bishop 2002; Hodgson 2002).

That is not all. It has in it loose philosophy, some of it fantastic. It also has in it a dilemma having to do with micro-determinism amplifying upwards into macro-determinism or not, up to the level of neurons and spoons. If there is amplifying up, to where there is no evidence of determinism, then indeterminism down below is put in question. If there isn't amplifying up, on the other hand, then even if there is indeterminism down below, there is no determinism where it would matter. Also, there is an obvious uncertainty as to whether some interpretations of Quantum Mechanics are really talking about events at all when they say some things are not effects. No determinist says any non-events are effects.

All of this is not put in doubt by the extent to which Quantum Theory *works*. Such a non-explanatory recommendation was also had by its predecessor in physics and is had by conceptions and the like elsewhere, say in medicine. And I propose to you, finally, that with determinism applied to our human existence, all physics has less authority than neuroscience. In that judgment I do not overlook the very shaky neuroscience-with-philosophy of Libet (Honderich 2004b), taken as evidence for and then as a successor to the large work of Popper and Eccles on the self and its mind (1977).

Do you need to be reminded, too, that affective attitude and the large and several-sided fact of subjectivity enters into or at least influences judgments as to truth? You can best divide consciousness into perceptual, cognitive, and affective, where the third part or side is at bottom a matter of diverse desire. That includes intentions, and hopes and life-hopes, and, most relevantly now, inclination to defer and conform. You are likely also to agree, maybe to say you know all too well, that our affective sides influence our cognitive sides. It is an inescapable fact. Some of affective states have to do with great practices or institutions and their history, and with consensus in them. One of those, indeed, is science.

There seems to me no doubt at all, despite my proper deference and indeed my esteem for scientific method, no less than my esteem for ordinary logic, that affective attitudes enter into what are taken as matters of only cognition with respect to science. These attitudes, part of a certain hegemony of science owed to its great usefulness, have issued in tolerance of what cannot be tolerated, which is the mentioned contradiction and the rest. It is no good, of course, celebrating inconsistency as deep mystery. It is possible to forget that to say light is waves and also not waves is to say nothing.

It is my hopeful guess that the heyday of physics-inspired indeterminism is over or on the way to over. In this connection I also mention in passing, if not with heavy intention, renowned skepticisms having to do with what might be called fashions in science (Kuhn 1962), and acute judgments with respect to realities of scientific method (Godfrey-Smith 2003). Can we toy with the idea that indeterminism with respect to our choices and decisions will one day be looked back on in the way we now look back on *animism*, the attribution of living souls to plants, inanimate objects and natural phenomena?

Do you now observe, very properly, that my proposition that a part of physics does not disprove determinism, including the rest of science, is itself in part a matter of attitude? I cannot possibly declare otherwise. We're all human, aren't we? What I can do, in passing, is note a couple of other things.

It is not clear what significant personal satisfaction determinists are supposed to gain from their theory. Indeed, as we will be noticing, disadvantage is at least more likely. It was of course speculated (Pagels 1983, 20–23) that Einstein's determinism was owed to some fact of personality, some insecurity, but that silly proposition was of course never made clear and persuasive. Was it a 'need' for order in the universe? Maybe something to do with his good politics? Now, with the decline of Freudianism, tied to decline in belief in Freud's veracity, I take it that the possibility of an accepted diagnosis of Einstein, let alone of determinists generally, is yet more remote. It may be that this progress with Freudianism may have contributed to recent general and strong advocacies of determinism (e.g. Oerton 2012).

It is clear, on the other hand, what personal satisfaction indeterminists get from their theory, what non-rational motivation there is. There is a lot of it. Their indeterminism goes with a pervasive morality having to do with desert, of which you will be hearing a bit more. It goes with personal impulses almost all of us have, of which you will also be hearing a bit more. It goes with having the support of consensus, also to be known less reassuringly as democracy about truth. It goes with respectability and what is taken as non-crankiness. It goes with mystery, whose allure in much human existence is clear. It goes with religion.

INCOMPATIBILISM AND COMPATIBILISM

But come away from the subjects of determinism itself, its truth, and certain affective attitudes. Come away towards a matter as great as the truth of determinism, which is its consequences for us in our lives and our thinking of our lives.

The matter is best viewed by way of thumbnail sketches of the historical responses to what has been, for philosophers, the principal problem with respect to determinism. What follows for us from determinism? What follows with respect to our freedom and responsibility? That has been or maybe was the principal philosophical dispute about determinism from at least as far back as before Hume's flying the flag of the regiment that followed him thereafter (1748/1963, 95), and Kant's insulting him for it (1788/1949, 99) and raising another flag.

Kant's regiment is now not standing so firmly, except perhaps in more remote and backward states of America and outer counties of England and like places. Still, the regiment defends a proposition about our being free in the primary ordinary sense, the sense that matters. It is that our being free, and hence our being held responsible and credited with responsibility for our actions, not to mention our prospect of heaven, is our being free in a way logically incompatible with determinism.

This is so since free and responsible action, as we are all supposed to know and obliged to know, is action *owed to choice or decision that is uncaused and yet within the control of the actor*. It is random in the first and clear sense—being uncaused—but not in the obscure second sense. Speaking of action being in control of an actor may come to little more than that it is action such that the actor is open to affective attitudes of holding him responsible or crediting him with responsibility—but that is to say *something* (cf. Strawson 2002). It is to not to say nothing of sense. It makes some sense.

So much for Kant's regiment of *Incompatibilism*. It defends freedom that is best named as *origination*, maybe what is most commonly meant by talk of *free will* as against just *freedom*.

The other regiment, more on parade still, defends the proposition that our being free and responsible, as we are all supposed to know, is our being free in a way perfectly logically compatible with determinism. This is so since, as we are told we all know or should know, free action is action owed not to no causation but to one kind of causation. Free action is owed to self-determination, inner causation, say embraced desire (Honderich 1988, 394; 2002, 95), rather than compulsion or constraint. This is *Compatibilism*.

These two tired traditions (Honderich 1988, 451–87; 2002, 105–21) have been elaborated and refurbished over time, and to some lesser extent continue to be. Arguments of ingenuity have been offered, mostly on the incompatibilist side (van Inwagen 1983). I respect them, but respect more the attraction of many philosophers to the clarity of the idea of voluntariness. It is at least an aid to truth, something hard to say for the tolerance of their opponents. That is a tolerance of at least the relative obscurity, the exceedingly general and thus thin content of the idea of origination—decisions and choices not caused, not explained in that obvious way, but still gestured at as in the control or the like of the actor. Self-causation, cause of itself, is the worst of this story.

Incompatibilism in its assertion of the freedom of origination cannot be true or probable for the reason, a first reason, that determinism *is* true or probable. What of the idea shared by Incompatibilism and Compatibilism that we have but *one* idea of freedom—the idea about which the two regiments disagree as to what it is?

I myself cannot take at all seriously this shared proposition that we have only one idea of freedom, anyway one idea worth attending to. Incompatibilists say our only idea of freedom and of responsibility in a primary ordinary sense is the idea of origination and the responsibility based on it. Compatibilists say our only idea of freedom and responsibility has to do with voluntariness. If there are now Incompatibilists and Compatibilists who have retreated to safer positions, who say that their idea of freedom and responsibility is the one that matters, or the one favored by a better class of thinkers, that does not save them.

I cannot but put aside in passing a third contention, semi-compatibilism, original but to me factitious. It is that our single idea of freedom and our single attitude and practice of responsibility are such that one is a concern with origination and the other is a concern with voluntariness (Fischer 2002). This ecumenicalism seems to me to face an indubitable obstacle.

Prior to all theorizing, all dispute between the two regiments, it is clear that any attitude and practice having to do with responsibility is inseparable from a conception and belief having to do with freedom. The attitude and practice simply has a content that in one of its two main parts is a matter of freedom—the other part having to do with action being right or wrong (Honderich 1988, 379–450; 2002, 91–104). And, to come to the main point, it is to me inconceivable that if, as supposed, we have one principal and fundamental idea of freedom, and one principal and fundamental attitude and practice of responsibility, the second does not have the first as intrinsic or integral to it. Semi-compatibilism, I suspect, collapses into the truth that we have two ideas of freedom going with two attitudes and practices of responsibility (Honderich 2002, 120).

To return to Incompatibilism and Compatibilism, Incompatibilism is false both because of determinism and the only-one-idea proposition, and Compatibilism is false because of the only-one-idea proposition. As far as I know, recent Incompatibilists and Compatibilists have not set out explicitly to argue, let alone succeeded in arguing, that we do not also have the idea of freedom and responsibility to which they are not inclined. They would have had a job to do so, for at least two large sorts of reason.

I myself am not and never have been a member of a party that no longer exists, that of Oxford ordinary-language philosophy associated with J. L. Austin (Warnock 1989). But I have no hesitation about citing the best repositories of our concepts and conceptions, these repositories being dictionaries, and in particular the best shorter dictionary I know. *The New Oxford Dictionary of English*. It defines freedom in the primary or core sense as "the power or right to act, speak, or think as one wants without hindrance or restraint." It then gives the two relevant subsenses—being free is (i) "having the power of self-determination attributed to the will, the quality of being independent of fate or necessity," and being free is (ii) not being subject to enumerated kinds of compulsion, constraint, and domination.

In the face just of this evidence of our two ideas of freedom, both Incompatibilism and Compatibilism are nonsense. Moritz Schlick, the Logical Positivist of Vienna, said Incompatibilism as against Compatibilism is the greatest scandal of philosophy (1956, 143–44). He should have added into his declaration its assumption of there being only one conception of freedom and responsibility. But you may have more reservations about lexicographers and Logical Positivists than I. So consider some other evidence, some other stuff of reflective empiricism. Consider two examples or rather large cases, certainly not the only cases.

We hear much, rightly, of human rights, and of denials of them. They are rights to an array of things, from enough food to sustain life to education to a lot else. To have such a right, plainly, is to have a freedom, a freedom implied to be justified. Excuse my not elaborating that plain truth. To claim such a right is to claim a freedom. What freedom? What kind of freedom?

In this case of human rights it would be mad to say it is origination. It would be mad to say people who want a freedom from hunger and starvation or from invasion of their indigenous homeland want an alteration of their human natures so that they can originate actions, become mysteriously in control in their causeless actions. They are not under the influence of mediaeval or Kentucky or Dorset theologians. What they want is a change in things outside of themselves, not *in* their nature as deciders. What they want, obviously, is the freedom which is not being compelled by a lack of food, or more particularly by others or an economic and social system, to be hungry or to be ignorant.

Now the other case, our yet more personal and sometimes private lives. We also hear a lot in both covert and overt ways with respect to what purports to be another many-sided fact. The fact, so to speak, includes what people *deserve* in terms or punishment or income or respect or whatever. If I give this paper as a talk in Kentucky or Dorset, and a clever fellow manages really to insult me effectively in public, call in question my intelligence, I am unlikely to be able to respond only by thinking and feeling that his insult was voluntary. I shall feel an impulse of retribution that presupposes that as things had been in his life and were then, he could then have done otherwise. He could have done otherwise in the sense not that his insult was not compelled or constrained but in the sense that he could have done what his power of origination or free will allowed.

If we cannot for this second reason alone respond to determinism in the single-minded Incompatibilist way or in the single-minded Compatibilist way, by way of their shared mistake, how are we to respond to it? Evidently we have to give up on the idea of origination and the responsibility attached to it. What of the obvious alternative of responding by means of voluntariness alone? The alternative of taking it that we need to live with only the idea of voluntariness and the responsibility attached to it?

It remains my view that part of the answer must be neither what was called Dismay or Intransigence, but rather something called Affirmation (Honderich,1988, 488–540; 2002, 122–32). You can also think about the reassurance of being your own man, being your own woman (Honderich 2002, 142–47). But there is more to be said, more to be thought about and worked on. Consider a proposition of the foremost contemporary philosopher of Incompatibilism, the acute Robert Kane (1998). He has the great recommendation of explaining that not only Incompatibilists but also the rest of us want something of a general kind that Incompatibilism and in particular origination would give us. This is distinct from the motivations of Incompatibilism already mentioned. It is *standing*.

We want a human standing that separates us from what used to be called *nature*, or anyway the rest of nature, in some sense puts us apart from or even above *the objective physical world* or the rest of that world, which origination would have done. Or, to state a better and more respectable requirement, we want an explanation of what there is reason to call a truth, that we *have* such a standing, at least that we *are* somehow different in kind from the rest of nature. We have a true sense of our lives such that determinism and voluntariness do not satisfy it.

ACTUAL CONSCIOUSNESS AND SUBJECTIVE PHYSICAL WORLDS

What can be added as quickly is that the subject of freedom and responsibility has never been separable from the subject of consciousness. It is not just that there is no question at all of freedom and responsibility with respect to what is unconscious. It is that consciousness gives to any species, and in a special way to our species, a kind of distinction different from and greater than, say, the distinction between the living and the non-living, a distinction that is bound up with freedom and responsibility.

Is it the case that *any* conception of our consciousness serves this argument? That the conceptions are the same in this respect? If the answer is not easy, it is still no. It is clear enough that a really flattening objective physicalism about consciousness, say a physicalism that makes no effective distinction between consciousness in the or a primary ordinary sense and the rest of the mental, no effective distinction between such consciousness in seeing, thinking and wanting as against the rest of mentality, will not provide a distinction that is useful. So with Block's two ideas of consciousness, phenomenal and access consciousness (1997, 2007). The situation is not much complicated by the fact that all of what I am calling flattening physicalisms do of course maintain they are not such. Dennett's is a strong and fortitudinous exemplar (1984, 1991).

Is it the case that any conception of consciousness other than flattening physicalism will serve the end in question as well? The short answer must again be no. It is no for the reason that the couple of dozen existing theories of consciousness contain so many that are open to serious objections that make them of at least limited use in the way we are considering (cf. Caruso 2012). Abstract functionalism, which is standard functionalism, and such associated lines of life as a kind of cognitive science, as against a conceivably physical functionalism, share the disability of traditional dualism or spiritualism. I myself have reservations not much less serious against the Higher Order Theory of consciousness (Rosenthal 2005) and various others. They include strong doctrines of supervenience (Kim 2005), general representationalisms (Dretske 1995), and biological naturalism (Searle 1992).

I end with anticipation of a very different theory of consciousness, that of the forthcoming book entitled *Actual Consciousness*, and then with a hope, a grand hope, what you can properly call a hope of mankind.

The speculation attached to the different theory is that there are different facts on which we can rest, facts that gives us a standing or standings that may leave us content despite the loss attendant on giving up origination. Certainly it is a speculation that makes us different in several related ways from the rest of nature. If its beginnings (Freeman 2006) include nothing whatever about freedom and responsibility, but much about an adequate initial clarification of consciousness in the ordinary sense, it does give to us a standing given to us by no other theory.

Let me say quickly that it is in part an externalism or anti-cranialism different in kind from those of Putnam (1975), Burge (2007), Noe (2009), and Clark (2011). It is an externalism with respect only to perceptual consciousness as against cognitive and affective consciousness—the latter consisting in representations having to do with truth and desire.

A first thing to be said or promised with respect to this theory of consciousness (Honderich 2013), is that an arguable account of all consciousness in the primary ordinary sense is open to summary in a certain way. This consciousness, in accordance with a lot of data we have, is *something's being actual*. In the present speedy report, I add no more to that than the following general proposition. It is possible to give an account of what can be called *actual consciousness* that separates it from the rest of what there is, not by a retreat to dualism as against physicalism, but to a recognition of a fundamental kind of physicality, as fundamental as any.

If a sentence of anticipation is worth anything, the theory is to the effect that for you to be perceptually conscious in particular now is for there to be *a subjective physical world* external to you, a world of space outside you, in causal relations, and so on. This world, say this room, whose particular physicality cannot be in doubt, is dependent on the objective physical world. It is also dependent, crucially, on you, on you neurally. You have this standing lacked by anything that lacks perceptual consciousness. On this theory, as someone else might give in to the temptation to say, and I do not, you have standing of being a little demigod, if one among very many indeed. We are all creators, alongside the objective physical world, of myriad subjective physical worlds, no less real for being myriad.

HUMANITY

Coming on now to the grand if faint hope, it has something to do with what has been mentioned already, that we are all, or all save a very few of us, inclined to impulses of retribution, what can as well be called impulses of desert, impulses that have within them an idea or anyway something like an image of origination. The grand hope, however, has much more to do with something much larger—practices and institutions of retribution and desert that are fundamental to our societies and also to relations between them. Punishment in a society will come back to your mind immediately. So should our systems of reward by desert, systems having to do in one part with income and wealth.

These systems in our societies, the hierarchic democracies of Britain and United States and those others along similar lines, are of course open to classification and theorizing of many kinds. To my mind, they are most generally classified as being systems of *Conservatism*. This includes at least much Liberalism, such as that of the Liberal Democrat party in the coalition government of the United Kingdom as of now. You ask what Conservatism is, and I must reply with outrageous brevity.

It is the self-interest, a self-interest of individuals and classes, that has no arguable principle of right and wrong to defend itself (Honderich 2005). It has, for a start, on account of the truth of determinism and the non-existence of origination, no general principle of desert to defend itself. There is also the difficulty, not so particular to this conversation, that it can be argued that no principle of desert succeeds in understanding propositions of the form *X is deserved* in such a way to distinguish them from *X is right*—with the upshot that every principle of desert is fundamentally of the circular form *X is right because it is right*.

Conservatism is different, to say the least, from what I shall call The Left in politics, a tradition of as much self-interest but with a principle of right and wrong that defends it in pursuing that self-interest. That is the *Principle of Humanity*. It is, in a sentence, that what is right is what is rational, only what is rational, with respect to the end of getting and keeping people out of bad lives, these being lives to different extents deprived of the great human goods, frustrated in the great desires of human nature. These goods and desires have to do with length of conscious life, bodily well-being, freedoms and powers, respect and self-respect, goods of relationship, and the goods of culture.

The practices and institutions of desert in our societies are owed less to any intrinsic or genetic or ordinarily evolved human attributes than to something else. They are owed to the tradition of Conservatism, the self-interest incapable of justifying itself. My great hope, a hope in which I invite you to join, is the grand if faint hope of The Left in morals and politics. My invitation, in the context of this moment, has to do with determinism, freedom, the non-existence of origination, and wrong and right.

It is that the abandoning of Incompatibilism, Compatibilism, ordinary belief and inclination with respect to origination, and the politics of desert that is a main source of the belief and inclination, has the recommendation of serving the end of the great principle of right and wrong, the Principle of Humanity. We can have the support of that principle, so to speak, in living with what follows from the falsehood of the proposition of origination.

It is not only that we can, in truth, see that our standing is greater by reflection on perceptual consciousness as conceived in the theory of Actual Consciousness. We can hope for our human successors an escape from at least the temptation to an attitude that is a means of those of us who are wrongly defending our societies as they are.

One more thought. You will agree, maybe, that there is at least the possibility of consolation having to do with perceptual consciousness in the necessary escape from the stuff about origination. With respect to the great hope, you are less likely to agree, maybe, in what you may call my intruding of morals and politics into our inquiry.

I make no apology at all. I merely remind or inform you of something. The very best account of the whole history of the questions of determinism and freedom is that one by Mortimer J. Adler and what was The Institute for Philosophical Research. This account, *The Idea of Freedom: A Dialectical Examination of the Conceptions of Freedom*, divides the history into thinking about origination, voluntariness, and a third thing—what is called self-perfection. I reduce the latter idea by remarking that it has to do with the freedom that is the circumstance of *the good man, the good woman*, and I reduce it horribly by saying that it has to do with, in its very least persuasive conception, the freedom of *he or she who is free from sin*.

You will note the consonance between this tradition of thinking on freedom and my remarks about the Principle of Humanity and the hope. I add, finally, that the part of Adler's history that considers the thinking of freedom that is thinking of origination and voluntariness, rather than self-perfection, adds in an extensive consideration of those bodies of thinking in so far as their content is social and political. A large part of the thinking on voluntariness, a part given separate attention, is on political freedom.

Chapter Four

The Stubborn Illusion of Moral Responsibility

Bruce Waller

The philosophical commitment to moral responsibility is stubborn, profound, and almost universal. Belief in moral responsibility is also strong among "the folk," of course; but while philosophers may be more familiar with the wide range of threats to moral responsibility, they seem even more devoted to its defense. When nonphilosophers consider the possibility of determinism they often conclude that determinism *might* be true, and that if determinism turns out to be true that could mean the demise of moral responsibility. Philosophers likewise acknowledge that determinism *might* be true, but insist that conclusive proof of determinism would not and should not result in doubts about moral responsibility. Thus P. F. Strawson (1962) claims that our moral responsibility system is held firmly in place by deep personal and social values and cannot be shaken by such theoretical considerations as determinism. John Martin Fischer agrees: "I am motivated in much of my work by the idea that our basic status as distinctively free and morally responsible agents should not depend on the arcane ruminations—and deliverances—of the theoretical physicists and cosmologists. That is, I do not think that our status as morally responsible persons should depend on whether or not causal determinism is true" (2006a, 5). And Peter van Inwagen makes it clear that though he would be distressed by the discovery that determinism is true, that could never lead him to doubt moral responsibility:

> If incompatibilism is true, then either determinism or the free-will thesis is false. To deny the free-will thesis is to deny the existence of moral responsibility, which would be absurd. Moreover, there seems to be no good reason to accept determinism. . . . Therefore we should reject determinism.

> This conclusion is, at least in principle, open to scientific refutation, since it is conceivable that science will one day present us with compelling reasons for believing in determinism. Then, and only then, I think, should we become compatibilists. (1983, 223)

So while proof of determinism might threaten the moral responsibility faith of the folk, philosophical faith in moral responsibility looks on tempests and is not shaken. Whether the tempests are in the form of determinism, neuropsychological research, or psychological studies, the philosophical commitment to moral responsibility remains firm.

Belief in moral responsibility is a powerful and deep-rooted belief, for philosophers and nonphilosophers alike. Even religious convictions seem to come out second best when they clash with belief in moral responsibility. The Christian New Testament teaches that humans have no moral responsibility: the godly potter makes each pot (each person) for damnation or grace, the pots have no power and no choice and no moral responsibility, it is all beyond human understanding, and it is blasphemous to question the potter's decision. While followers of John Calvin and Martin Luther reluctantly swallowed that dogma, today most Christians (including fundamentalists devoted to the literal truth of the Bible) simply ignore the plain but inconvenient Scriptures and insist that humans have a special power of miraculous free godlike choice that makes them morally responsible for their own eternal destiny.

Philosopher or Christian fundamentalist, belief in moral responsibility seems immune to challenge. And whether empiricist (like Hume), pragmatist (like William James), logical positivist (like Moritz Schlick), or Kantian rationalist (such as C. A. Campbell, or Kant himself), philosophers of all stripes seem to hold one belief in common: Belief in moral responsibility.

There is no stronger proof of the powerful hold of moral responsibility than the desperate philosophical efforts to make sense of moral responsibility, under increasingly difficult conditions. In the fifteenth century, Pico della Mirandola—with the aid of gods and miracles—had no trouble giving an account of human moral responsibility. As God states in Pico's *Oration on the Dignity of Man*, humans have been given a remarkable power to make themselves in any form:

> The nature of all other beings is limited and constrained within the bounds of laws prescribed by Us. Thou, constrained by no limits, in accordance with thine own free will, in whose hand We have placed thee, shall ordain for thyself the limits of thy nature.... We have made thee neither of heaven nor of earth, neither mortal nor immortal, so that with freedom of choice and with honor, as though the maker and molder of thyself, thou mayest fashion thyself in whatever shape thou shalt prefer. Thou shalt have the power to degenerate into the lower forms of life, which are brutish. Thou shalt have the power, out

of thy soul's judgment, to be reborn into the higher forms, which are divine. (1486/1948, 224–25)

By the twentieth century, philosophers were considerably less comfortable with explanations that appealed to gods and miracles and mysteries; but if moral responsibility requires miracles, then miracles there must be. C. A. Campbell (1957) posits "contra-causal free will" as a means of saving moral responsibility: A special power of choosing among alternatives, with *nothing* causing that pivotal choice save the choice itself; and Campbell insists that if this account of free will is inconsistent with our scientific understanding of the natural world then so much the worse for science. Richard Taylor proposes an account of human *agency* that makes us morally responsible for our behavior, but acknowledges its extraordinary requirements: "one can hardly affirm such a theory of agency with complete comfort, however, and wholly without embarrassment, for the conception of men and their powers which is involved in it is strange indeed, if not positively mysterious" (1963, 52). But embarrassment and mystery are apparently a small price to pay for saving moral responsibility. Roderick Chisholm specifies and embraces the godlike power required for moral responsibility:

> If we are responsible, and if what I have been trying to say is true, then we have a prerogative which some would attribute only to God: each of us, when we really act, is a prime mover unmoved. In doing what we do, we cause certain events to happen, and nothing and no one, except we ourselves, causes us to cause those events to happen. (1982, 32)

When contemporary philosophers are willing to posit miracles in order to save moral responsibility, the philosophical belief in moral responsibility obviously runs deep and strong.

Of course most philosophers—from Hume on—have rejected miracles, and made *compatibilist* efforts to save moral responsibility: moral responsibility is fully compatible with our naturalistic (even deterministic) world view. But what is remarkable is the amazing variety of competing compatibilist arguments for saving moral responsibility. Anyone making a candid survey of the enormous range and diversity of compatibilist arguments for moral responsibility would find it difficult to avoid two conclusions: First, that the defenders of moral responsibility are deeply divided among themselves, with small scattered groups clinging doggedly to favored compatibilist positions while each group regards all the other compatibilist arguments as clear failures. Second, that the efforts to defend moral responsibility are becoming increasingly desperate and dubious. For example, Daniel Dennett offers a rich variety of compatibilist arguments for moral responsibility, but never seems satisfied that they work. He continues to contrive new ones, until at last he recommends that we stop trying to find an account of human freedom that will justify moral responsibility, and instead simply take moral responsibility as given: obviously we are morally responsible, therefore *whatever* powers humans have *must* suffice for moral responsibility (2003, 297). Such an approach to justifying moral responsibility has its advantages; unfortunately, as Bertrand Russell might phrase it, Dennett's solution has all the advantages of theft over honest labor.

Whatever one thinks of the rich variety of libertarian and compatibilist arguments in defense of moral responsibility and their comparative strengths and weaknesses, one thing is clear: The philosophical *belief* in moral responsibility is much stronger than the *arguments* for moral responsibility. While few philosophers state their absolute adherence to belief in moral responsibility with the fervor of Van Inwagen—denying moral responsibility "would be absurd"—it is clear that philosophical belief in moral responsibility is as strong as it is widespread. Yet even the most dedicated philosophical defender of moral responsibility must acknowledge that there is no philosophical *argument* that can justify such confidence and commitment. So if we are seeking to understand the philosophical dedication to moral responsibility, that cannot be accomplished by examining philosophical *arguments* in support of moral responsibility. Those arguments are interesting, inventive, and instructive; but even if one believes that one or another of those arguments offers grounds for belief in moral responsibility, few philosophers would claim that their *arguments* and *reasons* in support of moral responsibility are as strong as their *belief* in moral responsibility. To find the roots of belief in moral responsibility we must dig deeper than philosophical arguments.

The most obvious, probably the strongest, and no doubt the deepest source for belief in moral responsibility is the visceral *strike-back* impulse: an impulse that philosophers share with the folk, that skeptics concerning moral responsibility feel as strongly as believers, and that we hold in common with chimpanzees, rats, and many other species. When we are harmed, we desire to strike back; at the source of the harm, if that is readily available, but the important thing is to strike back at something. Rats placed in a cage and then shocked through the floor of the cage immediately attack one another (Virgin and Sapolsky 1997). A chimp attacked by a larger and stronger dominant attacks a weaker subordinate (Kawamura 1967). This common response is an element of slapstick humor (Larry hits Moe, and Moe hits Curly) and sadly amusing cartoons (the boss berates a subordinate, who returns home to yell at his wife, who chastises the kid, who kicks the unoffending dog). But in fact there is nothing funny in the strike-back response. When the U.S. suffered a painful defeat in Vietnam, American citizens felt better after the U.S. launched an unprovoked attack on the defenseless island of Grenada; unscrupulous prosecutors know that when the evidence is weak, a conviction can still be obtained if the jury is convinced that a terrible wrong has been done and thus *someone* has to suffer (and the defendant is an easily available target). The research of Jonathan Haidt and other social intuitionist psychologists shows this retributive impulse to be a cross-cultural universal (Haidt 2001).

Whatever its actual motivating force, most philosophers are reluctant to appeal directly to the strike-back impulse as grounds for moral responsibility; but there are some noteworthy exceptions who openly advocate strike-back retributivism. Michael S. Moore gives a stark and unapologetic statement of his retributive view:

> Of course Dostoyevsky's nobleman [who has his dogs kill a small child in front of the child's mother] should suffer for his gratuitous and unjustified perpetration of a terrible wrong to both his young serf and that youth's mother. As even the gentle Aloysha murmurs in Dostoyevsky's novel, in answer to the question of what you do with the nobleman: you shoot him. You inflict such punishment even though no other good will be achieved thereby, but simply because the nobleman deserves it. The only general principle that makes sense of the mass of particular judgments like that of Aloysha is the retributive principle that culpable wrongdoers must be punished. This, by my lights, is enough to justify retributivism. (1997, 188)

Peter French regards retribution as an essential underpinning of morality:

> Personal and vicarious moral anger can be and ought to be placated by hostile responsive action taken against its cause. Wrongful actions require hostile retribution. That, despite its seeming lack of fit with the body of moral principles upheld in our culture, is actually one of the primary foundations of morality. It is a foundation that is settled in passions, attitudes, emotions, and sentiments, not in reason. (2001, 97)

Robert C. Solomon takes a similar view:

> Sometimes vengeance is wholly called for, even obligatory, and revenge is both legitimate and justified.... To seek vengeance for a grievous wrong, to revenge oneself against evil—that seems to lie at the very foundation of our sense of justice, indeed, of our very sense of ourselves, our dignity, and our sense of right and wrong. (2004, 37)

Thus the retributive principle that requires us to strike back at those who harm us is "at the very foundation of our sense of justice," it is "one of the primary foundations of morality" and is "settled in passions, attitudes, emotions, and sentiments, not in reason." It is a "foundational" starting point settled deep in our emotions.

When we look carefully at the strike-back emotion that we share with rats and chimps, we may question its legitimacy as a foundation for our moral thought. But looking carefully is what this visceral retributive emotion prevents. The powerful strike-back emotion overwhelms careful reflection; indeed, we have experimental proof of its power to overwhelm reasoned reflection, as demonstrated in an experiment conducted by Shaun Nichols and Joshua Knobe (2007). They first presented subjects with an account of a determinist universe, proceeding according to deterministic laws (Universe A). They then divided the subjects into two groups, and asked the first group this question: "In Universe A, is it possible for a person to be fully morally responsible for their actions?" Fewer than 5 percent said that a person could be fully morally responsible in that deterministic universe. The second group was given a more concrete case within the same deterministic Universe A, in which a man named Bill is attracted to his secretary, and decides that the only way to be with her is to kill his family. Bill places an incendiary device in his basement that burns down the house while he is away on a business trip, killing his wife and three children. Is Bill fully morally responsible for killing his wife and children? For the latter concrete case, 72 percent of the subjects responded that Bill was fully morally responsible.

In discussing that experiment, Joshua Knobe and John M. Doris (2010) suggest that the concept of "moral responsibility" is not an "invariantist" concept, but instead operates under different criteria in different circumstances; that is, rather than a single concept of moral responsibility with a single set of criteria, we use different criteria for moral responsibility in different cases: one set of criteria in the abstract setting and a different set in the concrete situation. But that multiplies criteria beyond necessity, for there is a simpler explanation. We have settled criteria for moral responsibility, and concerns about determinism challenge the criteria for moral responsibility and result in reflective doubts concerning moral responsibility. But when we encounter a concrete case (the murder of an innocent woman and her three children) then our strong emotions overwhelm careful deliberation (Sherman, Beike, and Ryalls 1999; Hafer and Bègue 2005, 137), we demand retribution, and the belief that the individual is morally responsible and justly deserves punishment follows smoothly, effortlessly, and nonreflectively.

The strong feeling in favor of retributive moral responsibility not only overwhelms careful reflection, but blocks it. It *feels* right to strike back, and thoughtful consideration—for example, of all the factors that shaped the wrongdoer (Watson 1987; Nichols 2007)—tends to block the expression of that feeling. Thus there is a strong tendency to avoid the careful scrutiny that would get in the way of expressing our retributive impulses. So the belief in moral responsibility—the belief that it is right and just to punish those who cause harm—is both supported and protected by the desire to strike back: that emotion not only provides the basic support for belief in moral responsibility but also blocks the careful scrutiny that calls moral responsibility into question.

The underlying motives for philosophical belief in moral responsibility are not, however, confined to the strike-back emotion we share with rats.

While the powerful retributive emotions are an obvious source for belief in moral responsibility, there are also sources that function more subtly. One of those sources is a belief that exerts a powerful nonconscious influence, but which most philosophers *consciously* reject. Psychologists have studied "belief in a just world" for several decades, but those studies have received scant philosophical attention. Basically, the belief in a just world is the belief that wrongs will be righted (or at least requited), virtue rewarded, and justice will (ultimately) prevail; and this deep belief is an important foundation for belief in moral responsibility.

The suggestion that philosophical belief in moral responsibility is supported by belief in a just world will seem implausible to philosophers. Whatever the folk may believe about the world being just, philosophers do not share that illusion. Many philosophers believe in moral responsibility, but few believe that God is in His Heaven and all is right (or ultimately will be right) with the world. Whatever the deeper source of philosophical belief in moral responsibility, it is not a belief that the world is just.

When we carefully consider it, philosophers and folk alike find little *reason* to believe in a just world. But belief in a just world runs deeper than our conscious philosophical thought, and as part of our nonconscious belief system it exerts a powerful influence on folk and philosophers alike: an influence that is facilitated by being *non*conscious. While the visceral strikeback emotion is painfully evident, the deep human belief in a "just world" rarely rises to consciousness; when we do consciously consider whether this world is just, we may well deny it—though without eliminating the deep nonconscious belief. The powerful influence of nonconscious belief is not strange nor implausible nor Freudian. In similar manner, one may consciously and honestly repudiate racial prejudice while nonconsciously retaining deep and influential prejudices (Quillian 2008; Lane et al. 2007). And as automaticity theorists (Bargh and Chartrand 1999) and situationist psychologists (Doris 2002) have emphasized, motives and influences that do not rise to consciousness can exert a powerful influence on both our conscious thought and behavior.

Psychologist Melvin Lerner calls belief in a just world a "fundamental delusion" (1980). When we think carefully, it is quite obvious that the world is not just. The world news provides depressing and constant examples of innocents caught in the midst of terrible wars and ethnic conflicts, dying from industrial pollution or industrial accident (think of Bhopal), losing life or loved ones in tsunamis and earthquakes, dying slowly and painfully in drought and famine stricken regions; and our daily lives among our friends and families and communities include cases of tragic traffic deaths, terrible genetic diseases that kill or disable children, abuse of children and spouses, the deeply depressing loss of jobs and homes and pensions among good hardworking people. Philosophers are very familiar with the ancient "problem of evil": the unjust suffering of the innocent—on an enormous scale, and produced by famine, flood, war, and pestilence—is the major argument against belief in a just, caring, and omnipotent deity; and the only "solution" to the problem of evil requires appeal to a deity whose ways are beyond our understanding ("God's justice is not our justice," "from the divine perspective, this is the best of all possible worlds," "God has arranged an afterlife in which all the many wrongs will somehow be righted"). Whether philosophers or folk, belief in a just world cannot survive conscious scrutiny; but the deeper *non*conscious belief in a just world avoids such scrutiny and continues to exert a powerful influence.

While belief in a just world is certainly implausible, the *non*reflective nonconscious underlying belief in a just world is powerful, pervasive, and well-established by a body of psychological research spanning several decades and encompassing dozens of studies (Furnham 2003; Hafer and Bègue 2005). This deep belief is both common and cross-cultural, though not quite universal; and it is stronger in some than in others. Psychologists have learned a great deal about the belief, its resilience, and its unfortunate effects (as well as some of its benefits). In his extensive review of the psychological research into belief in a just world, Adrian Furnham gives a succinct statement of the basic belief in a just world (BJW): "The BJW asserts that, quite justly, good things tend to happen to good people and bad things to bad people despite the fact that this is patently not the case" (2003, 795). Lerner and Miller note that this belief, though false, serves a valuable function in motivating behavior and avoiding a sense of helplessness:

> Individuals have a need to believe that they live in a world where people generally get what they deserve. The belief that the world is just enables the individual to confront his physical and social environment as though they were stable and orderly. Without such a belief it would be difficult for the individual to commit himself to the pursuit of long range goals or even to the socially regulated behaviour of day to day life. (1978, 1030–31)

It is hardly surprising that such a deep and widespread belief (false though it be) serves some useful function: otherwise it would not have become so pervasive. It gives us a sense of a well-ordered world and thus encourages our positive efforts. But the benefits of this false belief are bought at a high price; and ironically, the costs of belief in a just world are paid in fundamental *in*justice. As Lerner and Miller note:

> Since the belief that the world is just serves such an important adaptive function for the individual, people are very reluctant to give up this belief, and they can be greatly troubled if they encounter evidence that suggests that the world is not really just or orderly after all. (1978, 1031)

The many ways and circumstances in which people *avoid* recognizing that the world is *un*just have been a major focus of research into belief in a just world. While belief in a just world can have limited positive effects, the efforts to preserve that belief in the face of powerful contrary evidence generates profoundly harmful results, including additional injustices toward those whose suffering threatens our just world belief.

Consider first the positive. When an innocent is harmed, one way of maintaining belief in a just world is by *aiding* the victim, and thus restoring the world to a just state. Lerner and Simmons (1966) found that when people believed that without great difficulty they could effectively aid innocent victims, then they were likely to provide such aid. But there are three conditions for such aid: the suffering victim must be *innocent* (must not have brought the suffering on herself), the aid must be *effective* (if the suffering is likely to continue, then people are not inclined to provide aid), and it must be possible to provide the aid without great difficulty. The problems start when we encounter the suffering of an innocent victim whom we cannot restore to a state of justice. That, after all, is commonly the case: the woman who has been brutally assaulted and raped, the child who is dying of untreatable disease, the victims of widespread famine, those trapped in harsh discriminatory social environments, the victims of a terrible ethnic conflict. When we cannot easily and effectively help innocent victims then our belief in a just world is severely threatened, and the most convenient and common way of preserving that belief is to change the status of the victim from innocent to guilty. The case of rape victims is the most obvious and extensively studied example of this phenomenon. Rape is a brutal, demeaning, and trauma-producing crime; in a just world, no innocent person would be subjected to such a horrific fate. Thus there is a powerful tendency to see rape victims as really not quite so innocent: they dressed provocatively; they were "loose" women; they did something to put themselves in that situation (they were careless about where they walked, or they drank too much); they "led him on" or were "asking for it" (thus in some parts of the world, rape victims are subject to death by stoning). Harsh cross-examinations of those who claim to be rape victims are notoriously common; those harsh cross-examinations are common because they are often effective; and they are often effective because juries—eager to preserve their belief in a just world—are already inclined to see the victim of this terrible ordeal as other than innocent.

The treatment of rape victims is an obvious way that belief in a just world leads to condemning the victim, but by no means the only way. The poor deserve their fate, because they are lazy. The unemployed don't really want to work. The victim of disease "brought it on himself." Those in famine-stricken regions are victims of their own corruption, or their own laziness, or their own lack of foresight. This blaming of victims (in defense of belief in a just world) has been established by numerous studies, including studies showing that the stronger the belief in a just world the greater the likelihood of blaming victims for their unfortunate fates (Wagstaff 1983; Furnham and Gunter 1984; Harper and Manasse 1992; Dalbert and Yamauchi 1994; Montada 1998).

Belief in a just world exerts enormous power for transforming innocent victims into guilty actors who get what they deserve. One of the most striking examples of that power can be found in the views of Eileen Gardner, who gained a few minutes of infamy when she was selected by Reagan's Secretary of Education, William Bennett, as his special assistant in the Office of Educational Philosophy and Practice. After her appointment, some of her views concerning severely disabled children came to public notice. In her writings, Gardner had complained that resources dedicated to helping disabled children were draining resources that should go to "normal" children, and that disabled children were *not* innocent victims but instead were responsible for their own problems: "They falsely assume that the lottery of life has penalized them at random. This is not so. Nothing comes to an individual that he has not, at some point in his development, summoned" (1984). (And if the disabled child did not summon it in this life, then he must have summoned it in an earlier life.) Severely disabled children are suffering now not because they are innocent victims, but because of their "level of inner spiritual development."

Not only do we blame innocent victims for their unfortunate fates, but belief in a just world often motivates victims to blame themselves (Lerner 1980, 123–25). Think of the sad cases of abused children who are convinced that they bring the abuse on themselves by their bad behavior, and that if only they could manage to be "good children" then the abuse would stop. Children who suffer when their parents divorce often blame themselves for the divorce. The story of Job presents in cosmic form the key elements of belief in a just world. Job is acclaimed by God to be "a perfect and an upright man, one that feareth God, and escheweth evil"; but Job—through no fault of his own—becomes the subject of a cosmic wager: his children are killed, his possessions lost, and his body is covered with painful bleeding sores "from the sole of his foot unto his crown." When his friends come to visit, they conclude that Job must have done something terribly wrong to have suffered such terrible misfortune. Ultimately, even Job concludes that he brought this suffering on himself by his own pride, and he repents "in dust and ashes." Job's judgment matches the conclusion innocent victims often draw: I must have done something to deserve this, somehow this must be my fault (a judgment facilitated by their own enduring belief in a just world, often coupled with the judgment of those around them: "Are you really sure you didn't do anything to lead him on?"). Blaming ourselves is less painful and disturbing than the belief that the world and its gods are arbitrary and unjust. In fact, the story of Job is so disturbing that, Biblical scholars generally agree, an epilogue (from some other source, probably a more ancient story) was added, which gives the book of Job a storybook ending: God acknowledges that Job is righteous, severely reprimands all those who had called Job evil, and commands them to apologize to Job, "lest I deal with you after your folly"; and "the Lord gave Job twice as much as he had before," and all his brethren came to him and comforted him and "gave him a piece of money, and every one an earring of gold." The moral of the added epilogue is much more comforting, though starkly different from the central story: "So the Lord blessed the latter end of Job more than his beginning." Job is just, the world is just, God is just, and a just man gets his just rewards.

We might be tempted to suppose that the "folk" are inveigled by belief in a just world, while philosophers rise above it. But in fact the history of Western philosophy is permeated with belief in a just world. As Bernard Williams (1993) makes brilliantly clear, the belief that the world is ethically well-ordered and just—the virtuous will receive their just reward, and the wicked will not prosper—has exerted a powerful influence on the history of philosophical thought. Among philosophers committed to belief in a just world, Plato insists that one who acts justly will invariably experience a better life than one who acts unjustly; Aristotle maintains that living a morally good life will result in genuine flourishing; Kant insists that the world *must* be such that it is never impossible to meet our moral obligations. As Williams notes: "Plato, Aristotle, Kant, Hegel are all on the same side, all believing in one way or another that the universe or history or the structure of human reason can, when properly understood, yield a pattern that makes sense of human life and human aspirations" (1993, 163). That is, they all believe that somehow justice is built into the *structure* of the world. Williams notes that contemporary philosophers have given up that belief, and thus have more in common with the ancient Greek tragic dramatists than we might realize:

> We are in an ethical condition that lies not only beyond Christianity, but beyond its Kantian and its Heglian legacies. . . . We know that the world was not made for us, or we for the world, that our history tells no purposive story, and that there is no position outside the world or outside history from which we might hope to authenticate our activities. We have to acknowledge the hideous costs of many human achievements that we value, including this reflective sense itself, and recognise that there is no redemptive Hegelian history or universal Leibnizian cost-benefit analysis to show that it will come out well enough in the end . . . we are like those who, from the fifth century and earlier, have left us traces of a consciousness that had not yet been touched by Plato's and Aristotle's attempts to make our ethical relations to the world fully intelligible. (1993, 166)

But while we know this consciously—ask any contemporary philosopher whether the world is fundamentally just, and a dozen painful examples of massive injustice, from slavery to the Holocaust, will spring to mind and demand a negative answer—we are still subject to the deep influence of the Platonic-Kantian justice tradition coupled with our profound nonconscious belief in a just world. The result is that the deep belief in a just world still manifests itself in contemporary philosophical views, and particularly in propping up belief in moral responsibility: belief in a just world and just deserts is built deep into our belief system, our justice system, and our system of moral responsibility. The deep nonconscious belief in a just world predisposes us to believe in *just* deserts: people generally "get what they deserve," whether those just deserts are meted out by society or circumstances. Thus when someone is punished, or one person is wealthy while another lives in poverty, or one group enjoys privilege while another (perhaps the impoverished refugees denied access to a wealthy country) suffers deprivation, there is a deep tendency to suppose that somehow justice still prevails. This is not a conscious belief that can withstand serious scrutiny: there is no *reason* I could possibly give to support the view that I justly deserve my privileged place in a wealthy society, while the child born to poverty in Jamaica or Guatemala justly deserves to suffer. But the deep nonconscious belief in a just world that hands out just deserts is enough to prevent me from worrying too much about the obvious injustice.

Lest we suppose that belief in a just world is a delusion to which Plato and Kant might have succumbed, but not more sophisticated and psychologically subtle contemporary philosophers, consider arguments for moral responsibility offered by two of the most insightful and psychologically well-informed philosophers on the contemporary scene: Daniel Dennett and George Sher. In *Elbow Room*, Dennett offers a charming folksy argument for moral responsibility. Dennett claims that (with rare exceptions) we are morally responsible for the outcome of our lives, because although we don't start exactly even, differences in "racing luck" even out the breaks and advantages: "After all, luck averages out in the long run" (1984, 95). We don't all get an even start, Dennett readily acknowledges; but the race of life is a marathon, not a sprint, and so "racing luck" balances out: One who starts from a somewhat disadvantaged position of genetic abilities or early environment has offsetting luck later in life, and so overall we have roughly equal opportunities. Obviously Dennett knows that racing luck doesn't "average out." Early advantages are seldom balanced by later "racing luck," but instead the early advantages tend to be cumulative. The more naturally talented youthful player gets more playing time, plays in better leagues, receives better coaching, is selected for all-star teams and plays more games against better competition; the child of a wealthy family who receives the benefits of superb (and very expensive) preschools also has the benefits of superb prep schools (or at least the best suburban schools), more advanced placement courses, tutors for the SAT, and probably a legacy advantage in applying to the most selective universities.

George Sher presents a very similar argument:

> Even if M is initially stronger or more intelligent than N, this difference will only entail that M does not deserve what he has achieved relative to N if the difference between them has made it impossible for N to achieve as much as M. However, differences in strength, intelligence, and other native gifts are rarely so pronounced as to have this effect. The far more common effect of such differences is merely to make it more *difficult* for the less talented person to reach a given level of attainment. He must work harder, husband his resources more carefully, plan more shrewdly, and so on. (1987, 31–32)

But Sher obviously knows—when not in the grip of nonconscious belief in a just world—that the "natural lottery" does not distribute talents and powers so even-handedly. Fortitude and self-confidence are not distributed independently of other talents; to the contrary, the person with initially greater intelligence experiences more frequent success in efforts at solving challenging problems, and thus develops a stronger sense of self-efficacy (Bandura 1997) as well as greater fortitude together with a greater "need for cognition" (Cacioppo and Petty 1982) and thus a greater eagerness to engage in careful rigorous thinking. The less gifted and less successful student does not develop greater fortitude, but instead repeated failure is more likely to generate a weaker sense of self-efficacy and thus less power of perseverance, and the student is more likely to become a "cognitive miser" (who seldom and reluctantly engages in careful deliberation) in contrast to the more fortunate student's tendency to become a "chronic cognizer" (who eagerly takes on tough deliberative challenges). Strengths in one area are likely to foster other strengths, just as the more talented basketball player gets more playing time and better coaching and develops greater fortitude and stronger "court savvy" and a superior sense of "basketball self-efficacy."

The diligent tortoise triumphing over the swift but dilatory hare is a wonderful children's story; but however much our deep belief in a just world prompts our approval of the story, cold sober reflection recognizes it as fantasy. We all have equal opportunities—viewed from a longer perspective, luck and talents and opportunities balance out in this *just* world—so we all justly deserve the benefits or detriments of what we accomplish. Dennett and Sher both know that breaks and talents do *not* even out, even roughly; and it is a mark of the power of this deep—but seldom consciously recognized—belief in a just world that it can lead even such insightful philosophers as Dennett and Sher to make such transparently false claims. The tortoise finished last; but he deserves it, the world *is* just, and so somehow the tortoise *must* have had a fair and roughly equal chance at success.

A striking manifestation of deep philosophical belief in a just world is the widely held principle that "ought implies can." The principle could, of course, be treated as merely a stipulative definition, something like the following: It is correct to say that a person *ought* to perform a certain act if and only if that act is morally obligatory and it is within the power of that person to perform the act. However, when people make the "ought implies can" claim, they typically suppose themselves to be making a statement that is more than merely analytic, a moral claim that is more than definitional. "All our moral obligations are within our power to perform." That is a claim concerning the nature of our obligations and our moral world: a metaethical assertion that is claimed to be true, and not merely true by definition.

But assuming it is not merely a definitional stipulation, is it true? Certainly it is widely believed to be true; but on what grounds? Why should we believe that we cannot have moral obligations that we *cannot* meet? In fact, it seems quite easy to think of examples that contradict that claim. You have generously loaned me (at no interest) a significant sum of money, on the condition that I will repay the loan two years hence, when you will be in particular need of funds. Unfortunately, my financial plans take an unanticipated bad turn: my investment in real estate looked rock solid, but the bursting of the real estate bubble left me impoverished and my credit rating ruined. I have no money, and no means of obtaining money. I *ought* to repay your loan, but I *cannot* do so. Indeed, we can embellish this example a bit, and find a whole host of oughts that do not imply cans. You made the loan as a no-interest loan out of kindness to a friend, and I now have an obligation to reciprocate that I ought to fulfill, but cannot. You desperately need the money for life-saving surgery, and I ought to help you, out of an obligation to prevent the suffering of others; but I cannot. I promised to repay you, and I ought to keep my promise; but I cannot.

Rather than requiring vivid imagination, such cases are simple to construct. My child is threatened by a fire, and I ought to rescue her; but I am an abject coward, and find it impossible to overcome my profound fear. I ought to rescue her, but I cannot. My friend is in the hospital, and I ought to visit him and bring cheer; but I have a deep dread of hospitals, and cannot overcome that psychological impediment. My family is enslaved by a brutal slave master, and when the opportunity arises, I ought to lead the escape and carry them to freedom. But I have tried to escape on several occasions, and each time I have failed and suffered brutal treatment. This series of painful failures has caused me to descend into a deep depression and a state of learned helplessness, in which—like Seligman's dogs (Seligman 1975)—I no longer have the capacity to exert effort toward escape. I *ought* to escape and help my family escape, but I cannot.

The counterexamples are so obvious that the interesting question is: Why should anyone (much less almost all philosophers) find "ought implies can" plausible? The answer is that in a just world, ought *should* imply can. After all, it does not seem fair that there are things that I ought to do, that I am morally obligated to do, but that I *cannot* do. *If* the world were just—as we deeply but not consciously believe—then whenever there is something we *should* do, then we would be capable of doing it; and then, since we are always capable of doing whatever we should do, since we are always capable of doing what we are morally obligated to do, it makes sense to blame us for failing to do as we ought. But the powerful nonconscious belief notwithstanding, when we look carefully—as Daniel Kahneman would say, when we think *slowly* (2011)—it is clear that the world is *not* just, and instances of moral obligations which we cannot fulfill are painfully common.

The easy acceptance of ought implies can discourages us from looking slowly, carefully, and hard at the details of situations in which someone *ought* to perform some obligatory act (since Jane *ought* to have done it, obviously she *could* have done so). But careful scrutiny of the details raises troubling questions. Jane *ought* to have taken her child to the doctor when the child ran a high fever and broke out in a rash. That is what a conscientious, caring, competent parent would have done; Jane *ought* to have done so, she has a moral obligation to care for her child; it is obvious that she *could* have fulfilled that obligation—ought implies can—and so she deserves blame for neglecting the welfare of her child. But if we slow down and look carefully, then the easy belief that Jane *could* have recognized the problem and taken her child to the doctor does not seem nearly so plausible. Of course, it will seem quite plausible if we believe that human volition has miraculous powers to overcome any obstacles (that no matter what Jane's capacities and shortcomings, she had the special power to rise above all limits and impediments and do the right thing). But leaving miracles aside, and looking closely at the actual conditions in which Jane was operating, the claim that Jane could have done as she *should* have done seems not only implausible, but plainly false. It's true that Jane *should* have thought more carefully about the needs of her child; but assuming she did *not* have some special miraculous power to switch into careful slow critical thought (Kahneman 2011) no matter her situation and shaped character, it is just false to say that she *could* have done so. True, she could have done so if she were a chronic cognizer rather than a cognitive miser (Cacioppo and Petty 1982); it's true that she could have done so had she been in a different situation, with different situational cues and primes; she could have done so had she not experienced severe ego-depletion (Baumeister et al. 1998) during the course of the previous couple of hours; she could have done so if she had greater medical knowledge; that is, she *could* have done so *if* the circumstances had been different. But the relevant question is whether she *could* have done so in precisely those circumstances with precisely the powers and limitations she actually has; that is, could she *actually* have done so. And when we examine it carefully and in detail—precisely what belief in moral responsibility discourages—it is implausible to suppose that she actually could have done so. *You* would have done so; but you have a stronger sense of cognitive self-efficacy (Bandura 1997), and you have an internal locus-of-control (Rotter 1966) in contrast to Jane's external, and you are a chronic cognizer while Jane is a cognitive miser, and you have not had to make any difficult decisions recently and thus you are not in a state of ego-depletion, while Jane is. Jane *should* have thought more carefully; but when we scrutinize the details rather than ignore them, and we recognize that Jane's capacity to focus critical attention when and where it needs to be focused is—like ours, whether ours is better or worse—not a miraculous power; then we must conclude that Jane *could not* have done otherwise. But until we look carefully, our deep nonconscious belief in a just world ("Jane *ought* to have considered carefully, so in a world that is justly ordered she *could* have considered carefully") slides smoothly and easily to the comfortable conclusion that Jane *could* have acted otherwise, and so justly deserves blame.

Jane is morally flawed, certainly; as all of us are, in various ways. No doubt Jane *should* have taken steps to correct her flaws; but supposing that therefore she *could* have corrected her flaws will turn us in a very small circle. And there are a few people who insist that by acknowledging that Jane is morally flawed, we have already admitted that she is morally responsible. Such a claim proposes either a very special definition of "moral responsibility" or a very implausible claim concerning moral responsibility. It is easy to think of philosophical examples of persons who are profoundly flawed whom we would not count as morally responsible and deserving of blame: the congenial, peaceful philosophy professor whose morning coffee is drugged by the proverbial mad scientist, and who is immediately and irreversibly transformed into a brutal killer who deeply and reflectively approves of her murderous motives. And it is easy to think of real world examples that have the same moral: Robert Harris—shaped by an almost unimaginably brutal childhood and adolescence to become a callous, cruel, and calculating killer—was certainly a person with profound moral flaws; but even if one can (very implausibly, by my lights) conclude that Robert Harris is morally responsible for his brutal behavior, it is obvious that drawing such a conclusion will require a big step *beyond* simply claiming that Robert Harris has deep moral flaws.

Unconscious belief in a just world underlies the easy acceptance of ought implies can, and it also helps explain the enthusiasm for the "plateau" or "threshold" argument for moral responsibility. All of us "competent" ones live on the plateau of moral responsibility; and once on this plateau, we are all roughly equal in abilities—or at least equal enough that we can all be held morally responsible, and the insignificant differences in our abilities and opportunities can be ignored—and thus we can be justly blamed for our failures and credited for our successes. The idea seems to be that we started unevenly, with different talents; and neither racing luck nor talents balanced out. Eventually, however, we all arrived at roughly the same level, or close enough so that any differences are not worth worrying about, and certainly not worth scrutinizing; so the world turned out to be just—at least for almost all of us—after all. Daniel Dennett gives the clearest picture of the plateau model:

> moral development is not a race at all, with a single winner and everyone else ranked behind, but a process that apparently brings people sooner or later to a sort of plateau of development—not unlike the process of learning your native language, for instance. Some people reach the plateau swiftly and easily, while others need compensatory effort to overcome initial disadvantages in one way or another.
>
> But everyone comes out more or less in the same league. When people are deemed "good enough" their moral education is over, and except for those who are singled out as defective . . . the citizenry is held to be composed of individuals of roughly equivalent talents, insofar as the demands of such citizenship are concerned. (1984, 96)

So differences in starting points, the genetic lottery, and racing luck don't really matter: almost all of us wind up "more or less in the same league," roughly equal, and so the world is fair and just after all. We are all competent morally responsible adults "of roughly equivalent talents," and so what you do with your equal share of the talents is up to you—and you justly deserve reward or punishment for the results.

This "plateau" comes in several shapes and sizes, but the basic idea is the same. John Martin Fischer develops the most sophisticated plateau model: almost all of us are "moderately reasons-responsive" (2012, 125) which means that we are capable of recognizing under various circumstances that there are sufficient reasons not to perform a certain act and at least sometimes we refrain from doing that act due to the recognition of such reasons. Since almost all of us have such capability, we are roughly equal in our capacity for acting well and avoiding bad acts, and thus we are in a "just world" which affords almost all of us the resources for acting virtuously. And again, since this key capacity is one we all enjoy, the differences in resulting behavior will be differences that it is fair and just to reward and punish. A world in which we have distinctly different capacities for moral behavior would not be a *just* world (especially if we punish and reward on the basis of differing results that stem from significantly different capacities); and so when we get to the really important capacities for behavior, we must be roughly equal—at least equal enough so any differences in capacities are insignificant.

But the remarkable ingenuity and creativity of these plateau models notwithstanding, their fundamental problem is obvious; obvious, that is, unless our thinking is shaped by a deep belief in a just world. However we describe this plateau, the differences among its residents will be very significant indeed. The differences include important differences in intelligence, self-control, fortitude, sense of self-efficacy, talents, and cognitive fortitude among those judged to be on the "plateau of moral responsibility"; and when we look carefully at those differences—look carefully in ways that are discouraged by belief in moral responsibility—the importance of those differences is clear. Consider John Fischer's "moderate reasons-responsiveness" plateau of moral responsibility. Rachel and Sarah both qualify as moderately reasons-responsive: for both, there are circumstances under which they recognize good and sufficient reasons for *not* breaking a promise to a friend (say, a promise to help a friend who is struggling to meet a publisher's deadline); and both, having recognized those reasons, will under at least some circumstances keep their promise. On the plateau of moderate reasons-responsiveness, any remaining differences are hardly worth mentioning. But we know that small subtle differences are critically important, and that is obvious when we look *closely*—slowly and carefully—at the details of the case. Rachel and Sarah are both moderately reasons-responsive; both have promised to spend the weekend helping a friend meet a difficult deadline; both have the unexpected opportunity for a delightful beach holiday; Rachel rises to duty and Sarah succumbs to desire. But if we ask *why* the striking divergence in the behavior of Rachel and Sarah, that is not a question Fischer investigates: Both were moderately reasons-responsive, and so both are morally responsible for their behavior. But closer scrutiny reveals all manner of significant differences in Rachel and Sarah—their common "moderate reasons-responsiveness" notwithstanding—that undercut any confident conclusions concerning moral responsibility.

Rachel is a "chronic cognizer" who often and easily switches into careful rigorous "slow" deliberation, while Sarah is a "cognitive miser" who finds careful deliberate thought more aversive. Rachel has a strong sense of cognitive self-efficacy, and is confident that she can effectively work out the right path through her own critical powers, while Sarah has much less confidence in her ability to rationally reach the right conclusion. Rachel has a strong internal locus-of-control, and believes that what happens in her life is largely under her own effective control; Sarah has an external locus-of-control, and regards herself as largely under the control of external powers. Rachel has not been faced recently with any challenging decisions, while Sarah has struggled with a number of very difficult problems over the past couple of hours and is currently in a state of severe ego-depletion (Baumeister et al. 1998) that makes her particularly likely to avoid hard deliberation in the present case. Rachel deliberates carefully and thoroughly about her present choice, reflecting fully on the importance of friendship, honoring her commitments, exercising self-control and thus becoming even stronger. We might well conclude that Rachel is a better person: more trustworthy, more competent, firmer in her commitments, reflectively committed to her own values, stronger in her powers of self-control. In contrast, Sarah is wishy-washy at best, not someone who is worthy of great trust, not a friend on whom you can depend. It does not surprise us when Rachel, acting from her strong and steadfast character, does the right thing; nor when Sarah, with her much weaker character, acts selfishly and betrays a trust and breaks a promise. But when we scrutinize the *details* of the contrasting characters and circumstances of Rachel and Sarah, belief in their moral responsibility faces severe challenges. Both Rachel and Sarah are moderately reasons-responsive; but Rachel will do right almost every time, while Sarah will do so sporadically at best—any breeze, and any temptation, can blow her off course.

While both Rachel and Sarah have some degree of self-control, Rachel's self-control powers are robust while Sarah's are very modest. This is a very important difference, resulting in major differences in behavior (Baumeister 2008a, 70–71). But *why* is there such a significant difference? The libertarian "explanation" that Rachel simply *chooses to exert the self-control effort* while Sarah does not has little plausibility; it has even less when we discover that this important difference in self-control was shaped at a very early age: psychologists find that pre-school children exhibiting high levels of self-control are much more likely to exhibit high levels of self-control as adolescents (Mischel, Shoda, and Peake 1988; Shoda, Mischel, and Peake 1990); and high levels of self-control are positively correlated with better grades, better adjustment, and greater interpersonal success (Tangney, Baumeister, and Boone 2004). Thus the basic foundation for adolescent and adult levels of self-control is set in place at an age at which it would be ridiculous, not to mention grossly unfair, to hold Rachel and Sarah morally responsible for their differing self-control capacities.

This does not imply, of course, that one's degree of self-control is written in the book of fate: by *exercising* one's powers of self-control one can strengthen that capacity. So Rachel—who is already a chronic cognizer with a strong internal locus-of-control and at least moderately good powers of self-control, reads Roy Baumeister's excellent book on how to strenghen one's self-control capacities and the importance of undertaking such exercise (Baumeister and Tierney 2011), and she becomes even better at self-control. But that is not grounds of blaming those with more modest capacities who fail to take such steps; and when we recognize that Rachel's capacity for strengthening her powers of self-control were dependent on abilities not of her own making or choosing, the grounds for holding either Rachel or Sarah morally responsible are soon eroded away. While both Rachel and Sarah meet the standard for moderate reasons-responsiveness, when we give careful attention to the substantial differences in the histories that shaped their very different capacities, then attributions of blame seem fundamentally unfair, and claims of moral responsibility ring hollow. Viewed from a comfortable distance, the plateau of moderate reasons-responsiveness may seem sufficiently level to support moral responsibility; viewed more carefully and closely, the plateau is far too uneven to provide a secure moral responsibility foundation. Such differences do not lessen the importance of making our own decisions and enhancing our powers of self-control, which remain psychologically valuable; but they do undercut claims of moral responsibility.

Why does Fischer, whose facility for delving deep into philosophical details is abundantly clear, halt inquiry at that point? In Fischer's case, no explanation in terms of cognitive miserliness is remotely plausible. The answer might be found in the deep nonconscious commitment to a just world: We condemn Sarah and commend Rachel, and that dramatically different result is surely *just* (it is, after all, a natural and almost universal reaction to their behavior); and so no further scrutiny is needed, since the justice of the result is obvious. The grounds for their moral responsibility *must* be adequate, because we feel justified in condemning and commending.

The plateau argument for moral responsibility is supported by deep nonconscious belief in a just world; but it also gains support from a third major source for the stubborn belief in moral responsibility, and this source is very conscious indeed. The "plateau" is how the *system* of moral responsibility works: when you reach a "competence" level we hold you morally responsible, and the significant differences among competent adults are irrelevant. The powerful and pervasive presence of our moral responsibility *system* makes the truth of moral responsibility seem obvious, and objections to moral responsibility appear silly or even incoherent. It becomes very difficult to step outside the system and consider criticisms against it.

Is Jones really morally responsible for the murder of Smith? The immediate tendency is to ask that as an *internal* question. That is, does Jones meet the conditions that the moral responsibility system sets for being morally responsible? If so, then Jones is morally responsible. And of course if Jones *is* morally responsible, then belief in moral responsibility is justified. But the real question is not the conditions for holding Jones morally responsible *within* the moral responsibility system, but whether the moral responsibility *system* is itself justified. If we have an elaborate and almost universally accepted belief system for the existence of witches, then it may be clear—by the carefully elaborated and developed rules of that system—that the Widow Jones is a witch (she has a strange birthmark and three cats, a cow died inexplicably after she walked by the farm, and when thrown into a lake the widow floated); and the system will be *reliable*, in the sense that there will be general agreement on who counts as a witch. But that reliability will do nothing to establish the legitimacy of the *system* of belief in witchcraft. Likewise, the fact that we have clear reliable standards for who is morally responsible does nothing to establish the legitimacy of the moral responsibility system. Daniel Dennett and John Martin Fischer (along with many others) have fashioned excellent accounts of who counts as morally responsible within the moral responsibility system; in particular, they have elucidated the sort of control that qualifies one as morally responsible within the moral responsibility system (Fischer's "moderate reasons-responsiveness" is a model of such philosophical elucidation). But the question remains of whether the moral responsibility *system* is itself fair and genuinely just.

Is it fair to hold people morally responsible when (though they meet the basic competence standard) they are weaker in self-efficacy, or have a strong *external* locus-of-control, or are cognitive misers (they can reason, but they find reasoning aversive rather than appealing), or are in situations in which careful thinking rarely occurs? In short, is it really fair to blame someone when we know that their bad behavior was ultimately the product of causes over which they had no control? That basic fairness question is difficult, as Shaun Nichols makes clear (2007). But however one answers that question, it is clear that it is *not* answered by internal claims about a plateau of moral responsibility. Because we almost invariably ask the *internal* question, it seems obvious that sometimes people *are* morally responsible.

When we are deeply immersed in the moral responsibility system the denial of moral responsibility generates ridiculous results. This can be seen most clearly in the arguments of P. F. Strawson. Strawson's elaboration of the moral responsibility system and its deep roots is masterful; but when he argues against those who would deny moral responsibility, his arguments start from the assumptions made *within* the moral responsibility system. Strawson gives a marvelous internal account of the circumstances under which we *excuse* people from moral responsibility: When people are profoundly impaired by delusion or lack of any moral capacity—either temporarily or permanently—then we adopt the "objective attitude" toward them and excuse them. If someone denies moral responsibility altogether, then—viewed from *within* the moral responsibility system—they must permanently excuse everyone, which implies that "...nobody knows what he's doing or that everybody's behavior is unintelligible in terms of conscious purposes or that everyone lives in a world of delusion or that nobody has a moral sense, i.e., is susceptible of self-reactive attitudes, etc." (1962, 74). And of course if that is the case, then nobody could possibly have genuine *reasons* for anything, including the denial of moral responsibility. So the denial of moral responsibility crashes and burns under its own weight of universal derangement.

Strawson is correct: if we start from the assumptions of the moral responsibility system (common deep assumptions that are difficult to escape) then the *denial* of moral responsibility is self-defeating. But the universal denial of moral responsibility does *not* start from the assumption that under normal circumstances we are morally responsible, and then enlarge and extend the range of excuses to cover everyone (so that *everyone* is profoundly flawed). Rather, those who reject moral responsibility reject the basic system which *starts* from the assumption that all minimally competent persons are morally responsible. For those who deny moral responsibility, it is never fair to treat anyone—no matter how reasonable, self-efficacious, strong-willed, and clear-sighted—as morally responsible. Certainly one can reject the moral responsibility abolitionist view, for various reasons; but when rejecting moral responsibility appears to be absurd—as it is, for many people—that is because they are operating *within* the deep assumptions of the moral responsibility system and criticizing the moral responsibility abolitionists for violating those assumptions. It would be absurd to "permanently excuse everyone" on the grounds that everyone is permanently deranged; and from within the moral responsibility system, that is the only way that universal denial of moral responsibility can occur. But the basic challenge to the moral responsibility system does not accept the rules of that system.

The moral responsibility system is held in place by powerful forces of strike-back emotions, deep nonconscious belief in a just world, and a pervasive moral responsibility system that makes doubts concerning moral responsibility appear absurd. Those forces do not provide reasonable *justification* for belief in moral responsibility, but instead give an *explanation* for steadfast belief in moral responsibility in the absence of good reasons. The moral responsibility system has served a useful function in controlling and moderating the desire for revenge, but it now blocks the path to a better understanding of the causes of both good and bad behavior while sustaining a pattern of profound injustice in both punishment and benefits. In order to scrutinize the moral responsibility system for what it is and the harm it causes we must break through the powerful systemic and emotional and nonconscious forces that guard belief in moral responsibility. Recognizing the actual nature of those basic forces—a strike-back emotion we share with rats, a just world belief that is plainly delusional, and a pervasive moral responsibility system that swallows up questions and stifles careful inquiry—is a small first step toward breaking their powerful spell.

Chapter Five

Be a Skeptic, Not a Metaskeptic

Neil Levy

In *Hard Luck* (Levy 2011), I argued that agents are never morally responsible for their actions. At the heart of my view was the following dilemma: either actions are subject to present luck (luck around the time of the action), or they are subject to what Thomas Nagel (1979) influentially named constitutive luck (luck that causes relevant properties of agents, such as their desires, beliefs and circumstances).[1] In either case, I argued, luck undermines moral responsibility. Present luck undermines moral responsibility when it is a matter of luck that an action has the moral character it has (that it is morally good rather than bad, or vice-versa); constitutive luck undermines moral responsibility because it accounts for the *absence* of present luck. It is always in part due to the influence of constitutive luck that an action fails to have its moral character settled (in part, once more) by present luck, I suggested. *Hard Luck* is organized around this central argument.

In developing this argument, I appealed to my intuitions about fairness. I appealed to a simple and—I claimed—intuitive fairness principle, according to which "agents do not deserve to be treated differently unless there is a desert-entailing difference between them" (2011, 9). Further, I appealed to intuition to establish that present luck and constitutive luck are inconsistent with desert-entailing differences. If you don't accept that an agent who performs morally bad action A doesn't deserve blame in cases in which it is a matter of present luck that he performs A *rather than* morally neutral or good B, then there is little I can do to convince you. Or rather, there is little I can do to convince you that doesn't involve attempting to bring you to share my intuitions: I can fill in the details of the case, and present others like it; I can point out its similarities to other cases in which I and others are disposed to excuse agents from moral responsibility, and I can point out its differences from other cases in which we are more disposed to blame. But if you do not share my intuitions with regard to these other cases, as well as this one, there is little more I can say.

In this paper, I want to respond to an argument which, if successful, spells trouble for my view. Indeed if successful, it spells trouble for the entire range of views about moral responsibility, skeptical and non-skeptical. In *Relative Justice*, Tamler Sommers (2012) argues that in appealing to our intuitions, as I do in *Hard Luck*, we are appealing to dispositions to respond in ways that are culture-bound. We therefore systematize *our* views on moral responsibility, not (as we think) discover *the* necessary and sufficient conditions of its attribution to agents. Sommers' argument targets all theories of moral responsibility, because he believes that appeal to intuitions is essential to normative philosophy. Since appeal to intuitions is appeal to culture-bound dispositions, there is no non-question-begging way to settle disputes between rival conceptions of moral responsibility (where a 'conception' refers to a particular set of conditions associated with a concept). Sommers therefore advocates *metaskepticism* about moral responsibility, rather than skepticism. The skeptic believes that the necessary conditions for agents' being morally responsible are (necessarily or contingently) unsatisfied by actual agents. The metaskeptic believes that there is no fact of the matter what the necessary conditions for moral responsibility are.

In this chapter, I will argue that metaskepticism is an unstable position. As it stands, it threatens to collapse into good old-fashioned skepticism. Even if it can avoid this collapse, it is vulnerable to refutation, and it can avoid this refutation only by expanding to embrace all normative properties, becoming what I shall call normative nihilism. I shall suggest that the most attractive way out of this quandary is for the metaskeptic to embrace skepticism: only thus can he defend the values he endorses.

METASKEPTICISM

In cultures like ours, the conception of moral responsibility is closely linked to individual causal responsibility. Sommers argues that other cultures have conceptions of moral responsibility that are much less tightly linked to individuals. He focuses on two kinds of cultures in which the conception of moral responsibility is much less individualistic: East Asian cultures, which are supposedly more collectivist than Western cultures, and cultures which develop a strong honor code. Let's focus on the latter kind of culture (I will very briefly return to East Asian cultures later in the paper).

In honor cultures, when someone is wronged the victim is expected to retaliate. If they fail to retaliate, they are shamed and may be treated contemptuously by third-parties. It is very important that the victim respond personally; it is much less important that the target of their response be the very person who harmed them. Someone who belongs to the same group as the offender will do nearly as well, and the death of the offender—say by accident—may not reduce the obligation for the victim to retaliate.

In cultures like ours, though, when someone is wronged the focus is more on the offender than the victim. The offender is an appropriate target of punishment only if they meet certain demanding conditions, in particular control and epistemic conditions. In these cultures, it is far more important that the offender be punished than that the victim retaliate; third-party punishment is adequate or even preferable to victim retaliation. Moreover, it is the offender himself who must be punished; no one can stand in for him.

Sommers claims that these two kinds of cultures have conflicting conceptions of what it takes for an agent to be morally responsible for an action. Further, he claims, these different conceptions are the products of the ways of life in these societies, and that these ways of life are adaptations to local ecological conditions (such that changing their ways of life would come at a cost in human well-being). Honor cultures are those in which wealth is portable and concentrated. They are typically cultures dominated by livestock production. In these cultures, an individual's livelihood is relatively easily threatened: if someone makes off with one's herd, one may be reduced to penury literally overnight. The precariousness of life in these cultures, its vulnerability to criminality, is what causes the hair trigger responses in these cultures. Because agents living in these conditions are so vulnerable to crime, they have a strong interest in making it known that offense—even a comparatively minor slight—will be met with overwhelming force. Because these societies have weak (or no) state apparatus, moreover, the norm develops that the victim be the person to retaliate. If the victim loses the chance to retaliate—say, because a third-party intervenes on his behalf—he does not shore up his own reputation. Given the unreliability of third-party punishment in these societies, he therefore becomes vulnerable.

In cultures like ours, though, the norms aim at discouraging free riding. We aim to deter wrongdoing more generally. We can (quite literally) afford to be more lenient in our assessments, because our livelihoods are not vulnerable in the same kind of ways as the livelihood of herders. The kind of norm that governs our societies grow up in sedentary agriculture societies, in which theft is harmful but rarely devastating, so long as the rate of crime remains at acceptable levels. Since our interest is in discouraging free riding generally, and because—being sedentary—societies like ours can develop strong institutions, we are generally happy to turn punishment over to third-party institutions.

Sommers claims that the different frames constituted by these different ways of life generate conflicting intuitions with regard to who is the appropriate target of response to wrongdoing—roughly, intuitions with regard to moral responsibility—and that because each way of life is an adaptive response to prevailing ecological conditions, we cannot judge one better than the other. Since these intuitions are building blocks that are indispensable in the construction of a theory of moral responsibility (such that agents with different intuitions will construct conflicting accounts of moral responsibility), and given that we have no rational grounds for judging one framework better than another, we cannot rationally adjudicate between the rival accounts of moral responsibility each tends to generate. So we should regard our own preferred theory as unjustified.

Sommers maintains that his argument supports not skepticism but metaskepticism, because the argument undermines all accounts of moral responsibility, including skeptical theories. He claims that "there is no set of conditions for moral responsibility that applies universally," so no theory of moral responsibility is "objectively correct" (2012, 5). Sommers' strategy for defending metaskepticism is familiar: he argues for culture relativism with regard to moral responsibility. The cultural relativist argues that moral norms—*tout court*—differ and conflict from culture to culture, and there is no non-question-begging-way of settling the question which culture is best. Giving this basic argument an evolutionary twist, Sommers argues that the intuitions upon which theories of moral responsibility are built vary from culture to culture, and that these intuitions and the practices they sustain are adaptation to local ecological conditions. Because they are adaptations to local ecological conditions, he argues, agents whose intuitions support the local practices cannot be accused of being irrational. Rather, their responses are rational, relative to local conditions.

Because it is true that even under the ideal conditions of reflective equilibrium, agents in different kinds of cultures would converge on quite different conceptions of moral responsibility, we can't rationally settle debates between them unless we can show that some cultures are better justified than others. But if cultures are adaptive responses to prevailing ecological conditions, we don't have any grounds to choose between them. So we can't choose between different conceptions of moral responsibility. Views like this—whether advanced in support of metaskepticism about moral responsibility or in the form of standard cultural relativism—are *framework relativisms*: they claim that particular normative judgments are caused by a framework, and that justification questions must be addressed to the conflicting frameworks rather than the judgments internal to each.

Sommers' argument has interesting parallels (as he notes) to recent evolutionary arguments against moral realism (e.g., Joyce 2006; Street 2006). These arguments appeal to our evolutionary history in place of the framework of individual cultures. They point out that had evolution taken a different turn, we might have had quite different moral responses to those we human beings actually have. On that basis, they argue that our actual moral responses cannot be taken to be reliable guides to moral truth: since we would respond as we do no matter what the moral truths were—because our moral responses are shaped by processes sensitive to fitness, not moral truth—we can't regard them as reliable guides to moral truth.

The parallel between these arguments and Sommers' claims might actually seem to be bad news for him. The opponents of moral realism rightly take their arguments to aim at showing that claims to moral truth are *unjustified*, not false. If successful, they undermine our right to appeal to our intuitions in constructing a normative theory. They do not show that there are no moral truths. But Sommers does not take his argument to establish the parallel claim, that all theories of moral responsibility are *unjustified*. Rather, as we have seen, he takes it to establish that there is no "objectively correct" account of moral responsibility. Why this difference?

Sommers does not address the question, but he does seem to have grounds for arguing that there is a difference between the evolutionary argument against moral realism and his argument against moral responsibility. The difference is this: he assumes the truth of *constructivism* about moral responsibility. That is, for him the truth of claims about moral responsibility is (in part) "*constituted by* our attitudes, practices, and norms" (2012, 189). Because variation across cultures is variation in the truth-makers for claims about moral responsibility, rather than just variation in the intuitions that might give us insight into the truth regarding moral responsibility, framework relativism undercuts truth, not justification (alternatively, and more or less equivalently, it might be taken to establish a thoroughgoing relativism about moral responsibility: if the truth-makers *themselves* vary across cultures, perhaps different accounts of moral responsibility are genuinely, if locally, true in different cultures).

In what follows I will argue that metaskepticism can avoid refutation only by collapsing into a more thoroughgoing relativism. Before turning to showing how this might occur, however, I will note that even as it stands—before it contorts to avoid refutation—metaskepticm threatens to become good old fashioned standard skepticism.

THE COLLAPSE INTO SKEPTICISM

Sommers accepts that there is a link between moral responsibility and how people get treated. He (like me) accepts what he calls a "desert entailing" conception of moral responsibility, according to which those who are morally responsible deserve to be praised or blamed, punished or rewarded, "independent of any practical or consequentialist benefit of doing so" (2012, 10). Now, different accounts of moral responsibility (so understood) distribute burdens differently. Focusing on the examples canvassed in Sommers' book, for instance, we can represent the differences between them, and between them and skepticism, roughly as follows:

> *Honor cultures*: In addition to those people who must be burdened in order to secure practical or consequentialist benefits, burden *those who have caused harm or others who are appropriately linked to those who have caused harms*.
>
> *Individualistic cultures*: In addition to those people who must be burdened in order to secure practical or consequentialist benefits, burden *those who satisfy some kind of control condition*.
>
> *Skepticism*: In addition to those people who must be burdened in order to secure practical or consequentialist benefits, burden *no one*.

This schema is rough, because the description of how honor cultures and individualistic cultures will distribute burdens, in addition to burdening those who are judged morally responsible on their theories, is only roughly true. Some such cultures may accept some kind of restrictions on who may be burdened for consequentialist reasons. Still, I think it clear that accepting these theories of moral responsibility entails burdening more (almost certainly many more) agents than the skeptic would burden. After all, skeptics will refrain from distributing burdens unnecessarily, and will do so only when the consequences of refraining involve greater burdens. So skepticism entails burdens on fewer people.

These facts about how many people each theory is committed to burden entail that metaskepticism has quite different implications for each. All three theories accept (roughly) the same baseline; moreover, unless they are skeptical about human flourishing, this is a (rough) baseline that everyone should accept. The three theories therefore differ in who they would burden *over and above* that baseline. Now—again, unless one is a skeptic about normative claims more generally—everyone accepts that harms require justification. But according to metaskepticism, none of the theories has any justificatory advantages over any of the others. In that case, however—if non-skeptical views cannot justify the additional harms they entail—skepticism, which entails that no one is burdened over and above those people we have independent (non-responsibility-related) reasons to harm, wins by default. Holding that no account of moral responsibility is justified just is extensionally equivalent to holding that skepticism, not metaskepticism, is true. Because the other theories shoulder additional justificatory burdens, attacks on justification fall mainly on them.[2]

I think therefore that unless Sommers' relativism extends beyond moral responsibility to other normative properties—such as the normative properties to which consequentialists appeal—his metaskepticism collapses into skepticism. I also think, though, that metaskepticism may indeed tend to become more pervasive, infecting other normative properties. Sommers may therefore evade the objection just sketched, but at a cost he is not willing to pay. Let's turn to this issue.

CREEPING RELATIVISM

One problem Sommers must confront is the standard objection to relativism. The standard objection is that the relativist claim undercuts itself. If our judgments are the product of our culture, what happens to the judgment that cultural relativism is true? It is true only relative to a particular culture? What would that mean? Or does the relativist making the judgment somehow float free of culture? If she can do it, why can't others (say, in making normative judgments)? Objections like this seem to gain purchase on Sommers' view. Sommers advances the following argument (argument r): the justification for all particular accounts of moral responsibility is undercut by the discovery that accounts of moral responsibility rest heavily on intuitions, but that intuitions are generated by frameworks. Now what about argument r? Isn't it too undercut by the discovery that our intuitions are generated by frameworks? Argument r is vulnerable to undercutting if two conditions are met: if r relies on intuitions at crucial points, and these intuitions vary across cultures.

Since r is vulnerable to undercutting in this kind of way only if both the two conditions mentioned above hold, Sommers can defend it by denying that either (or both) are true: either that r does not depend on intuitions, or that these intuitions fail to vary across frameworks. It is far from clear to me that this strategy will work. It is true that arguments like r do not depend on thought experiments and cases in the same way in which theories of moral responsibility often do, but it seems to me that they nevertheless depend on intuitions—for example, concerning what kinds of considerations are relevant to theory choice—and that these intuitions do indeed vary across cultures. I think many people will be unmoved by r as a matter of empirical fact. More than a century and a half ago, Mill pointed out that "the same causes which make [a man] a churchman in London, would have made him a Buddhist or a Confucian in Peking" (1859, 78). This fact is surely well-known to many religious believers who do not thereby find their confidence in their faith undermined. Of course, they may be wrong in rejecting the framework relativism that Mill's thought can motivate, but that fact is helpful to Sommers only if we can demonstrate that they are wrong on grounds that are not question-begging.

Sommers may well believe that normative claims are not in the same boat as descriptive claims. Since normative claims include among their truthmakers human attitudes, beliefs and practices, they are uniquely vulnerable to r. Claims about God concern the non-mental properties of the world, and are therefore not vulnerable to framework relativism. This might be so, and appeal to this fact may be helpful in preventing framework relativism in becoming a universal acid that eats away at all our theories. But it will not prevent framework relativism from undermining the normative claims that Sommers wants to protect, since they too are partially constituted by human attitudes, beliefs and practices.

It is worth noticing how much relativism of values Sommers already allows. Fairness falls to metaskepticism; at least so I think it is reasonable to conclude from Sommers' remarks that it is neither objectively fair nor unfair to hold people responsible (112). Rights seem to fall; at least so I conclude from Sommers' contention that the individualistic emphasis on autonomy and a distinct self is no better justified than alternatives (120). Individual liberty goes too, for related reasons (127).[3] Sommers maintains, however, that some values will remain above the tide of creeping relativism. But it is unclear to me that this claim is consistent with metaskepticism.

How might a defense of some normative principles against creeping relativism go? Sommers might appeal to features of human beings that fail to vary across cultures, because they are part of the common human condition. There are a number of relatively fixed facts about us, that constrain what kinds of environments and what kinds of institutions and practices are conducive to our flourishing. Appeal to them might stop creeping relativism. The problem is that it might succeed *too well*. This seems to be a strategy that might allow us to choose between conceptions of moral responsibility as well as to defend moral values. I turn to this issue next.

REJECTING RELATIVISM

It is essential to Sommers' view that even under ideal conditions, agents living in different cultures will fail to converge on a particular theory of moral responsibility. That is, even when their intuitions and judgments are in reflective equilibrium, they will continue to disagree on exactly who is morally responsible and how they should be treated. I shall suggest that though Sommers is correct in thinking that even under ideal conditions rational agents will not converge on a single theory, this is not the appropriate test to apply when asking whether one theory is better justified than another. We can choose between competing theories even when we should acknowledge that those who reject them are not guilty of irrationality.

Most philosophers (including Sommers himself) now advocate *wide* reflective equilibrium: our theories must not only be internally consistent, but also consistent with our best theories in natural and social science, as well with whatever other sources of genuine knowledge we possess. Wide reflective equilibrium is not the kind of test that lends itself to Sommers' test. We ought not to expect agents in other cultures or at other times to think themselves into wide reflective equilibrium with us, because our starting points are too far apart. They will accept non-scientific theories that are so far at odds with ours that they can't reject them in favor of ours; not and remain the people they are. They may live in lifeworlds shot through with supernatural properties. I don't expect these people to be capable, through some reasoning procedure, of accepting our scientific theories. Yet I do not take this fact to cast any doubt on our scientific theories. Nor should it cast doubt on our normative theories.

That is not to say that we can simply take our normative views to be untroubled by disagreement. As Sommers says, normative theories seem to be in a different category to scientific theories, inasmuch as their truth-makers include human responses. It is only to say that the mere fact of faultless disagreement is not by itself a worry for normative theories. We should set out to vindicate our moral views—or to alter them—by reference to our shared human condition, applying the method of wide reflective equilibrium. Of course I do not aim to engage in that project here. Instead, I want to make a start on a small aspect of that project, demonstrating that *our* moral responsibility intuitions are better justified than those stemming from honor cultures. I turn to this project now.

One ground for rejecting honor-culture derived accounts of moral responsibility is that they seem to be metaphysically extravagant. We make best sense of several otherwise puzzling aspects of their conception of moral responsibility—if indeed they *have* a conception of moral responsibility; this is an issue to which I will return—if we suppose that they have an extremely unparsimonious moral ontology. I think we make best sense of some of the features of the practices of honor cultures (or collectivist cultures more generally) if we suppose that they take demands for retribution to be grounded in claims about the nature of a non-natural moral reality. Some evidence: consider, first, the practice of third-party punishment in these cultures. Unlike third-party punishment in individualist societies, the target of third-party punishment in these societies is not the offender, but the victim. The person who was originally harmed may be mocked, insulted and treated with contempt unless and until they retaliate. From an evolutionary perspective, this is somewhat puzzling. Why should third-parties care about whether retaliation has been delivered? Notice that this kind of behavior is (technically) altruistic punishment: even though the victim may have signalled his relative unwillingness to retaliate, in mocking him a third-party risks becoming the victim of his anger. Why would third-parties take this risk? Second, consider Agamemnon, forced to sacrifice his daughter and then held responsible for it. It is one thing to have a hair-trigger response to offense; that (as Sommers argues) is an explicable upshot of certain ecological conditions. But it is quite another to retaliate, as the Greek gods did, to offenses that they themselves deliberately caused.

I think we can make best sense of the responses by supposing that the moral ontology of those who respond in this manner is richer than Sommers seems to think. Rather than having a conception of moral responsibility like ours, differing from ours only in its extension, I think that agents in these cultures have a radically different concept, founded on a *cosmic order*. The rough idea is that these people think that there is a moral balance in the universe. Offenses, *no matter their etiology*, disturb this order, and the order is set right by some kind of comparatively harsh response, by the victim of the wrong, to the person who caused the offense, or failing that to someone who is appropriately linked to that person. This suggestion explains third-party mockery of the victim. Third parties have an interest in whether retaliation is delivered because the offense disturbed the cosmic order. This also explains the gods' response to Agamemnon. It doesn't matter how Agamemnon was brought to his offense. What matters is simply that he caused it, and the cosmic order can be set aright only if he suffers some appropriate consequence.

Indeed, discussions by classicists of the Greek concept of *dike* indicate that this was how the Greeks saw things.[4] Dike indicates the way; the path things must (normatively) follow. Now, if Dike indicates a concept of a cosmic order, and if other honor cultures also postulate such an order, then they have a moral ontology that is richer than ours (and richer, moreover, in a way that seems inconsistent with naturalism). Richness in ontology requires justification. In the absence of a justification for these metaphysical extras (and Sommers will certainly agree that an appropriate justification is unlikely to be forthcoming) we can shave off the extras with Occam's razor. If the extras are essential to these conceptions of moral responsibility (or—more likely in my view—to an account of response to offense so different from ours that it should not really be regarded as an account of moral responsibility at all), then we have a good reason to prefer our more parsimonious conception to theirs.[5]

There are several replies available to Sommers. He might say that the metaphysical extravagance of honor cultures is an inessential extra; we can shave it off with Occam's razor and leave their practices untouched. Alternatively, he might say that such a system shorn of excess *might* have developed, and argue that this possibility is sufficient to motivate metaskepticism.[6] We need to know therefore whether a conception of 'moral responsibility' akin to that of an honor culture, but shorn of its metaphysical excesses, is possible. Things get very tricky very quickly here, as they always do when issues of modality arise. What sense of possibility is at issue? Clearly such a culture is conceivable. However, I think some much more demanding sense of possibility is needed for Sommers' purposes. I think an entirely naturalistic sense—might such a system have developed given the right ecological conditions, say over the past 10,000 years—is the right one to invoke here. In this sense of "possible," is such a system possible?

The question is a difficult one to answer. It depends on the role that belief in a cosmic order is playing in the system. If it is required to stabilize the honor system, then it is not dispensable. Any system that mandates punishment places those who dish it out at risk of retaliation. A purely rational self-interested agent will not run this risk under many of the conditions in which punishment is required by the prevailing norms, because the cost/benefit ratio favors failing to enforce the norm. Even when the cost/benefit ratio (measured in terms of inclusive fitness) favors punishment, moreover, the agent may often be badly placed to grasp this fact, because the rewards are delayed, or delivered to conspecifics (who share a sufficient proportion of his genes, say). In order to secure these delayed or obscured rewards, and in order to secure benefits which come from the disposition to punish (though not from *actually* punishing), humans have evolved emotions that often bring them to behave in ways that circumvent rational assessment of costs and benefits (Frank 1988). That is, plausibly, the evolutionary function of the reactive attitudes. Now, it may be that belief in a cosmic order plays precisely the same kind of function. It allows the agents who could not without it secure the benefits of the hair trigger response to bridge the gap. A lot depends on how wide the gap is, and whether emotions might evolve to bridge it. But it is quite likely that metaphysical excess is an expected concomitant of honor-like systems. As a result, such systems fall to Occam's razor.

Sommers might reply by pointing out that what evolves is not necessarily the most adaptive response to a problem. For a variety of reasons, norms and behaviors may stabilize at frequencies that are suboptimal from the evolutionary point of view. They are stable when, for instance, there is a kind of collective action problem involved in defection; when any individual who attempts to replace the suboptimal behavior with a better one pays a high cost unless a sufficient number of other individuals follow suite immediately. It might be that for whatever reason metaphysical excess has a large basin of attraction, such that honor cultures tend to develop this kind of unparsimonious moral ontology, but this fact is not the direct upshot of the ecological problems that honor systems are designed to solve.

The problem with this response is that while it is true it threatens to generalize. The reminder that norms can stabilize at suboptimal forms is salutory and we ought to bear the fact in mind when examining all the aspects of honor systems, and not merely their unparsimonious moral ontology. Bearing this in mind, we see that it is in fact far from obvious that Sommers' central claim that these systems are justified inasmuch as they are adaptive responses to ecological conditions is really true. Their central features may be suboptimal.

It is a commonplace in anthropology that honor cultures suffer from a risk of pathology. In particular, they are at risk of a death spiral arising out of feuds (Elster 1990). Suppose a member of clan A (advertently or not; it doesn't matter for members of these cultures) kills a member of clan B. That injury justifies (and requires) a representative of B in killing a member of A. Sometimes, the cosmic order is seen to be restored by the retaliation, but very often honor cultures work with a conception of the order that requires the last act of violence be revenged, no matter its cause or justification. A member of A may therefore be required to retaliate against B. And so on. Whole villages have been wiped out in this manner on more than one occasion. It is far from obvious that a system that is at risk of spiralling out of control in this manner is really as well justified (as a response to prevailing ecological conditions) as rivals.

It may be that this propensity to feuds can be eliminated (though Elster thinks that the risk is endemic to honor cultures). But this vulnerability is just one issue we need to consider. The general point is that in assessing rival frameworks, we need to ask about more than their internal consistency. We need to ask about how well they secure important goods: human flourishing, in brief. When we ask about honor cultures with the overarching question of human flourishing in mind, we begin to see the myriad ways in which these violent, stressful societies are suboptimal as they stand. Key features of these societies are symptoms of problems that are fixable, not justified as responses to prevailing ecological conditions.

Consider for example, the opposition to third-party punishment in these societies. As Sommers points out, honor cultures put the onus on the individual to retaliate and therefore regard third-party punishment not only as unsatisfactory but even as a new offense against the original victim, since they deprive him of the chance to retaliate. This, as we have seen, is supposed to be justified by the fact that individuals must establish reputations as big men, so that their risks of predation are minimized. But an opposition to third-party punishment *tout court* can't be justified in this kind of way. All that can be justified is an opposition to *unreliable* third party punishment. Reliable third-party punishment would be at least as effective in protecting property as the existing system (indeed, since institutions can benefit from economies of scale and other efficiencies, one would expect them to be better). But they fail to develop, due to the opposition to third-party punishment Sommers mentions. Honor systems look like good responses to prevailing ecological conditions only if we set aside other possibilities like stronger institutions. Compare them to these other possibilities and they no longer seem attractive.

One might also consider the position of women in these cultures. I don't think their subordinate status is an accident or an extraneous feature. Rather, a patriarchal system, centered around older males (fathers, uncles and brothers) who constitute the forces of retaliation is an expected upshot of these systems. Women are unlikely to possess genuine political power in these groups, nor to have many opportunities for developing capabilities beyond those needed in the home. These systems therefore do a bad job at promoting female flourishing (it is likely that they do a relatively bad job at promoting male flourishing too, since the male roles will be almost as circumscribed as the female roles, and perhaps just as stunted).

Sommers might reply that though these societies pay a cost in human flourishing, nevertheless this is a cost they are (all things considered) justified in paying: prevailing ecological conditions make this way of organizing society the least bad option. This *might* be true (though once again we must recall that suboptimal equilibria may have large basins of attraction, so we can't argue from the fact that these costs are often paid that such societies have no real choice but to pay them). However, it is true only if we hold these ecological conditions fixed. Now, from the point of view of the application of wide reflective equilibrium, there is no more reason to hold fixed ecological conditions than there is to hold intuitions or theories fixed. Sometimes, the best response to prevailing ecological conditions is to change them.

That is, the best response to an environment in which life is harsh and always at risk from predation is to alter the environment. Sommers gives us no reason why we ought to accept the conditions in which these people find themselves as a baseline against which we should measure various responses. Human beings are niche-constructing animals. Our niches are part of our extended phenotype, and along with other features of our extended phenotype (our behaviors, our clothes, our rituals and practices) they can be altered. Even if it is true, as he contends, that honor cultures are the best responses to certain harsh environments, this gives us no reason to think that the norms of these cultures are as well-justified as the norms of rival societies, *when the norms of the first are less conducive to human well-being than rivals*. It may be that honor cultures are rational for those who live in them, but internal consistency is not all that matters in assessing rival theories. It is a familiar response to Inuit infanticide to point out that the practice was justified by the harsh environment in which the Inuit lived (Rachel 1995). They might thereby have achieved the highest degree of human flourishing they could. But that fact does not show that infanticide is as good as alternatives. It is justified as a response to harsh conditions, but when a better response is available, it is no longer justified.[7]

I think this objection can be avoided, but only at the cost of embracing more relativism than Sommers wants. Sommers can avoid the appeal to human flourishing by claiming that human flourishing, too, is a merely local affair: intuitions concerning it, too, are the product of an optional and (non-question-begging) unjustifiable frame. Similarly, he can avoid the objection, sketched above, that skepticism wins by default as the least harsh view, if no view is better justified than any other, by claiming that intuitions about harming others, too, are framework-relative. I think this move is implausible: though I share Sommers' constructivism, I think that the best account of morality will identify a core set of norms and values, constructed out of the facts about human lives that constitute our shared human condition as well as our shared dispositions to respond in certain ways. But this is not the place to begin the defense of this view. It is enough, for our purposes, to show that Sommers cannot pull off the highwire act he aims at. He can't have framework relativism confined to moral responsibility. Either we should be normative nihilists, or we should be skeptics.[8]

CONCLUSION

I want to conclude by considering how things stand with regard to the view I defended in *Hard Luck*, in the light of the remarks made above. As we saw, Sommers' metaskepticism is a challenge to my view. If metaskepticism is true, my view is false because it alleges that no one is morally responsible, at all times and in all places. Though Sommers shares my skeptical intuitions (or at any rate sufficiently similar intuitions to motivate a similar kind of view), he thinks that these intuitions are merely local, and therefore unjustified. Though we have good reason to advocate for skepticism round here, he thinks, it would be a mistake to regard skepticism as *true*.

If, as I have argued, the metaskeptical view is unstable, this argument fails. We have seen that metaskepticism is either false, or it collapses, either into skepticism or into normative nihilism. It collapses into skepticism if it accepts that we can choose between rival conceptions by reference to normative considerations such as how burdens are distributed across agents. It collapses into normative nihilism if it attempts to avoid refutation by denying that we can choose between rival frameworks by reference to broader normative considerations. If it takes this route, it becomes a straightforward and pervasive relativism. Obviously, if metaskepticism collapses into skepticism, my view is safe. Obviously, too, if the considerations adduced here are straightforward refutations of metaskepticism, my view is also unchallenged. But what if metaskepticism collapses into nihilism?

Normative nihilism is a challenge to my view. If all norms fall to creeping relativism, then my appeal to norms of fairness can no longer have a claim to being guides to truth. But if all norms fall to creeping relativism, we have bigger worries than that. While it is true that normative nihilism is a threat to my view, and to other views of moral responsibility, too, it is hardly a specific threat. Rather than target skepticism, or even moral responsibility, normative nihilism sweeps the board clear of all values. Normative nihilism is a threat akin to global skepticism: indeed my views are threatened by skepticism about the external world, but rebutting that skepticism is not a burden that falls on me (*qua* theorist of moral responsibility). Rebutting the normative nihilist is not my burden either. Though I think that normative nihilism is false, and demonstrably so, the demonstration is not my task. I conclude that there is no specific threat from metaskepticism to good old-fashioned skepticism.[9]

NOTES

1. Nagel actually distinguishes constitutive and circumstantial luck. For some purposes we ought to keep them separate, but clearly circumstances can help to cause agents' attitudes and beliefs.

2. In constructing his argument that those who belong to his intuition group should reject libertarianism, Sommers appeals to the "moral hardness" of such views (2012, 150), citing Double (2002) in support. It is morally hard, Double maintains, to blame individuals while also believing that the theory that justifies blaming them has scant epistemic support. I think this is a mistake: libertarianism is no morally harder than compatibilism. Double is mistaken in thinking that libertarians accept that there is scant epistemic support for moral responsibility; rather, I think that most would follow van Inwagen in maintaining that the disjunction of compatibilism and libertarianism is overwhelmingly likely true (even, self-evident). Perhaps because he accepts this claim, Sommers cashes out Double's claim not in terms of the views accepted by libertarians, but on (what he takes to be) the actual empirical plausibility of libertarianism. But since he rejects compatibilism as well, he ought to accept that libertarianism and compatibilism are in the same boat. Since moral hardness objections apply to all non-skeptical theories, Sommers should reject them all. He can avoid this collapse of metaskepticism into skepticism only by maintaining that the moral hardness intuition is framework relative. As we shall see, this move has its own costs.

3. In correspondence, Sommers has confirmed that he is willing to countenance relativism about fairness, rights and (on some construal of liberty) individual liberty. However, he denies that his relativism would extend much further.

4. At least this is true of later Greek thought. Gagarin (1974) notes that in archaic Greek thought *dike* was an essentially legal term, but in Heraclitus and Parmenides its meaning expands so that it refers to a universal cosmic force of balance and order. By the fifth century, and especially in Aeschylus, it was decisively identified with "a universal force of balance and order in human affairs" (Gagarin 1974, 197).

5. There comes a point at which it is no longer appropriate to say that two cultures have different conceptions of a common concept; they diverge so radically that they have rival concepts. It may well be that honor cultures should be regarded as lacking a concept of moral responsibility, rather than advocating a rival conception of it. Now if this is true, it is important, because it demonstrates that relativism is not after all confined to the concept of moral responsibility. Hence conflicting concepts makes the problem of creeping relativism all the more serious.

6. In correspondence, Sommers suggests a difference response, maintaining that individual autonomy and the control condition are as metaphysically extravagant. Surely this is false: individual autonomy does not require us to postulate the existence of constituents of the universe other than those that are physicalistically acceptable. A better response along similar lines was suggested by Gregg Caruso, who notes that the concept of agent causation is metaphysically extravagant. But there is no good evidence that the folk are committed to anything like agent causation. The empirical evidence on folk intuitions concerning moral responsibility and free will is equivocal (as Sommers 2010 himself shows), but it is consistent with all the evidence to hold that ordinary people are not committed to anything incompatible with contemporary science, even *if* we think that they are libertarians. In any case, the skeptic is not

committed to anything more extravagant, so even if it were possible to show that some individualistic theories are in the same metaphysical boat as the theory extant in honor cultures, we would still have grounds for choosing skepticism over rivals.

7. Sommers himself recognizes that broader considerations, such as flourishing, are relevant to theory choice in this arena (2012, 174). But he does not take this insight far enough, and fails to see how it can lead us to reject the framework in which his questions are posed.

8. Sommers rightly points out that many of the points made here, concerning both the metaphysical extravagance and the alleged dysfunctionality, of honor cultures do not apply to East Asian cultures. There seems no basis for saying that these cultures are dysfunctional and it is contentious whether they have a richer metaphysics than ours (though they might: settling this question would regard difficult work in social ontology as well as anthropology). However, it is far from clear to me that East Asian societies actually have a conception of moral responsibility that is sufficiently different from ours to establish an interesting relativism. As Sommers shows, East Asians may feel shame, and even a tinge of responsibility, for offenses committed by other individuals who belong to their group. But they seem to share with us the view that the agent causally responsible for the action alone is responsible for it in a special way, such that only that agent deserves the full force of blame.

9. Special thanks are due to Tamler Sommers and Gregg Caruso for perceptive comments on this chapter. This research was supported by grants from the Australian Research Council.

Chapter Six

Free Will as a Case of "Crazy Ethics"

Saul Smilansky

I would like to introduce and explain the idea of a "crazy ethics," to illustrate why the free will problem is a striking example of this notion, and then to draw some tentative conclusions. My use of the term "crazy ethics" should be unfamiliar to the reader. I am not using the term "crazy" pejoratively for ethical views I disagree with (as when one says "that view is just crazy"), nor am I referring to views that everyone should think are crazy, such as Nazi genocidal views. Rather, I use "crazy ethics" (or CE) as a semi-descriptive term for moral views which in spite of being *true* (or at least plausible) are in this sense crazy. To say that the free will problem is "crazy" in this sense is to say that we have good reasons to believe that plausible views on the free will debate strongly exhibit the characteristics of crazy ethics. This paper aims both to illustrate the unfamiliar notion of crazy ethics through the free will problem, and to illuminate unfamiliar aspects of the free will problem through the notion of a crazy ethics.[1]

WHAT IS CRAZY ETHICS?

The "craziness" of views might exhibit any of several characteristics. An ethical view might be considered crazy if it clearly could not serve as a basis for social life. A society that tried to function in the light of such a view would quickly fail. Similarly, an ethical view might be considered crazy if it is self-defeating, so that attempting to implement it would make things worse, in terms of that very view. A view that would be considered far too demanding and thus would be overwhelmingly rejected would also earn the label "crazy"; as would a view that flies in the teeth of fundamental reflective moral beliefs: no matter what arguments are offered for it, it could never be accepted. And an ethical view that needs to be kept apart from the vast majority of the people to whom it applies, an "esoteric morality," also involves craziness.

These characteristics themselves explain why ethical views that posses them are "crazy," and why grouping them together under this heading can contribute to our understanding that something larger seems to be going on here, beyond the specific difficulties of each. Although the craziness does not present a single common denominator but comes more in the form of a "family resemblance," the "crazy" features share the idea that *common, important and seemingly reasonable expectations from morality are disappointed, in significant ways, leading to a surprising, discordant and to some extent even irrational situation.* True moral views are expected to be coherent and more or less consistent both in themselves and, at least broadly, with our most dependable moral convictions. They need to be capable of being accepted and implemented by most people. If implemented, they should not be destructive in a major way to the society within which they are implemented, let alone destructive in the terms the view most values. Those seem to be natural and fairly minimal expectations from moral views, and not to meet them in a big way makes for manifest craziness, in the senses specified above, on both the theoretical and practical level.

Putting these diverse features under the single heading of "crazy ethics" also helps us to see the complex ways in which our given expectations from morality can be disappointed, and how we are all too often apt to deceive ourselves into an undue optimism on this matter (more will be said on this, in the free will context, towards the end of the paper). Finally, as we shall see when we explore the implications of the free will problem for CE, some of these features emerge together and lead to each other, thus enhancing the craziness of the emerging situation even further, beyond any one familiar feature.

I focus here on "craziness" within normative ethics, and assume a more or less optimistic metaethics. Assuming that morality has a stable metaethical grounding (any of various metaethical views could serve) is helpful in examining the possibility of "crazy" normative views. I also treat the free will problem as essentially ethical, rather than, say, essentially metaphysical or logical. I will not defend these assumptions here, but even those who are inclined to doubt it are likely to find interest in some of the discussion.

THE BASICS OF THE FREE WILL PROBLEM

I believe that the best way to understand the problem of free will is as a combination of four questions; the first two are the more familiar ones but, as we shall see, the last two are also crucial. The questions are:

1. Is there libertarian free will (LFW)? (Here would be included as sub-questions the issue of determinism, the question of whether libertarian free will is at all coherent, and so on.) Libertarians of course think that there is libertarian free will; compatibilists (typically) and hard determinists disagree. This first question is metaphysical or ontological.

2. If libertarian free will does not exist, do we still have moral responsibility and the related notions such as desert? This is, of course, the familiar compatibility question: is moral responsibility compatible with determinism or, better, is it compatible with the absence of libertarian free will irrespective of determinism? Compatibilism and hard determinism are opponents on the compatibility question. This issue, in my opinion, is mostly ethical.

3. If we have no moral responsibility in light of the absence of libertarian free will, or if moral responsibility is at least seriously weakened by the absence of libertarian free will, is this good or bad? In other words, are we better off without (or with much less) valid attribution of moral responsibility, so that we ought to welcome the absence of libertarian free will, or are we worse off?

4. What can and should we do about the replies to Questions 1-3? (Here would be included as sub-questions descriptive questions that concern the nature of folk belief and the possibility of radical change, and normative questions such as whether the continuation of widespread false belief can be tolerated.)

Just by way of an outline of my view on free will, I offer pessimistic answers to the first three questions. In response to Question 1, I hold that there is no libertarian free will. In response to Question 2, I believe that compatibilism is insufficient, and that we must opt for a Fundamental Dualism or compatibility-dualism, that attempts to combine the limited but crucial insights of both compatibilism and hard determinism. And in response to Question 3, I hold that this insufficiency is very important, and indeed tragic. This pessimism has complex and surprising implications for Question 4. Illusionism concerning free will relates to this fourth question. I will not in this essay attempt to defend my overall view on free will in a systematic way (for such an attempt see, for example, Smilansky 2000; Smilansky 2011a). I will try to show why I see central aspects of the free will problem—primarily, compatibilism and hard determinism—as "crazy."

   I believe that a robust libertarian free will does not exist. A robust notion of libertarian free will would go much beyond compatibilism, and offer a large qualitative advantage in grounding desert, responsibility and justice.

The most prominent current libertarianism, based upon event-libertarianism (e.g., Kane 1996; Ekstrom 2000) is not robust. It adds a measure of indeterminism to the initiation of action, which might be thought to limit and harm compatibilist control, but even when it does not, it does not add much to it. Robust libertarian free will is typically thought of as involving agent-causality (cf. Clarke 2003). Many, including libertarians, believe that there is no reason to think that what we know empirically about human beings supports this sort of libertarianism. Some people, including myself, even think that the very notion of a robust, transcendent metaphysical libertarianism is incoherent. Galen Strawson (e.g., 2002) argued convincingly, in my mind, for this claim; my attempt at presenting this argument in ethical garb is not very different (Smilansky 2000, ch.4). In any case, what I have to contribute to the free will problem lies elsewhere, namely in confronting Questions 2-4 above rather than Question 1. From now on I will assume that libertarian free will does not exist, and focus on trying to understand what follows.

If there were libertarian free will, then I believe that the free will problem would not provide fruitful ground for crazy ethics. But I believe that libertarian free will does not exist, and hence we must go on and explore the implications of a life without it.

HARD DETERMINISM AND JUST PUNISHMENT: A STUDY IN CRAZINESS

Hard determinism is the view that there is no free will, moral responsibility, and desert. In a recent paper (Smilansky 2011b), I explored the results of an attempt to implement hard determinism in the field of punishment. Here I shall summarize the ideas of that study, a practical *reductio* of hard determinism; and show why it implies crazy ethics. To the extent that the insights of hard determinism are true—and I believe that they encompass a lot of the relevant truths here—we must take this result very seriously (later we shall explore how well compatibilism can do). This means that our ethics is in large measure crazy, in the sense under discussion in this paper.

Hard determinists may not punish people. Under hard determinism, no one has the requisite free will and moral responsibility to deserve punishment. If no one deserves punishment, and he or she are punished, then this punishment is unjust. So hard determinists cannot put people in the sort of institutions of incarceration as we presently do with criminals. But while hard determinists cannot punish people, they still may separate and incarcerate severe wrongdoers away from normative people. Under hard determinism punishment will be substituted by "funishment," where every effort is made so that the wrongdoers will not be badly off, or worse than they would be on the outside. Since the separation from normal society and the deprivation of the freedom that others share is in itself a grave harm, it needs then to be compensated for, in making the life of those being "funished" otherwise delightful.

I cannot elaborate in full detail here on the way things would unfold, but the crux is that hard determinism is seen to collapse upon itself: institutions of "funishment" will lose their ability to deter, and prove self-defeating. The number of people who would need to be kept apart from lawful society would increase enormously. Many people who would otherwise not have become involved in crime, nor ever suffer detention, would be caught up in that very life. In the meantime, the rest of us would be living in the worst possible world: suffering unprecedented crime waves while paying unimaginable sums for the upkeep of offenders in opulent institutions of funishment.

Even in hard determinist terms, all this is a very bad state of affairs. Hard determinists have sought to limit the number of people that the justice system must deal with, to reduce public hatred of offenders, and to beneficially reform the social conditions that generate crime. But hard determinism itself defeats all those idealistic goals. If implemented, the view would generate more rather than less crime, more criminals would be caught up in the system and incarcerated apart from society (albeit under improved conditions), and public sentiment would hardly move toward an offender-sympathetic stance, once crime blossoms, and the taxation required to finance the regime of funishment mushrooms. A backlash against hard determinist reforms would be inevitable. But that result is philosophically less interesting than the consequences of full implementation of hard determinism itself: it is not only that implementing hard determinism would result in a traumatic reaction and an abandonment of hard determinist policies. A hard determinist order would be nightmarish, even for hard determinism, if *correctly* implemented. Hard determinists themselves cannot desire the results of the reforms required by their own position (such as rising crime and much higher levels of incarceration). Hard determinism, thus interpreted, is, in practice, self-defeating.[2]

My "funishment" argument has focused on the clear-cut case of punishment. But matters would not stop there. The broad framework of human reactive attitudes would be similarly disrupted. Most human reactions have the potential to make people feel bad, whether directly or comparatively. But according to hard determinism no one can come to deserve to suffer such negative (or comparatively deficient) reactions; no one is blameworthy. Yet it is hard to imagine interpersonal life without them. Presumably those who are made either directly or comparatively unhappy by such reactions would need to be compensated, in the psychological equivalent of funishment. The negative attitude, if it were not to make the targeted person unjustly despondent, would presumably need to be immediately accompanied by a stronger, compensating, positive emotional response, which would make him or her feel good about him or herself. But not only would this be artificial and disruptive of natural human interaction—it would typically and at once empty the negative reactions of their purpose and effectiveness.

In sum, I am claiming that (irrespective of its philosophical merits and demerits), the idea of applying a genuine, morally principled hard determinism cannot be taken seriously. It lies at too great a distance from human nature and cannot be implemented in personal or social life, except at the margins.

A further danger is that this may lead hard determinists to give up their principles, and adopt utilitarian or other such theories. Like many, I am a normative pluralist, and of course see a role for consequentialist considerations in the justification of punishment or other matters. That is not, however, the issue. It is one thing to say that we punish people also because the institution of punishment does good, overall, but a very different thing to say that we may punish the innocent. Hard determinists can remain with the insights of their position, in which case the theory breaks up as a source of guidance for personal and social behavior. Alternatively, once they recognize the impossibility of implementing their position, hard determinists can deny its moral core, and turn to utilitarian-like forms of consequentialism. If they do so, their position will lose its interest as a position on the free will problem, and morally, it will not matter anymore. The whole impetus of the free will problem follows from the idea that free will matters. It matters if we have it, but it also matters if we believe that we do not. To the extent that hard determinism, as a deep moral position and not just as a form of incompatibilism that denies LFW, cries out that because there is no free will no one deserves to suffer, then it is an important moral position, but if it betrays its principles and opts for something like utilitarianism, we lose all interest.

So, a genuine, morally important hard determinism may well be to a large extent true, but it cannot be implemented. Hard determinism is, in practice, self-defeating. *This makes it squarely an example of crazy ethics.*

COMPATIBILISM, INJUSTICE AND KNOWLEDGE: A STUDY IN CRAZINESS

In order to explore whether compatibilism can do better than hard determinism, we need first to explore the incompatibilist perspective against compatibilism. There are many arguments which seek to show the inadequacy of compatibilism. The most familiar one is van Inwagen's "Consequence Argument," whereby since we can control neither the past nor the laws of nature, yet everything that we do is a consequence of those two, then we cannot control what we do (van Inwagen 1983). Such arguments have been much discussed, and I will not aim to review the huge literature. I would like to present my own version of the attempt to clarify the incompatibilist discomfort, an argument that I call The Trap (Smilansky 2012).

Assume a world without libertarian free will. In fact, just for the sake of simplifying the story (compatibilists will not object), assume that it is a deterministic world, rather than one which combines determinism with random indeterminism, which does not enhance human control. Consider further a person who is paying a very high price as a result of his choices; various possibilities could be contemplated, but let us begin by thinking of a person serving very many years in prison, in a way that for all practical purposes ruins his life. He will be deprived of the best years of his life, spend them in horrible surroundings, and the experience will stop him from being truly happy even after he is released. Assume that this person is in prison for committing a real offense, not for one that needs to be de-criminalized. All compatibilist conditions have been fully satisfied; he is a model of the deserving wrongdoer, according to compatibilism. This means that he is an adult, cognitively competent and mentally stable. He did the deed for which he is in prison, intentionally, purposefully, and after due reflection. He has no justification or excuse (setting aside here the incompatibilist threat from the free will problem). There are even no mitigating circumstances in his case, as philosophical compatibilists (and the courts) would evaluate matters.

Let us assume, now with far less empirical basis but not in a way that should matter to us for present purposes, that it was known years in advance that he would commit the sort of crime that he committed, and then end up in prison. The available technology is such that this could be predicted and, as long as nothing further would be done (and as long as the prediction remains unknown to this individual), it would be fulfilled. Assume further, and now very plausibly, that there are things that, were they to have been done, would have prevented him from committing the crime. Let us focus on ways that merely extend current manners of functioning, such as reducing socio-economic inequality, or increasing the severity of the (threat of) punishment, or increasing the likelihood that an offender would be caught. Such changes, had they been implemented, would have in fact deterred our criminal.

Let us further assume that we, as a society, have good reasons not to change our procedures in a major way: we choose to keep the current level of inequality, limit the severity of punishment, and not increase significantly the chances of detection and capture. This we do for a host of reasons based, for example, upon the benefits of a market economy, of liberal penalization, and of limiting the resources that we devote to policing and related efforts. Our practices work pretty well, *statistically*, in limiting crime to a manageable degree, for us as a society; and the way in which we balance all the relevant values and considerations is reasonable. Now in fact it is unlikely that social practices on all these matters are fully justified, and to the extent that they are not, this will help my argument, but I would like to make my case under optimal conditions for my opponents.

Even if all that is the case, it seems to me that not only is the convicted prisoner a victim of circumstances, but—recall that we knew that he would commit the crime—he is *a victim of our decisions*. We knew that if everything were kept as it is, this person would commit the crime, and end up spending many years in prison, a ruined man. We also knew that if we changed some of the factors I noted in the previous paragraph, then he would *not* go on to commit any crime, and would not go to prison. The *failure in deterrence*, broadly conceived, is also *ours*. In compatibilist terms, we could have prevented the crime as well as the punishment. However, we established the social institutions and, *despite knowing that he would fall were we not to change things*, we nevertheless decided not to. *The man is trapped, and we are responsible for the parameters that trapped him.*

This does not mean that, all considered, we are doing wrong; that we are not justified in operating as we are. Let us first set aside the free will problem as it now applies to *us*, and assume compatibilism here, for the sake of this argument: in other words, let us assume that we can be blameworthy for the way we treat wrongdoers. The compatibilist should see no problem with our being potentially blameworthy. Nevertheless, the problem with The Trap is not that it follows from our wrongdoing—the purpose of this thought experiment is to indicate the limitations of compatibilism, to show why even under ideal compatibilist conditions, *when we do right*, according to compatibilism, injustice prevails. Recall that we were assuming that for our society, the decisions (on economic, penal, and policing policies) may well have been reasonable, given the balance of values at stake. But we are nevertheless responsible for the victimization of our criminal: we have set up our social institutions knowing full well that they would lead him to his ruin, yet chose to persist in making these arrangements.

It is crucial to see that compatibilists find no fault in this practice. What my story is intended to emphasize is the sense in which the person is trapped by our policies: to repeat, we know beforehand what he is destined to do unless we save him but we decide—for *our* reasons—not to do so. We let him develop into a criminal, harm his victim, and (compatibilistically-justly) fall to his doom.

This story is unreal only in one important respect: we do not in fact possess the high level of knowledge described here, and hence we are incapable, as a rule, of such prediction on the *individual* level. We do, however, have reason to believe that, statistically, many people are going to fall in this way, unless we change our economic, penal, or policing policies, which we do not change. Morally, the fact that our knowledge is only statistical does not seem to matter much. The setup I have described, whereby in effect we socially construct a trap in which people then fall, is in place even if our knowledge about the details is sketchy. This sketchiness serves to hide from us the nature of what is going on and thereby helps the setup to function more smoothly, but it does not change its nature. *We know that, in a deterministic world, The Trap is set, whether we are aware of the details or not. The difficulty is practical, and epistemic; metaphysically matters are already settled.*

The sort of scenario that I have tried to capture in The Trap is the anti-compatibilist move that I find most salient. The challenge facing the compatibilist is directly ethical: the very people whom the compatibilist describes as free, morally responsible, and deserving of blame and punishment for committing a given criminal act are seen to be, in fact, trapped. They are literally the victims of circumstances. Moreover, they are trapped by us. We are all familiar with utilitarian arguments sacrificing some for the greater good of others. But compatibilism is a position within the free will debate, which values free will-based justice. The basic moral idea is that a person must not be punished unless he has permitted this through his free actions: "Justice simply consists of principles to be observed in adjusting the competing claims of human beings (i) which treat all alike as persons by attaching special significance to human voluntary action and (ii) forbid the use of one human being for the benefit of others except in return for his voluntary actions against them" (Hart 1970, 22). Compatibilism allows such exceptions. But once we take the broad perspective and see that in fact there is a trap here, then it becomes much more difficult, I feel, to give this fact no weight; the victimization begins to seem quite similar to the notorious one permitted (or indeed often required) by utilitarianism. In other words, society knowingly and willfully follows a path where certain people will be sacrificed for the sake of the general good (or some such goal). This is not to deny all validity to compatibilism; I defend a more modest version of it myself. But the question here is whether the compatibilist can continue to deny the deep moral problem involved in punishing people on the basis of their compatibilist free will, moral responsibility, and desert, once we see the compatibilistically free criminal as being, all along, in The Trap, our trap.

That The Trap works through rather than bypasses people's voluntary actions (suitably enhanced according to compatibilist requirements) cannot be the only thing that matters. The idea that it is fine for the person to be punished, since he has forfeited the constraint against harm through his voluntary actions, is seen in a much darker light once we see the role that this person plays as, simply, his being *in* The Trap. From one perspective, he deliberates, takes his chances, chooses, and is then punished for his choices. It is not as though he is punished when he did nothing, or when he showed only good will; he is not (say) framed by the police and falsely accused of a crime he did not commit. But on a deeper view, what we see is merely a person who is doomed. Under such and such circumstances, he will do such and such things, and end up very badly off, blamed and severely punished.

What role does the idea that it is we (as a society) that set The Trap, play? It might be thought that it only harms my case. After all, even if people had robust libertarian free will, and were thus deserving of punishment in the strongest sense, then some would commit crimes. Even then it would still be the case that, were we to make certain changes, then those people would not choose to commit a crime of their own libertarian free will. Even libertarians, after all, believe in incentives, and in situational moral luck. But our role matters in a different way here. With libertarian free will, while circumstances are important, they do not determine the outcome. Thus if we as a society have otherwise been reasonable in setting up the moral game, it is the criminal—rather than we—who is morally responsible for his ending up in prison, because of the way he chose to play the game. But given determinism, it is no longer clear why we should say that *he* is at fault for our failure to deter him. There is a casual nexus leading to a person's ending up in prison, with a ruined life. He plays his role, according to the way he is built. That is the role he will play, unless we change things. Were we to change matters, we could save him (and his victims). We see it coming, and yet (for our own reasons) we continue; we see that unless we do something, he will be doomed, but we change nothing. And we blame him.

Michael McKenna discusses my criticism of compatibilism in considerable detail (McKenna 2008a, 192-98), responding primarily to Smilansky (2000) and Smilansky (2003). He concludes his interesting discussion in this way: "In closing this section, my challenge to Smilansky and other advocates of the Ultimacy Argument is to produce some positive account of the element of free action that ultimacy affords and that a compatibilist cannot provide. Until then, I remain skeptical that any argumentative force should be granted to the U condition as an aid in an argument for incompatibilism" (McKenna 2008a, 198). Now, if the compatibilist means by a "positive account" a creditable account of libertarian free will, then that demand is unreasonable: one can be an incompatibilist (or a partial incompatibilist, like myself), who thinks that libertarian free will cannot exist. Nevertheless it is possible to claim that compatibilist forms of free will are insufficient, so that the absence of LFW matters. It matters that we cannot have the sort of things that LFW was supposed to provide. Here again The Trap seems to me to help and flesh out the difficulty: quite simply, *our choosing to proceed in blaming and punishing a person who was all along trapped in a course leading to his doom.* Were this person to have libertarian free will (and were LFW possible), he could, of course, have escaped The Trap; he would *not* be doomed. That presumably is what LFW would allow. Once we see the nature of social life as a trap for those unfortunate enough to fall into our (compatibilist) hands, we see why compatibilism falls short, in not recognizing the unfairness and injustice involved.

In parallel to the issue of punishment, people end up in unpleasant places in their lives in other respects, also through their (compatibilistically-free) choices; in their economic lives, in their personal relationships, and so on. So parallel cases to the one I have made here concerning punishment can be made in other areas.

The compatibilist can reply that even assuming determinism, the fact that certain people end up very badly off does not make the process through which they got there unjust. If a system victimizes people who are not able to understand rationally their options or control their actions (e.g., are acting under compulsion), then indeed their ending up in prison would be unjust; but then such people lack compatibilist free will, or at least have it only in mitigated form, and in an adequate compatibilist society they would not end up in prison. However, if we are considering the compatibilistically-free, then they themselves chose to participate in social encounters, accepted responsibility for their actions, and benefited from the responsible behavior of others. If they then happen to lose out through the free exercise of their compatibilist capacities, they cannot morally complain. The importance of a compatibilist Community of Responsibility is something that I have and continue to affirm. But at issue here, to repeat, is not whether there is something in compatibilism, but whether it is *sufficient*. Or, in other words, the issue is whether the hard determinist case, which I have just made through the story of The Trap, captures an important sense of *injustice*. And this seems to me now very hard to deny. The absence of predictability means that the criminal to be did not know that he was doomed through our socially-designed setup, but this ignorance does not change the reality, which is that, in fact, he was doomed.

So, in one way, compatibilists are in a better state than hard determinists: while implementing hard determinism would be self-defeating in terms of that theory, and hence hard determinism could simply not serve as a basis for our social practice, compatibilism can, by and large, serve as such a basis. While hard determinism thus involves crazy ethics of the first order, compatibilism does not. However, the CE element comes in with compatibilism as well. In order to see why we need to first see the practical vulnerability of compatibilism.

If people became aware of the absence of libertarian free will and of incompatibilist arguments (such as The Trap), there is a significant chance that they would lose confidence in the idea that our social practices and institutions are just. However, as we saw from the gross inadequacy of hard determinism, while there is always room for reform, such practices and institutions are required. We need to establish a Community of Responsibility (I have argued for this in detail elsewhere; see, e.g., Smilansky 2000; Smilansky 2005a). Yet if we become aware of how deeply unjust even our best practices (under ideal compatibilist conditions) can be, simply in light of determinism, would this not make us *care* less about those standards and constraints, and opt more for pragmatic compromises and considerations? There is surely a constant temptation to get things done, to use people, to achieve good social results at the expense of individuals, in short, to bypass "respect for persons," particularly if interpreted in an individualistic and liberal manner. History is full of examples. Whether in the form of bigotry that cares nothing for choice and responsibility, or in the form of the dominance of the need to manage things and the call for efficiency, which bypasses them, the temptation is always present. But constraining such natural social and political tendencies is no mean feat. Traditional free will-related beliefs have played a major role here. Consider, for example, the idea of the *sanctity of innocence*: the view that the innocent must not be harmed, while those who freely chose to do bad may be harmed, at least if this would produce good results. This, of course, connects directly to a robust sense of desert—which must exist to allow negative sanctions, and which is the ground for positive reactions and rewards. Now, all these important matters can have some, limited, local justification through broadly compatibilist forms of thought. But surely the libertarian story grounds them in a much *stronger* way.

When we look backward, we frequently see what made us choose as we did, to understand the causal mechanisms that led to our choices and actions. But then there is little to stop us from being led to the thought that we simply operated as we were molded; facing the equivalent of The Trap, only going much beyond the penal examples. Unless we believe in libertarian free will, in which case the backward gaze poses no inherent danger.

We often want a person to blame himself, feel guilty, and even see that he deserves to be punished. Such a person is not likely to do this if he internalizes the ultimate perspective, according to which in the actual world nothing else could in fact have occurred, he could not strictly have done anything apart from what he did do and, in fact, he had no real opportunity to escape The Trap. Again, with a belief in libertarian free will all this is not necessary.

Compatibilism is partly justified, often salient, and in any case must form the backbone of our moral life, for hard determinism is inherently "leveling" and cannot adequately distinguish and motivate. Nevertheless, compatibilism is also *vulnerable*, and dangerously so. It is a widespread topic for conversation among philosophers teaching the free will problem, how difficult it is to convince many of our students to see the force of compatibilism: the abandonment of libertarian beliefs typically leads to a free fall into the philosophical denial of free will and moral responsibility.

Take the most influential contemporary form of this position, John Martin Fischer's semi-compatibilism. According to this view, while determinism rules out the "ability to do otherwise," it does not rule out free will and moral responsibility, which do not require that people have the ability to do otherwise at any point (Fischer 1994). But irrespective of its philosophical merits, does it really make sense to think that such a view can be widely accepted? In other words, is it likely that the vast majority of people can be convinced of the idea that, while even compatibilists admit that no one could have ever done anything else except what they in fact did, yet nevertheless all these people were free and may deserve blame and punishment for their actions?

I cannot enter here into a detailed discussion of the experimental philosophy results of the investigation of folk belief (for a thorough recent survey and discussion, see Nichols and Knobe 2007). The field is, in any case, still in early stages of development. But the robust results we already have do not lead to confidence concerning to the ability of compatibilism to capture the folk. When asked abstractly, it turns out that there is an overwhelming degree of belief in something like libertarian free will, and tacit incompatibilism, around. The great majority of people are not ready to accept a philosophical compatibilist understanding of free will, moral responsibility, desert and justice. On the other hand, the situation is reversed and compatibilist replies are given by most people when asked concrete questions about specific situations. This disparity in itself is highly unstable and disturbing. Moreover, the compatibilist-like results seem to follow in large measure because of (a) emotional priming, that is, when people are presented with highly charged emotional situations in concrete situations; and (b) to be highly moralized, for example, the answers seem to depend upon how worried the respondents are about bad deeds going unpunished. Much of this moralization seems to me to indicate a pragmatic concern rather than any real acceptance of a compatibilist perspective. I conclude that if libertarian beliefs are shaken, there is little reason to think that compatibilism can fill the gap, and maintain the proper free will-related beliefs, reactions, and practices, in a dependable way. Compatibilism is vulnerable, and dangerously so.

As a compatibility-dualist, I believe that some forms of free will and moral responsibility are possible, and some not, and both conclusions matter. Hence we need to try and combine the true, if limited, insights of both compatibilism and hard determinism (see Smilansky 2000, Part I; Smilansky 2005a; Smilansky 2011a). Such theoretical complexity raises its own practical difficulties, but clearly these do not dispel the specter of crazy ethics, which is our current concern. Even if one is a monistic compatibilist, there are strong reasons to doubt whether compatibilism can suffice, in practice. It suffices for the purpose of seeing that crazy ethics follows under compatibilism, to think of the practical issues. A position such as semi-compatibilism is at such great distance from common assumptions and sentiments that, whatever its theoretical merits, it seems clear that it cannot serve as a basis for social and personal practice. To the extent that compatibilist-like beliefs, reactions and practices need to dominate, they will need to be supported, in practice, by illusions, primarily by (false) libertarian beliefs.

And so, unless illusion intervenes the partial validity of the compatibilist distinctions is unlikely to overcome the *practical* salience of the ultimate hard determinist perspective in such a situation. Determinists are not likely to cherish and maintain adequately the respect due to people in the light of their free actions, nor a free will-based moral order in general. The ethical importance of the paradigm of free will and responsibility as a basis for desert should be taken very seriously, but the ultimate perspective threatens to present it as a farce, a mere game without foundation. Similarly with the crucial idea of a personal sense of value and appreciation that can be gained through our free actions: this is unlikely to be adequately maintained by individuals in their self-estimates, nor warmly and consistently projected by society. A broad loss of moral and personal confidence can be expected. Applying the sort of perspective that leads us to see the incompatibilist worry (e.g., The Trap) more generally, to our whole view of ourselves and others, can be very dangerous. The risks of understanding and internalization are great. Fortunately, however, so far most people live under illusion. This need not involve a firm, explicit, libertarian system of belief. All that is needed are general and vague libertarian assumptions, to the effect that people are free in the libertarian sense, and thereby are typically responsible, deserving, blameworthy and praiseworthy, and the like. At the minimum, it might be sufficient simply to persuade oneself that there is no clear threat to the idea of moral responsibility and free will-related justice.

I have argued in the past in detail for the crucial and largely necessary role of illusion on free will, and in particular of the advantages of the widely prevailing but false belief in libertarian free will (e.g., Smilansky 2000, Part II; Smilansky 2001). I do not wish to repeat this here, but will just briefly illustrate how I think that things operate.

One way which seems to work is where we *keep ourselves* on the level of compatibilist distinctions about local control and do not ask ourselves about the deeper question of the "givenness" of our choosing self; resisting threats to our vague, tacit libertarian assumptions. As Bernard Williams put it: "To the extent that the institution of blame works coherently, it does so because it attempts less than morality would like it to do . . . [it] takes the agent together with his character, and does not raise questions about his freedom to have chosen some other character" (1985, 194). The result is not philosophically neat, but that, after all, is its merit. By not inquiring too deeply, by taking care to keep things vague, we can continue to function.

But a firmer set of beliefs should be more effective. They will, for example, be the familiar belief, when we think of some past junction, *that we could have actually done otherwise in it*, that doing so was up to us in a literal, real and deep sense. Therefore we can be blameworthy for our wrongdoing, we accept this and feel remorse and compunction, and acknowledge that we might even deserve punishment. Likewise, when choosing and acting we know all of this, and therefore realize that in the future we shall be judged, and judge ourselves, according to whether we function responsibly now, thinking that (unless unusual circumstances apply) we shall have no excuse if we do not fulfill our duties. And so forth.

This, I believe, is a central feature of human life. We cannot live with the full truth on the free will problem and related matters; illusion is necessary, and by and large positive. I will not repeat more lengthy elaborations and defenses of this claim presented in my previous writings. What matters here is to see how with compatibilism as well, we do not escape crazy ethics. The threat of the ultimate, hard determinist perspective, even if it is only part of the truth on the free will problem, looms over compatibilism, and threatens to submerge it in practice, leading many people here to some measure of nihilism, or turning them away from valuing free will, towards utilitarianism or such views. We saw this threat in a focused way with the help of The Trap. The implication is that compatibilist distinctions, and a largely compatibilist Community of Responsibility, need to be the foundation of social and personal life—yet they require the support of illusion.

The free will-related illusions are not easily dispelled. They are deeply ingrained culturally, socially, and probably also biologically. Nevertheless, it is complacent to feel assured that there is nothing to worry about (cf. my criticism, in Smilansky 2001, of P.F. Strawson's famous position on this matter in his "Freedom and Resentment"; Strawson 2003). The sort of threat illustrated by The Trap is always there, once people become aware of the free will problem and realize, and try to internalize, its implications. As we saw, there is a double danger here: first, the truths themselves are grim and dispiriting. Second, this may lead to an over-reaction, to the neglect of the partial, true insights of compatibilism in favor of nihilism or a consequentialist abandonment of the inherent importance of free will. The main solution seems to be that most people continue to live with the false belief in libertarian free will, and with the deep ideas of responsibility, desert, and justice that follow from it. In other words, the dangers of the truth make illusion by and large positive, arguably a morally necessary illusion. But here we are well within crazy ethics-territory: except within the confines of philosophy, it is not clear whether true morality can or ought to be attempted to be lived upon. Morality becomes esoteric.

CONCLUSION

It is far too early to gauge the significance of our being bound to live with a crazy ethics. The notion of a crazy ethics is an unfamiliar one, and the topic needs to be thought out almost from the ground up. In this paper I have merely sought to present the notion of a crazy ethics, and to explore how the free will debate helps us to see that we must consider it. Further work needs to be done, both in understanding the philosophical-ethical implications of this notion, and in exploring what it might mean for actual moral lives.

I began by introducing this new notion of a crazy ethics. This craziness in ethical views does not indicate that the views are mistaken; on the contrary, the craziness can be a feature of true beliefs. Ethical craziness can take various forms: in manifestly dysfunctional or self-defeating ethical positions, extreme demandingness, moral conclusions that are indubitably unacceptable, or in proposing an esoteric morality. I explained why those features are indeed crazy, in a public morality, and tried to show why thinking of them together, under this one heading of CE, rather than of each individually, may be fruitful.

I next explored the free will problem. Various aspects of this problem seem to show that major corners of our moral universe are "crazy" in some of the above senses of craziness. We focused on the idea of just punishment, and saw that the two major contenders on the free will problem, hard determinism and compatibilism, do very badly, even if in different ways. These failures give rise to the overwhelming presence of crazy ethics. A hard determinism that remains true to its own moral principles is self-defeating on punishment. Compatibilism is not self-defeating, but is vulnerable and requires massive support by illusion in order to be maintained. The truth on free will is dangerous, and the idea of an esoteric morality, for all its unattractiveness, seems to raise its head.

Finally, I reflected briefly on the meaning of the occasional craziness of morality, and concluded that we probably need to lower our expectations from normative ethics (and consequently from applied ethics as well). The major example we saw concerned justice: in the light of the free will problem, punishment could not be just. Of course matters could be better or worse; we could always make things even more unjust, say, by punishing at random or victimizing particular racial groups. But even under the best conditions, punishment cannot be fully just. To the extent that we follow hard determinism and aim for the proper form of punishment, "funishment," we will face self-defeat. To the extent that we follow (as by and large we should, in practice) compatibilism—we will still have gross, ultimate injustice. Together with our hopes from justice, we should (as philosophers) therefore also give up the idea of an open, transparent morality, guiding personal and social practices. Just as the fantasy of the reign of justice must go, so must that of the reign of truth.

Thinking about the idea of a crazy ethics puts into relief the importance of the free will problem in a new and grim form: the absence of libertarian free will and the insufficiency of compatibilist desert mean that justice in punishment (and other desert-based social practices and reactions) is impossible. The necessity of the belief in libertarian free will, in order to support the partly valid but vulnerable compatibilist distinctions and concerns, means that illusion seems to be morally necessary. In both these respects the free will problem appears to be a fertile ground for "ethical craziness." This illustrates why the free will problem means that crazy ethics is widely prevalent in life. Arguably, the free will regions are the craziest territory of all.

NOTES

1. I discussed the topic of this paper in the philosophy blog Flickers of Freedom in November 2012, and am grateful for the input of contributors to the debate. I am very grateful to Gregg Caruso, Iddo Landau and Daniel Statman for helpful comments on drafts of this chapter.

2. In his response to my chapter, Neil Levy (2012) raises the possibility for a consequentialist alternative for dealing with the absence of libertarian free will in punishment. I cannot discuss here the merits of his case, let alone of consequentialism in general, but will just note that such an option confronts two difficulties: first, under typical interpretations of consequentialism which do not involve desert (such as utilitarianism), such a position lies outside the free will problem, for it has no inherent concern for free will. It might care whether or not people believe in free will for its own pragmatic reasons, but the position itself is indifferent to the problem. We blame people or hold them responsible not because they deserve such attitudes or reactions in light of their actions, but because it is thought to be beneficial for the general good that they be so blamed and punished. So, rather than a position on the free will problem, this would seem to be a view that bypasses giving any moral weight to the concern over free will (or the implications of its absence). Second, such a radical move outside of the free will fold would involve the familiar difficulties of consequentialism. One difficulty is with justice (see, e.g., on the punishment of the innocent, Smilansky 1990). Likewise, as we have already learned from Sidgwick, such consequentialist views are themselves notoriously sympathetic to thoughts of "truth-rationing" and an esoteric morality. So even "going consequentialist" is unlikely to help us avoid crazy ethics.

Chapter Seven

The Potential Dark Side of Believing in Free Will (and Related Concepts)

Some Preliminary Findings

Thomas Nadelhoffer and Daniela Goya Tocchetto

Perhaps you've chosen to read this essay after scanning other articles on this website. Or, if you're in a hotel, maybe you've decided what to order for breakfast, or what clothes you'll wear today. You haven't. You may feel like you've made choices, but in reality your decision to read this piece, and whether to have eggs or pancakes, was determined long before you were aware of it—perhaps even before you woke up today. And your "will" had no part in that decision. So it is with all of our other choices: not one of them results from a free and conscious decision on our part. There is no freedom of choice, no free will. And those New Year's resolutions you made? You had no choice about making them, and you'll have no choice about whether you keep them. The debate about free will, long the purview of philosophers alone, has been given new life by scientists, especially neuroscientists studying how the brain works. And what they're finding supports the idea that free will is a complete illusion. —Jerry Coyne, *USA Today* (2012)

Humanity is fortunately deceived on the free will issue, and this seems to be a condition of civilized morality and personal sense of value. Illusion and ignorance appear to be conditions for social and personal success. —Saul Smilansky, *Free Will and Illusion* (2000)

While the free will debate has traditionally been the fairly cloistered haunt of philosophers and theologians, a growing number of scientists have recently become increasingly vocal about their skepticism concerning free will (e.g., Bargh 2008; Cashmore 2010; Greene and Cohen 2004; Harris 2012; Haynes 2011b; Montague 2008; Wegner 2002, 2008; cf. Baumeister 2008a; Walter

2001). With articles appearing in *The New York Times*, *The Economist*, *Forbes Magazine*, *WIRED*, and *USA Today*, the debate about free will has finally hit the mainstream. One common theme in the way free will has been discussed in the popular press is that recent scientific advances (especially in neuroscience) threaten or undermine our traditional pictures of agency and responsibility.[1]

Addressing whether the alarmism coming from the scientific skeptics is well-motivated (or misplaced) is a complicated task that would take us too far afield for present purposes (see, e.g., Mele 2009, 2010a, 2010b, 2010c, 2011, 2012a; Nadelhoffer 2011, forthcoming; Nahmias 2011b, forthcoming-b). So, rather than focusing on whether the scientific skeptics are right either about what free will is (they say laypersons are committed to both libertarian, contra-causal free will and dualism about the mind and the body) or about whether we have it (they say free will can't be squared with the gathering data in neuroscience on the relationship between the mind and the brain), we are going to focus on the potential *ramifications* of their skepticism. For regardless of whether the scientific skeptics are correct about the purported tension between science and free will, their proclamations in newspapers and magazines could still have an impact on people's moral beliefs and behaviors.

As Dennis Overbye noted in *The New York Times* a few years ago, "the death of free will, or its exposure as a convenient illusion, some worry, could wreak havoc on our sense of moral and legal responsibility. According to those who believe that free will and determinism are incompatible. . . . It would mean that people are no more responsible for their actions than asteroids or planets. Anything would go" (2007). This is an age-old worry and not just a skeptical tempest in an academic teapot—a worry that was once expressed very poignantly by Shakespeare in the following way:

> This is the excellent foppery of the world, that when we are sick in fortune, often the surfeits of our own behavior, we make guilty of our disasters the sun, the moon, and stars; as if we were villains on necessity; fools by heavenly compulsion; knaves, thieves, and treachers by spherical predominance; drunkards, liars, and adulterers by an enforced obedience of planetary influence; and all that we are evil in, by a divine thrusting on—an admirable evasion of whoremaster man, to lay his goatish disposition on the charge of a star. (1610/2005)

If the great Bard of Avon were alive today, he would no doubt be unsurprised to learn that there is gathering evidence in social psychology which suggests that manipulating people's beliefs about free will influences their moral behavior in a variety of ways. Consider, for instance, the following research:

1. Vohs and Schooler (2008) show that participants who are exposed to anti-free will primes are more likely to cheat than participants exposed to pro-free will or neutral primes.
2. Baumeister, Masicampo and DeWall (2009) show that participants who are exposed to anti-free will primes behave more aggressively than participants exposed to pro-free will or neutral primes. Moreover, these researchers show participants who naturally believe more strongly in free will are more likely to behave helpfully towards strangers.
3. Stillman, Baumeister, Vohs, Lambert, Finchman and Brewer (2010) show that participants who naturally believe more strongly in free will have more positive careerist attitudes and their bosses and co-workers give them better job performance ratings.
4. Stillman and Baumeister (2010) show that believing in free will facilitates learning from self-conscious emotions and inducing disbelief in free will hinders learning.
5. Rigoni, Kuhn, Sartori and Brass (2011) show that participants who are exposed to anti-free will primes display reduced activation in the motor cortex compared to participants who received a pro-free will or neutral prime.

These (and similar) findings suggest that even if the scientific skeptics turn out to be right that we don't have free will, believing in free will could nevertheless be a so-called "positive" illusion (Taylor and Brown 1988, 193).

In the social psychology literature, it is now widely acknowledged that illusions of control, self-other biases, and other cognitive errors are much more common in human cognition than previously assumed. More surprising still is the fact that these epistemically problematic inferences, beliefs, and judgments appear to be adaptive in a wide variety of domains. As Taylor and Brown (1988, 204) point out:

> Evidence from social cognition research suggests that, contrary to much traditional, psychological wisdom, the mentally healthy person may not be fully cognizant of the day-to-day flotsam and jetsam of life. Rather, the mentally healthy person appears to have the enviable capacity to distort reality in a direction that enhances self-esteem, maintain beliefs in personal efficacy, and promotes an optimistic view of the future. These three illusions, as we have called them, appear to foster traditional criteria of mental health, including the ability to care about the self and others, the ability to be happy or contented, and the ability to engage in productive and creative work.

If believing in free will ultimately turns out to be a positive illusion along similar lines, then this would add additional urgency to the aforementioned worry expressed by Overbye, Shakespeare, and others. Minimally, it would suggest that the public pronouncements made by the scientific skeptics may be imprudent from the dual standpoints of positive psychology and public policy.

Saul Smilansky has recently raised similar concerns in motivating his own novel view about what we ought to do concerning the purported death of free will—a position which he calls "free will illusionism" (2000, 2001, 2002; cf. Nadelhoffer and Feltz 2007; Nadelhoffer and Matveeva 2009). In short, Smilansky claims (a) that beliefs in libertarian, contra-causal free will are both widespread and illusory, and (b) that these illusory beliefs confer a number of positive benefits to individuals and society more generally. On this view, because people's illusory beliefs concerning libertarian free will undergird their notions of deep desert and ultimate moral responsibility (among other things), these free will beliefs should be preserved as much as possible (2000, 150). As Smilansky says, "To put it bluntly: people as a rule ought not to be fully aware of the ultimate inevitability of what they have done, for this will affect the way in which they hold themselves responsible" (2001, 85).

Similar illusionist views are hinted at in the social psychology literature. For instance, Kathleen Vohs and Jonathan Schooler claim that, "the fact that brief exposure to a message asserting that there is no such thing as free will can increase both passive and active cheating raises the concern that advocating a deterministic worldview could undermine moral behavior" (2008, 53). In the event that the scientific skeptics are right that we don't have free will, these (and similar) findings from psychology concerning the social utility of free will beliefs would provide prima facie empirical support for illusionism. But we simply don't have enough data at this point to draw any firm conclusions about the overall value of believing in free will. Making things even more difficult still is the fact that the empirical evidence that we do have is mixed. For while most of the studies have focused on the potential *upside* to believing in free will, there are some recent findings which suggest that there may also be a potential *downside* as well—which is an underexplored issue we plan to address in the following pages.

Accordingly, one of our primary goals in the present chapter is to survey some recent findings from moral and political psychology on the possible dark side of believing in free will (and related concepts) in order to shed some empirical light on the illusionism debate. In doing so, we first briefly discuss two of the most recently developed psychometric tools for measuring people's agentic beliefs—namely, the Free Will and Determinism Scale (FAD-Plus) (Paulhus and Carey 2011) and the Free Will Inventory (FWI) (Nadelhoffer et al. in prep.)—and we explore some of the interesting (and sometimes surprising) correlations that have been found between people's free will beliefs and their other moral, religious, and political beliefs (§§1-2). Then, we present and discuss the results of two exploratory studies we recently ran to further explore the moral and political psychology of believing in free will (§3). Finally, we say a few words in closing and lay the groundwork for future research (§4). As we'll see, there is a lot of psychological spadework and philosophical analysis that remains to be done.

1. MEASURING BELIEFS ABOUT FREE WILL, DETERMINISM, AND DUALISM: FITS AND STARTS

Given how much seems to be at stake when it comes to whether humans have free will, it is surprising how little empirical research has traditionally been done that specifically explores people's beliefs about free will, determinism, and responsibility. For while there was some pioneering work done in the 1980s on the psychology of believing in free will (e.g., Viney, Parker-Martin and Dotten 1988; Viney, McIntyre and Viney 1984; Viney, Waldman and Barchilon 1982; Stroessner and Green 1989), it wasn't until fairly recently that a critical mass of researchers started to take a renewed interest in what role (if any) believing in free will plays in our daily lives. As a result, during the past few years, free will beliefs have finally started receiving the attention they deserve among psychologists and experimental philosophers. And even though the results have admittedly been mixed thus far—e.g., there is (seemingly) conflicting evidence for (both) folk compatibilism (e.g., Nahmias, Morris, Nadelhoffer and Turner 2005, 2006; Nahmias and Murray 2010) and folk incompatibilism (e.g., Nichols and Knobe 2007)—it has become increasingly clear that making progress in understanding how people think about free will requires us to have valid and reliable techniques and tools for measuring people's beliefs and attitudes about free will and related concepts.

Fortunately, several psychometric instruments have been developed for precisely these purposes (Viney et al. 1984; Stroessner and Green 1989; Paulhus 1991; Rakos, Laurene, Skala and Slane 2008). And while each of these tools has its own unique features, uses, and advantages, for present purposes we are going to focus on two of the most recently developed tools. The first instrument is The Free Will and Determinism Scale (FAD-Plus) developed by Del Paulhus and Jasmine Carey (2011).[2] FAD-Plus is a 27-item scale that consists of four primary subscales: (a) Free Will—which measures intuitions about responsibility, free will, and "ultimate" control, (e.g., "People have complete free will"); (b) Scientific Determinism—which measures intuitions about the biological and environmental causes of human behavior (e.g., "As with other animals, human behavior always follows the laws of nature"); (c) Fatalistic Determinism—which measures intuitions about the inevitability of the future (e.g., "Whether people like it or not, mysterious forces seem to move their lives"); and (d) Unpredictability—which measures intuitions about the potential impossibility of predicting human behavior (e.g., "Chance events seem to be the major cause of human history"). FAD-Plus has recently been the most widely used tool for measuring beliefs about free will and related concepts (e.g., Baumeister, Sparks, Stillman and Vohs 2008; Baumeister et al. 2009; Baumeister, Crescioni and Alquist 2011; Stillman, Baumeister and Mele 2011; Vohs and Schooler 2008). And while one might object to the way a number of the items from FAD-Plus are worded—e.g., "Whatever will be, will be—there's not much you can do about it" seems a bit too tautological for our tastes to be a good indicator of specifically fatalistic beliefs—Paulhus and Carey found some noteworthy results during the course of developing their scale.

One of the more surprising findings from the work on FAD-Plus for many readers will be that people's intuitions about free will and determinism appear to be driven by two largely independent psychological constructs. According to the traditional way the free will debate has often been framed, especially by incompatibilists, the more determined we are, the less free we are (and vice versa). As such, one might expect free will and determinism to anchor the two opposite ends of a single, bi-polar scale ranging from free to determined (and hence, unfree). However, this expectation is not borne out by the work by Paulhus and Carey. Instead, they found that the scores for both the free will items and the determinism items reliably load onto largely independent factors—which explains why there are *distinct subscales* for free will, on the one hand, and scientific and fatalistic determinism, on the other hand.

Paulhus and Carey perhaps unsurprisingly suggest that their work on FAD-Plus "supports the conclusion that lay judges see freewill and determinism as quite compatible" (2011, 102). Whether Paulhus and Carey are right that their work on FAD-Plus provides conclusive evidence that compatibilism is the default view among the folk is an open question. We have our doubts for reasons we'll discuss below. For now, let it suffice to say that figuring out the contours of people's beliefs about free will, responsibility, and related concepts is a messy affair and conflicting data lurk around every corner. As we'll soon see, for every piece of evidence that seems to support compatibilism as the folk view, there is competing evidence that suggests that people find incompatibilism every bit as intuitive.[3]

But for present purposes, we are going to turn our attention to another one of the noteworthy findings from the work on FAD-Plus—namely, that free will beliefs correlate in interesting ways with other moral, political, and religious beliefs, attitudes, and practices (Carey and Paulhus, in press). During the course of validating FAD-Plus, Paulhus and Carey administered their scale along with measures of religiosity, political conservativism, just world beliefs, and right wing authoritarianism.[4] Based on the recent work in moral and political psychology as well as the traditional philosophical discussions about the nature and limits of free will, Paulhus and Carey predicted that believing in free will would correlate with religiosity, punitiveness, and politically conservative beliefs and attitudes such as just world beliefs and right wing authoritarianism (Carey and Paulhus, in press). These predictions were largely borne out by their data. But before we discuss the salient findings, we want to pause to highlight just how worrisome some of the predicted associations between free will beliefs and political ideology happen to be. Consider, for instance, a few sample items from two of the scales that Paulhus and Carey used to validate FAD-Plus:

The Just World Belief Scale (JWB: Lerner 1980):

- "By and large, people deserve what they get."
- "Although evil men may hold political power for a while, in the general course of history good wins out."
- "People who meet with misfortune have often brought it on themselves."

The Right Wing Authoritarianism Scale (RWA: Altemeyer 1996)

- "The established authorities generally turn out to be right about things, while the radicals and protestors are usually just 'loud mouths' showing off their ignorance."
- "Our country desperately needs a mighty leader who will do what has to be done to destroy the radical new ways and sinfulness that are ruining us."
- "It is always better to trust the judgment of the proper authorities in government and religion than to listen to the noisy rabble-rousers in our society who are trying to create doubt in people's minds."

We suspect that most readers will find that these items express some troublesome (and perhaps even potentially dangerous) ideas. Yet, based on the work by Paulhus and Carey, it appears that these sorts of beliefs and attitudes may go hand in hand with believing in free will. For instance, in one study (N = 222), scores on the FAD-Plus free will subscale were positively correlated with religiosity ($r = .34$, $p < .001$) and just world beliefs ($r = .28$, $p < .005$). And while the raw scores on the free will subscale correlated with both political conservativism ($r = .22$, $p < .001$) and right wing authoritarianism ($r = .30$, $p < .001$), controlling for religiosity eliminated the latter two associations (although doing so didn't eliminate the aforementioned association between free will and just world beliefs).

So, while the results concerning the relationship between free will beliefs, religiosity, and political psychology were a bit messier than they had hoped, Paulhus and Carey nevertheless found roughly what they expected. Their prediction concerning the relationship between beliefs about free will and punishment held up as well—e.g., in one follow-up study (N = 118), Paulhus and Carey found that believing more strongly in free will was correlated with punitiveness (r = .33, p < .001) (Carey and Paulhus, in press; cf. Viney et al. 1982, 1984; Stroessner and Green 1990). This, too, is unsurprising. It makes a priori sense that people who believe more strongly in free will would be more interested in giving wrongdoers their just deserts.

However, Paulhus and Carey also found some less intuitive results that are more difficult to interpret. On the one hand, they found that scores on the FAD-Plus scientific determinism subscale were positively correlated with just world beliefs (r = .16, p < .05). On the other hand, they found that scores on the FAD-Plus fatalistic determinism subscale were correlated with right wing authoritarianism (r = .27, p < .001). Both of these findings are admittedly a bit puzzling. We will try to shed some additional light on these otherwise curious results downstream in §3 when we discuss the results of our most recent two studies.

For the time being, we would like to turn our attention to the second scale for measuring free will beliefs that we are going to examine in this section—namely, The Free Will Inventory (FWI) that was recently developed by one of the present authors and his collaborators (Nadelhoffer et al. in prep.). FWI is a 29-item tool for measuring (a) the *strength* of people's beliefs about free will, determinism, and dualism (Part 1), and (b) the *relationships* between these beliefs and related beliefs such as punishment and responsibility (Part 2).[5] Each item of FWI is scored on a 7 point Likert scale ranging from 1 (strongly disagree) to 7 (strongly agree). Part 1 of FWI consists of three subscales: (a) Free Will—which measures intuitions about free will and the power to do otherwise (e.g., "People always have the ability to do otherwise"); (b) Determinism—which measures people's intuitions when it comes to whether the universe is purely deterministic (e.g., "Every event that has ever occurred, including human decisions and actions, was completely determined by prior events"); and (c) Dualism/Non-Reductionism—which measures intuitions about both the existence of an immaterial soul and the irreducibility of the mind and the body (e.g., "The fact that we have souls that are distinct from our material bodies is what makes humans unique").

Part 2 of FWI, on the other hand, isn't technically a scale, properly speaking. Instead, it is a series of fourteen statements designed to probe people's more fine-grained intuitions concerning the nature and limitations of free will and how free will relates to responsibility, determinism, dualism, punishment, and scientific explanation. So, whereas some items from Part 2 probe people's more nuanced understanding of the nature and limits of free will—e.g., "Free will is the ability to make different choices even if everything leading up to one's choice (e.g., the past, the situation, and their desires, beliefs, etc.) were exactly the same"—other items probe instead people's intuitions about the relationship between free will, the soul, prediction, punishment, and moral responsibility more generally—e.g., "To have free will means that a person's decisions and actions could not be perfectly predicted by someone else no matter how much information they had." While one might once again quibble with the wording of some of the items from FWI, Nadelhoffer and collaborators also found some interesting results during the course of developing and validating their instrument.

For starters, the work on FWI supports the earlier research by Paulhus and Carey on FAD-Plus when it comes to the independence of the psychological constructs that appear to drive people's intuitions about free will and determinism. As before, scores for the free will items and the determinism items loaded onto distinct factors (as evidenced once again by the fact that FWI has distinct subscales for free will and determinism rather than one bipolar scale). More surprising still, these distinct factors aren't even negatively correlated as one might minimally expect. This provides some additional prima facie evidence for folk compatibilism. After all, the work on both FAD-Plus and FWI suggest that people's intuitions about free will and determinism are driven by largely independent cognitive mechanisms—which is a surprising finding that we believe has not received sufficient attention in the extant literature.

Another related finding by Nadelhoffer and collaborators is that people's intuitions about free will and dualism are similarly independent. Given the theological and metaphysical connections that have historically been drawn between free will and the soul, this, too, will likely be puzzling to some readers. And while weak yet significant correlations were sometimes found between the scores on the dualism and free will subscales during the development of FWI, scores on the two subscales reliably loaded cleanly onto distinct psychological factors—which adds yet another wrinkle to the debate between the scientific skeptics and the illusionists. After all, if people's beliefs about free will aren't necessarily dependent upon (or even directly related to) their beliefs about the soul and the relationship between the mind and the brain, then it's unclear that advances in neuroscience will directly challenge (or undermine) people's views about agency and responsibility as the skeptics have assumed. Minimally, the work by Nadelhoffer and collaborators suggests that the scientific skeptics are wrong to assume that most people treat having free will as simply co-extensive with having a soul (see, e.g., Montague 2008).

However, this same research also suggests that the skeptics are *right* that people ordinarily think that having free will requires contra-causal agency (i.e., the unconditional ability to do otherwise). For instance, in one of the final validation rounds (N = 330), participants were presented with FWI and asked to state their level of agreement with each of the twenty-nine items. Here are the responses to two items that are especially germane to our present discussion:[6]

- Libertarian 1 (L1): "Free will is the ability to make different choices even if everything leading up to one's choice (e.g., the past, the situation, and their desires, beliefs, etc.) was exactly the same": 6 percent disagree; 15 percent neither agree nor disagree; 79 percent agree (mean = 5.44; standard deviation = 1.30).
- Libertarian 2 (L2): "To have free will is to be able to cause things to happen in the world without at the same time being caused to make those things happen.": 17 percent disagree; 36 percent neither agree nor disagree; 46 percent agree (mean = 4.53; standard deviation = 1.45).

These kinds of results reveal that many people explicitly endorse precisely the kinds of libertarian views about free will that are often attributed to the folk by the scientific skeptics and illusionists.[7] So, as we saw earlier, while there is clearly a compatibilist element to how people ordinarily think about free will, it is becomingly increasingly clear that there is also an *incompatibilist* element to people's free will beliefs that is every bit as deeply ingrained. Indeed, it is hard to see how to square the findings concerning the widespread endorsement of explicit statements of libertarian free will with the fact that both FAD-Plus and FWI have distinct subscales for free will and determinism—which is why we have chosen to remain agnostic when it comes to the debate about folk incompatibilism for present purposes.

At this point, there are simply too many unanswered questions and too much conflicting evidence. So, trying to provide a unified model of the extant data on folk intuitions about free will and related concepts is beyond the scope of the present chapter. Our suspicion is that the debate about folk incompatibilism is ultimately based on a false dichotomy—namely, that people must either be compatibilists or incompatibilists.[8] It is becomingly increasingly clear that in some sense people are *both*, depending on the circumstances, depending on their unique psychological temperaments and needs, depending on their cultural practices, etc. Given how intractable the traditional free will debate has been, perhaps the complicated empirical data on folk intuitions about free will and responsibility shouldn't come as a surprise. Minimally, we believe that it is clear at this stage that if we are to make any progress when it comes to the illusionism debate, we first need to ensure that we have a balanced understanding of the possible upsides and downsides to believing in free will (and related concepts). But before we discuss our own attempts to fill in a few of the missing empirical details (see §3), we would first like to take a closer look at some of the work from political psychology that motivated our research.

2. MORAL PSYCHOLOGY MEETS POLITICAL PSYCHOLOGY

In the last section, we surveyed some preliminary data from moral psychology that suggested that people's beliefs about free will may hook up in potentially problematic ways to their other moral, political, and religious beliefs. After all, if believing in free will goes hand in hand with inflated just world beliefs or right wing authoritarianism, this is something we ought to carefully consider before taking sides in the illusionism debate. However, while we paused very briefly earlier to consider why some of the recent findings on free will beliefs are potentially worrisome, we didn't spend much time exploring the actual research from political psychology. So, we thought it would be helpful to briefly say a bit more about some of the salient work on this front.

During the past few decades, the gathering empirical data has made it increasingly clear that "different psychological motives and tendencies underlie ideological differences between the political left and the right" (Jost, Glaser, Kruglanski and Sulloway 2003b, 339). As a result, a number of political psychologists have explored the underlying cognitive and ideological differences that distinguish liberals from conservatives. One of the goals of the research in motivated-social cognition is to provide a unified yet multifaceted account of moral and political ideologies that embraces social, cognitive, and motivational factors. In order to empirically investigate people's political psychology, researchers have developed a series of scales intended to measure the different facets of the political mind.

The first scale that we would like to discuss is the aforementioned Right Wing Authoritarianism Scale (RWA: Altemeyer 1996). The notion of right wing authoritarianism was originally developed by Theodor Adorno and the intellectual successors of the Frankfurt School, and subsequently improved by Altemeyer (1981). Right wing authoritarianism is typically defined in the literature in terms of submission to established and legitimate authorities, sanctioned general aggressiveness towards various persons, and adherence to the generally endorsed social conventions. It is also closely related to a larger set of ego-justifying tendencies that provide support for social ideologies such as intolerance of ambiguity, dogmatism, terror management, uncertainty avoidance, and need for cognitive closure. The idea is that these broader cognitive-motivational factors constitute the general framework under which authoritarian personalities tend to function. Consequently, the goal of the RWA Scale is to measure the degree of obedience to authorities and adherence to the existing social conventions. Scores on the RWA scale have been found to reliably correlate with an array of worrisome beliefs and attitudes such as punitiveness, racial prejudice, homophobia, religious orthodoxy, and victim blaming. Moreover, scores have also been found to correlate with a wide range of conservative attitudes such as abortion rights, diversity on university campuses, and opposition to environmentalism (Jost, Blount, Pfeffer and Hunyady 2003).

The second scale we would like to discuss is the Just World Belief Scale (JWB: Lerner 1980). The origin of the *just world conception* can be traced back to the original empirical findings of Lerner and Simmons (1966); namely, that persons have a tendency to blame the victims of misfortunes for their own fate. Based on these empirical findings, Lerner (1965) formulated the Just World Hypothesis, whereby individuals have a need to believe that they live in a world where people generally get what they deserve. In order to measure the degree to which persons are willing to believe that everyone deserves what happens to them, Lerner (1980) developed the JWB scale. Scores on this scale have been found to correlate with the presence of frail religious beliefs (Sorrentino and Hardy 1974), an internal (as opposed to an external) locus of control, and with the likelihood of derogating innocent victims (Rubin and Peplau 1975). In addition, people who score high on JWB are more likely to trust current institutions and authorities, and to blame the poor and praise the rich for their respective fates (Jost et al. 2003).

A third and related scale is the Economic System Justification Scale (ESJ: Jost and Thompson 2000). Advocates of system justification theory claim that the justification of the status quo is generated by (sub-conscious) processes that work at the expense of personal and group interests; but in the best interest of the maintenance of the existing social system. One example of these processes is the adherence to unfavorable stereotypes undertaken by disadvantaged groups. For instance, evidence shows that African American respondents generally accept self-derogating stereotypes as lazy, irresponsible, and violent (Sniderman and Piazza 1993). Closely related to the system justification theoretical approach, the ESJ scale measures the tendency to perceive socioeconomic and political arrangements as inherently fair and legitimate—even at the expense of individual or group interests. The scores on ESJ correlate with JWB, RWA, opposition to equality, and self-deception.

The final scale that we would like to discuss is the Social Dominance Orientation Scale (SDO: Pratto, Sidanius, Stallworth and Malle 1994). Social Dominance Theory, unlike economic system justification, is a group justifying approach that views the minimization of group conflict as the crucial factor in the evolution of human societies. This theory suggests that this minimization is facilitated by the social embracement of ideological belief systems that justify the hegemony of some groups over others. The SDO scale measures the degree of adherence to conservative legitimizing myths that attempt to rationalize the interests of dominant group members. The scores on the scale have been shown to correlate with beliefs and attitudes such as nationalism, racism, sexism, RWA, JWB, and militarism (Jost et al. 2003b).

In short, the important research from political psychology on right wing authoritarianism, just world beliefs, economic system justification, and social dominance orientation has collectively revealed a disturbing constellation of related beliefs, attitudes, and behaviors that is not only associated with both religiosity and political conservatism but which is also associated with sexism, racism, homophobia, nationalism, militarism, and the like. Fortunately, the aforementioned work by Paulhus and Carey on FAD-Plus helped bridge the gap between the work on motivated-social cognition from political psychology and the work in moral psychology on free will beliefs. Our overarching goal when we ran the studies we are going to discuss in the following pages was to both replicate and build upon this earlier research. After all, if believing in free will makes it more likely people rely on stereotypes to justify inequality, perceive social inequality as legitimate and fair, or blame victims of violence and injustice, as the earlier work on FAD-Plus suggests, then this challenges the claim that believing in free will is a *purely* positive illusion. But before we can pass judgment on the overall utility (or disutility) of believing in free will, we need more data on the relationship between people's beliefs about free will, responsibility, determinism, dualism, and their other moral and political beliefs and attitudes. Filling in some of the missing empirical details was the goal of the following two studies.

3. THE POTENTIAL DARK SIDE OF FREE WILL: TWO NEW STUDIES

Study 1:

Recruitment

Participants were 152 undergraduate students at the College of Charleston who participated for research credit in introductory psychology classes: 82 percent were female and the mean age was 18.77 (standard deviation = 1.85).

Procedure

The data were collected as part of an online survey on Qualtrics.com. Participants logged on to the website and completed roughly thirty minutes of questionnaires at their leisure. The participant pool was organized to maximize confidentiality, so participants' responses could not be linked to their names or their student I.D. numbers.

Measures

Participants received the following psychometric inventories (see §§1-2 for details):

- The Free Will Inventory
- The Right Wing Authoritarianism Scale[9]
- The Just World Belief Scale
- The Social Dominance Orientation Scale
- The Economic System Justification Scale

We also collected data concerning participants' religious and political beliefs.

Predictions

Based on the aforementioned work on both FAD-Plus and FWI (see §1) and the research from political psychology (see §2), we made a number of predictions:

1. Free Will and Dualism: We predicted that scores on the FWI free will subscale and the dualism subscale would both correlate with right wing authoritarianism, just world beliefs, social dominance orientation, economic system justification, retributivism, religiosity, and political conservativism.
2. Libertarianism: We predicted that scores on the two explicit statements of libertarianism from FWI Part 2—namely, L1 and L2 (see §1)—would be even more predictive than scores on the free will subscale when it comes to right wing authoritarianism, just world beliefs, social dominance orientation, economic system justification, retributivism, religiosity, and political conservativism.
3. Retributivism: We predicted that scores from the explicit statement of retributivism from Part 2 of FWI[10] would correlate with scores on the free will subscale, libertarianism, right wing authoritarianism, just world beliefs, social dominance orientation, economic system justification, religiosity, and political conservativism.
4. Determinism: We predicted that believing in determinism would correlate with right wing authoritarianism, religiosity, and political conservativism. We also predicted that determinism would negatively correlate with libertarianism but that it would be uncorrelated with scores on the free will subscale more generally.
5. Political Ideology: We predicted correlations between right wing authoritarianism, just world beliefs, social dominance orientation, and economic system justification.

While we were fairly confident in some of our predictions—e.g., between free will and just world beliefs and right wing authoritarianism—we were much less confident about others. For instance, because no data had previously been collected when it comes to the relationship (if any) between people's beliefs about free will, determinism, dualism, and retributivism, on the one hand, and constructs such as economic system justification and social dominance orientation, on the other hand, we made these latter predictions based partly on our a priori assumptions and partly on the previous work done in moral and political psychology.

Results

As predicted, free will beliefs correlated with right wing authoritarianism ($r = .22$, $p < .01$) and just world beliefs ($r = .29$, $p < .001$). However, contrary to our predictions (as well as previous findings), scores on the free will subscale did not correlate with religiosity, political conservativism, retributivism, social dominance orientation, or economic system justification. The latter finding was especially surprising given the close associations between economic system justification and just world beliefs. Unfortunately, our predictions concerning libertarianism fared only marginally better. On the one hand, as expected, the combined scores on L1 and L2 correlated with dualism ($r = .23$, $p < .01$) and trended towards a negative correlation with determinism ($r = -.15$, $p < .06$). On the other hand, we didn't find the other correlations involving libertarianism that we anticipated.

As for our predictions concerning dualism, while scores on the dualism subscale correlated as expected with right wing authoritarianism ($r = .18$, $p < .05$) and religiosity ($r = .40$, $p < .001$), we did not find correlations between dualism and political conservativism or just world beliefs. Similarly, while scores on the determinism subscale correlated with right wing authoritarianism as predicted ($r = .21$, $p < .01$), we didn't find the expected associations with political conservativism and religiosity. Finally, our predictions concerning retributivism yielded mixed results as well. For even though retributivism correlated as expected with just world beliefs ($r = .28$, $p < .001$), right wing authoritarianism ($r = .31$, $p < .001$), and economic system justification ($r = .23$, $p < .01$), it did not correlate with free will beliefs, dualism, libertarianism, political conservativism, or religiosity.

Unsurprisingly, we also found a number of correlations between religiosity, conservativism, and political ideology. For instance, right wing authoritarianism was strongly correlated with political conservativism ($r = .50$, $p < .001$), religiosity ($r = .40$, $p < .001$), social dominance orientation ($r = .33$, $p < .001$), just world belief ($r = .24$, $p < .01$), and economic system justification ($r = .29$, $p < .001$). Similar correlations were found between the other political ideology scales as well.

Discussion

As we said earlier, our goal in this first preliminary study was to try to replicate and build upon the earlier work on believing in free will (and related concepts). At least in this limited sense, the study was a success. For while a number of our predictions missed their mark, we nevertheless (a) replicated some of the earlier work that had been done on free will beliefs, and (b) shed some new light on the relationship between free will beliefs and other moral, political, and religious beliefs. However, one of the main weaknesses and limitations of our first study was that our sample was not very representative. Because the participants in Study 1 were undergraduates who were both young and overwhelmingly female, we wanted to rerun the study using a more representative and gender-balanced participant pool. So, we would now like to discuss the results of this follow-up study.

Study 2:

Participants

Respondents were 118 general population participants who were both recruited through (and compensated by) the Qualtrics.com fee-based panelist service: 53 percent were female and the mean age was 49.92 (standard deviation = 13.42).

Procedure

The data were collected as part of an online survey on Qualtrics.com. Participants logged on to the website and completed roughly 30 minutes of questionnaires at their leisure. The participant pool was organized to maximize confidentiality, so the participants' responses could not be linked to their names.

Measures

Participants once again received the following psychometric inventories:

1. The Free Will Inventory
2. The Right Wing Authoritarianism Scale
3. The Just World Belief Scale
4. The Social Dominance Orientation Scale
5. The Economic System Justification Scale

We also collected data concerning participants' religious and political beliefs.

Predictions

Because Study 2 relied on the same experimental design as Study 1, we decided to once again make the same predictions that we made earlier under the assumption that using general population participants this time around—who tend to be older, more conservative, and more religious than their undergraduate counterparts—would yield the results we expected (but did not find) in Study 1. Our main hope was that we would not only find the same correlations that we found the first time around—e.g., correlations between free will beliefs and right wing authoritarianism—but that we would also find the predicted correlations this time that we failed to find earlier—e.g., correlations between free will beliefs and political conservatism. If so, that would tell us something interesting about the role that age, conservatism, and religiosity play when it comes to the relationship between free will beliefs and other moral, political, and religious beliefs. If not, then this would at least strengthen our confidence in whatever similarities we find in common between the data sets from the two studies while at the same time highlighting the issues that still need to be addressed in future research. Either way, the results have the potential to advance our understanding of the moral and political psychology of believing in free will.

Results

As predicted, believing in free will was once again associated with right wing authoritarianism ($r = .19$, $p < .05$), just world belief ($r = .23$, $p < .01$), and dualism ($r = .20$, $p < .05$). However, just as before, free will beliefs were uncorrelated with social dominance orientation or economic system justification. We once again got similarly mixed results when it came to libertarianism as well—which correlated with economic system justification ($r = .40$, $p < .001$), right wing authoritarianism ($r = .22$, $p < .01$), dualism ($r = .35$, $p < .001$), and retributivism ($r = .19$, $p < .05$), but which did not correlate with religiosity or political conservatism as predicted.

While our predictions concerning free will beliefs didn't fare as well as we'd hoped in either Study 1 or Study 2, the findings concerning dualism in Study 2 were much more in line with our initial expectations—e.g., dualism correlated with economic system justification ($r = .23$, $p < .01$), right wing authoritarianism ($r = .48$, $p < .001$), political conservatism ($r = .22$, $p < .01$), and religiosity ($r = .35$, $p < .001$). Unfortunately, our predictions concerning determinism yielded mixed results this time around as well—e.g., determinism correlated with both social dominance orientation ($r = .24$, $p < 01$) and right wing authoritarianism ($r = .38$, $p < .001$), but it did not negatively correlate with libertarianism as predicted. Finally, just as before, correlations were found once again between the different political ideology scales—e.g., right wing authoritarianism correlated with just world beliefs (r

= .20, p < .05), social dominance orientation (r = .28, p < .01), and economic system justification (r = .36, p < .05).

Discussion

The goal of Study 2 was to see whether our earlier predictions from Study 1 fared better with general population participants than they did with undergraduates. Lamentably, however, the results were once again mixed. For while we found many of the correlations we were expecting in Study 2 (thereby both replicating and extending the results from Study 1), a number of our predictions missed the mark. Given the complexity of people's beliefs about free will and related concepts, this should perhaps be unsurprising. After all, the results of these two studies suggest that our beliefs about free will, determinism, and dualism hook up to a cluster of related moral, political, and religious beliefs in a number of multi-faceted (and sometimes surprising) ways. Some of the correlations we found in both Study 1 and Study 2 make a priori sense whereas other findings are harder to interpret and understand.

For instance, between the earlier work on FAD-Plus and FWI and the recent findings we've presented in this chapter, it's clear that there is a correlation between believing in free will, just world beliefs, right wing authoritarianism, and intuitions about punishment. But there are still a number of unanswered questions. For instance, it's unclear why determinism also correlates with some of these constructs from political psychology. It's also strange that social dominance orientation and economic system justification were uncorrelated with free will beliefs despite the fact that both the latter and the former correlate with right wing authoritarianism and just world beliefs. One possible explanation is that each of the scales from political psychology that we've discussed measure related but nevertheless dissociable constructs. For instance, while RWA is supposed to probe the *personality trait* of authoritarianism, SDO and ESJ were both designed to probe people's tendency to engage in *ideological rationalization*. So, this may partly explain why even though these scales correlate with one another, they don't all correlate with beliefs about free will, determinism, dualism, and the like. The next logical step is to design studies that do a better job at getting at the more fine-grained data we need before we can take sides in the illusionism debate. For now, we merely wanted to try to shed some preliminary light on these and related issues in the hopes that doing so would motivate others to pursue similar research down the road.

In light of both our exploratory findings and the previous work on FAD-Plus and FWI, it's clear that it isn't going to be easy to disentangle the complex web of beliefs and attitudes that shape our intuitions about agency and responsibility. But hopefully the work that has been done thus far can help us figure out how best to proceed in our efforts to better understand the moral and political psychology of believing in free will. One clear shortcoming of all of the extant work on this front is that the findings have been mostly correlational. So, even though this kind of exploratory research represents an important first step in the process of discovery, we ultimately want to understand the *causal* relationships between believing in free will and related moral, political, and religious beliefs, attitudes, and behaviors. For while it's helpful to know that free will beliefs correlate with retributivism or right wing authoritarianism, what we really want to know is whether believing in free will drives our retributive or authoritarian beliefs (or vice versa). This is something we are already exploring (see Nadelhoffer and Baril, in prep.). For now, we'll have to settle for the admittedly incomplete picture concerning free will beliefs that we've been trying to piece together in this chapter. Hopefully, our findings (however preliminary and messy they may be) will nevertheless help point researchers in the right direction moving forward.

4. CONCLUDING REMARKS

Our primary goal in this paper was to discuss some recent work from moral and political psychology on believing in free will in the hopes that it would shed some light on the illusionism debate. Along the way, we surveyed the extant empirical literature on free will beliefs and we presented the results of our most recent attempts to better understand how believing in free will ties into our other beliefs, attitudes, and practices. Unfortunately, our findings raised more questions than they answered. But that's nothing new when it comes to free will—which has always been one of the thorniest problems in philosophy. Minimally, we think that the results of our two latest studies make it clear that researchers still have a lot of empirical spadework to do before we'll be in a position to better understand the potential psychological and social consequences of widespread skepticism about free will. As things presently stand, we simply don't have enough data to know what the impact would be if people came to believe that they don't have free will. For while widespread free will skepticism would likely have some negative consequences, it could also lead to some positive consequences as well. We just hope that what we've said in this chapter encourages more psychologists and philosophers to roll up their sleeves and work together towards developing a better understanding of the complicated role that believing in free will plays in the economy of our daily lives. For unless and until we have a better grasp on whether (and to what extent) there is a dark side to believing in free will, we won't know whether to counsel revolution or illusion.

NOTES

1. We would like to thank Galen Baril for his invaluable assistance along the way.
2. It is called FAD-Plus because there were several earlier, unpublished versions of FAD.
3. For some recent discussions of the debate about folk incompatibilism, see Nadelhoffer forthcoming; Nahmias forthcoming; Sommers 2010.
4. We will say more about the recent work in political psychology on right wing authoritarianism, just world beliefs, and related constructs in §2.
5. The two parts of FWI can be given either together or separately (depending on the researcher's specific interests).
6. For ease of presentation, we are going to lump together the responses by those who strongly disagree, disagree, and somewhat disagree under the heading "disagree" and we are going to lump together the responses by those who strongly agree, agree, and somewhat agree under the general heading "agree." For full details, see Nadelhoffer et al. (in prep).
7. Nadelhoffer and colleagues also found that L1 and L2 correlated in predictable ways with other beliefs and attitudes. On the one hand, responses to L1 were correlated with scores on the free will subscale ($r = .25$, $p < .001$), the dualism subscale ($r = .19$, $p < .001$), political conservativism ($r = .13$, $p < .01$), and retributivism ($r = .13$, $p < .01$). On the other hand, responses to L2 were correlated with scores on the free will subscale ($r = .17$, $p < .001$) and retributivism ($r = .12$, $p < .05$). More importantly, responses to L1, unlike scores on the free will subscale, were negatively correlated with scores on the determinism subscale ($r = -.15$, $p < .01$)—which suggests that L1 may be the best available empirical tool we have for discriminating libertarians from compatibilists.
8. For some early suggestions along similar lines, see Nichols and Knobe (2007); Sinnott-Armstrong (2008).
9. We created a short version of RWA based on previous analyses which revealed that the positively worded items and the negatively worded items of RWA may pick out distinct factors. So, for both Study 1 and Study 2 we used only the positively worded items from RWA since these are the items which clearly get at authoritarian attitudes and not just social conservative attitudes more generally. See Nadelhoffer and Baril (in prep.) for a full discussion of this and related issues with RWA.
10. Retributivism item from FWI (Part 2): "People who harm others deserve to be punished even if punishing them won't produce any positive benefits to either the offender or society—e.g., rehabilitation, deterring other would-be offenders, etc."

Chapter Eight

The People Problem

Benjamin Vilhauer

Philosophers who are skeptical about free will have to contend with an issue that I will call "the people problem." Do we have to treat human beings as if they have free will to treat them as *persons*, in the sense that matters for morality and the meaning of life? A lot is at stake in this question. If the answer is "yes," then a world in which human beings no longer treated each other as having free will would be impoverished in some important ways, and it would be natural for this to motivate some to argue against the view that we lack free will. If the answer is "no," on the other hand, then we have one less reason to resist this view. This question has received a fair bit of discussion in the literature, but a lot more effort has been invested in arguing for "yes" than for "no." My goal here is to contribute to the "no" side (with a caveat that I will mention shortly). I will argue that a primary concern of philosophers in the recent literature who argue for "yes" is the worry that if we stop treating people as if they have free will, then we are driven to consequentialism, and we end up instrumentalizing human beings and treating them as mere means to social ends. I will argue that this concern is misplaced, since there is a broadly Kantian ethics available to free will deniers which holds that we must always treat people as ends, and never merely as means.

Let me explain a few terms before proceeding. "Free will" refers to whatever satisfies the control condition of moral responsibility. I will sometimes use "treating as free" as shorthand for "treating as having free will." "Moral responsibility" refers to the relationship to our actions which is necessary for us to be appropriately praised or blamed for our actions. "Free will believers" claim that we have free will. "Free will deniers" claim that we lack free will. "Free will skeptics" claim that we don't know whether we have free will or not. I will occasionally refer to both deniers and skeptics as "philosophers who take skeptical approaches to free will theory."

I will not try to establish that a particular sense of "treating as persons" is *the* one that matters for morality and the meaning of life. There are different senses that matter for different aspects of morality and life-meaning, and I do not want to deny that there is indeed a sense of "treating as persons" that does imply "treating as free," which really does matter for some aspects. My own position is free will skepticism rather than denial. I agree with Kant that it is possible that we have free will, but we do not know that we do. I also agree with Kant that the mere possibility of free will can be enough to justify us in treating each other as free.[1] But while Kant thinks the mere possibility of free will justifies us in treating each other as free across the board, I think it justifies us in treating each other as free only in some contexts, for example, when we seek to justify some kinds of praise.[2] The mere possibility of free will is not sufficient to justify retributive punishment, at least not when significant harm such as imprisonment is at issue.[3]

However, despite my own preference for skepticism over denial, I think that the free-will-implying sense of "persons" is necessary for much less of morality and life-meaning than many philosophers seem to believe, and that we can do quite well without much of the stuff for which it is necessary. I do not wish to claim that we lose nothing worth having. But I think we lose less than many think. My main effort in this paper will be to focus on a particular sense of "treating as persons" which does not imply free will in any way, and which is therefore readily available to free will deniers—a sense which has been mentioned in the literature but does not seem to have received detailed discussion. I have in mind the Kantian notion that to treat human beings as persons is to treat them as ends in themselves, rather than as mere means to ends.[4]

I will not presuppose any background in Kant's philosophy. However, philosophers with even a passing acquaintance with Kant will probably know that Kant's own account of personhood and treating others as ends is not compatible in all respects with a philosophy that denies free will.[5] For example, Kant is a retributivist who holds that criminals can only be treated as ends when we punish them if we hold them morally responsible for their actions. He is also a strident advocate of the death penalty. I will discuss these points later, and argue that Kant would be better off without his retributivism. However, in light of Kant's actual position, it may seem confused to look to Kant's philosophy for a notion of "treating as persons" that does not imply "treating as free." But Kant's work is noteworthy for how much effort he expends in providing multiple explanations of his basic ideas, and how little effort he devotes to showing how those different explanations fit together. Commentators still argue about whether Kant's different explanations of treating others as ends cohere. To my mind, Kant's most helpful explanation of treating others as ends is in terms of treating them as they would rationally consent to be treated. Even if Kant thought that treating others as they would rationally consent to be treated implies treating them as having free will, I think it can be demonstrated that it does not. This thread in Kant's thought is helpfully drawn out in Rawls' notion of original position deliberation. Properly understood, original position deliberation serves to "filter out," as morally irrelevant, desert claims that involve attributions of moral responsibility (what I call our "action-based" desert claims) and focus our attention instead on what we deserve just by virtue of being persons (what I call our "personhood-based" desert claims). Choosing the basic principles for society in the original position allows us to identify appropriate norms and practices for a society in which we can treat each other as persons in a robust Kantian sense without treating each other as having free will. But before we can see how this works, it will be helpful to briefly review a few points in the recent history of the people problem, which is cast in its distinctive form for the contemporary literature in P. F. Strawson's "Freedom and Resentment" (1997).[6]

1. SOME HIGHLIGHTS IN THE RECENT HISTORY OF THE PEOPLE PROBLEM

The idea that there is a special connection between treating human beings as persons and treating them as having free will has been a part of philosophical reflections on free will for a very long time. But P. F. Strawson's "Freedom and Resentment" prompted a renewed interest in this issue. Most readers will know his basic story, so I will treat it in summary fashion.

Strawson frames his thoughts in terms of a debate between "optimists" and "pessimists." Optimists think that the concept of moral responsibility still works just fine if determinism is true, because praise encourages people to continue doing more of what we want them to do, and blame encourages people to behave differently. Pessimists not only disagree, but find the optimists' vision of the world deeply disturbing. They see the optimist vision as depersonalizing, and they hold that we can only legitimately hold people morally responsible if we have libertarian free will. Strawson thinks both sides in this quarrel have a point. He thinks optimists are right to insist that we must find a way of going on with our practices of holding morally responsible which does not presuppose libertarianism, because libertarianism is merely a fantasy. But pessimists are right to see the optimist vision as depersonalizing. Optimists recommend that we regard each other with what Strawson calls the "objective attitude," rather than the "reactive attitudes" which are essential components of "ordinary inter-personal attitudes." The reactive attitudes are the attitudes involved in our holding each other morally responsible, including praise and blame, as well as any other attitudes that have praise or blame as essential elements. Strawson thinks we avoid the depersonalizing effects of the objective attitude by maintaining the reactive attitudes. But on his view, the pessimists are wrong to suppose that we need libertarian free will to justify the reactive attitudes. In some sense that is a bit mysterious, Strawson sees the reactive attitudes as self-justifying—the reactive attitudes themselves "fill the gap" in the optimists' vision. For purposes of studying the people problem, the key point here is the claim that we can avoid a depersonalizing objectivity of attitude if we maintain the reactive attitudes.

But why, exactly, would it depersonalize us if we relinquished the reactive attitudes and took up a permanent objectivity of attitude? Strawson's remarks here are not as clear as one might wish. At first pass, we can discern (at least) two sub-problems. One is about a profound sense of isolation Strawson thinks would ensue. The other is about consequentialism. Ultimately they may best be viewed as the same problem, the former being a consequence of the latter, but the literature seems not always to have connected them. The isolation issue has already received a fair bit of discussion in the literature, so I will discuss it briefly, and then move on to discuss the consequentialism problem which is my main concern.

Strawson claims that a world where the objective attitude was universal would be a tragic world of "human isolation" (Strawson, 129). He thinks this because he thinks that the reactive attitudes are essential elements of a very wide range of human emotions and relationships, including friendship and love (124). John Martin Fischer endorses this view, and claims that such a world would be "colorless and cold," and would be missing one of the "key normative ingredients in the notion of personhood" (Fischer 1995, 2–3).

But it is not clear that love and friendship are essentially reactive, i.e. that they are intrinsically bound up with holding people morally responsible. Consider love. Suppose Anisha successfully acts in ways designed to cultivate virtues such as fidelity and courage, and Bud loves Anisha because of these virtues. If Bud supposes that Anisha is morally responsible for these actions, then he can take his love to be a response to her that she can claim to deserve. But suppose that he instead believes that she has done nothing to cultivate her character. She has always been this way—it is simply her nature. Would this give him a reason to love her any less? As Derk Pereboom puts the point,

> Explaining love is a complex enterprise. Besides moral character and action, factors such as one's relation to the other . . . and her affinities with persons or events in one's history all might have a part. . . . But even if there is an important aspect of love that is essentially a deserved response to moral character and action, it is unlikely that one's love would be undermined if one were

to believe that these moral qualities do not come about through free and responsible choice. For moral character and action are loveable whether or not they merit praise. Love of another involves, most fundamentally, wishing well for the other, taking on many of the aims and desires of the other as one's own, and a desire to be together with the other. (2009, 20)

To take the next step in reflection, now suppose that Bud comes to see his love for Anisha as simply a consequence of his own nature, rather than something he has in any way willed or cultivated. It is not clear that any of this should make him see this love as shallower, or less valuable. As I discuss in more detail elsewhere, the same sort of argument can be made regarding many other attitudes that Strawsonians sometimes claim to be essentially reactive, such as friendship, and respect. (We can respect people for their fidelity and courage without liking or loving them for it, even if we do not suppose that it involves free will.) There are no doubt some attitudes that are essentially reactive, such as the attitudes involved in praise and blame, and some species of gratitude, anger, resentment, and vengefulness. A world devoid of these attitudes would be a different world, without question. But if the worry is that it would be so devoid of emotional engagement that the human beings populating it could no longer be counted as persons, then the recognition that it could still contain love, friendship, and respect should suffice to allay this worry.[7]

Now I want to turn to the problem about consequentialism. Consequentialists hold that the rightness of actions is determined entirely by the consequences they produce. Non-consequentialists deny this. They hold (among other things) that there are some actions we cannot take, no matter what the consequences may be. Utilitarianism is probably the most widely discussed form of consequentialism. Utilitarians hold that the morally correct end is maximum overall happiness, and that whatever means maximizes overall happiness is the means we should take.[8] Strawson associates optimism and the objective attitude with utilitarianism. He explains that the optimist finds "an adequate basis for certain social practices in calculated consequences," an approach which he calls "a one-eyed utilitarianism" (140). When the optimist "undertakes to show that the truth of determinism would not shake the foundations of the concept of moral responsibility and of the practices of moral condemnation and punishment, he typically refers, in a more or less elaborated way, to the efficacy of these practices in regulating behavior in socially desirable ways. These practices are represented solely as instruments of policy, as methods of individual treatment and social control" (137). The pessimist "is apt to say . . . that the humanity of the offender himself is offended by *this* picture of his condemnation and punishment" (137). Strawson acknowledges that we should have "some belief in the utility of practices of condemnation and punishment" (139). But he goes on to say that "the social utility of these practices, on which the optimist lays such exclusive stress, is not what is now in question. What is in question is the pessimist's justified sense that to speak in terms of social utility alone is to leave out something vital in our conception of these practices." He thinks that the "vital thing can be restored by attending to the complicated web of [reactive] attitudes and feelings which form an essential part of the moral life as we know it, and which are quite opposed to objectivity of attitude" (139). As Susan Wolf puts it, in commenting on Strawson,

> To justify praise and blame in the way the optimist suggests is to ... leave out of account any question of whether it is an individual's fault that he has done something wrong or whether it is to the individual's credit that he has done something right. In short, to justify the praise and blame of persons in the way the optimist suggests is ... to justify these practices only as a means of manipulation or training. The pessimist's fear may now be expressed as the fear that if determinism is true, this consequentialist justification of praise and blame is the only kind of justification that would be available to us. (1981, 390)

If I may gloss Wolf's claim in the final sentence of this excerpt in slightly broader terms, the worry seems to be that attributions of free will and moral responsibility are not just *a* way for us to avoid a slide into consequentialism, but are *necessary* if we are to avoid a slide into consequentialism. It is probably fair to assume that this is Strawson's view too, even if he never quite states it explicitly. But philosophers who take skeptical approaches to free will can resist this view.

Wolf goes on to ask us to

> Imagine for a moment what a world would be like in which we all regarded each other solely with the objective attitude. We would still imprison murderers and thieves, presumably, and we would still sing praises for acts of courage and charity.... But these actions and words would have a different, shallower meaning than they have for us now ... they would be bits of positive and negative reinforcement meted out in the hopes of altering the character of others in ways best suited to our needs. (1981, 391)

Tamler Sommers (2007b) argues that Strawson and Wolf are too grim about the implications of rejecting the reactive attitudes. He considers a world of universal objectivity of attitude in which a character named Sally loses a wallet and a helpful stranger finds it and returns it to her:

> Sally should thank the woman, but not only because it may reinforce the behaviour. She should also thank the woman because she deeply appreciates the gesture. And while it is true that the woman is not ultimately deserving of praise for her actions (ultimately, Sally believes, it is a matter of luck that she

> became the kind of person who performs them), there is no reason for Sally to be coldhearted to her. She can warmly appreciate the gesture and the person who performed it without attributing desert-entailing responsibility to her. Sally can exult in the gesture, if she wants to; she can think "What a nice world it is that produces clumsy, absentminded people like me who drop money-stuffed wallets, and sweet unselfish women like her who return them." And the greater the heroes—the Danes, for example, who protected Jews during the Holocaust—the more profound one's feelings of appreciation will be. (2007b, 229–330)

I take part of Sommers' point here to be that even if we endorse a consequentialist, behavior-reinforcement justification of thanking people who do good turns for us, we are not required to think of this as a calculating, cynical manipulation of them. We can have a sincere, emphatic, emotionally rich experience of this appreciation. This is what a utilitarian would encourage, since we will probably contribute more to the maximization of overall happiness in this way. But this point does not go far enough to resolve the consequentialism problem (though in fairness to Sommers, he does not claim that it does—he does not appear to take up this broader worry about consequentialism). I see Sommers' point here as adding another reply to the isolation issue. That is, one might think that the root of the isolation issue is the fear that a thoroughgoing consequentialist justification of all our interactions would mean that we should always be calculatingly putting on a show when interacting with others, trying to reason out what sort of emotional experiences we should be pretending to have, in order to cause the people around us to behave as we desire. If we looked out across our social world and saw that all our potential interlocutors were manipulative, dissembling play-actors, then this would be isolating indeed. I take Sommers' point to be that if that is not what we want our lives to be like, then the mere fact of relinquishing the reactive attitudes gives us no reason to try to make them that way. This is an important point, but the problem about consequentialism extends further. Sommers goes on to say that

> Kantian proclivities may begin to rebel at this picture, but the rebellion can be suppressed, at least for now. True, we are not attributing to these heroes a dignity and respect as autonomous agents. But this does not prevent us from admiring and applauding their characters and the actions that arise from their characters. We are grateful to the world for having such people in it, and we appreciate the heroes themselves for being what they are (even if they are not morally responsible for it). This is a deep, warm, *un*bleak, *un*barren, *un*ironic appreciation, and it is entirely consistent with denying free will and taking the objective attitude. (2007b, 330)

I think Sommers is correct that Kantian proclivities need not rebel when what is at issue is whether we can legitimately have sincere and heartfelt emotional experiences in contexts where they raise no moral qualms, barring misplaced concerns about the objective attitude. But what about when confronted with the issues that more traditionally divide consequentialists and Kantians—issues about human rights, for example? To treat each other as persons is surely not only to have sincere, engaged emotions in our interactions, but also to respect each others' rights, and to develop social institutions together that safeguard our rights. What should free will deniers say about a situation in which, by depriving just a few agitators of their right to vote, or their right to free speech, we can dramatically improve social harmony, thereby maximizing overall happiness? Or, what if, by punishing criminals with torture, we will get such vigorous general deterrence that the overall crime rate will be dramatically lower, and overall happiness dramatically higher? Many philosophers seem to think that free will deniers have to accept consequentialism, and then choose between accepting disturbing answers to these questions, on the one hand, or on the other, taking on the burden of complex consequentialist attempts to offer less disturbing answers. But I think free will deniers should develop a non-consequentialist theory which allows them to attribute to human beings what Sommers calls "a dignity and respect as autonomous agents." Free will deniers can make such dignity and respect for people a central moral principle if they respect people as *rational* agents rather than as *free* agents, and if they regard agents as autonomous not with respect to the laws of nature, but instead with respect to the undue influence of other agents. There is of course a long and rich consequentialist tradition of developing sophisticated strategies for accommodating rights—rule consequentialism, indirect consequentialism, and so on. But it is widely held that it is harder for consequentialists to explain rights in a satisfying way than it is for non-consequentialists. So it seems worthwhile to explore a non-consequentialist alternative.

2. A KANTIAN DEONTOLOGY FOR FREE WILL DENIERS

It may be easier to determine what free will deniers need in a non-consequentialist ethics if we a have better understanding of why so many accept the view that eschewing attributions of moral responsibility requires us to be consequentialists.[9] I think this view derives from an impoverished picture of what we might call "directions" of justificatory grounding in ethics. The impoverished picture is that, when justifying claims about how people ought to be treated, we have two options: we can either offer "forward-looking" justifications, or "backward-looking" justifications. Forward-looking justifications are consequentialist justifications: they justify treating people in particular ways based on the future consequences of that treatment. Backward-looking justifications justify treating people in particular ways based on events prior to the proposed treatment. Backward-looking justifications can in principle refer to any sort of event prior to the proposed treatment. In principle, they can refer to the event of being born under a bad sign. But the only sort of reference event that mainstream ethicists typically accept in backward-looking justifications is action—more specifically, actions that they take agents to be morally responsible for performing (if they suppose that there are such things). According to backward-looking justifications of this form, we deserve to be treated in particular ways because of how we have acted. I will refer to such justifications as *action-based desert claims*. Since we can only deserve to be treated in particular ways based on our actions if we are morally responsible, action-based desert claims imply that the agent at issue acted with free will. Those who accept this "two directions" picture, and who think that action-based desert claims are the only legitimate backward-looking justifications, see action-based desert claims as the only way to constrain consequentialist justifications.

With a little reflection, however, this "two directions" picture looks like an oversimplification, because there certainly seem to be non-consequentialist justifications that do not look backward. Care ethicists think we can justify kinds of treatment by referring to the ways in which we care about, or are attached to, other people. Virtue ethicists refer to the virtuousness of treating people in particular ways. Deontologists refer to our duties to treat people in particular ways. The things these views refer to, in grounding their justifications, are not facts about the past or future in any obvious way. So it seems reasonable to speculate that we might develop a variety of any of these theories that avoids a depersonalizing consequentialism and still eschews attributions of moral responsibility.[10]

Some may object that the very idea of ethics without free will is absurd, since there is nothing we *ought* to do if there is no free will, because "ought" implies "can," and this "can" implies free will. But there is an epistemic interpretation of this "can" which does not involve free will: I can do x so long as it is possible *to the best of my knowledge* for me to do x. Even if determinism and incompatibilism are true, there typically will be a variety of mutually exclusive actions that I can take, in the epistemic sense of "can," at any given point in the future, given the limits of our predictive abilities.[11] Objectors may go on to claim that, in a non-consequentialist ethics, there cannot be any right or wrong way to treat people if we're not praiseworthy or blameworthy for how we treat people. But this is simply to assert that no sense can be made of a non-consequentialist ethics that dispenses with action-based desert claims, and that is precisely what is in question here.

Objectors may now lodge a more specific objection: the only way for human beings to have the moral status necessary for a non-consequentialist justification to be plausible is for human beings to be morally responsible. The objection I have in mind states that when we justify something on the basis of it being required by, say, duty or virtue, we aren't necessarily offering an action-based justification, but for creatures to have the right sort of moral status for us to have duties to them, or for virtue to require us to treat them in particular ways, they must be creatures with the capacity for morally responsible action. Let me frame this objection in different terms. I think that everyone should acknowledge the pull of consequentialist justifications. Even staunch non-consequentialists typically accept the legitimacy of consequentialist justifications when it comes to the lower animals. If saving most of the inhabitants of an overpopulated earthworm farm means killing a few, most non-consequentialists will not be too burdened by non-consequentialist qualms, because they do not regard earthworms as having the right sort of moral status to impose non-consequentialist obligations on us. What makes human beings different? A common explanation in the philosophical tradition is that human beings have free will, which allows them to (for example) set their own ends, and consequentialist justifications go wrong in (for example) setting their ends for them.

I think the best way to reply to this objection is to work out a counterargument in detail, with respect to one of these non-consequentialist theories, and in this paper I am focusing on Kantian deontology. Kantian deontologists are non-consequentialists who hold that we distinguish permissible and impermissible means to our ends by applying the principle that *persons must always be treated as ends, and never as mere means*. It may be objected that personhood itself implies free will, so that human beings cannot have the moral status of persons unless they are free. At points, Kant himself advocates this view. In the *Metaphysics of Morals*, he states that "A person is a subject whose actions can be imputed to him," while "A thing is that to which nothing can be imputed. Any object . . . which itself lacks freedom is therefore called a thing" (1996, 6:223).[12] For Kant, to impute something to someone is just to hold them morally responsible for it, and by "freedom" here he means free will. But Kant does not need to define persons in this way. He can define persons as beings who autonomously set their own ends, and who must therefore be treated only as they would rationally consent to be treated. Free will skeptics can follow Kant in making respect for our right to independently set our own ends a central moral principle. So long as we understand the influence that we are independent from, in autonomously setting our own ends, as the undue influence of others, rather than the influence of the causal nexus constituting the world, this view is entirely compatible with free will skepticism. We might think this was a specious distinction if we thought that doing things for reasons implies doing things with free will. But I have never seen an argument for this view which does not include controversial compatibilistic or libertarian premises, and it seems to be a straightforward matter for free will skeptics to draw a line between the kind of control involved in doing things for reasons and the kind of control necessary for moral responsibility.

We can have a robust Kantian deontology without looking backward to action-based desert. We need only look to the people with whom we are interacting to find a basis for desert-claims that constrain consequentialist justifications. Personhood can provide a basis for desert-claims which is irreducibly different from action, and which does not depend upon free will in the way action-based desert does. Persons deserve to be treated only as they would rationally consent to be treated, just because they are persons.

Let me explain the distinction between personhood- and action-based desert in more detail. Action-based desert claims are very diverse—examples include claims about praise and blame, the Lockean claim that we come to deserve property when we "mix our labor" with objects, and the retributivist claim that criminals deserve the suffering of punishment based on their criminal actions. But on reflection, it seems clear that not all desert claims are action-based.[13] Some are based on the mere fact of being a person.[14] For example, when we claim to deserve the right to free speech, to be granted due process, and to be respected as persons (the sort of respect that Darwall calls "recognition respect"[15]), these claims are not based on facts about our actions, but instead on the fact that we are persons. Since personhood-based desert does not depend on how we act, we do not need to appeal to moral responsibility to make sense of it. Therefore free will deniers can endorse personhood-based desert claims even though they must reject action-based desert claims. Our rights to due process offer an especially clear illustration of personhood-based desert. It is part and parcel of our understanding of due process that there is nothing anyone could conceivably do to deserve not to be treated as innocent until proven guilty. And consider the concept of *inalienable* rights—rights can only be inalienable if they are disconnected from action-based desert, because they are by definition rights that we cannot lose through action. I think that personhood-based rights can all be seen as ramifications of a more basic right to be treated as ends and not mere means. Since many of the desert claims that we are pretheoretically inclined to accept are action-based, we would be in for substantial revisions of everyday notions of desert if we excised action-based desert claims from our thinking. But I think that enough of the rights that make up our pretheoretical ethical understanding are personhood-based that free will deniers need not entirely lose grip on that understanding.

I think Kant's most helpful way of explaining how to treat others as ends is as follows. We refrain from coercing, deceiving, or otherwise manipulating other people into serving as means to our ends, by causing them to do things they would not rationally consent to do, and (at least some of the time) we actively share others' ends, by taking on their ends as our own. The "others as ends" principle doesn't require us to avoid treating each other as means in all cases, because it is sometimes rational to consent to serving as a means to another's end, for example, when he is a collaborator reciprocally serving as a means to one's own end. If I have the end of teaching philosophy, then the students I teach are among the means to my end. If they have the end of learning philosophy, then I am among the means to their end. Since our ends are complementary in this way, we can rationally consent to this interaction, and treat each other as ends as well as means.

3. RATIONAL CONSENT WITHOUT FREE WILL

To my claim that rational consent doesn't imply free will, some may object that consent is only morally significant insofar as someone *acts* to give or withhold consent, in a way that makes them morally responsible for consenting or withholding consent. But this is a mistake—one which can be avoided if we properly distinguish between actual consent (consent given in the actual world) and hypothetical consent (counterfactual consent, consent that would have been given under different circumstances). When we properly understand the ethical significance of consent, it is clear that sometimes (though by no means always) the rationality of consent matters more than actuality of it. Sometimes what matters is hypothetical rational consent, and we quite properly disregard actual consent. Since we can only be morally responsible for what we actually do, we cannot be morally responsible for what we would hypothetically consent to do. So it follows from the moral significance of hypothetical consent that moral responsibility is not essential to the moral significance of consent.

Let me explain in more detail. There are times when we disregard actual consent precisely because it is *ir*rational—in other words, we care about what the agent would consent to *if he thought rationally about things*, not what he actually consents to, because he is not reasoning properly for one reason or another. Imagine a situation in which someone has been kidnapped by a cult and brainwashed into accepting his own enslavement. We kidnap him back and force him to undergo deprogramming therapy. After brainwashing but prior to deprogramming, he actually consents to enslavement, and actually refuses consent to deprogramming. But in this case it is clearly appropriate to tell the cult members that his actual consent to enslavement does not license them to enslave him, and to force him to undergo deprogramming therapy even though he actually refuses consent. It is appropriate because in this case his actual consent is clearly irrational, and it is his hypothetical rational consent that determines how he should be treated. He would consent to deprogramming therapy if he thought rationally about things, and it is that consideration which carries the day. Respecting autonomy sometimes means treating people as they would rationally consent to be treated, rather than as they actually consent to be treated.

When we turn from extreme cases like the brainwashed slave to subtler cases in everyday life, there will of course be more debate about when it is appropriate to override actual consent in favor of hypothetical rational consent. Too often in our society, labeling someone's viewpoint as irrational amounts to nothing more than a prejudiced rejection of his perspective. A great deal turns on how we understand what it would be rational to consent to do. A bit later, I will offer an account of rational consent that draws on Rawlsian original position deliberation. I think this is a good way to proceed, but I will not argue that here, and I will certainly not try to argue that it is the only way, or the best way, to proceed. I will merely claim that this seems to be an approach in the Kantian tradition which is worth exploring. There may be others that are worth exploring too.

I must also emphasize that I am in no way claiming that actual consent is not morally significant. In many cases, it is clearly wrong to override actual consent based on claims about hypothetical rational consent. These include cases where we are not sure what would be rational to do, or we think it important to tolerate disagreement about what is rational. Salient examples include voting, and choosing our friends and romantic partners. In pluralistic societies like those of the contemporary West, most of us agree that it is important to tolerate quite a lot of disagreement about what is rational. Kantians should hold that when in doubt, we ought to assume that an agent's actual consent is rational, and that claims about hypothetical rational consent have to meet a very high standard to justify overriding actual consent. But it is nonetheless important to see that we all draw the distinction between actual and hypothetical rational consent, and we all acknowledge that there are cases where hypothetical rational consent is what matters. This point severs the connection that may initially seem to exist between the ethical role played by consent, on the one hand, and the concept of moral responsibility, on the other. As mentioned above, this is because we can only be morally responsible for things that we actually do—not for things we would do if we acted rationally. Since moral responsibility plays no role in explaining the moral significance of hypothetical rational consent, moral responsibility is not essential to the moral significance of rational consent. This point gives us no reason to get more comfortable with overriding actual consent. It is a metaethical point about the modal structure of actual and hypothetical consent, not a normative claim that actual consent matters less than we might previously have thought. A Kantian deontology for free will deniers should recognize the moral importance of both hypothetical and actual rational consent.

Objectors may now take a different tack—they may argue that the metaphysics of moral responsibility is still crucial to explaining the moral significance of hypothetical consent, because hypothetical consent can only be morally significant if agents *could have* rationally consented in cases where they did not actually do so, and this implies that a possible world in which they rationally consented was *accessible* to them. Objectors could point out that the metaphysics of accessible alternatives depends on the concept of free will, which is a prerequisite for moral responsibility. They might claim that this shows that the moral significance of hypothetical consent depends on free will, even if it does not directly depend on moral responsibility. This would pose just as much of a problem for free will deniers as a direct dependence on moral responsibility would pose.

The problem for this way of objecting is that if we look at how claims about hypothetical consent are typically formulated and applied, it is clear that they do not imply accessibility. That is, a claim about hypothetical consent typically states that an agent *would* have consented *if* he had thought rationally about things, but this does not imply that he *could* have thought rationally about it. And this is not simply a quirk of phrasing. Let us return to the case of the kidnapped and brainwashed cult slave. It is obviously morally significant that he would have refused consent to enslavement, and consented to deprogramming, if he had thought rationally about it, but it is just as obvious that *as things were*, in his brainwashed state, he *could not* have thought rationally about it. In other words, in his brainwashed state, his hypothetical rational consent remains significant even though a possible world in which he thought rationally about things was not accessible to him. This demonstrates that neither moral responsibility nor free will are prerequisites for the moral significance of hypothetical consent.

Objectors may persist—they may claim that moral responsibility and free will are crucial to the significance of rational consent in the cases where actual consent matters, even if they are not in the cases where hypothetical consent matters. But given that these concepts have no role when it comes to explaining the significance of hypothetical consent, it seems unmotivated to insist on a role for them in an account of actual consent. It seems entirely adequate to say that respecting actual consent is the best way to respect autonomy in cases where we do not have extremely good grounds for favoring hypothetical consent. We can, after all, respect actual consent without supposing that actual consent is important because it is an expression of free will. Further, treating people as they would hypothetically consent to be treated, instead of as they actually consent to be treated, often involves coercion, which we must assume to be an invasion of autonomy unless we have extremely good grounds to believe otherwise.

Presumably all will agree that law enforcement is an area where coercion is necessary. Broadly speaking, Kantians should prefer the least invasive legal system consistent with the protection of human rights. But given human nature, whatever laws we do have will have to be enforced, and this seems to imply coercion. On the view I am advancing here, law enforcement sometimes requires us to disregard actual consent and instead treat people as they would rationally consent to be treated. The notion is that even when we sanction or punish law-breakers, we are obligated to treat them as they would rationally consent to be treated. On this view, it is legitimate to garnish the wages of a tax cheat, or imprison a violent criminal, so long as it is the case that if these law-breakers had thought rationally about things, then they would have consented to this treatment.

This approach can be worked out in more detail with the help of social contract theory, which can be used to model rational consent. If it would be rational to choose to join in a social contract with a particular institutional structure, then we can view that institutional structure as one to which we would rationally consent. Kantian free will deniers should model rational consent based on personhood- but not action-based desert. The Rawlsian social contract seems especially well-suited to this approach, because original position deliberation has the effect of "filtering out" action-based desert claims. The original position is an idealized standpoint in which the members of a society choose the basic principles that will govern their society. It is formed by drawing what Rawls calls a "veil of ignorance" between the people who make up a society and all their particular characteristics. Original position deliberators must choose principles to govern society without knowing where they will end up within society. In the original position, one cannot know whether one is among the best or worst off, what one's religion, ethnicity, or sex is, or what patterns of action one exhibits, for example, whether one is industrious or lazy. Rawls holds that the veil of ignorance ensures that the principles chosen in the original position will be just, since one will not be able to choose principles that make any of one's particular characteristics advantageous. Further, since people are self-interested and risk-averse in conditions of uncertainty, deliberators will worry most about ending up among the worst-off members of society, and they will therefore choose principles which make the circumstances of the worst-off members of society the best they can be.

When it comes to human rights and distributive justice, Kantian free will deniers can take on board Rawls' view of original position deliberation in its entirety. Rawls thinks that original positions deliberators will insist on equality of rights and basic liberties, as well as what he calls the "difference principle." This is the principle that economic inequalities are just if and only if they improve the conditions of the worst-off members of society. This implies that it is just for the industrious to derive advantages from their industry to the degree that it produces economic dynamics that raise the standard of living for the worst-off, for example, by creating incentives for hard work, and by making redistributive taxation possible. Once we raise the veil of ignorance, we can justly disregard a wealthy person's actual withholding of consent to taxation, because original position deliberation demonstrates that he would rationally consent to the taxation of the wealthy.

Rawls himself refuses to apply original position deliberation to penal justice. He allows us to assume that we will be able to follow the laws we choose in the original position. It is a matter of controversy why Rawls takes this approach.[16] But free will deniers should part ways with Rawls on this point, since applying original position deliberation to penal justice makes possible a non-retributive justification of punishment that avoids treating criminals as mere means. This means that we must assume ignorance about whether we are law-followers or law-breakers. It is more difficult to apply original position deliberation to punishment than to distributive justice, since there is no singular worst-off position here in the way there is with respect to distributive justice. That is, potential victims of crime and the people punished "compete" for the position of the worst-off, and also with one another, in the sense that if we assume that punishment deters, then modifying the penal system to improve things for one party tends to worsen things for the other party, and vice-versa. If the purpose of original position deliberation is to ensure fairness, then I think original position deliberators must assume that they have an equal chance of finding themselves among the punished, and among those protected by the institution of punishment. Under these circumstances, it would be rational to choose to imprison violent criminals in benign prisons (prisons much less harmful than contemporary ones). But it would not be rational to choose an institution of punishment that included the death penalty, or torture, or imprisonment under harsh conditions. For people with normal social attachments, and a normal desire to be free from interference in the pursuit of their ends, prison would inevitably be harmful, even under benign conditions, and would therefore serve as a deterrent. But it would make sense to risk that harm if it significantly diminished our chances of being murdered or seriously injured by a violent criminal.

This justification of punishment countenances using criminals as means, since the rationale for accepting an institution of imprisonment is that it protects potential victims. However, since we would choose this approach to punishment in the original position, with the understanding that we might well turn out to be criminals when the veil of ignorance is lifted, we all satisfy the hypothetical rational consent requirement for punishment. So we can punish criminals without treating them as mere means, given their hypothetical rational consent. In other words, once we raise the veil of ignorance, we can justly disregard a violent criminal's actual withholding of consent to imprisonment, because original position deliberation demonstrates that he would rationally consent to punishment.

4. CONCLUSION: REFORMING KANT'S OWN THEORY

To conclude, I would like to apply the results of this inquiry to reforming Kant's own theory. As I mentioned toward the beginning, Kant himself is a retributivist. That is, he holds that punishment must be justified in terms of action-based desert. Kant bases his argument for the legitimacy of the death penalty on the claim that murderers deserve to die. The core of Kant's argument goes like this:

> Punishment . . . can never be inflicted as a means to promote some other good for the criminal himself or for civil society. It must always be inflicted on him only *because he has committed a crime*. For a human being can never be treated merely as a means to the purposes of another . . . (1996, 6:331)

In this passage, Kant seems to accept the "two directions" picture I criticized earlier. He assumes that if we do not hold that criminals deserve punishment based on their actions, then the only other way to justify punishment is with a consequentialist appeal to the positive consequences of punishment for society. But as I have argued, there is another alternative—a personhood-based justification of punishment that turns on the claim that criminals would have rationally consented to punishment—and Kant's own theory has helped provide the resources to demonstrate this. In a nearby passage (1996, 6:335) Kant denies that, in the social contract, one has "consented to lose his life in case he murdered someone else," and he is certainly right here, at least insofar as we take a Rawlsian approach to social contract theory. Original position deliberation about punishment can justify benign imprisonment, but not seriously harmful measures. It may be that the only way to justify the death penalty is with action-based desert claims. But contemporary ethicists should see this as a point against the death penalty, rather than a point in favor of justifications that include action-based desert claims. Kant's own reasoning here may be driven by such a deep commitment to the death penalty that he cannot be content with any justification of punishment that will not support it. But this is not a part of Kant's theory that we should seek to preserve.

It seems quite clear that Kant's ethical theory as a whole becomes stronger if he gives up his retributivism and instead adopts a non-retributive justification of punishment.[17] As I mentioned at the outset, Kant holds that it is possible that we have free will, but we cannot know that we do. The mere possibility of free will is simply not adequate to justify retribution, at least not seriously harmful retribution of the sort that is involved in imprisonment under harsh conditions, and certainly not the sort involved in the death penalty. We recognize that we must meet a very high burden of proof to justify harming people when we impose the "reasonable doubt" standard on arguments in criminal courts, and we ought to apply the same standard in assessing justifications of punishment.[18] Kant himself acknowledges a parallel standard when he argues that the priests of the inquisition could not have known that God wanted the inquisition's victims to die, and that no evidentiary standard short of knowledge could justify anyone in imposing so severe a penalty (*Religion Within the Limits of Reason Alone,* 6:185). I think it is fair to ask Kant to apply the same high standard to claims about free will when they appear in justifications of serious retributive harm.

NOTES

1. Kant claims that we cannot have "theoretical knowledge" that we have free will, but that we can nonetheless have "practical knowledge" that we have free will. How to interpret this claim about practical knowledge is a matter of longstanding controversy. It seems to have something to do with the idea that it is necessary to think of ourselves as having alternative possibilities of action when we deliberate about how to act. But without an account of the sort of necessity Kant has in mind, it is not clear what moral implications it has. If it is a merely psychological necessity, due (for example) to contingencies of evolution, then it would be hard to see how it could have any moral implications at all. Kant clearly means something stronger than mere psychological necessity, but he also seems to mean a sort of necessity that is consistent with acknowledging that we may not *really* be free after all. In my view, such practical necessity is of little help if we seek to justify holding each other morally responsible. So I think that Kant's approach must ultimately rest on the notion that the mere possibility that we have free will is enough to justify the assumption that we have free will whenever we reason about our practices.

2. Influential views in the contemporary literature which bear interesting relationships to Kant's view include those of Pereboom and Smilansky. I take Pereboom to hold that it is possible that we have free will, but that it is impossible to provide evidence that we do, and that the mere possibility that we have free will does not justify us in treating anyone as free in any context. Smilansky holds that we can know we lack free will, but that free will is so important in ethics and practical reasoning that we are nonetheless justified in treating people as free in many contexts. See, e.g., Pereboom 2001 and Smilansky 2000.

3. I discuss this in more detail in Vilhauer 2009b and 2012.

4. See Pereboom (2001, 151) for some helpful points on Kant and free will denial.

5. I discuss Kant's free will theory in Vilhauer 2004a and 2010a.

6. All references to Strawson are from "Freedom and Resentment" (1997).

7. I make this argument in more detail in "Free Will Skepticism and Personhood as a Desert Base" (2009a).

8. A more detailed account of utilitarianism would have to distinguish between act- and rule-utilitarianism, but Strawson does not mention this distinction.

9. Parts of this section and the following section are adapted from Vilhauer 2009a and 2010b. I re-work ideas from those papers here in order to make them more general, explain their connection to Kant, and show their application to the people problem.

10. I discuss virtue ethics and attachment approaches for free will deniers in Vilhauer 2004b and 2008.

11. I discuss this further in Vilhauer 2012. Also see Pereboom 2001, 137.

12. All Kant citations are by Akademie pagination.

13. Philosophers who hold that all desert is action-based include Rachels (1978, 157) and Sadurski (1985, 131). Smilansky holds a related position, i.e., that giving up the belief that human beings are morally responsible for their actions implies giving up all our morally significant beliefs about desert (1996, 157-63).

14. Fred Feldman discusses this point, but not in the context of free will skepticism. (Feldman 1995a).

15. Darwall 1977, 38.

16. See Saul Smilansky (2006), Eugene Mills (2004), Jeffrey Moriarity (2003), and Samuel Scheffler (2000) for discussion of this issue.

17. Also see Wood 2010 for discussion of related issues.

18. Pereboom proposes applying the "reasonable doubt" standard in the free will debate (2001, 161). I also discuss this issue in Vilhauer 2009b.

Chapter Nine

Living Without Free Will

Susan Blackmore

Am I writing this chapter of my own free will?

No. I neither believe in free will, nor have the feeling of having free will. These two statements are different. The first is a purely intellectual claim and relates to the myriad arguments about free will that have raged over the centuries. In denying the existence of free will, I stand with many others on one side of this long debate. The second is a personal claim about how I live my life, and here I am in a very small minority. Indeed people have often told me that the way I live my life is impossible, or that it's possible but if everyone lived this way morality and the rule of law would collapse and all hell would break loose. But unless I am deeply deluded (which is possible), they are wrong.

I shall not say much about my intellectual position on free will. This book contains far better and subtler arguments than I can muster. In summary, the kind of free will I deny is the sort most ordinary people believe in—a contra-causal kind of free will, the idea that their thoughts or conscious decisions are the ultimate cause of their actions and that those thoughts and decisions are free from prior causes of their own.

There is a danger in making assumptions about what other people believe, but in lectures I often ask the audience to carry out some simple action of their own choosing and they typically clap, or stand up, or scratch their noses, or tap the tops of their heads. Asked why, some call on biological, social or physical causes (such as brain events, my actions, or the temperature in the room) but many claim simply that "I" decided to do it, or that "my mind" or "my thoughts" caused it to happen.

This is the common intuition that underlies belief in free will, and there is plenty of research suggesting that it is both false and misleading. One line of research stems from Libet's original work on the timing of voluntary actions

(1985). This has been amply replicated and deeply debated ever since. Another is the rapidly developing neuroscience of volition which reveals the many areas in the prefrontal cortex, supplementary motor area and parietal lobe which manage decision making and impulse suppression (e.g., Haggard 2008). A third explores the mechanisms involved when people come to believe that they did or did not cause their own actions. This research, pioneered by Wegner (2002), shows that the feeling that I did, or did not, do something is not proof of causation but is a post-hoc attribution based on sequence, timing and other variables.

Despite all this knowledge, the powerful feeling that "I" can freely cause "my" actions persists.

Inherent in that last sentence is the difficulty of writing about self. If that sentence appears to refer to two different things in the words, "I" and "my" that is because it does. The first is the fictional inner self who seems to be a persisting entity with consciousness and free will: the second is the whole human being; a brain and body carrying out actions and being held, or not held, responsible for them. The feeling of having free will amounts to the idea that the inner self can freely cause the body to act.

I (the whole human being) have written elsewhere about the illusion of self (Blackmore 1999, 2010). By "illusion" I do not mean something that does not exist but something that is not as it seems, and our inner self is like this. Most people confidently claim that they have, or are, a self, and that this self is a continuing and powerful entity; it feels like a conscious agent who lives inside their body, experiences their "stream of consciousness" (Blackmore 2002) and is the one who decides what to do. Without such an inner self, many people say, their life would have no meaning. No wonder they are reluctant to give it up.

Yet what we know about the brain, even at the most basic level, appears incompatible with the existence of such an entity. The human brain is a massively parallel system with decisions being taken at multiple levels, at different rates, and in multiple parallel streams all at once. Even though we may feel as though we are a continuous mental entity who is the subject of our experiences and issues instructions from some central command headquarters, there is no central place where this self could live and no means by which it could interfere with all these different on-going processes (Dennett 1991). In other words, we humans are clever decision-making machines that are prone to a number of powerful illusions, in particular the illusion of a persisting inner self that has consciousness and free will (Blackmore 2010; Hood 2012; Metzinger 2009). I am arguing that free will, in this sense, is an illusion.

Proponents of many popular compatibilist arguments often agree in rejecting contra-causal or magical free will. Yet they seem to be trying, at all costs, to rescue some snippet of freedom from the obvious fact that everything that happens in this universe is either caused by something that went before or is a truly random event. Neither of these alternatives provides any room for what most people would call free will. Of course human beings make choices. I am not denying this. Nor am I denying that we can be more or less constrained in the choices available to us, nor that we can be held responsible for some choices and not others. But we should not confuse the decision making powers of a living creature with freedom of the will.

This, it seems to me, has caused a lot of confusion. For example, Dennett's (2003) book *Freedom Evolves* is a wonderful description of how humans and other animals have evolved the ability to make ever more complex choices in ever more complex environments. But these choices are not free in the sense that most people want them to be free. They are the result of the evolved complexity of the perceptual and motor systems that Dennett so ably describes. A more apt title would therefore be *Choice Evolves*.

But I want to leave aside the complexities of philosophical discussion and turn to a different question—a question that arises for anyone who, like me, rejects the notion of contra-causal free will—if there is no free will, how should we live our lives?

There are two possible responses: One is to go on living "as if" we have free will—in other words, to accept that free will is an illusion and yet choose to remain deluded (not a free choice of course, but one caused by prior events and circumstances). The other is to reject the illusion and aspire to live entirely without free will.

I have chosen the second option, but the first of these is by far the more common. Indeed, when I was lucky enough to be able to interview many leading philosophers and neuroscientists about consciousness, I was amazed by the number who chose to live "as if."

LIVING "AS IF"

Daniel Wegner is well known as a neuroscientist who believes that free will is an illusion. He has published extensive research on the psychological processes that lead people to believe they have control over their own actions. He claims that "Our sense of being a conscious agent who does things comes at a cost of being technically wrong all the time" (2002, 342). I asked him how his work in general, and this conclusion in particular, affects the way he lives his life. He replied "I do the 'as if.' And I think almost everybody who's happy and healthy tends to do that."

He argued that our minds produce a sense of virtual agency, the feeling that we are a self who does things and, he said "this ends up being a very useful accounting system and a useful way of keeping apprised of our actions as opposed to those of others, or of the world" (Blackmore 2005, 254).

According to Wegner, the fact that the sense of agency is illusory doesn't mean that it's any less important since it still guides our subsequent behavior. In other words, we should carry on living "as if" we have free will because the illusion is useful and we wouldn't be happy or healthy without it.

Pat Churchland expressed a similar view when I asked her whether she has free will. Although she thinks the human brain is a causal machine, she replied ". . . you just hold those two things in your mind at the same time" and added that the brain "has this user illusion—that your decisions are made according to, shall we say, the standard model—that you consciously identify the options, you consciously do an expected utility calculation, you consciously choose, and then at some point later in time, the action's executed. That's a useful user illusion." When I pressed her further by asking "So do you mean that you're happy to think this is an illusion and then just behave as though it's real?" she replied "It's like the illusion with morality . . . it's also very useful for people to have the illusion that these are really true" (Blackmore 2005, 62).

The idea that illusions are useful is also found in Daniel Dennett's (1991) description of the self as a "benign user illusion of its own virtual machine." I have argued that the user illusion is actually malign and we might be better to try to throw it out and live without it (Blackmore 1999, 2000).

Some argue not just that the illusion might be useful but that it would be positively dangerous to give it up. According to Susan Greenfield there might be "terrible consequences." She poured scorn on my suggestion that it might be preferable to try to live without it, saying "I believe very much in my own free will. So I can see that you might be, in your Sue Blackmore way, sitting there and saying, 'I wonder what she's going to order' and so on, and that might be quite fun; but I don't think that every minute of your life you think, 'I wonder what she's going to do.' Well, you might if you have schizophrenia, but I think for most people most of the time, you have to assume that other individuals are acting of their own free will, and that you yourself are a cohesive entity" (Blackmore 2005, 100–101). In fact, as I told her, I do frequently think "I wonder what she's going to do."

Referring to further "terrible consequences," she said "I think you have to make that choice, because a lot of other things follow: if you don't do that, what do you do with the criminal justice system? For example; if no one has free will, it means that no one should be in prison . . . how can it provide a deterrent for people if they don't have free will; it's not up to them" (Blackmore 2005, 99).

In contrast, I think that the criminal justice system would be stronger and fairer if it were not based on the notion of free will. Certainly we would lose the idea of retribution; of punishing people because they acted badly of their own free will and so deserve to suffer. But people would be sent to prison for other reasons: to keep them away from doing any more harm, for training or rehabilitation, or as a deterrent to them or others in the future. We know that appropriate rewards and punishments can change people's behavior. So the relevant question would not be "does this person deserve to be punished?" but "would this punishment do any good to them, to their victims, or to society in general?" In many cases, the answer would be "yes."

Arguments of the "my genes made me do it" type would become irrelevant if we agreed that every action everyone carries out is caused by their genes, their memes, and the environments they have lived in. Arguments of the "I didn't know what I was doing" type would not hinge on whether or not the person was really responsible of his own free will, but on whether any punishment would be effective. For those too young or mentally incapacitated the answer would often be "no" and there would be no point in putting them in prison. These are complex issues, but in principle there is no reason to believe that our society and its criminal justice system would collapse and crime would run amok if we dropped the idea of free will.

All this assumes that it is possible to give up believing in free will, but some argue that it is not: we do not live "as if" we have free will because the illusion is useful or because giving it up would destroy society or make us mentally ill, but because we *cannot* give it up. Among my conversationalists, Stuart Hameroff claimed "I have no choice but to believe in free will" and John Searle said "Well, I don't have a choice about that."

Searle referred to his well-known example of ordering food in a restaurant. When the waiter asks for the order "I cannot say 'I'm a determinist, I'll just wait and see what happens,' because even that utterance is only intelligible to me as an exercise of my free will." He has famously claimed that "We cannot get rid of the conviction that we are free even if we become philosophically convinced that the conviction is wrong" (2004, 219). To me he added "when I go to the restaurant and I look at the menu, I might decide 'Well, I'll have the spaghetti,' but I'm not forced to have the spaghetti; the other options are open to me; I could have done something else. So we can't think it away or pretend that we don't really have free will . . ." (Blackmore 2005, 204-5). Of course I disagree with him.

A more surprising example of this view was that of neuroscientist, Kevin O'Regan, who told me that he had wanted to be a robot from childhood. He described poring over a book on neuro-anatomy at the age of ten and wondering how on earth the little neural circuits could give rise to experience. He not only thought of himself as a robot but said, of others, "I knew that they were all robots, and that they were just labouring under the illusion that they weren't." All this might imply that he would also have given up the feeling of having free will, and yet when I asked him "And do you believe you have free will?" he replied "Yes, everybody does. Even robots believe they have free will, even if they don't" (Blackmore 2005, 172).

The temptation to compare ourselves with robots is strong, and yet can produce very different responses. Almost the opposite reaction came from philosopher Paul Churchland, who explained to me that it comforts him to know that brains are non-linear dynamical systems whose behavior is exquisitely sensitive to infinitesimally small differences and therefore unpredictable. "So one mustn't fear the story science seems to tell, that we are just robots." I was surprised to learn that he needed comforting in the face of what science seems to tell us, and asked him about this "Sure," he said "I am just like everybody else."

But he is not like everybody else. Some scientists simply accept that they have no free will, including Francis Crick, who told me that he agreed with Wegner, not Dennett, and was happy to see his own life as thoroughly deterministic. Christof Koch said "It doesn't bother me too much." Others find it does bother them. It bothers them very much, and yet however useful the illusion might be they cannot go on living "as if" there is free will when they don't believe in it.

I am one of those. For as long as I can remember I have struggled to bring what I have learned as a scientist together with how I live my life.

REJECTING THE ILLUSION

It's a cold Sunday evening in December. If I'm going to go down to the village to see the Christmas lights switched on I need to put on my boots and coat now. It's warm by my wood fire. It's cold, windy and drizzling outside. Yet I like to support our village events, perhaps especially when so many people will stay away because of the horrible weather. This simple dilemma is typical of the many small decisions each of us has to make every day. So how do I decide? Do I agonize over the right course of action? Do I exert the freedom of my will? No. I sit by the fire and the arguments, pro and con, come and go. I might even think "I wonder whether she'll go or not?" Then suddenly I am up, reaching for my coat, and heading out of the door into the rain.

This sounds very easy. It is reminiscent of William James' brilliant analysis of how we get out of bed on a freezing morning in a room without a fire. We struggle and remonstrate with ourselves. We keep postponing the act. "Now how do we *ever* get up under such circumstances?" he asks. "If I may generalize from my own experience, we more often than not get up without any struggle or decision at all. We suddenly find that we *have* got up" (James 1890 ii, 524–25). He goes on to suggest that what prevents us from getting up in the first place is all those "contradictory or paralyzing suggestions"; the thought of the cold, the delicious warmth of the bed, the duties of the day ahead.

So who or what was responsible for the decision? James goes on to analyze "that peculiar feeling of inward unrest known as *indecision*" (1890 ii, 528). As long as the competing ideas are attended to, we are said to *deliberate* but when finally the action happens, or else is quenched by its antagonists, "we are said to *decide*, or to *utter our voluntary fiat* in favor of one or the other course. The reinforcing and inhibiting ideas meanwhile are termed the *reasons* or *motives* by which the decision is brought about." James does not reject the possibility of free will, and his analysis of self is subtle. Yet, one hundred years before Wegner's research, he beautifully exposed the retrospective attributions we routinely give to an imagined self. "We" are said to deliberate, "we" decide, and those voluntary fiats, reasons and motives are ours.

Wouldn't it be more honest to accept all these attributions for what they are, drop the notion of the self who decides, and simply let the competing ideas get on with it without interference? Might life even be easier, and making decisions less agonizing, if we could? This is what I am suggesting.

Let's take that simple example of going out on a cold night. Living without free will means letting all those "contradictory or paralyzing suggestions" carry on their battles without thinking they have to be settled by an inner self who ultimately wants one course of action rather than the other. It means treating them as just lots and lots of thoughts about warmth and cold, effort and relaxation, obligation and consequences. Eventually they settle their battle and one action prevails. Then afterwards—and this is perhaps the critical part—it means desisting from making those retrospective attributions of free will. As I walk along the road in the dark and the rain I do not claim that "I" freely made the decision to go down to the village but simply that the decision was made. Of course that decision has consequences and this person has to accept those consequences and the responsibility that goes with them. But this is not because "I" made the decision of my own free will. It is because this is the decision that the whole universe came up with for this person under those circumstances.

When I mention this attempt to live without free will people often ask me what I did or how long it took. I have met many people who are trying to do something similar, but I find their questions hard to answer. I have faint recollections of struggling with questions of causality and the impossibility of free will as a child. I remember, much more clearly, having deep and delightful arguments with my then boyfriend, John Dupre, at Oxford when he was writing on "Weakness of the will." Then last year, with the sad and unexpected death of my first husband, I took out my diary for 1977 to read about our first meeting. There I had written about our discussions of life, the universe and everything, and about the book *Zen and the Art of Motorcycle Maintenance* which I was reading at the time. In my diary I described exploring the effects of different kinds of "wanting," and two weeks after we met I wrote "It occurred to me that I can now understand how it is possible to give up one's will and *not* become a vegetable. One still wants, but in only this (way of) non-striving, or wanting possession or clinging." This is just one aspect of the task I was apparently already struggling with thirty-five years ago.

This might give some perspective on a task that has lasted most of a lifetime. It has been a slow process. Yet I suspect there may be an entirely different route—perhaps an instantaneous realization that does away with the illusion all in one go. I shall say more about this later, but for now I want briefly to explore a few aspects of the hard, slow route.

FEAR OF LETTING GO

Here's a simple question, asked of me again and again by students in my consciousness courses, some of whom found their studies deeply upsetting. As they learned neuroscience and philosophy many of them concluded, intellectually, that free will must be illusory. Yet they feared the consequences of accepting this conclusion in their own lives. So they would ask something like this: "But if I don't have free will why would I ever get up in the morning?" or more generally, "Why would I bother to do anything at all?"

My response (apart from referring them to William James) was to suggest that they try the exercise and see what happens. What happens is that they lie there for some time, some of them getting anxious, others enjoying the lie-in. Then they get bored, or they are desperate for a cup of coffee, or they need to go to the toilet, and so they get up. Once in the bathroom it seems tempting to have a hot shower and then they realize they'd like clean teeth. By then they are hungry and go and make breakfast. And so the day goes on and things get done.

Practicing in this way, motivation itself does not disappear, but the sense of wanting or being motivated begins to change. Indeed, it becomes increasingly obvious that one's motivations do not all come from "me," or from some unified inner person or agent; they spring up all over the place in a complex organism living in a complex world. Some of these motivations are available to introspection; they can be thought about, discussed and compared. Others cannot.

We may be tempted to say that the former "come into consciousness" or that "I am conscious of them," while the others are "unconscious." But this is another temptation that I have been systematically trying to root out because I think it is false. I should say that I am in a tiny minority here as well, although my view is close to that of Dennett who describes the temptation to fall into what he calls "Cartesian Materialism"; "the view that nobody espouses but almost everybody tends to think in terms of . . ." (1991, 144) "the view that there is a crucial finish line or boundary somewhere in the brain, marking a place where the order of arrival equals the order of 'presentation' in experience because *what happens there* is what you are conscious of" (1991, 107). Like Dennett I reject this view.

I also reject another unstated assumption that permeates the neuroscience of consciousness, and on which the search for the neural correlates of consciousness is based. This is the idea that some brain processes or ideas or thoughts are "conscious" while others are "unconscious." This assumption seems so natural and is so common throughout the neuroscience of consciousness that it is rarely questioned. Yet it implies what I call a "magic difference"; that some of the things that go on in our heads give rise to, or create, or are, subjective experiences while others are not; that the hard problem of consciousness applies to some neural processes and not others (Blackmore 2010).

This magic difference depends upon the fictional inner self who is supposed to experience some things going on in its body or brain and not experience others. It may seem bizarre to try to give up this very natural illusion, but I think it is intimately related to the task of giving up free will. So I have spent a great deal of time peering into the sensation of what I am conscious of to try to see what is going on. For example, right now I can easily look out of my window at the field opposite, at the shadows on the green grass and the stark outline of the trees against the sky, and think "right now I am conscious of those shapes and colors"; these are the contents of my consciousness.

What could be wrong with that? One way of investigating this has been through the exercises I set my students each week during my consciousness courses. In the first of twenty weeks they were given the question "Am I conscious now?" and told to ask themselves this question as many times as they could every day for a week and then report back. Many of them found this incredibly hard, but those who managed it reported that something very odd sometimes happened. It was as though asking the question made them become more conscious, as though they were not quite sure whether they were conscious a moment before or not. This led naturally onto the second week's exercise which was to ask "What was I conscious of a moment ago?"

I practiced this exercise along with my students for many years. I also set myself solitary retreats during which I meditated on this, and other questions, for long periods of time (Blackmore 2011). This persistent personal inquiry led me to the following conclusions: first, "I" am only conscious when I ask myself whether I am, and second, when I look back into what was happening a moment ago I can recall many things happening but I cannot say which I was conscious of and which not. If I cannot say, then who can?

Those who are searching for the NCCs expect to find an answer, but if my view is correct they never will. The idea that I am conscious of some things and not others depends on the construction of an illusory conscious self. This self is fleetingly constructed when required but most of the time is absent. Part of the illusion is that this self is a persisting entity who is always conscious of something or other. This is the idea that I reject.

These conclusions, reached through personal inquiry, are essentially the same as those I came to intellectually, as described above. They imply that most of the time for most of us, there is no answer to the question "What was I conscious of at time t?" There is no fact of the matter about whether a thought, action or brain process was conscious or unconscious. There is no Cartesian Theatre and no magic difference.

So how does one live with this in ordinary life? I am sure there are countless ways, but whenever I find myself thinking "I am now conscious of the rain pounding on the roof," or "I've just realized I am hungry," I don't imagine that the rain or the hunger have just "entered consciousness" or "become conscious" but rather that the self and what it is supposed to be conscious of have both popped up together. Neither was there a moment ago. If the Cartesian temptation persists, I might repeat the exercise of looking back into the immediate past and seeing, once again, that I have no idea whether I was conscious of the clock ticking or the crackling of the fire, or not. There is no answer because a moment ago I was not thinking about what I was conscious of. So there was no one to be conscious. When I do this, the sense of a continuous conscious self loses some of its power. This is the same self who would, if it existed, have free will, and dismantling this self is part of the task of living without free will.

MORALITY AND RESPONSIBILITY

Letting go of the illusion of free will can be frightening. In addition to the fear of not doing anything at all, there is the fear that if I stop exerting my free will then I (or something else) will make the "wrong" decisions. What counts as "right" or "wrong" may be deeply moral or may be purely selfish. For example, if I decided not to go to the village to see the Christmas lights, I might later hear that it was great fun and so I missed a brilliant evening. In that case I might selfishly conclude that I made the "wrong" decision, because I would have been happier if I had gone. I might even get cross with myself for being so stupid. Such thoughts often accompany the everyday decisions we all have to make. Should I accept this invitation, eat this or that for lunch, ring that friend back now or later, go on holiday here or there? If I make the wrong choice I will be unhappy, so I should have done otherwise.

It is perhaps obvious that the process of agonizing over these decisions, the anger with oneself for getting it wrong, and the potential for regret, are all causes of distress. It is perhaps less obvious that these all stem from the illusion of having free will and that without it they would be lessened or would disappear altogether.

Dan Wegner, although he lives "as if" there is free will, described to me some of the ways his research has affected his own life. "I would have to say that it gives me a sense of peace. There are a whole lot of things that I don't have to worry about controlling because I know that I'm really just a little window on a lovely machinery that's doing lots of things. It also gives, not so much a sense of inevitability, but perhaps a sense of correctness to the behaviors I do—that not all of them have to be chosen; I don't have to worry about every little thing; things will happen well, and have happened well throughout my life, as a result of simply allowing this machinery to do its operation" (Blackmore 2005, 255). He went on to describe how this had helped him with a major life decision.

This is the process I'm trying to describe here—allowing that "lovely machinery" to get on with its decisions and choices without interference from little me.

A deeper and even more upsetting fear is that without free will we might become wicked creatures who would go around harming others, stealing, raping, pillaging or committing whatever other evils one can think of. It's as though people cannot trust themselves to act well unless they keep conscious control over everything they do; as though they think that if they stop believing that "they" are in control of their body (or whatever part of their brain or body they think of as "not me") its behavior will somehow degenerate into evil.

This is surely a recipe for unhappiness. It means falsely dividing oneself into the controller and the controlled; siding with some impulses and not others. The conscious part that is "me" has to control the unconscious part and so of course battles ensue. When James wrote about getting out of bed, his "contradictory or paralyzing suggestions" were conscious ones (available to introspection) battling against each other, but here I am talking about the additional fear that if my conscious self does not adjudicate over such battles then the result will be something terribly bad. So to avoid this terrible outcome "I" must keep a firm control over all my evil impulses and choose good over evil. And for that I have to exert my free will.

This fear, that deep down we are all wicked, is, I suggest, completely unfounded. Yet it is both understandable and widespread. It can be seen in many religions, especially in the Christian doctrine of original sin and the idea that God created us for a purpose and gave us the choice between good and evil. If one asks "who" has this choice, or "who" is good or evil, Christians will refer to the human soul or spirit; that non-material, thinking, acting, persisting being that ultimately takes responsibility and in time will be rewarded by going either to heaven or to hell.

How can people believe such things? The deep roots of such beliefs and fears came home to me some years ago when I had a wonderful conversation with my ninety-year-old demented father. I had gone to spend a few days with my parents and one evening was due to give a lecture nearby. So before I left, I sat down by the fire with my Dad.

I should add that my father left school at fifteen, fought in the Second World War, was one of the few survivors of the sinking of the Prince of Wales, and then came home to take over his father's printing business and, as far as I know, never read a book the rest of his life. He was a kind, honest and practical man whom I admired but he did not share my mother's strong Christian faith, nor did he enjoy discussing life, the universe and everything. So when he asked, for the second or third time, "Where did you say you were going dear?" I did not expect to get into a philosophical discussion.

"To Sharpham House." I said, "It's a Buddhist center near Totnes."

"Why are you going there, dear?"

"I'm giving a lecture on free will."

"Free will? What is there to say about that?"

I hesitated, wondering what on earth I could say to my dear old Dad who just about knew who I was but had no idea what day or year it was, and whose entire world consisted of his bed, his fireside chair, and the daily paper he kept on his lap all day even though he could no longer understand it. But I had to say something. So I said that in my lecture I would explain some of the science of how brains work and why human brains have no need of any inner self, or spirit or soul, to direct them. There are parts of the brain that make decisions and organize movements but no center in which a self or soul could live, and no need for it to do anything if it did. So there's a problem—I seem to be in control but I cannot really be. This, I said, is what I was going to be talking about.

To my complete surprise this set my old Dad alight. He said he was quite sure that his wayward daughter was wrong. "I know I have a soul," he said "It stands to reason. It's me." I asked him what it was made of and he said it was spirit. I asked where it came from, and he said it came from God. I protested that there was no God, and that spirits controlling a body would have to be magic, and he replied with a question I have never forgotten:

"Then why do we want to be good?"

He didn't ask why we are good, or argue about what good is, he simply asked "Why do we *want* to be good?" I went off to my lecture with a far better appreciation of why so many people believe in free will and fear giving it up. And I kept asking myself his question.

So why do we want to be good? Perhaps not everyone does want to be good, but many of us do, and there are good evolutionary reasons why, including the fact that in a social species with reciprocal altruism, the way one person treats another determines how they are treated in return. If you are generous, you are likely to have favors returned. If you are helpful, you gain friends and allies, have a wider social circle, and gain status which translates into future genetic success. Some of our natural desire to be good, or to be thought to be good, is bred into us.

So maybe it is not really so dangerous to give up the illusion of a self in control. Psychologist Guy Claxton agrees. "The thing that doesn't happen, but of which people are quite reasonably scared, is that I get worse. A common elaboration of the belief that control is real . . . is that I can, and must control 'myself,' and that unless I do, base urges will spill out and I will run amok." Luckily, he says, this is false because I never was split into controller and controlled, although the sense of strain and the self-recrimination were real enough. "So the dreaded mayhem does not happen. I do not take up wholesale rape and pillage and knocking down old ladies just for fun." Instead guilt, shame, embarrassment, self-doubt, fear of failure, and much anxiety fall away, and contrary to expectation I become a better neighbor (Claxton 1986, 69).

Where does that leave responsibility? If there is no inner self that exerts control through free will, there is still a whole living being that can take responsibility and can be held responsible by others. And that is sufficient.

PAYING ATTENTION

When Claxton described giving up control, it was in the context of Buddhism, with its training in meditation and mindfulness, and its concepts of no-self and not-doing. The practice of mindfulness, now becoming increasingly popular in education, therapy and business, as well as in sitting meditation, is all about paying attention. In mindfulness one pays attention to everything happening now, but without discrimination, judgment or response. One simply stays with everything that is. Done with single-minded determination this is a tough task. Our minds just do seem to slip off into speculations about the past or the future, into imagined conversations with other people, into regrets about past actions, into annoyance at things we cannot control, or into wishing to change things for the better. This is how minds are.

Letting go of all this can seem terribly scary. As we stop interfering and allow thoughts just to come and go as they will, we seem to become isolated in a present world which is just as it is, and not under our control. Indeed the sense of being a self who could control anything begins to slip away. With the steady practice of mindfulness, whether in everyday life or in sitting meditation, the mind becomes slower and gentler. It becomes less eager to grasp onto what it thinks is good, and push away what it thinks is bad; to identify with some thoughts or events and not others.

Even more unnerving is that the imagined continuity of self begins to fail. As sounds come and go; as thoughts arise and fall away, a terrible fear can arise—that unless "I" keep on watching them and connecting one to the next in an ongoing stream of consciousness, then I will disappear. I will fall into the gaps. But then comes the discovery that the continuity was always in the world, and never in that mythical inner self that seemed so strong before. In this, and in many other ways, the simple practice of attending to the present moment can wreak havoc. The self who would have had free will begins to lose its grip.

Although this can be frightening, it has always seemed to me to be a fear worth facing. Many years ago, when intensively practicing mindfulness, I began to notice that more and more decisions simply made themselves. I did not have to interfere with them or tell myself that "I" was making them. I could let go of the sense of personal control and trust the body I once thought I inhabited to get on with its work unhindered. These decisions included difficult choices that took days to resolve, as well as quick and trivial ones. But one that sticks in my mind was both simple and potentially dangerous.

When I lived in the country near Bristol, my route home took me to a set of traffic lights where I could either turn right along the main road or left into the narrow lanes. Straight ahead was a dry stone wall. One route was a bit faster; the other was slower but prettier. It really did not matter which I took but I would often approach the junction in an agony of indecision—beset by James' "contradictory or paralyzing suggestions." The lanes are more fun but what if I meet a herd of cows or a slow tractor? The main road is faster but it uses more fuel. Then one day I simply stopped bothering. I paid attention to the present moment in which the light was red and I was sitting still. Then the light changed and . . . . I forget which way she went but it was not into the stone wall.

Has the feeling of having free will completely gone away? For me, no, not entirely. Sometimes the feeling comes back, usually in the form of "Oh, I can't decide whether to accept that invitation, to work a little longer, to tell that person I . . ." and so on. In these cases I am helped by remembering Dan Dennett's (2001) remark about the Zombic Hunch (the powerful intuition that there could be beings that act and speak exactly like a normal person but are actually devoid of consciousness). He says of that hunch "I feel it, but I don't credit it." So when the feeling of free will comes along, so do those words, along with an acknowledgment that this feeling of having free will is both natural and understandable.

Could it go away completely? Christian mystics describe a final "unselfing" in surrender to the divine will. Surrender to God is said to be the essence of Islam. But the clearest exposition is found in the "sudden and revolutionary change" described in Zen Buddhism, in which the self, with all its fear, clinging, choosing, and deciding, ends.

In his classic book *The Way of Zen*, Alan Watts says that "We just decide without having the faintest understanding of how we do it. In fact it is neither voluntary nor involuntary . . . a decision—the freest of my actions—just happens like hiccups inside me or like a bird singing outside me" (Watts 1957, 141). In the way of Zen one simply walks on, wholeheartedly engaged in every action. Yet "we cannot realize this kind of action until it is clear beyond any shadow of doubt that it is actually impossible to do anything else" (1957, 161). This is "unmotivated non-volitional functioning." It is "non-action" or "not-doing." It is how things are because really there is no entity to act; no entity to be either bound or free (Wei Wu Wei 2004).

So could I be completely free of the illusion? Wei Wu Wei suggests "asking yourself whether you are not still looking as from a phenomenal centre that has only an imaginary existence. If so, you will be misled; if not—you will understand at once" (163). Clearly, as long as I wish to be free of the illusion, I am not.

Chapter Ten

If Free Will Doesn't Exist, Neither Does Water

Manuel Vargas

There are now many thoughtful people who insist that science has shown us that there is no free will. In one way, this is unsurprising. The march of science has a long history of overturning a variety of beliefs that have seemed obvious, even vital to those who have had them. In another way, though, the triumphalism among free will skeptics is surprising. As much as science has a track record of overthrowing beliefs, it also has a distinguished history of changing the details of what we believe without abandoning the general outline. Skepticism is not always the result when science shows us something troubling about how we understand the world.

Consider that at one point many educated people thought that water was one of the four basic indivisible substances of the world, that race was a strict biological kind, that marriage was a property exchange between two men, and that the normative force of laws depended entirely on the God-sanctioned powers of the sovereign. Most of us now have little trouble accepting the chemical theory of water, that race is mainly a social kind, that women aren't property to be exchanged between men, and that law is not just the divinely sanctioned threat of a sovereign. Some of these transitions went easier than others, and the role of experimental science played larger or smaller roles in each of these cases. However, it is also clear that anyone who would now deny the reality of water, race, marriage, or the law is going to have to explain themselves.

It is not obvious that our current notion of free will is an immutable feature of our conceptual framework. But many scientists seem to think that it is, and that the operative conception of free will was fixed by commitments that no physicalist should accept. For example, neuroscientist P. Read Montague (2008) asserts that:

> Free will is the idea that we make choices and have thoughts independent of anything remotely resembling a physical process [. . .] From this perspective, your choices are not caused by physical events, but instead emerge wholly formed from somewhere indescribable and outside the purview of physical descriptions. This implies that free will cannot have evolved by natural selection, as that would place it directly in a stream of causally connected physical events. Consequently, the idea of free will is not even in principle within reach of scientific description. (R584)

In a similar vein, John Bargh and co-author Brian Earp (2009) have maintained that:

> Free will may be defined as an agent's ability to act on the world by its own volition, independently of purely physical (as opposed to metaphysical) causes and prior states of the world.

Most scientists who are "no free will" enthusiasts fail to consider whether free will might be something—like water, marriage, race, law, and so on—about which we change our views regarding its fundamental nature. To them, elimination of the concept of free will seems to be the only live option, and the basis for the elimination is (in part) that they think free will must be as they happen to conceive of it.

However, skepticism about free will has to be *earned*, just as it does in the case of eliminativism about water, marriage, race, and laws. The free will skeptic has to, at the very least, show that free will skepticism is a more plausible view than its alternatives. Crucially, when one of those alternatives is that we are mistaken about what free will entails, skepticism can't be demonstrated simply by observing that there is something problematic about free will if we understand it in pedestrian ways.

My task here is to show why eliminativism or nihilism about free will has not yet been earned, at least in those quarters that tend to say some form of science shows that we lack free will.[1] The target of my discussion is limited in an important way. My present target is work by contemporary scientists—Montague, Haggard, Bargh, Greene and Cohen, Pockett, and Cashmore, among others—who claim that something about the state of contemporary science shows that we lack free will. The present account is *not* intended to function as a reply to free will skeptics whose work is grounded in largely philosophical considerations. I've engaged with that work elsewhere, and while my grounds for resisting it are not unrelated to some of what I say here, the details are distinct (see Vargas 2013, esp. chapters 2, 3, and 9).

My engagement with scientific free will skeptics is not motivated by a more broadly anti-scientific, anti-physicalist, or anti-naturalist view of these matters. I accept, as they do, that science is relevant to our understanding of free will, and that our growing grasp of the physical constituents of abilities will change how we understand ourselves. Nevertheless, I maintain that our concept of free will is more resilient and flexible than most free will skeptics tend to acknowledge, and given their concerns, there is typically better reason to prefer a revisionist conception of free will over free will skepticism.

I make my case in four parts. First, I will distinguish between several distinct problems associated with free will, and identify the strand that I take to be central (or, at least, central to the issues discussed here). Second, I turn to criticism, illustrating what is confused or mistaken about some of the main paths to contemporary forms of scientific free will skepticism. There, I will argue that many of its familiar forms turn on overly-ambitious claims about determinism, characterizations of free will, and what follows from a commitment to a scientific worldview. Third, I argue that even the best forms of scientific skepticism fail to block the possibility of revisionism. Finally, I offer a revisionist alternative that captures much of what motivates skepticism about free will, without giving up the integrity of our ordinary judgments and practices.

I.

What is free will? One can, of course, define any term as one sees fit, if mere stipulation is the name of the game. However, a proposed definition is only interesting if it corresponds to either ordinary usage or some technical notion whose appeal or function can be established. So, when someone claims that free will is some or another thing, we should ask ourselves whether there is any reason to think that the proposal does capture ordinary usage, or whether it represents a specialized notion, the interests of which should be stated.

Free-will-doubting scientists are not univocal about what they think 'free will' means. For example, Wegner has characterized it as "the feeling of conscious control" (Wegner 2002). This notion is markedly distinct from "undetermined choices of action" (Bargh 2008, 130) and the idea that we choose "independent of anything remotely resembling a physical process" (Montague 2008, R584–85). So, for any of their accounts, we should ask whether such characterizations are intended to reflect folk or technical discourses.

Although these are serious, thoughtful scientists doing important work in their primary fields, what is striking is that none of them give any evidence that their definitions of free will track either ordinary *or* standard technical discourse. In the articles from which these quotes are extracted, there is no appeal to any empirical or experimental work on how it is that ordinary folks actually think about free will, nor argument for why we should think of free will as they characterize it, nor any engagement with those whose professional occupation it is to think about these things.[2]

This might be reasonable if there were no disagreement about the meaning of free will, or whether it exists, but that is surely not the case. Indeed, looking at the specialist literature on free will, it is clear that there is disagreement about all of these things. Philosophers have variously characterized free will as the ability to do otherwise, decision-making in accord with reason, a mesh between one's actions and values or privileged desires, and so on.

These considerations suggest that we do better to characterize free will in some way that does not beg the question against the various accounts and the ensuing disagreements about its existence. One way to do this is to consider the how and the why of our concern for free will. If we start with why we are supposed to be worried about free will, we can move to consider what sorts of powers would be adequate to secure that thing.

Indeed, a cursory examination of the sprawling literature on free will reveals that free will is rarely presented as significant for its own sake.[3] More commonly, it is invoked as a key ingredient in some other, more readily apparent concern. We are usually told that free will matters because it is crucial to, for example, the truth of our beliefs about ourselves when we deliberate, our deservingness for moralized praise and blame, all of morality, the idea of human agency itself, or our general distinctiveness in the natural order.

The version of free will at stake in the present essay is this: free will is the power or capacity characteristic of agents, in virtue of which they become appropriate targets for moralized praise and blame. This is a "responsibility-centric" notion of free will. On this way of putting things, the stakes are whether we have the power required to license moralized praise and blame. The free will nihilist holds that we lack the sort of power necessary for moral responsibility, so that our inferences about responsibility are mostly false, our responsibility practices (including praising, blaming, and punishing) are unjustified, and our attitudes are unwarranted, even if inevitable.

One advantage of making explicit an understanding of free will as linked to responsibility, is that it anchors philosophical concerns in something comparatively concrete and undeniably important to our lives. This is not a sense of free will whose only implication is whether it fits with a given philosopher's particular speculative metaphysics. It is not a sense of free will that is arbitrarily attached to a particular religious framework. Instead, it is a notion of free will that understands its significance in light of the role or function it plays in widespread and recognizable forms of life.

There are two things to notice here. First, this way of characterizing free will doesn't rule out the possibility that, as Montague and Bargh suggest, free will requires something like substance dualism. Nor does it rule out Wegner's characterization of free will as nothing more than a kind of experience. What it does clarify, though, is what general sort of thing free will is supposed to be, or what is supposed to be important about the property of free will—i.e., it is supposed to be a power ordinarily necessary for culpability.

A second point concerns the scope of the account. Although a responsibility-centric notion of free will is plausibly the notion that animates at least a plurality of philosophical discussion under the label "free will," it is not the only notion with some claim to the label. I will have little to say about other notions, but by the end of this essay it should be clear that the basic lessons about alternatives to skeptical views about free will generalize across alternative construals of the role of free will.

What is at stake here is whether responsibility-centric versions of "no free will" views are warranted or true. There is no standard terminology to refer to such views. I will interchangeably use the phrases *free will skepticism, free will nihilism*, and *eliminativism about free will* to refer to views on which free will does not exist, and I will use the phrase *scientific free will skeptics* to refer to those who maintain that, on scientific grounds, we should conclude that free will does not exist.[4]

None of this unduly stacks the deck against the nihilist. In treating free will in roughly functionalist terms—in offering a specific approach that makes central its role for responsibility practices, judgments, and attitudes—traditional skeptical worries remain live. For all I have said, the role in light of which we understand free will may be incoherent. Or, it might be that nothing in the world can fill the role. Or, it might be filled, but on balance there are other reasons why we are better off not deploying a notion of free will in our linguistic and social practices. If so, then free will and moral responsibility nihilism or a related view might well follow. Accepting a responsibility-centric conception of free will does not guarantee the tenability of the ensuing first-order accounts of free will. What it does ensure, though, is that we are clear on the stakes, clear on the kind of power the nihilist is denying, and clear that our target concept is plausibly connected to the long-standing philosophical and scientific traditions concerned with free will.

II.

In this section, I present three challenges to standard forms of skepticism that purport to be grounded in scientific concerns. The first concerns difficulties in the invocation of determinism. The second concerns the widespread failure of scientists to see the view known as *compatibilism* as something other than verbal or semantic subterfuge. The third involves a basic challenge to simple forms of scientific reductionism. The overriding theme in this section is that it is difficult to get an interesting scientific conclusion about free will without helping yourself to a substantive—and usually contested—account of free will. Or, to put the point differently: if science drives your free will skepticism, you better be prepared to do a lot of philosophy too.

Determinism

There are many paths from science to free will skepticism. Perhaps the most venerable path goes through determinism. Although it is a less common refrain than it once was, one sometimes still hears assertions that science in general is deterministic.[5] For example, psychologists Lee and Harris have claimed that, "most scientists are intrinsically deterministic" (forthcoming, ms 3).[6] More reservedly, some merely claim that determinism describes some or another particular field of science. For example, neuroscientist Patrick Haggard has claimed that, "Neuroscience is fundamentally deterministic in its methods, its assumptions and its outlooks" (2011, 8).

Whatever else is true, on pain of denying standard interpretations of quantum mechanics, no scientists with passing familiarity with 20th century developments in physics should think determinism is an obvious feature of *every* part of the world subjected to scientific investigation. Of course, there is a minority of scientists and philosophers who have rejected the standard interpretations of quantum mechanics.[7] Doing so, however, requires a good deal of work and at the very least it involves swimming against the dominant scientific current of the time.

Moreover, many particular subfields (including neuroscience) provide no clear home for determinism either, despite Haggard's assertions. As his fellow neuroscientists Atmanscpacher and Rotter note, "the descriptions of brain behaviour currently provided by neuroscience depend on the level and context of the descriptions. There is no clear-cut evidence for ultimately determinate or ultimately stochastic brain behaviour. As a consequence, we see no solid neurobiological basis to argue either in favour of or against any fundamental determination or openness of human decisions and actions" (2011, 85).

Although appreciation of this point is not as widespread as it perhaps should be, there is growing recognition among neuroscientists and philosophers that whatever the temptation to presuppose lurking deterministic explanations in neuroscience models, nothing in the neuroscientific data or current models of it actually supports philosophically significant conceptions of determinism (Roskies 2006, 2010; Koch 2012, esp. ch.7).

Matters are not different in psychology more generally. There is virtually nothing in the experimental data to support deterministic generalizations of notable human behavior. It would be nothing short of a miracle if we were to regularly produce behavioral studies that isolated the variables that produce notable target behavior at rates in the 90-95 percent range—and this would still fall short of demonstrating determinism as it is conventionally understood.

So, whatever its venerable path to worries about free will, there are no easy generalizations to be had about science's deterministic significance. Scientists might yet give us reason for thinking determinism is true, but given the complexity of the issue in physics—where our most nuanced models of determinism are to be found—it seems unlikely that science will issue any definitive edicts about determinism anytime soon.

Compatibilism as a Definitional Gambit

The path to scientific skepticism is relatively straightforward if (A) one thinks that we face a choice between determinism on the one hand, and a form of non-deterministic agency on the other and (B) one thinks there is no good evidence that we are non-deterministic agents. In the philosophical literature, *libertarianism* is the name for the sort of free will that is incompatible with determinism. So, one might conclude that the dearth of evidence for libertarianism is sufficient warrant to conclude that free will does not exist.[8]

Even allowing that one can't show that determinism is true, what this familiar "free will *or* determinism" picture leaves out is, arguably, the most influential view in the 1000+ years in which people have been grappling with these issues. The alternative view is known as *compatibilism*, and it is the view on which free will is compatible with determinism. Compatibilism's string of proponents date back to at least the ancient Stoics. Unfortunately, recognition of compatibilism as a live possibility seems largely absent in typical scientific discussions of free will. Moreover, if compatibilism gets any airing at all among scientists, it is usually to dismiss it (Nahmias forthcoming-b; Mele forthcoming). Although there are plausibly diverse motivations involved in the dismissal of compatibilism, the motivation for dismissing it seems most often connected to the thought that compatibilism amounts to a kind of semantic subterfuge that sidesteps the real issue. So, for example, in this volume Susan Pockett claims that "Compatibilism is simply a definitional choice, and as such can not be either proved or disproved by any variety of science" (ch.15).

Pockett's claim provides an especially useful illustration in the present context because it brings together two threads of the scientific dismissal of compatibilism: (1) the idea that compatibilism is something of a definitional gambit, and (2) that the commitments of compatibilist theories are somehow insulated from or orthogonal to scientific matters, and thus, the core of the free will debate. Neither is tenable.

Consider the second idea, in which compatibilist accounts are cabined off from scientific matters and the core of the free will debate. As Pockett portrays it, this follows from the idea that compatibilism is a "definitional choice." If "definitional choice" just means "proposed definition" then this fact hardly suffices to show that compatibilist construals of free will are immune to scientific discomfirmation. To see why, consider a different sort of case where one might plausibly make a "definitional choice" but where it is manifestly clear that scientific findings impinge on the tenability of the choice.

Suppose I choose to define 'race' as a heritable biological kind. It does not follow that because the biological proposal for understanding race is a "definitional choice" that it can be neither proved nor disproved by any variety of science. Famously, scientists and philosophers have argued both for and against biological conceptions of race, and most of the involved participants have agreed that if we are clear about the definitional matter, we can show (or not) the existence of race, thus understood.[9]

Even if we can make non-trivial sense of the idea that compatibilism is somehow "definitional" it is hard to see how compatibilism entails isolation from scientific issues in the way Pockett claims.[10] Whether compatibilists models of agency can be squared with what we have learned from social, cognitive, and neuropsychology is something a good number of philosophers and scientists have been worried about.[11]

These concerns do not disappear if we shift from the general position of compatibilism to the particulars of individual compatibilist theories. Whether we have identifiable mechanisms for recognizing and responding to reasons (Fischer and Ravizza 1998), whether we have a general capacity to recognize moral reasons (Wallace 1994), whether we have the kind of self-knowledge required to be able to identify with our motives or values (Frankfurt 1971; Watson 1982), all these accounts invoke commitments vulnerable to experimental disconfirmation. If we could empirically demonstrate that our responsiveness to reasons was an illusion, or that we lack particular mechanisms to recognize reasons, or that we consistently lack robust self-knowledge of our motives and values, then we would, by those compatibilist accounts, lack free will. Contrary to Pockett's characterization of compatibilism as insulated from science, we should instead think that science can inform, threaten, and refine philosophical accounts of compatibilism.

Let's put aside the implications we might draw from the allegedly "definitional" nature of compatibilism. A more charitable way to characterize recurring doubts among scientists about compatibilism is to portray disputes between compatibilists and incompatibilists as engaged in something like David Chalmers' (2011) notion of a "verbal dispute." On Chalmers' account, "a dispute between two parties is verbal when the two parties agree on the relevant facts about a domain of concern and just disagree about the language used to describe that domain" (515). Perhaps the picture is this: there is consensus that we have the powers described by compatibilists. Whether such powers are labeled "free will" or not is a verbal dispute in the sense just given: we can call it free will, but the scientific status of compatibilist powers is hardly in dispute. What is in dispute, on the picture under consideration, is whether the additional powers postulated by libertarians of various stripes are scientifically plausible.[12]

As initially appealing as such a view of the free will problem might be, it importantly misconstrues the operative stakes in the bulk of serious work on free will over the past 40 years or so. What is (and has been) at stake in the compatibility debate is whether the powers identified by compatibilists are sufficient to support, justify, or explain attributions of responsibility (or the ability to do otherwise, or the ability to form true beliefs under deliberation—depending on the particular theorist's interests). If such powers are insufficient, then what we need to know is whether different powers—namely, the diverse powers invoked by various strands of incompatibilism—would be sufficient.

If the dispute were merely verbal, then the compatibility debate should have withered away once the involved parties recognized that the powers appealed to by compatibilists were different than those appealed to by libertarians, and that we could mark that difference by referring to "libertarian free will" and "compatibilist free will."[13] That hasn't happened, and for good reason. The disagreement between parties really is over *which* powers are sufficient to support the relevant practices, judgments, and attitudes. It is a disagreement about what sorts of agents we need to be for our suite of responsibility-characteristic phenomena to be in good standing. It is only with some grip on the answer to *that* question—what's required for moralized praising and blaming?—that we are in a position to evaluate whether we have such forms of agency. Incompatibilist and compatibilist accounts represent different camps in a substantive disagreement about that question.

Scientific verdicts about our agency typically help to resolve questions about free will only when coupled to a substantive (and usually contested) view about the requirements of free will. Given that one can't resolve this philosophical issue without doing some philosophy, it is better that such work be done straight on, rather than inadvertently.[14]

So, compatibilism is not a definitional gambit, and disputes with compatibilism are not merely verbal disputes. If one wants to show that science demonstrates the nonexistence of free will, one will have to contend with the richly developed compatibilist accounts of free will out there. To my knowledge, no scientist proclaiming the non-existence of free will has seriously undertaken this task.

Reduction and Sourcehood

Here is one way to characterize much of the foregoing: most interesting claims about what science does or does not show about the free will debate turn at least in part on substantive and frequently contested philosophical positions on free will. In some cases, though, the philosophical presuppositions are less apparent. Consider the recent remarks by distinguished biologist and member of the National Academy of the Sciences, Anthony Cashmore (2010). Cashmore claims that

> Many discussions about human behavior center around the relative importance of genes and environment, a topic often discussed in terms of nature versus nurture. In concentrating on this question of the relative importance of genes and environment, a crucial component of the debate is often missed: an individual cannot be held responsible for either his genes or his environment. From this simple analysis, surely it follows that individuals cannot logically be held responsible for their behavior. (4499)

At first blush, Cashmore's discussion seems to trade on a regress argument akin to the one that motivates Galen Strawson's views on the impossibility of moral responsibility (Strawson 1994). However, there are a variety of reasons to resist the conclusion that from non-responsibility for genes and environment we get non-responsibility for behavior.[15] Perhaps the most obvious is this: unless the particular inference is defended (which Cashmore doesn't try to do) it appears that he is simply helping himself to a dubious principle on which if the origin (or constituents) of something (responsible behavior) lacks a particular property, then the product (or constituted entity) lacks that property. At least as stated, that principle cannot be right. Such a principle would show that because hydrogen is not a fluid and refreshing to drink, water cannot thereby be a fluid and refreshing to drink.

So, it simply does not follow from Cashmore's "simple analysis" that individuals cannot "logically be held responsible for their behavior." But suppose we decide that this disagreement is a draw. Cashmore goes on to object that proponents of the view that we have free will simply fail to provide the kind of explanation that any serious account of free will should possess. He writes: "Whereas much is written claiming to provide an explanation for free will, such writings are invariably lacking any hint of molecular details concerning the mechanisms" (4499–4500).

Now Cashmore's engagement with philosophical accounts is fairly limited, if his references are any indication.[16] So, perhaps he just hasn't read the various accounts of, for example, the mechanisms of reasons-responsiveness or identification or value-coherence or quantum amplification or so on, that are thought to be involved in free will. Or, perhaps he is looking for a different kind of explanation. (Perhaps he means "molecular details" to mean "an account of the constituent parts of the ordinarily invoked notions" or perhaps he simply means *molecules*. The text is not clear on how this passage is meant.)

If Cashmore is simply unaware of the literature, then we can put his objection to the side. However, I suspect that he is giving expression to a deeper worry connected to broader issues in ontology. What I have in mind are worries about reductionism and the level of description at which the problem of free will arises.

I have speculated elsewhere that scientists are sometimes motivated by something philosophers call "source" intuitions, i.e., the thought that moral responsibility requires that we must be the ultimate origins of at least some strands of the causal nexus. On such accounts, free acts must be partly free of causal antecedents prior to the relevant decisions of the agent or the agent's free formulation of the relevant characterological inputs to that decision (Vargas 2009, forthcoming). For those who take such views to capture the essential element of free will, the requirement is that we must sometimes be, in some suitable fashion, the ultimate sources of what we do.

As a purely conceptual matter, there are a variety of ways we might satisfy that demand.[17] The important idea for scientific free will skeptics of the sort suggested by Cashmore is that scientific results impugn the possibility of satisfying the sourcehood requirement. The real worry, I'm suggesting, seems to be this: Cashmore and others are afraid that science shows that we are ultimately constituted by the same stuff as everything else. As a consequence, the only powers we have are those afforded to us by those (physical) things that constitute us. Since humans are composed of lower-level physical entities—molecules, as a start, but more fundamentally atoms, and even more fundamentally energy—the powers we have are limited to the powers of our constituents. Since those elements and their powers are just part of the universal causal nexus, there is no room left over for humans possessing some special, originating or ultimate source of what they do. So, free will and moral responsibility must be rejected.

On this picture, then, it is a broadly reductionist impulse that motivates a great deal of free will and moral responsibility skepticism among scientists.[18] As they see it, the arc of the scientific worldview shows that there are no good hooks on which to hang the hope for sourcehood. Substance dualism is untenable, but so is nearly any other approach that tries to find a place for special human powers for originating causes in the universe.

Questions of reduction and emergence are thorny issues, and they involve a good deal more than debates about free will. However, there is reason to be skeptical about versions of reductionism that proceed on the basis that Cashmore and others have offered. The operative idea in Cashmore seems to be that if we don't get to molecular details in an account of the mechanisms of responsibility, we aren't properly explaining things. It is not clear why a molecular-level account (as opposed to, say, an account at the level of cognitive mechanisms on one hand, or atomic properties on another) is privileged.

The impulse to treat "lower" level explanations as privileged may be well founded in some cases. However, matters are much less simple with social-normative notions like moral responsibility (and on the present account, free will). The more plausible view of these things is that our explanatory interests and social practices play some role in settling what is a relevant and irrelevant explanation for social-normative notions.

For example, suppose a Martian came to visit and proceeded to invite us to write something up about the nature of touchdowns. We comply, writing all the customary things, such as "a touchdown is worth 6 points" and "touchdowns are earned when a player in possession of the ball during play breaks the plane of the opposing goal with the ball" and so on. We would be surprised if the Martian replied to this treatise by saying (or telepathically articulating): "Whereas much is written claiming to provide an explanation for touchdowns, such writings are invariably lacking any hint of molecular details concerning the mechanisms."

At this point, we would have good reason to insist that the Martians are looking for the wrong sort of explanation. For some kinds of explanations, we might say, what is at stake are relatively high-level phenomena. They might be *constituted* by lower-level things, but the *relevant* properties and their significance to us are simply not to be found at those lower levels. If you go looking for the core of an explanation of touchdowns in the molecules of the players, the field, and the pigskin, you are just looking in the wrong place.

Of course, it is unremarkable that biologists are interested in biological things, that physicists are interested in physical things, and that sociologists are interested in social things. But there's an old carpenter's lesson here: we shouldn't think everything is a nail just because we are carrying a hammer. Perhaps Cashmore really is interested in the biology of moral responsibility for its own sake. That's fine. However, at least for any conception of agency that is interested in the powers that license praise and blame, biology is relevant only as a realizer or constituent, and not as the principal source of puzzles and solutions. At first blush, the interesting agentive and social-normative dimensions of free will and moral responsibility should be higher order properties. As in football, the molecular details matter less, and our high-level concerns may tolerate mutiple, distinct realizers when it comes to the molecular constituents of fields, football players, end zones, free will, and moral responsibility.

One *could* ask questions about the biology of free will, just as one could ask about the molecular features of touchdowns. Sometimes, the answers to such questions will be interesting—for example, the molecular constituents of footballs might have some role to play in whether touchdowns are more or less likely in some conditions and not others. Again, our theories of free will and moral responsibility are not obviously altogether insulated from scientific developments.

What will make scientific developments interesting and informative for free will and responsibility, though, is *how* they connect to the social-normative roles that drive the basic philosophical problem. As a matter of framing the general free will problem—what powers suffice to license moralized praising and blaming?—starting from biology, physics, or some other sub-agential science is an altogether circuitous path to discoveries about what's at stake. Moreover, as we have seen, such an approach hardly avoids taking uncontested stands on a wide range of substantive philosophical issues—including the possibility of emergent causal powers, whether free will has a sourcehood requirement, how that requirement should be construed, and so on.

In sum, it really is difficult to go from science to free will skepticism without taking a stand on substantive, usually disputed philosophical matters.

III.

There is something powerfully appealing about free will nihilism, despite the shortcomings in the particular claims by scientists. Free will appears to be an artifact of a prior conception of the world, the sort of thing that would not be taken seriously if we had not inherited it from important cultural and moral authorities.

Such thoughts may be driven, in part, by the sense that close inspection of the apparently distinctive powers of humans reveals that they are not radically disconnected from the physical nature of the world. This fact alone can be unsettling to those whose image of humans is that they are radically set apart from nature. Indeed, reflection on the more general trajectory of the sciences may fuel the worry that free will is just another instance of metaphysical nonsense that the sciences gradually expunge from "the manifest image" of ourselves—that is, our widely received, pre-scientific self-conception.

These are potent considerations against any case for free will. Thus, even if we have reason to find wanting the standard paths to free will skepticism, it is not hard to believe that science threatens *something* that seems quite important to us. The question, then, is what we are to say about these matters, given dissatisfaction about the familiar paths to skepticism on the one hand, and on the other hand, uneasiness about supposing that science changes nothing. One path is to cast about for a new challenge from some or another branch of science. Perhaps we will find that there is some further distinct scientific threat to free will, unreliant on the sorts of claims canvassed thus far. Although I cannot hope to vindicate the claim here, attention to the literature on these issues strongly suggests that the recurring lesson herein tends to generalize: there is no clear path from science to free will nihilism that does not involve significant philosophical engagement.[19]

A second path is to shift gears, accepting the need to hitch free will skepticism to philosophical commitments. That is, we could pursue philosophical free will nihilism. As I noted at the outset, the scope of my arguments in this paper leave untouched the possibility that there might be good philosophical grounds for adopting free will nihilism. So, one could elect to take up the familiar philosophical issues, among them, debates about the metaphysics of agency, the analysis of capacities, the conceptual demands of freedom and responsibility, the whether and how of a raft of thought experiments, and so on. Doing so is no guarantee of a skeptical conclusion, though. Indeed, skeptical views remain something of a minority view in the literature. Antecedent to doing the work, there is no special reason to think that philosophical free will skepticism will be sustained.

There is a third path. It is a path that accepts the skeptic's concerns about our manifest image, while insisting that we can retain a commitment to free will if we refashion our understanding of it. This is the *revisionist* path. Revisionism about free will is the view that either: (A) we've misunderstood the nature of free will, or (B) we have misunderstood what it requires, or (C) at least all the conceptual and practical work for which free will has been invoked can be done with forms of agency that are compatible with the going scientific worldview.

To appreciate the basic idea of revisionism, it helps to first distinguish between an account of what we think about some domain or idea (e.g., free will) and what we ought to think about it. Call an account of the former *diagnostic*, and an account of the latter *prescriptive*. An account is revisionist to the extent to which the prescriptive account recommends a view about the subject matter that conflicts with aspects of the diagnostic account. We can say that an account is revisionist when it tells us that what we ought to think is in conflict with what we do think about that thing. Ergo: a revisionist account of free will is at odds with how we think about free will.

What making this distinction permits us to see is that the ordinary grist for the free will skeptic's mill tends to license conclusions only about how we think about free will. If I give you an example of how a universe, deterministically characterized, undermines our convictions about free will, I've only shown you something about how you and I think about free will. It remains an open question whether you and I have accurate beliefs about free will and/or whether we should change our minds about what free will requires.

In the absence of some independent account of why our ordinary convictions about free will should be thought to tell us about the Real, True, Essential nature of free will, we should only think that our reactions to experiments—whether imagined or real—tell us only about the best diagnostic theory of free will. They do not, by themselves, settle what the best prescriptive account is of how we ought to understand free will, all things considered.

One might protest that any revisionist about free will needs to explain why we should think that free will is, or could be, different than we ordinarily suppose. Why should we tolerate the idea that we somehow have importantly mistaken beliefs about free will? Isn't this just a dodge?

In reply, there are a variety of reasons why we should take seriously the possibility that the best prescriptive account of free will could conflict with how you and I intuitively understand free will. First, there is just the fact that there might not even be much agreement in our linguistic community about what free will means. You and I constitute a pretty limited data set, and it might turn out that there are important divergences in our linguistic community, or that there are notable differences across communities.[20] If so, then we would face questions about whether some or another of these usages are better or worse, and on what grounds we could plump for one or another notion of free will.

Second, it might turn out that we are confusing the metaphysics of free will (what it requires) with the "epistemological pragmatics" of our practices, that is, with the heuristics we use given our limited knowledge about people's intentions and beliefs and the like (Vargas 2006). Disentangling our conception of free will's ontology from our cognitive shortcuts used to track it in the real world is no easy task. And, to the best of my knowledge, no one has a particularly good account of when ordinary judgments about some philosophically contested matter reflect an assessment of only the metaphysics of the matter and when it amounts to the fallible deliverances of our (correctly or incorrectly) deployed epistemological heuristics.[21]

Third, there are reasonably familiar pictures in the philosophy of language for thinking that at least some terms function in ways that don't entirely depend on how the speaker intends to use the word. At least sometimes, I don't need to know what water is, in order to refer to water. It might well turn out that I have some deeply confused or mistaken beliefs about water (that it is a basic, indivisible substance, for example). Nevertheless, water exists and I can talk about it, despite my confused beliefs.

This sort of picture—a broadly referentialist picture—is not the only one that tolerates divergence between how we think about something and what it is. Suitably sophisticated "internalist" accounts allow for some flexion between beliefs and the world, as well. For example, one can hold that a term refers to whatever property it is that renders most platitudinous sentences about some subject matter true. Here, reference derives in part from what we think about things, but also from the fit our usages have with the properties of the world. In either case, there is room for 'free will' to pick out something distinct from our naive uses of the term.

Fourth, it might turn out that our traditional or naive interest in free will (assuming it is reasonably unified), doesn't uniquely underpin anything practically significant (say, deservingness for praise and blame). So, for example, suppose that *if* we had a libertarian form of agency it would suffice to justify praising and blaming. Even if we discovered we lacked libertarian free will, we might yet discover that some other form of agency or some other feature about us and our practices justifies deservingness for praise and blame. If so, whether we keep free will talk (in the present responsibility-centric sense) or not appears more a matter of convention than anything substantive about philosophy or science.

To be sure, I haven't here shown that any of these things are indeed the case in a way that definitively demonstrates the viability of revisionism about free will. That's a case I have tried to make elsewhere (Vargas 2013a). Nevertheless, the considerations presented here weigh heavily against our simply supposing that revisionism is a non-starter. If that's right, then skeptics about free will have a good deal more work to do before they have shown that we must accept nihilism about free will.

What do revisionist accounts look like? I will say more about this in a moment, but for now let us just assume they will look a lot like any number of compatibilist accounts, e.g., emphasizing elements like reasons-responsiveness, identification, or what have you. The main difference is that the revisionist does not claim that such accounts capture ordinary notions of freedom, but are instead replacement accounts, or accounts of what we ought to mean, all things considered. Indeed, the revisionist thinks that the skeptic may well be right about something important: science (or philosophy, or what have you) shows that our ordinary understanding of free will is flawed, and compatibilists are wrong to claim otherwise.

With these pieces in place, we can now begin to see how the dialectic between the revisionist and skeptic unfolds. If the free will skeptic wants to show that free will doesn't exist, as opposed to the revisionist's claim that free will exists but is (say) more like what compatibilists talk about, we need to know *why* the skeptic thinks we should conclude that free will doesn't exist.

One instructive reply is provided by a widely-cited paper by Greene and Cohen (2004) that makes just that case. They argue that "when it comes to the issue of free will itself, hard determinism is mostly correct. Free will, as we ordinarily understand it, is an illusion" (1783).[22] The core idea in their paper is that the emerging picture in neuroscience threatens free will and responsibility as we intuitively understand those terms, and that despite the law's neutrality about the metaphysics of free will, a growing appreciation of the deterministic threat will lead us to jettison our commitments to free will, responsibility, and retribution. They conclude that this will ultimately reshape the law on matters of punishment.

Perhaps neuroscience can and does threaten these things in just the way they claim. The operative question here is *why* neuroscience threatens these things. On this point, Greene and Cohen offer a familiar villain: determinism. They claim that "contrary to legal and philosophical orthodoxy determinism really does threaten free will and responsibility as we intuitively understand them" (1780). To illustrate, they introduce the idea of "Mr. Puppet."

Mr. Puppet is characterized as an engineered person, created with a particular personality and behavior profile through powerful control of his genetics and environment. Mr. Puppet's architects ensure that he has the relevant experiences and opportunities so that, by design, he commits a murder during a failed drug deal. Greene and Cohen contend that Mr. Puppet ought not be held legally responsible because once we realize the engineered nature of his actions, "it is hard to think of him as anything more than a pawn" (1780).

This is an elegant, intuitively powerful argument. However, as it stands, it does not show that determinism undermines responsibility. For starters, as Greene and Cohen themselves note, the example doesn't actually guarantee an outcome in the way we would expect from ideal deterministic control. Mr. Puppet's architects, they note, have a 95 percent success rate in controlling his action. Perhaps there is measurement noise, or some other error in prediction and control of a deterministic system. Still, even if we assume the control is deterministic, a similar example would show that it isn't determinism that is doing the undermining of responsibility. If Mr. Puppet's architects simply had a hard metaphysical limit of 99.9999 percent effective control over Mr. Puppet, given otherwise maximal control over Mr. Puppet's constitution and environment, that degree of control would presumably make us wary of assigning responsibility even if, by stipulation, Mr. Puppet's behavior was not deterministic.

So, if an example like Mr. Puppet can show a threat under both determinism and indeterminism, it looks like a mistake to present *determinism* as the threat. Instead, something like a regress worry arising from *causal embeddedness* or "being embedded in a system of causes" seems to be the root of the problem. To their credit, Greene and Cohen are not entirely insensitive to this point, sometimes appealing to the "mechanistic" nature of decision-making as the real threat.[23] (Although, notice that even if we somehow concluded that Mr. Puppet's architects could control his behavior through ectoplasmic manipulation or emotional vibrations in the ether, the same exculpatory intuitions get going. Mechanism, understood in a physicalist sense seems—like determinism—a special case of worries about causal embeddedness.)

Here, though, some of the revisionist tools mentioned above can do some work for us. Granting that we have the reactions Greene and Cohen describe for the Mr. Puppet case, this does not yet tell us anything about free will or moral responsibility, or what prescriptive account we should have of it. What it does tell us about are our received, i.e., naive *judgments* in this particular case. It is, at best, understood as a diagnostic account that is (one suspects) being taken to license a prescriptive account.

The move from diagnosis to prescription is not so easily warranted. Suppose that we could get convergence about both the substance of our judgments about the Mr. Puppet case, and that we could explain the psychological mechanisms that yield that judgment. For all that, we would not have obviously shown anything about whether people have free will. After all, showing that naive judgments about physics fall into recognizable patterns because of identifiable psychological mechanisms of judgments does not show anything about physics. So, why would showing the same about our judgments of free will show us anything about free will?

There are a number of ways to appreciate the force of this point. Consider why highlighting the fact of causal embeddedness might undermine our existing judgments of responsibility. It could be that we have residual worries about the possibility of agency in the face of reductionism about causes. However, as we've seen in the discussion of sourcehood concerns and Cashmore's concern for molecular details, there is a lot of heavy philosophical lifting to be done if someone wants to make the case that such judgments are *correct*.

A different potential source of our exculpatory intuitions may lurk in the idea that Mr. Puppet is controlled or manipulated. The scope of control and manipulative power by Mr. Puppet's architects may drive our intuitions simply because of how remote and unusual such powers are from the circumstances in which we ordinarily deploy our responsibility judgments. It may also be the case that we are particularly disposed (whether by evolution or socialization) to detect "cheaters," or social norm violators.[24] For that matter, the name "Mr. Puppet" presumably primes our "not responsible" judgments. I imagine if we described the agent as Will Power, this would color our reactions in various ways. Finally, some of our reluctance to ascribe responsibility may simply be a byproduct of the habit of looking to find a best candidate for responsibility, generally ignoring lesser candidates. However, responsibility is not a zero-sum thing. You and I might both be fully responsible for some outcome, without either of us being solely responsible. So, to some extent, our thinking about this case may reflect more about sloppy habits of mind than careful thinking about the conditions of responsibility.

The proponent of prescription-by-diagnosis theorizing might provide replies to each of these objections in turn, but the revisionist has more to say. Let us even suppose that we can show that convergence in judgments that Mr. Puppet is not responsible does not hinge on the errors I have noted. Before we accept the truth of our initial judgment, we might wonder whether the case has been under-described. Has Mr. Puppet (or better, Will Power) been subjected to manipulations that rob him of the requisite powers to recognize and respond to reasons? If they have, then why isn't *that* the reason he is not responsible?

If Mr. Puppet/Will Power does retain his powers to recognize and respond to reasons, then why shouldn't we think he is, after all, responsible?[25] For the sake of argument, let's suppose that we persist in thinking Mr. Puppet is not responsible. We still might ask whether something about Mr. Puppet's circumstances unduly burdened the operations of those powers. Ordinary dollops of self-control tend to fare badly in light of extraordinary temptations. If a problem with Mr. Puppet is that his ordinary degree of self-control has been subjected to extraordinary stress or temptation, then this might be the source of exculpatory impulses, depending on what it is that we think praise, blame, and responsibility are *for*, what they *express*, and what they *do*.

It should be evident that there are lots of places to get off the train going from diagnosis to prescription. For all that, though, one might insist that the troubles with skepticism are just as strong a reason to adopt agnosticism as they are to adopt revisionism.

It is here that the onus is on any account with revisionist aspirations. If we wish to concede that there are problematic threads to our ordinary conception of free will, while still insisting that the notion can be fruitfully recast, the revisionist needs to offer an account of the basis of the revision.

IV.

There is no single way to construct a revisionist account. In the previous section, I noted that a revisionist account can look a lot like compatibilism, absent the pretension to describe our convictions as we find them. Nevertheless, given that standard compatibilist accounts were constructed with non-revisionist aspirations, it might turn out that the best revisionist account will have some distinct contours. In what follows, I present a revisionist framework that is indebted to many compatibilist accounts, but that has its own distinctive features as well.

Start with the idea of why we care about free will. What I claimed at the outset was that, at least in many corners, the stakes are moralized praising and blaming and related assessments of moral responsibility. If free will is going to be worth the name, it will need to be the sort of thing that helps make sense of those practices and judgments. However, the skeptical scientists are right: if free will requires substance dualism, the power to initiate causal chains *ex nihilo*, choices completely causally independent of features of the world, or even decisions that always involve alternative possibilities, it seems unlikely that we have such powers. It might be nice if we did have such powers, but there is little in the book of science that would lead a disinterested viewer into thinking that we obviously have such powers. So, the question is whether anything else could be the sort of thing that helps makes sense of those practices and judgments. If there is, then we have a good candidate for a revised notion of free will, i.e., one that is not exactly what we had hoped for, but one that can do what we want from a notion of free will.

One power that we plausibly have is that we recognize and respond to reasons. What this power comes to, its limits, the circumstances of its best use, and so on, are all difficult matters. Nevertheless, the existence of this power is a familiar enough feature of our lives. If standard scientific views about us turn out to be correct, this power is physically instantiated. It need not be a property of an ectoplasmic substance or an immaterial soul. Rather, it is most plausibly a power of physical systems that, at least in principle, can be studied in considerable detail.

We need a few more ideas. One is that there is a class of reasons that are especially important to creatures like us. Call them *moral considerations*, or reasons that are tied to a characteristic suite of concerns we have, presumably derived from our imperfectly rational but social natures and the patterns of emotional reactions and judgments that follow in their wake.[26] How exactly we should characterize moral considerations, whether ordinary understandings of morality are accurate, and what exactly defines the boundaries of the moral are important questions. The present account, however, only requires that at least sometimes we recognize moral considerations and can be moved by them. And, in the ordinary course of things, normal mature adults are such that we possess the ability to recognize and respond to moral considerations, and this is not a fact to which we are indifferent. We value this capacity in ourselves and in others, we seek to cultivate it in our children, and we generally regard it as desirable that this capacity should be maintained and even flourish. The capacity to recognize and suitably respond to moral considerations is, in many respects, a prerequisite for us to be taken seriously as fully participating members of the social sphere. We care a great deal about being seen as creatures who, to a suitable degree, recognize and respond to those considerations that our groups regard as morally significant.

Moral considerations may well be explicable in terms of more basic and familiar mechanisms. When I see you are hurt, and stop to help you, we can say that I saw a reason to stop and aid you. That explanation might decompose into more detailed explanations about the mechanisms by which I perceive and evaluate the pain of others, the interaction of those systems with my attention and sense of time pressure, and so on. At least in form, though, these do not explain away our acting for moral reasons so much as they explain what it is to act for moral reasons.

Here is the final element we need: our ordinary practices of moralized praise and blame, the norms emphasizing how we treat each other, and our reactive dispositions to violations and supererogation in light of those norms, over time support, reinforce, extend, and fine-tune our capacity to recognize and respond to moral considerations. This does not mean that they do so in each and every instance. Nor does it mean that our responsibility norms are or should be baldly consequentialist. Indeed, part of the efficacy of these norms plausibly rely on their having robust backwards-looking elements and licensing retributive attitudes. The point is that we collectively have an interest in these norms and practices having currency in our societies. They do something for us, something that we should be loathe to lose—at least so long as we value the form of agency they support and, in time, refine.

I can now state the substantive proposal baldly: free will should be understood as the capacity to recognize and suitably respond to moral considerations. The account is revisionist, but it is not unprincipled. The capacity to recognize and suitably respond to moral considerations matters in part because it is valuable to us to be those kinds of agents who are good at such things. However, the capacity also satisfies an important desideratum. It is the sort of thing, the presence and absence of which, suffices to support the relevant roles in the characteristic patterns of judgments and practices we associate with responsibility. Where that capacity is absent we typically lack grounds for holding someone responsible, and when it is present we typically have good reason to praise and blame. Crudely put, praise and blame, as mechanisms that enhance an already present capacity, cannot fulfill that function when that capacity to recognize and respond to moral considerations is absent.

These brief remarks are only a suggestive sketch at what a fully developed revisionist account can say about the basis on which we might recast our understanding of free will and moral responsibility. The point here, though, is that such accounts exist, and they offer a good deal of what the free will skeptic insists on (Vargas 2011a, 2013a). For example, such accounts allow that contemporary science may threaten our naive view of ourselves. They also allow that compatibilism is inadequate, at least as a theory of how many of us, at least sometimes, think about free will. Moreover, the positive, revisionist aspect of the account does not ask us to pretend that free will is some anti-natural, mysterious counter-causal force. Instead, it is the kind of thing that may well be distinctive of us, but that is nevertheless entirely natural in its composition.

Science also retains a role and remains a potential threat on the account just sketched. It may yet turn out that the kinds of powers required to support our practices are insufficiently had, even on the best revisionist account. Or, we might learn that our practices only undermine the forms of agency we find morally salient. These are matters that cannot be settled by moral philosophy alone, and on these and related matters the discoveries of science will be vital for our understanding of our moral world.

This is not to say that this account does everything we might have hoped. It will not give us back our immaterial souls or our contra-causal freedom, if that's what we thought free will required. But it does get us most or even all the things for which we wanted those powers, including an explanation of why we can and should praise and blame. Revisionist free will might not be what we thought we were looking for, but it is exactly what we need, and science has not given us a reason to doubt that we have it.

V.

The principal task of this essay has not been to muster a sustained defense of the idea that there is, in fact, a set of powers and practices sufficient to justify moralized praising and blaming and ascriptions of free will. What I hope to have done is to have offered some reasons why those inclined to scientific skepticism about free will should, at worst, only embrace agnosticism, and more optimistically, may find cause to adopt a revisionist picture of free will and responsibility.

In any event, it should be clear that several familiar paths to scientific skepticism about free will are deeply problematic in ways their proponents tend not to appreciate. Moreover, there are alternatives to skepticism. For all I have said, revisionist alternatives may yet prove unsatisfying. However, there are practical reasons to aspire to revisionism over nihilism. What the free will skeptic typically claims is that we should abandon our belief in free will. As a conceptual matter, we should be careful about dispensing with ideas that are at the center of so many aspects of our social worlds. However, some experimental data suggests that disbelieving in free will promotes antisocial behavior.[27] If that is right, then we have special reason to be careful about adopting nihilism without giving revisionism a lengthy hearing.

I began by noting that it seems apparent to many that our manifest image is defective in deep, perhaps fundamental ways. Although I have only gestured at it here, it is plausible to think that there are good reasons for insisting that there is a morally central, socially vital, and conceptually defensible set of powers we have that can legitimate familiar practices of moralized praising and blaming (Vargas 2013a, especially chapters 5 and 8). If this latter idea is right, then a scientifically plausible account of free will is not going to be precisely what ordinarily people—and most free will skeptics—tend to think it is. Rather, a scientifically credible notion of free will will have to be revisionist, departing in specific and principled ways from strands of our troubled, fragmented ways of thinking about free will.

This still leaves us with a lot to learn from scientific work on agency. But science about the nature and limits of human agency is not the end of the free will and responsibility story any more than it was the end of the water story, the story about race, the story about morality, or the story about legality. Depending on how we think about various social and normative issues, scientific developments will impinge on those stories, and maybe even threaten familiar equilibrium points for our thinking. Nevertheless, the details of our normative interests and practices seem here to play a special role in shaping the target of our metaphysical concerns. For example, rather than concluding, as Greene and Cohen do, that knowing the causes of someone's behavior necessarily undermines our conviction that someone deserves punishment (1783), it might turn out that knowing the grounds for punishment, doing the partly *normative* work of reflecting on the justification of punishment, can firm up our commitment to punish in some cases and not others. Science might someday tell us which of those cases falls into what categories, but this will be a collaborative result, not an edict about punishment handed down solely from a lab bench.

On this picture, rather than free will being a notion disposed of by good science, free will turns out to be an issue whose shape and nature is better understood by science. None of this is to deny the possibility that there are genuine threats (from science and philosophy both) to free will. However, on the view I have sketched, the structure of scientific threats is less sweeping. Instead, it will be more about whether in these circumstances we plausibly have those powers, and whether this condition or syndrome impairs those capacities. These are typically accounts of pockets of our world, rather than accounts of the global scenery. Threats to high-level, normatively structured social phenomena are partly a matter of science, but they also remain the stuff of philosophy.

At the outset, I noted that it is something of a puzzle why revisionist-style views of free will remain the path less taken by scientists. Many scientists (including Cashmore, Montague, and Pockett) work in fields where the progress of science became possible in large part because of the willingness of researchers to entertain the thought that various familiar (if somewhat mysterious) notions could be re-written by what we learn from experimental studies of the world. What it is to be alive, the nature of the mind, and the relationship of bodies to action-initiation, were all notions that were retained and re-written in light of scientific developments. We did not ultimately jettison commitment to the mind at the first hint of difficulties with substance dualism. And, of course, we did not despair that water never existed when its indivisibility was in doubt. Why then should we do differently with free will?

There were, of course, those who thought we should do without talk about minds, mental states, causes, and so on. Moreover, there have been concepts that we have ultimately discarded as not worth saving or re-writing. Nevertheless, it seems altogether contrary to the scientific spirit to neither consider what evidence there is about actual convictions (whether folk or specialist), nor to allow for the possibility that perhaps we need to revise our understanding of free will.

There is reason to end on an optimistic note. Despite the tide of work that presumes that conflict with science always entails elimination, there are sometimes hints that at least some scientists can be sensitive to the ways in which our interests in free will may be broader than the explanatory interests of particular scientific subfields.

In that vein, John Bargh sometimes provides a model of how one might reasonably endorse limited forms of skepticism. Bargh, for example, has claimed that we do not need free will "at the psychological level" to explain a range of psychological phenomena that free will has, he thinks, been historically invoked to explain (Bargh 2008, 143-45). Framing things in this manner allows for the possibility that there might be other roles or purposes for which it might make sense to admit ongoing utility to a notion of free will. If so, then a conception of free will tied to licensing moralized praise and blame can be compatible with an account of the psychology of action initiation which, by itself, need not posit an account of free will. This is, I think, one way in which serious psychological and neuroscientific work can coexist with serious philosophical work, even aspiring to be mutually informed by one another.[28]

NOTES

1. I am oftentimes skeptical that there is much use in talking about science, as though it were a single, unified thing with a consistent ontology across its fields. Nevertheless, it is striking how similar the arguments of scientists are about the non-existence of free will, whatever their field. So, despite my reservations about there being a uniform thing that is "scientific" skepticism about free will, I will use the phrase to refer to the collection of individual views of scientists that free will does not exist. In what follows, however, I try to focus on individual claims by particular scientists instead of appealing to generalizations about entire fields of scientific practice.

2. This is a point that has been emphasized in Mele (forthcoming) and by Eddy Nahmias (2010), among others. If one looks at the data on folk beliefs, things are interestingly mixed about what people believe about free will—but you wouldn't know it from scientists discussions of why some or another bit of science shows the non-existence of free will.

3. The point here is not that no one has ever thought free will was significant in and of itself, or that it could not be separated from other concerns that we have. The claim here is only about the ordinary paths to a concern about what is evidently a metaphysical, or at least traditionally philosophical claim.

4. The differences between views on which such non-existence is necessary, contingent, certain, or uncertain is immaterial for present purposes. However, there remains room to make use of greater terminological sensitivity to modal differences, e.g., holding that a skeptic might doubt the existence of free will, without actually believing in the non-existence of free will, or insisting that one kind of eliminativist might think free will is impossible, whereas another might think it is possible but not actual. I see nothing to be gained by insisting on these distinctions in the present context.

5. Here's a standard philosophical characterization of determinism. Let determinism stand for the following thesis: the state of the universe at any prior time and the actual laws of nature are sufficient for the state of the universe at any later time.

6. I take it they mean, roughly, that most scientists are committed to scientific explanations being deterministic, or even more ambitiously, that all events in the world are deterministically caused.

7. One prominent example is Honderich (1988).

8. Elsewhere, I have argued against libertarianism on grounds that it does not have the evidence it needs in favor of the requirements it posits. See Vargas (2013a, 52–72).

9. It does not follow that there is agreement about the definitional matter, what the folk notion of race is, and whether biologically useful phenomena map on to the folk notion (Spencer 2012, forthcoming).

10. She writes that "nothing can kill compatibilist free will" (ms 10) and elsewhere she has written that "Compatibilism is not interested in how a behavior is caused—it simply states that, in the absence of external (and arguably also internal) compulsion, acts are said to be freely willed. In intellectual terms this is a relatively weak definition" (Pockett 2007, 292) and "Philosophical compatibilists define free will in such a way that science is irrelevant. They concentrate purely on whether or not there were constraints on a particular action or whether the actor was 'free' to choose his own course. Constraints in this sense can be either external or internal." (284) These latter two characterizations of compatibilism would come as a great surprise to most self-identified compatibilists I know, even among the most enthusiastic defenders of the claim that "nothing can kill compatibilist free will."

11. For a sampling, see Doris (2002, forthcoming), Mele (2008, 2009, 2012b), Levy (2011), Nahmias (2007, 2010), Nelkin (2005), Roskies (2006, 2008, 2010), and Vargas (2013b).

12. Pocket claims that incompatibilism requires that "causal determinism [is] an illusion" but goes on to claim that libertarianism is distinguished from incompatibilist free will because it demands acts with "no physical antecedents" (ms 4). This way of characterizing things has the startling consequence that all event-causal libertarians and most physicalist agent causal libertarians are not libertarians.

13. For reservations about the recent uptick in usage of this distinction, see van Inwagen (2008). For a reply, in which I deploy something like what Chalmers calls "the subscript gambit" see Vargas (2011b). See also Chalmers (2011, 532).

14. For discussion of the difficulty of drawing substantive conclusions about various aspects of the free will problem from psychological research, see Doris and Murphy (2007), Nelkin (2005), Nahmias (2007), and Vargas (2013b).

15. For prominent responses to the strands of Strawson's work that embrace free will nihilism, see Clarke (2005) and Fischer (2006b). One difficulty with a regression principle is that it commits us to responsibility being essentially impossible. However, there are considerations in the philosophy of language that weigh against any picture that holds that responsibility is "essentially impossible." Briefly: disagreements about the meaning and requirements of "free will" and "moral responsibility" cut against the plausibility of any armchair-derived proposal for responsibility being an essentially impossible property, and essentially impossible properties lack suitable "explanatory depth" for the involved practices, so that even if we had once referred to something impossible we would have likely shifted to some nearby property that actually obtains (Hurley 2000; Vargas 2011a, 466).

16. He cites some work by Dennett and Searle. Dennett's work is obviously a reasonable place for a scientist to learn about philosophical work on free will, but the Searle text he cites has almost nothing to do with free will and moral responsibility.

17. Substance dualism and agent causation are some of the more prominent approaches.

18. To my knowledge, Eddy Nahmias and his collaborators were the first to consistently articulate this sort of concern in the contemporary free will debate (Nahmias et al. 2007).

19. There are a number of candidates lurking out there. One could think that, for example, epiphenomenalism is free will's silver bullet, or that automaticity, or situationism present more powerful challenges. I agree that they are challenges. I also think they have already largely been met, but again, that the details require taking substantive positions on philosophical

issues. See, among others, Doris (forthcoming), Mele (2008, 2009, 2012b), Nahmias (2007, 2010), Nelkin (2005), and Vargas (2013b).

20. The former has become increasingly plausible in light of experimental work (Nahmias 2011a; Sarkissian et al. 2010). The latter has been defended by Sommers (2012).

21. One might deny that our metaphysical commitments and our epistemological pragmatics can yield distinct answers. That would be a most fortuitous discovery. In many ordinary cases, our commitments about the nature of some thing ("water is H20") turns out to be rarely useful. In contrast, philosophically looser but practically efficient thoughts like "that wet, clear stuff that is refreshing to drink" tends to be relied upon a good deal, and a useful guide to finding water outside of bars.

22. In context, it appears that the "mostly correct" claim about hard determinism doesn't reflect doubts about the existence of determinism but confidence that responsibility, understood in terms of punishment, can persist.

23. "We submit that [questions about free will and desert] which seem so important today, will lose their grip in an age when the mechanical nature of human decision-making is fully appreciated" (1781) and "We do not wish to imply that neuroscience will inevitably put us in a position to predict any given action based on a neurological examination. Rather, our suggestion is simply that neuroscience will eventually advance to the point at which the mechanistic nature of human decision-making is sufficiently apparent to undermine the force of dualist/libertarian intuitions" (1785, n.6).

24. Thanks to Eddy Nahmias for this point.

25. As a matter of ordinary patterns of judgments about manipulation cases, it is not clear that the folk aren't compatibilists, at least sometimes. There is some evidence that even manipulated agents with intact reasoning mechanisms are sometimes judged to be responsible (Feltz 2013).

26. Talk of morality is not intended to be supernatural. Understand morality as naturalistically as you like. However, if you aren't a naturalist about morality, it seems reasonable to assume that you don't share the familiar scientific worries about free will and moral responsibility.

27. This is a point made in Nahmias (2011b). Nahmias argues for this in light of some interesting results detailed in Vohs and Schooler (2008) and Baumeister et al. (2009).

28. I'm indebted to Eddy Nahmias for many conversations about these things over the years, and for feedback on this paper. His influence on my thinking about these matters is considerable. Thanks, too, to Gregg Caruso, Daniel Speak, and Stephanie Vargas for helpful feedback on an earlier draft of this paper.

Chapter Eleven

Free Will and Error

Shaun Nichols

1. BACKGROUND

A growing body of empirical evidence indicates that people think that their choices aren't determined (Nichols and Knobe 2007; Sarkissian et al. 2010). It is not just that they don't have the belief that their choices are determined. Rather, they positively think that their choices are not determined. And this belief is implicated in their thoughts about free will. For instance, when presented with a description of a deterministic universe, most participants say that in that universe, people don't have free will (Roskies and Nichols 2008; also Deery et al. forthcoming). This provides reason to think that the everyday conception of free will is not compatible with determinism (see also Rose and Nichols forthcoming).

Libertarians, of course, think that we make indeterminist choices. If that's right, then the folk belief in indeterminist free will might well be true. For the purposes of this essay, let's set aside libertarianism. The issue of interest concerns the consequences of folk error on free will, so the issue can only be joined if we assume that there is something interestingly mistaken about the folk view. There are many ways that the folk view might be mistaken. For instance, it might be that the folk view falsely assumes that agents have free will of a sort that contravenes event causation. But to keep things as simple as possible, let's just assume that determinism is true.[1] That means that the folk falsely believe in indeterminism. One last stipulation is required. People use the words "free will" in lots of different ways. For the purposes of this paper, the term "free will" will be taken to pick out the kind of free will that is presumed to be in conflict with determinism. To summarize: we are assuming that the ordinary notion of free will is in error because it falsely presupposes that indeterminism is true. With that large set of assumptions, we can frame the key question: Does free will exist?

2. ELIMINATIVISM AND REFERENCE

It might seem that I have so thoroughly stacked the deck that it trivially follows from my assumptions that free will doesn't exist. If we take on all those assumptions, then eliminativists can claim an easy victory. However, does the fact that the ordinary notion of free will has a false presupposition entail that there is no free will? Over the last several decades, it has become clear that this is no trivial matter at all. The basic theme has played out over and over in contemporary philosophy. In ethics it appears in the debate over error theory (Mackie 1977; Blackburn 1985); in social-political philosophy, it's found in disputes over the existence of race (Appiah 1995; Andreasen 2000; Mallon 2006); in philosophy of science, it's endemic to debates about scientific realism (Feyerabend 1962; Laudan 1984; Boyd 2002); and in philosophy of mind, we find the theme in debates about eliminative materialism (e.g., Stich 1983; Lycan 1988). In each of these debates, eliminativists maintain that *K doesn't exist* (where *K* might be morality, race, belief, etc.). Typically shortly after an eliminativist claim of this sort is made another group of philosophers adopt a *preservationist* position. In effect, they say, *Ks aren't what we thought they were.*

To set out the problematic, I'll focus on the debate over eliminative materialism, since the critical themes to be discussed here were carefully charted in that debate (see esp. Stich 1983, 1996; Bishop and Stich 1998; Lycan 1988). One central argument for eliminativism went roughly as follows:

1. "belief" is a term (or concept) in a folk theory;
2. that folk theory is massively mistaken;
3. therefore beliefs don't exist.

Stich was characteristically pellucid in his presentation of the argument. He begins by setting out David Lewis' (1972) descriptivist account of how theoretical terms get their meaning and reference from the theory in which they are embedded (Stich 1983, 17–21). A theoretical term refers to whatever object or class of objects satisfies some critical set of claims in the theory. Stich then argues that the folk psychological theory that gives meaning and reference to "belief" is deeply erroneous; from this he concludes that beliefs don't exist. Lewis himself approves of a key component of this argumentative strategy. He writes: "If the names of mental states are like theoretical terms, they name nothing unless the theory . . . is more or less true" (Lewis

1972, 213). The salient difference between Lewis (1972) and Stich (1983) concerns the extent to which the folk theory is true. Unlike Lewis, Stich thinks the folk theory is deeply mistaken and this enables the eliminativist conclusion.

William Lycan reacted to these eliminativist arguments by calling into question the Lewisian account of how the reference of theoretical terms gets determined. Lycan writes:

> I am at pains to advocate a very liberal view . . . I am entirely willing to give up fairly large chunks of our commonsensical or platitudinous theory of belief or of desire (or of almost anything else) and decide that we were just wrong about a lot of things, without drawing the inference that we are no longer talking about belief or desire. To put the matter crudely, I incline away from Lewis's Carnapian and/or Rylean cluster theory of the reference of theoretical terms, and toward Putnam's . . . causal-historical theory. As in Putnam's examples of 'water,' 'tiger,' and so on, I think the ordinary word 'belief' (qua theoretical term of folk psychology) points dimly toward a natural kind that we have not fully grasped and that only mature psychology will reveal. I expect that 'belief' will turn out to refer to some kind of information-bearing inner state of a sentient being, . . . but the kind of state it refers to may have only a few of the properties usually attributed to beliefs by common sense. (1988, 31–32)

Lycan promotes a "liberal" view of reference fixing. On the approach to reference fixing adopted by Lycan, the reference of a theoretical term can succeed even if the theory is radically mistaken. For on this theory (again very roughly) the reference of a theoretical term is the entity or kind that was "baptized" when the term was introduced. As people transmit the term to others, the term continues to refer to the entity or kind that was baptized at the end of that causal-historical chain of transmission. As a result, people can have massive misconceptions about the objects that their terms (or concepts) refer to.[2]

Thus the core of the dispute between eliminativists and preservationists seems to be over what is required for a term or concept to refer successfully (see, e.g., Stich 1996; Bishop and Stich 1998).[3] For instance, the eliminative materialist says,

> There are no such thing as *beliefs*. Of course there are causally efficacious psychological states that are semantically evaluable, but there are no psychological states that have their causal efficacy *in virtue of* their semantic properties.

The preservationist replies:

> There are such things as *beliefs*. After all, even though there are no psychological states that have their causal efficacy *in virtue of* their semantic properties, there are causally efficacious psychological states that are semantically evaluable.

The eliminativist maintains that the fact that the concept of belief has a false presupposition about semantic causal efficacy means that beliefs don't exist. If a descriptivist theory of reference is right, then the fact that the concept of belief is critically associated with a false presupposition provides reason to think the eliminativist is right. The preservationist maintains that the fact that there is this false presupposition isn't enough to mean that beliefs don't exist. The concept of belief can allow for this amount of associated error. If a causal-historical theory of reference is right, then there is reason to think that "belief" continues to refer despite the fact that it is associated with a critical presupposition that is false.

The same kind of analysis applies to debates about eliminativism in the free will literature (e.g., Hurley 2000; Pereboom 2009b; Vargas 2005). Grant that determinism is true but that indeterminism is an important element of our folk notion of free will. The free will eliminativist might say:

> Free will doesn't exist; of course there is preference-guided information processing, but everything is determined.

And the preservationist might say:

> Free will does exist; after all, even though everything is determined, there is still preference-guided information processing.

Who is right in this exchange? It seems to depend on how liberal the reference-fixing relation is. If the causal-historical theory is right, then it's plausible that "free will" refers successfully despite the false presupposition. If descriptivism is right, then the fact that the concept of free will is critically associated with a false presupposition provides reason to think that "free will" fails to refer and consequently that the eliminativist is right.

3. THE GEOGRAPHY OF ERROR

The philosophical space we've been exploring starts with the assumption that some concept is enmeshed in significant error. In the philosophy of free will, the two most prominent reactions to this situation are eliminativism (e.g., Pereboom 2001; Strawson 1986) and "revisionism" (Vargas 2005, 2011a, 2013a). But these two views do not exhaust the space of possibilities. In this section, I will lay out the philosophical geography more fully (see figure 11.1). Let's say we agree that some concept has, as part of its associated content, an error. In some cases, the error might be specified. For instance, in metaethics, Mackie maintains that folk morality falsely presupposes that moral statements are objectively true. One might agree that Mackie has identified an error in the folk concept of morality and then proceed to consider whether moral eliminativism follows. That would be a case on which we have a specified error. But in other instances, we might acknowledge that there is an error associated with a concept, even though we do not know what the error is. Often in science, we have reason to think our theories have errors even when we don't know what the errors are. For instance, current theory surrounding neurotransmitter reuptake channels likely contains significant errors, even though we haven't yet identified them. Thus, the error can be *specified* or *unspecified*, and that provides the first branch in our tree.

For our purposes, the more important issue is whether to draw an eliminativist or a preservationist conclusion. If the associated error yields a failure of reference, then the argument sketched in section 2 suggests that eliminativism follows for the kind under consideration. If, however, the associated error does not stand in the way of successful reference, then the preservationist position stands. Let's start with the *unspecified error* branch. Philosophers of science typically acknowledge that current theories likely have a great deal of unspecified error. This admission is a first step in broad-scale anti-realist arguments based on the "pessimistic induction." Prominent versions of this argument explicitly appeal to reference failure. Laudan observes that many theories that were successful in their time are now acknowledged to contain "central terms that (we now believe) were nonreferring" (Laudan 1984, 121).

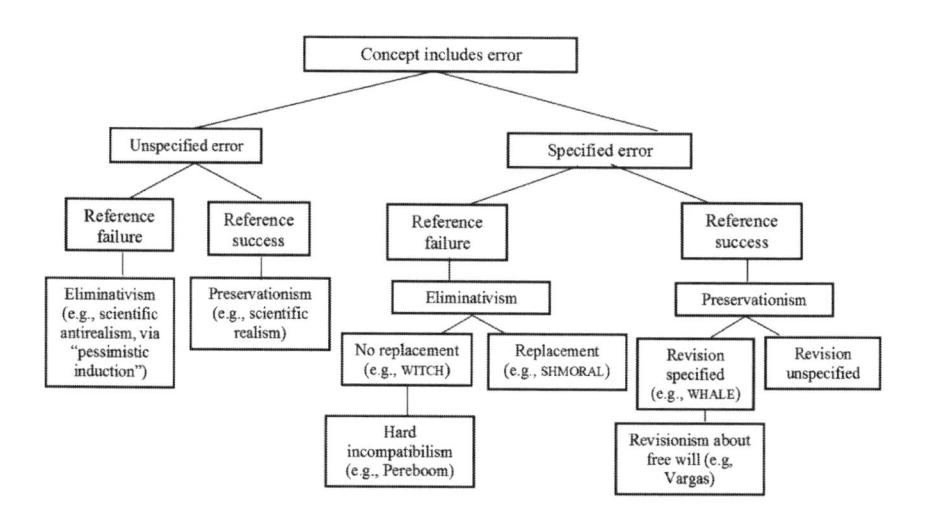

Figure 11.1. The geography of error

It's widely agreed that the entities posited by those terms, e.g., *phlogiston, caloric, humors*, don't exist. The anti-realist then notes that since our current theories are acknowledged to contain significant error, it's likely that current science is in the same boat—the theoretical terms fail to refer and the posits don't exist. Scientific realists maintain that the fact that there is a great deal of error in a theory doesn't entail that the theoretical terms fail to refer, and so preservationism stands. Like Lycan, scientific realists can draw on causal-historical theories of reference to defend the claim that a term can refer successfully even if it is embedded in a theory rife with error (Boyd 1983).

Let's turn now to the *specified error* branch. If we know what the error is, and the concept continues to refer despite the error, then preservationism holds. If we follow the preservationist branch and promote a revised concept, then we have a *revisionist* theory (Vargas 2011a).[4] This approach is familiar. To take a folksy example, the concept WHALE falsely presupposed that whales were fish. Taxonomy kept the label and adjusted the concept, moving WHALE onto the mammal branch. In the free will literature, Manuel Vargas has been the most systematic (and tireless) advocate of revisionism. He argues that the folk notion of free will is error-ridden, but the concept continues to refer; in addition, he proposes a revisionist account of free will on which the critical feature of free will is the capacity to respond to moral considerations (Vargas 2013a).[5]

Because of Vargas' careful work, revisionism is the preservationist view that has received the most attention (McKenna 2009; Pereboom 2009b; Fischer et al. 2007). But it's possible to be a preservationist even if one doesn't proffer a revision. One might know that a given concept has a specific error associated with it, and preserve the concept without having a revisionist proposal. Call this node "revision unspecified" (figure 11.1). If we know that the reference relation permits at least the amount of error associated with the concept of interest, then we might promote preservationism even in the absence of a revisionist proposal.[6] For instance, a causal-historical theorist will likely take preservationism as the default position regardless of whether one has developed a specific proposal for a revised concept. This is an important option for contested kind terms like "free will." For it's perfectly sensible to hold a preservationist view about *free will* even if one does not side with any particular revisionist proposal.

On to the eliminativist branch. Again, if the error associated with a term (or concept) yields a failure of reference, then eliminativism seems to follow. In the most familiar cases, eliminativism holds that the target concept is empty and should be entirely discarded. For instance, the concept witch falsely presupposed the existence of certain supernatural powers and, on the standard narrative, we have abandoned commitment to that kind without looking for a replacement. Hard determinists typically take a similar approach to FREE WILL, maintaining that there is no such thing as free will and that we should not seek a replacement concept but face the truth. It is, however, available to the eliminativist to proffer a replacement for the empty concept. In *Ethics: Inventing Right and Wrong*, Mackie famously maintains that because moral beliefs falsely presuppose objectivity, the concept of morality is empty and all moral claims are false. Almost equally famously, in that same book, Mackie proceeds to promote what looks very much like a moral philosophy. The apparent inconsistency can be avoided if we suppose that Mackie is replacing our concept, MORAL, with a closely related concept, SHMORAL, that doesn't carry the problematic presupposition of objectivity (see Blackburn 1985, 150).[7] (See figure 11.1)

That concludes my cartography of error. But with the map before us, the contrast between replacement-eliminativists and revisionists might seem rather precious. After all, the replacement theorist is free to adopt whatever proposal the revisionist offers for FREE WILL, and the replacement theorist can say that while FREE WILL is an empty concept, the revisionists describe a related concept that is not empty. Indeed, the replacement theorist is even at liberty to adopt a *homonym* to pick out his replacement concept. So what is the fuss about between eliminativists and revisionists? Well, the eliminativist (including the replacement theorist) maintains that there is *no such thing as* free will and that everyone is under the illusion that there is free will. The preservationist (including the revisionist) says that there *is* free will and that everyone has merely been under some misapprehensions about its nature. This seems to be a fundamental ontological disagreement.

4. REFERENCE CONVENTIONS AND ONTOLOGY

It is a tacit assumption behind these eliminativist debates that there is a single correct reference relation to be discovered for a class of terms. Once we figure out the reference relation for the relevant class of terms (e.g., natural kind terms), we can simply apply the theory to the terms and thereby find out whether *belief, race,* and *free will* exist. However, this might just be a mistake. It might be a mistake to assume that there is a single reference relation for kind terms. Instead, in different contexts, different reference relationships might be in play. This is a heterodox view, but it has an advocate in the philosophy of science, and there is a smattering of experimental evidence for this pluralist view.

In attempting to explain discourse in the history of science, Philip Kitcher maintains that different reference relations are in play in different contexts. He writes:

> Different tokens of the same type [of term] may be associated with different modes of reference.... A token's mode of reference is of the *descriptive type* when the speaker has a dominant present intention to pick out something that

satisfies a particular description and the referent of the token is whatever satisfies the description. The *baptismal type* is exemplified when the speaker has a dominant present intention to pick out a particular present object (or a set of objects, one member of which may be present). (Kitcher 1993, 77; see also Bishop 1999)

Kitcher goes on to use this approach to reference to analyze episodes in the history of science (1993, 101). In some cases, when phlogiston theorists used cognates of "phlogiston," the term is naturally read as tied to a particular description. Priestley writes that if he had burned a pipe "in the open fire, the phlogiston would have escaped" (Priestley 1775 (vol. 2) 251). Here we naturally interpret the reference of "phlogiston" to be fixed by the description *the substance released in combustion*. That description, we now know, is not satisfied by anything—there is no substance released in combustion. Hence, in those contexts, the reference of "phlogiston" is determined by the associated description and the term comes up empty. However, there are other times when Priestley uses cognates of "phlogiston" that seem more naturally interpreted in causal-historical ways. For instance, Priestley reports breathing in "dephlogisticated air" after he had tested its effects on mice. He writes, "I fancied that my breast felt peculiarly light and easy for some time afterwards . . . Hitherto only two mice and myself have had the privilege of breathing it" (Priestley 162). We now know that what Priestley and the mice were breathing was *oxygen*, and it's natural to think that *oxygen* is precisely what the term "dephlogisticated air" refers to in this context (Kitcher 1993, 100).[8]

In a recent paper, Ángel Pinillos, Ron Mallon, and I have defended this kind of pluralistic approach to reference. In particular, we provide experimental evidence that natural kind terms are systematically ambiguous. In some cases, the reference of a token term is fixed by a descriptivist convention; in other cases, the reference of a token term (of the same type) is fixed by a causal-historical convention. To support the ambiguity theory, we presented participants with descriptions of contested kind terms from natural history, drawn from medieval bestiaries. As we explained to the participants, the cases were real cases. In several different experiments, participants were presented with the following sketch:

> In the Middle Ages, animal researchers described a distinctive kind of mammal. They called it catoblepas. The catoblepas was said to be like a bull but with a head so heavy that the animal has to keep its head down at all times. It was also thought that the catoblepas had scales on its back. Of course there is nothing that meets this description, but researchers think that it was based on reports of encounters with wildebeests.

After reading that description of *catoblepas*, participants were presented with some questions that were expected to elicit a descriptivist interpretation and some that were expected to resist a descriptivist interpretation.

Our hypothesis was that if the participants are asked about the existence of a kind, this will lead people to apply a descriptivist convention to the kind term. It's a familiar point that the causal-historical theory of reference has difficulties accommodating empty terms (e.g., Devitt and Sterelny 1999). For instance, if the modern use of "Santa Claus" causally traces back to the historical Saint Nicholas, the causal-historical approach suggests that "Santa Claus" is Saint Nicholas, and hence Santa Claus exists. By contrast, descriptivism claims that the meaning of a term like "Santa Claus" is given by the associated description, and so it's easy for such a theory to accommodate the sad fact that Santa Claus doesn't exist. This led us to predict that people would be likely to respond as descriptivists when presented with an existence statement. Thus, following the description regarding *catoblepas*, participants were asked to indicate their level of agreement with the sentence "Catoblepas exist." As predicted, people tended to *disagree* with this statement (for related results, see Machery et al. forthcoming).

One reaction to the corroboration of our prediction is that descriptivism is simply the right theory of reference. But we suspected that people could be led to make judgments that are more naturally taken as causal-historical. Given that the description associated with *catoblepas* isn't satisfied by anything, descriptivism entails that the term doesn't refer to anything and thus suggests that *catoblepas* don't exist. Again, the previous result suggests that people did in fact interpret "Catoblepas exist" in this descriptivist way. But there are some sentence forms that actually presuppose existence. When a term occurs in the subject position with predication, there is a presupposition of existence. If I say, "Adderley's solo on 'So What' was lovely" this presupposes that Adderley had a solo on "So What." (To say "I disagree" would typically imply that Adderley had a solo but it wasn't lovely.) However, if I say "Miles listened to Adderley's solo on 'So What,'" this does not presuppose that Adderley had a solo on that song (To say "I disagree" would typically not imply that Adderley had a solo) (cf. Strawson 1950). Thus, our prediction was that if we placed "catoblepas" in the subject position and predicated something of it, people would be more likely to respond in concert with a causal-historical convention. To test this, after the description regarding *catoblepas*, participants were asked to indicate their level of agreement with the sentence "Catoblepas are wildebeest." As predicted, people tended to *agree* with this sentence (which predicates "are wildebeest" of *catoblepas*). Indeed, even when participants were given *both* sentences "Catoblepas exist" and "Catoblepas are wildebeest," they agreed more with "Catoblepas are wildebeest" than with "Catoblepas exist."

Thus, ordinary people seem to shift how they think about the reference relation depending on subtle features of discourse. This doesn't mean that people are confused. It can be perfectly right to say that that 1 is false and 2 is true:

1. "Catoblepas exist"
2. "Catoblepas are wildebeests"

The different statements are naturally associated with different conventions of reference, so there is no inconsistency.

We used simple statements for our experiments, to keep the design as clean as possible. We find that existence statements attract descriptivist interpretations of the kind term. But of course we don't mean to suggest that it is impossible to produce an existence statement that attracts a causal-historical interpretation. For instance, if a speaker says "Catoblepas are wildebeests, so catoblepas exist," the fact that existence statement (1) is included in the statement doesn't make the statement contradictory. Rather, in the context of that utterance, it's plausible that the causal-historical convention is in play and we would want to accept the existence claim (Nichols, Pinillos, Mallon forthcoming).

Now we can finally get to the issue concerning eliminativism and preservationism about free will. We have been assuming that the folk conception of free will contains significant error. If the foregoing story about the diversity of reference conventions is right, how should we interpret Galen Strawson when he says "Free will doesn't exist"? Descriptively, of course. He is keying on the false description associated with "free will," and pointing out that nothing meets that description. To interpret Strawson's use of "free will" causal-historically would be manifestly uncharitable. What reference-convention is in place when Manuel Vargas says "Free will isn't what we thought"? Presumably *not* restrictive descriptivism, or what he says is, by his own lights, false.[9] This allows us to say that Vargas is right and Strawson is also right. It's just that the term "free will" operates with a different reference convention in the different contexts.

This pluralist approach yields a pacifistic answer to the metaphysical debate over the existence of free will. The eliminativist is assuming a demanding convention of reference and so, given that an important presupposition about free will is false, the eliminativist is right to say (under that convention for reference) that there is no such thing as free will. The preservationist on the other hand is adopting a more liberal convention of reference, and so the preservationist is right to say (under that convention for reference), that there *is* such a thing as free will despite the false presupposition. This pluralism deflates somewhat the importance of the metaphysical dispute between eliminativists and preservationists. There is no univocal answer on whether eliminativism is true.[10]

The pacifistic answer I'm promoting should not obscure the fact that, regardless of which standard for reference we adopt, in giving up the indeterminist dimension of choice, we are rejecting an important and perhaps incorrigible part of the way we ordinarily think of ourselves. It is self-deception to deny that our normal understanding of our decisions is vertiginously problematic. That is the point stressed by the eliminativist. Still, as with other genuine philosophical perplexities (like skepticism), the fact that there is genuine perplexity here doesn't mean we need to obsess on it, and the preservationist can be seen as offering an alternative to obsession.

5. PRACTICAL INTERESTS AND ILLUSIONS

In his classic essay, "Deconstructing the Mind," Stich makes a provocative argument that socio-political factors have shaped metaphysics. His leading example is witches. Stich points out that some contemporary scholars maintain that witches do exist and that they also existed during the Inquisition (e.g., Luhrmann 1991). However, witches, according to these theorists, don't do black magic or have pacts with the devil. Stich says that in the comfort of liberal democracies, this is a fine and interesting thing to say. But when faced with witch trials that led to torturing and executing innocent people, Stich suggests that eliminativism provides a more politically effective position:

> In sixteenth-century Europe . . . people who held the view that none of the women accused of being witches had made a pact with the devil or caused any harm, and that these women ought not to be tortured or put to death, might be much more effective if they insisted that witches are myths—that they simply do not exist—and thus that all of the women accused of being witches are falsely accused. That, near enough, is what many of them did say and what most of us say as well. (1996, 69)

It was a politically powerful move to deny that witches exist, and this might explain how our cultural forebears arrived at witch eliminativism.

I will attempt to build on Stich's insight. But the history is somewhat complicated. In England, the early witch skeptics (e.g., Scot 1584; Ady 1656) were not eliminativists. It's easy to see why: the term "witch" was commonly thought to be used in the Bible, and many of the skeptics did not want to defy scripture (see, e.g., Notestein 1911, 132). Thus, many of the early skeptical attacks did in fact promote the view that witches were not what people thought they were—in particular, witches did not have compacts with Satan. The most important of the early skeptics, Reginald Scot, held that the witches of the Bible included poisoners and illusionists (Scot 1584,

136–37; see also Thomas 1971, 572–73), and he explicitly maintains a preservationist view: "My question is not (as manie fondlie suppose) whether there be witches or naie: but whether they can doo such miraculous works as are imputed unto them" (Scot 1584, 15).[11]

Within a society deeply committed to scripture, to defend witch-eliminativism required arguing that the Bible did not quantify over witches. This was explicitly done in the later seventeenth century. The first chapter of John Wagstaffe's book is entitled "That the Bible hath been falsely translated in those places which speak of witchcraft" (1671, 1). Rejecting any Biblical witches makes available the option of denying the existence of witches outright, and that's exactly what Wagstaffe (83–84) and later skeptics (e.g., Hutchinson 1718, 229) did. These later skeptics, of course, won the day and witch-eliminativism prevails (Notestein 1911, 343).

It remains unclear whether the success of witch-eliminativism was facilitated by the political effectiveness of eliminativism for abolishing witch trials. To be sure, all of the skeptical writings (both preservationist and eliminativist) reflected a deep concern about the welfare of those accused of being witches. In any case, what is quite clear is that both eliminativism and preservationism were in play in the seventeenth century. And it's not hard to imagine history having played out in the preservationist fashion, retaining commitment to non-supernatural witches. Indeed, the term "magician" provides a closely related counterpoint to "witch." In the middle ages, *magicians* were regarded as individuals with supernatural powers (e.g., Thomas 1971, 41).[12] Yet we now use that term with no supernatural commitment. For *witch*, we fixed the reference convention such that the supernatural component is essential, affording an eliminativist view; for *magician*, we adopted a much more liberal reference fixing convention.[13]

The role of practical interests in the ontology of witches and magicians is unclear. But it is very plausible that practical interests can have important effects on ontological claims about witches and magicians. Nonetheless, although practical interests can plausibly affect which statements about free will (or witches) are true, it would be more constructionism than I can credit to think that this settles the metaphysical question about free will (or witches). When we apply practical interests to fix a reference convention, we are affecting which sentences are true, but we are not descrying the structure of reality.

I've been arguing that there are different reference conventions available for kind terms. History provides examples in which we have taken a restrictive reference convention (e.g., *witch*) as well as examples in which we have taken a liberal reference convention (e.g., *magician*). It is a matter of considerable historical interest why we adopt one convention rather than another. But, borrowing from Stich, it does seem likely that practical considerations can impact which conventions we adopt. In addition, if Pinillos, Mallon, and I are right about the availability of different reference conventions, then there need be no mistake in adopting one convention or the other (Nichols et al. forthcoming). As a result, we might appeal to practical interests in deciding which convention to adopt and impose.

To return to free will, Strawson says "Free will doesn't exist" or "Free will is an illusion." Vargas says "Free will does exist" or "Free will is no illusion." Each is right, under the appropriate reference fixing convention. If practical concerns can be recruited to determine which reference convention to adopt, this might provide a new kind of argument for preservationism or eliminativism.

There is a growing body of work that suggests that telling people that they don't have free will has negative social consequence (e.g., Vohs and Schooler 2008; Baumeister et al. 2009). The experiments have their limitations, but they are certainly suggestive enough to merit consideration. In one study, participants in the *no free will* condition were told things like the following: "Science has demonstrated that free will is an illusion" and "Like everything else in the universe, all human actions follow from prior events and ultimately can be understood in terms of the movement of molecules." These participants indicated that they were less willing to engage in prosocial behavior (e.g., let a classmate use their cellphone) than participants who were either given no information on free will or information that hailed the existence of free will (Baumeister et al. 2009). More generally, telling myself that there is no free will is likely to interfere with my productivity (there is practical benefit in the chant of the Little Engine that Could). By contrast, telling myself "it's my free choice whether I do it" is plausibly productive, even when I think that the notion of "free choice" is enmeshed in error. These considerations are far from decisive, but they provide some reason to think that it can be in our practical interests to be preservationists about the notion of free will. Proclaiming "Free will is an illusion!" will likely impede the production of valued behavior. And, as noted, we can proclaim instead "Free will is no illusion!" without running rationally afoul. Since a liberal reference convention is available, we can simply adopt such a convention for the reference of "free will."[14] We can do this, it should be emphasized, even if we refrain from embracing a specific revisionist proposal. We can just maintain that our ordinary notion of free will can successfully refer despite the associated error (cf. Lycan on *belief*).

There is thus some evidence of practical advantages to sustaining preservationism about free will. But there are also practical advantages to adopting eliminativism. As Tamler Sommers notes, the denial of free will can undercut an ugly self-righteousness: "Recognizing that all the people whom we love, respect and cherish, including ourselves, do not deserve praise for being who we are may help to lessen the disdain and contempt we sometimes feel for those who are not fortunate enough to make it into this charmed circle" (Sommers 2007b, 15). Sommers also suggests that denying free will can help to assuage pathological guilt, "the kind of morbid hand-wringing that keeps us awake all night thinking about what might have been" (Sommers 2007b, 14). Indeed, invoking determinism is an explicit strategy in some prominent behavioral therapies. Wolpe and Lazarus (1966) write, "Since the patient has had no choice in becoming what he is, it is incongruous to blame him for having gone awry." Patients wracked by self-blame should, on this view, be counseled that "human behavior is subject to causal determinism no less than that of billiard balls or ocean currents" (Wolpe and Lazarus 1966, 16; see also Wolpe 1990, 59; Robertson 2010). Although self-blame might sometimes be productive, at the neurotic end of the spectrum, it is a powerful hindrance to well being. The recognition that we lack ultimate control might well moderate those reactions. These practical considerations favor adopting the eliminativist view and proclaiming "Free will *is* an illusion!" The refrain is familiar now—this proclamation is rationally available to us as a function of adopting a particular reference convention for "free will." Just as eighteenth-century English scholars came to identity the reference convention of "witch" as fixed by the description: *human with satanically-derived supernatural powers*, so we might decide to fix the reference convention for "free will" with the description "indeterministic choice" or perhaps "causa sui." Given our assumption that determinism is true, that reference convention would ground eliminativism.

Thus, practical interests can be brought to bear on both sides of the free will debate. There are practical advantages to preservationism and also to eliminativism. Where next? Do we just calculate which view has the greatest practical advantage and then adopt and impose the appropriate reference convention? Perhaps we don't need a univocal answer. We might be *discretionary* in whether we adopt compatibilism or incompatibilism. When it serves our interests to affirm free will, we can do so; when it serves our interests to deny free will, we can do that. There need be no inconsistency here. We have available different ways of thinking about reference conventions; in some contexts we think liberally, in others, restrictively. As a result, we can be strategic about the conventions we adopt when it comes to "free will," adopting preservationism in some contexts and eliminativism in others.

Can we sustain this kind of two-faced strategic approach to free will? Maybe not. But given how much we excel at hypocrisy (e.g., Valdesolo and DeSteno 2007), it seems like we are quite capable of keeping two books, shifting according to what serves our interests. In the case of free will, I've argued, our interests are sometimes best served by eliminativism and other times best served by preservationism. So if we can manage to be elastic in our practices, it would serve our interests to do so.

In this chapter, I've argued that the statement "Free will exists" is true under some available reference conventions and false under others. As a result, in some contexts, the statement is true—because in some contexts the right way to think about the reference of "free will" is liberal about associated mistakes; in other contexts, the statement is false—because the right way to think about the reference of "free will" in some contexts is restrictive about associated mistakes. Since it's reasonable to interpret the eliminativist as adopting a restrictive convention for fixing reference, his claim that free will *doesn't exist* is true; it's reasonable to interpret the preservationist as adopting a liberal convention, so his claim that free will *does exist* is true. My secondary objective has been to promote a discretionary (in)compatibilism on which we can be strategic in embracing eliminativism in some contexts and preservationism in others, based on what serves our practical interests. We have good practical reasons for embracing compatibilism in some contexts and eliminativists in others. The diversity of reference conventions makes this expedient possible. It might be prudent for me to be a compatibilist in the morning, as I look forward to a productive day of work; but then I can be an eliminativist at night, when I try to sleep after another day of failure.

ACKNOWLEDGMENTS

I'd like to thank Mike Bishop, Angel Pinillos, Michael McKenna, Gregg Caruso, Victor Kumar, Tamler Sommers, and especially Manuel Vargas for comments and discussion on an earlier draft of this chapter.

NOTES

1. The main points in this paper can be made if we assume instead that (i) in addition to the presupposition of indeterminism, people also have a presupposition that choice isn't random and that (ii) all events are either determined or random (cf. Russell 1995, 14; Kane 1996, 11). For the sake of readability, I am taking the simpler assumption that determinism is true.

2. Although Lycan's liberal view of reference fixing is causal-historical, a descriptivist can be more or less liberal about reference fixing. It all depends on how much of the theory has to be true in order for the term to refer. So the key distinction of interest is between theories of reference that are liberal and those that are conservative. However, for ease of discussion, I will often focus on causal-historical as the key example of a liberal theory and a restrictive descriptivism as the key example of a conservative theory.

3. Bishop and Stich (1998; Stich 1996) argue that the appeal to reference in these arguments only works if one assumes a substantive rather than a deflationary account of reference. Since this paper is already technical enough, let's just assume that the right theory of reference is a substantive one.

4. Revisionism in Vargas' sense requires (1) that the errors are specified and (2) that a specific revision of the concept is offered (Vargas 2011, 460). Preservationism is thus a broader category since one can be a preservationist even if (1) or (2) doesn't hold. In this paper, I use the term "revisionism" in Vargas' sense.

5. Vargas' position is actually more nuanced. He proposes two different ways to run revisionism, and I'm focusing on what he calls "connotational revisionism" (Vargas 2013).

6. This seems to be Lycan's attitude about *belief* when he writes: "I think the ordinary word 'belief' (qua theoretical term of folk psychology) points dimly toward a natural kind that we have not fully grasped and that only mature psychology will reveal" (1988, 32).

7. On Vargas' latest presentation of revisionism, the replacement view would count as "denotational revisionism." As noted earlier, what I call "revisionism" is his "connotational revisionism" (Vargas 2013).

8. In many cases, the presence of systematic ambiguity will not affect the truth of existence claims. For instance, in contemporary chemistry the concept OXYGEN likely refers successfully under both descriptivist and causal-historical reference conventions.

9. This is an oversimplification, since there are different assumptions about reference that will make Vargas' claim true. Causal-historical accounts provide one option. But another possibility is just that the reference convention in play is descriptivist but is very liberal about how much of the description must be satisfied for reference to succeed.

10. An obvious way to reject my pacifism is to insist that there is a single correct theory of reference for kind terms, and hence there must be a univocal answer to the eliminativist question. That maneuver reestablishes the battle, but it's a rather different battle—one about the univocal nature of reference.

11. Scot thinks that people accused of being "witches" in England are not witches in any Biblical sense at all: "But as for our old women, that are said to hurt children with their eies, or lambs with their lookes, or that pull downe the moone out of heaven, or make so foolish a bargaine, or doo such homage to the divell; you shall not read in the bible of any such witches, or of any such actions imputed to them" (137).

12. For uses of "magicians" as supernatural, see Casaubon (1670, 111), King James I (1597, 31), and Boulton (1715, 33). For uses of "magicians" in roughly the modern sense, see Wagstaffe (1671, 23) and Webster (1677, 166–67).

13. This parallels examples from the history of science. Historically, we have come to associate "phlogiston" with "the substance emitted in combustion." We have fixed that description as the reference convention. Since nothing is emitted in combustion, it follows (given this way of fixing reference) that "phlogiston" doesn't refer. We went exactly the opposite direction with "atom." In keeping with earlier atomic theories, Dalton maintained that atoms are indivisible. (Kitcher riffs: "Almost everything Dalton maintained about atoms is wrong" (1993, 106).) When chemists like Rutherford discovered that Dalton's "atoms" were divisible, one option would have been to claim that atoms don't exist, adopting the reference convention that welds indivisibility to "atom" (it is the etymology after all). Alternatively, Rutherford could have said that even if there are atoms, atoms are not what Dalton & co. were studying. Instead, Rutherford opted for a preservationist view on which one says, "Atoms aren't what we thought they were. Turns out they're divisible."

14. Some of Vargas' arguments for revisionism also work as practical reasons for adopting a preservationist-friendly reference convention. For instance, Vargas maintains that the affirmation of free will tends "to contribute to our better perceiving and appropriately responding to moral considerations" (2007, 155–56). Insofar as we want to facilitate perception and response to moral considerations, this would provide a practical reason for preservationism. (Vargas actually makes this point about the "responsibility-characteristic practices, attitudes, and judgments", but he would include the affirmation of "free will" among that set of practices, attitudes and judgments.)

II

Scientific Explorations: The Behavioral, Cognitive, and Neurosciences

Chapter Twelve

The Complex Network of Intentions

John-Dylan Haynes and Michael Pauen

Intentions are among those features that make humans special. According to many philosophers, intentions are of specific importance when it comes to the difference between mere behavior (stumbling, coughing) and goal-directed action (writing, problem-solving). However, recent psychological and neuroscientific evidence has been interpreted as putting the existence of intentions into question.

Here we review this evidence and discuss the consequences that it has for our understanding of intentions. We will argue that intentions might well play an important role in human action and decision making, but that this role differs significantly from what commonsense as well as some standard philosophical and folk-psychological accounts of intentionality assume. This, however, does not mean that intentions are mere illusions as long as we are ready to accept a moderate revision of our commonsense concept of intention which, as we will argue, is reasonable in itself.

Forming intentions is thought of as one of the most basic human abilities. Intentions play a specifically important role for the distinction between action and behavior. Typical cases of behavior are stumbling or sneezing, typical cases of action are writing a letter or driving a car. The obvious difference between action and mere behavior is that actions are guided by intentions while mere behavior is not. Stumbling or sneezing may just happen to you; it's almost like getting sick. Driving a car or writing a letter is different. Neither just happens to you; and it seems that forming an intention, say to drive somewhere or to write a letter to someone, is what makes the difference.

All this, however, assumes something like a commonsense theory of action and intention. Recent evidence has cast doubt upon this idea, particularly on the assumption that intentions are always conscious, that they simply determine our behavior, but it's also debated what role intentions play for our experience of agency.

On closer examination, it turns out that the problem at hand consists of two separate questions, and we have to answer both if we want to come up with a serious and somewhat complete account of human intention: First, we have to make clear what, exactly, we *mean* when we talk about intentions. This is a conceptual question. In order to answer it, we will have to determine what is specific for intentions and how intentions differ from other mental states, say from beliefs and desires. However, even if we have a fair idea of what counts as an intention it would still be open whether there *is* something out there in the world that meets these criteria. This is the second question and it's empirical: Do intentions exist and, if so, what is their role in the process of acting and decision making? All these questions deserve an empirical answer and this answer is far from being trivial.

Conceptual and empirical questions are substantially different—but they are far from being independent of each other: On the one hand, you need a sensible idea of intention in order to design experiments. On the other hand, even if you have a fair conceptual understanding of this phenomenon, you might want to know whether or not intentions exist. But what if empirical studies show that there is nothing that exactly meets these criteria, but some states meet most of them? This may be a reason to ask whether some of the conceptual criteria can be revised such that we can save intentions.

In what follows, we would like to show that this is actually the case: There is evidence against the commonsense notion of intention, but accepting a somewhat modified and even more reasonable understanding of intention might allow us to save the existence of this kind of state—or so we argue. We will start with an account of the "commonsense notion of intention." According to this notion, intentions are conscious mental states that guide actions and directly establish our feeling of agency. In the second section, we will discuss the most important empirical results. It will turn out that these results raise severe doubts whether something exists that meets the criteria of the commonsense notion of intention. But does this mean that there are no intentions? In the third and final part, we will argue that this is not so. Rather, it is much more reasonable to revise our commonsense notion of intention such that it does account for the empirical facts. If we do so, then it turns out that intentions do exist—even if they might be somewhat different from the commonsense notion.

1. THE COMMONSENSE NOTION OF INTENTION

As we have already mentioned, intentions play an important role when it comes to actions. The main difference between action and mere behavior is that actions are brought about intentionally while mere behavior is not. You may go down a staircase because you intend to leave the building, thus performing an action. But falling down a staircase is mere behavior that doesn't require any intention—it just happens to you.

But what, exactly, is the relation between an intention and the related action according to the commonsense point of view that is at issue here? In a nutshell, intentions provide a link between a person's self and their actions. In order to see what this means, think about someone who intentionally goes down a staircase because she wants to leave the building. The commonsense story about this event might go like this. The person themself has certain beliefs and desires, among them the desire to leave the building she finds herself in and the belief that you best take the staircase if you find yourself on the second floor of a building that you would like to leave. This can be expressed by five criteria: **(1) Goal representation:** Having an intention is to have a goal, say to leave the building, to take the staircase, to buy a car, or to smoke a cigarette. As a consequence, an intention can be understood as a goal representation. **(2) Embeddedness:** These goal representations do not come out of nothing. Intentions are embedded in an individual's other mental states, particularly their beliefs and desires. In order to see why this is important, consider the distinction between behavior and action. What sets actions apart from mere behavior is that they are guided by our beliefs and desires or, vice versa, that they allow our beliefs and desires and other higher cognitive states to become effective in the real world. Why would mother nature bother to give us the cognitive abilities to draw conclusions from past experiences, to write books, or to construct cars if these abilities would not enable us to act in the appropriate way such that we—at least sometimes—actually end up evading past errors, writing books, and constructing cars? The same goes for actions: Having the ability to act wouldn't make much sense if actions were not guided by our beliefs and desires, by our experiences, memories and other higher cognitive states. So we need a connection between beliefs, desires and other higher cognitive states on the one hand, and actions on the other. And it seems that intentions are essential for providing this connection. And in order to be able to do so, they have to be connected to our beliefs, desires, and other higher cognitive states. But this is not all that is needed. Another condition is **(3) causal efficacy:** In addition to being connected to other higher cognitive states intentions have to be effective, that is: They have to be able to bring about the action that fits to our beliefs, desires, and other higher cognitive states. Imagine that you had the experience that it's dangerous to take a certain route. You have the desire not to be mugged, you think hard how to evade this risk, and eventually form the belief that taking another route would solve the problem: So you form the intention to go that way. This, however, wouldn't help you very much unless the intention becomes effective, that is, it almost determines the appropriate action. Of course, all this is almost trivial and nobody denies that our experiences need to be effective. Nobody denies that our cognitive abilities have to become effective in some way or other. It's less trivial, though, that intentions play an essential role here. Still another requirement needs to be met, namely **(4) consciousness:** In order for our beliefs and desires and other higher cognitive states to become effective, intentions emerging from them have to be conscious. We typically know what our beliefs, desires and other higher cognitive states like experiences are. So how could they become effective and guide our behavior if all this would happen subconsciously? Conversely, lacking conscious intentions seems to be what sets mere behavior apart from real action. Finally, intentions seem to establish **(5) agency.** If agency, seen from the first person perspective,[1] is the experience of being an agent with respect to a specific action, then having a conscious intention should be necessary and sufficient in order to establish agency: After all, having the conscious intention to do x is what it takes to be the agent who does x. This holds on the assumption that the intention is effective, but as we have seen, being causally effective is a necessary requirement for being an intention anyway.

A Bit More Complexity

Putting all this together, intentions can be said to be conscious goal representations that permit higher cognitive states to control our actions and thus establish agency. It does seem that these five criteria capture our commonsense idea of intention. Still, even a proponent of this commonsense notion of intentions might admit that this picture is way too simple. Start with your beliefs and desires. Unlike the case above, you may not have prefabricated and unambiguous beliefs and desires in stock that fit exactly the situation you find yourself in.

In certain cases, you might know your desire but lack sufficient knowledge for satisfying it. Imagine you want to become a millionaire. The desire is clear but the beliefs that may guide your actions aren't. You first have to find out what to do in order to become a millionaire, that is, you have to do some problem solving. In other cases the desire might be unclear. Imagine choosing from fifty different TV programs. Unlike the previous example there is no problem to be solved—you already know what you have to do in order to satisfy your desire: Just press a button. What you don't know, though, is, what, exactly your desire *is*. All this becomes even more difficult if we consider that beliefs and desires may be in conflict with each other, e.g., if you want to lose weight but also have the desire to eat a piece of chocolate cake every now and then.

Finally, it seems plausible to regard these conditions as necessary if you want to hold someone responsible for what she does. It's another question whether they are sufficient. You might think that you have to go beyond the above requirements in order to establish sufficient conditions for "real" responsibility. In other words, you might want to exclude desires that are dictated by addiction or you might think that responsibility requires alternative possibilities. All this makes the commonsense story a bit more complicated, but it could still be true that intentions have to be embedded in our beliefs and desires, that actions depend on intentions, that intentions should be conscious and, finally, that they are constitutive for our feeling of agency.

So the basic picture that emerges from these considerations is that intentions are conscious mental states that link not only our beliefs and desires but our entire problem-solving capacities to our actions: Intentions, that is, give us control over what we do. That's why it's not really surprising that they are also constitutive for our feeling of agency and a necessary condition for responsibility.

However, in what follows, we will present evidence that is not compatible with the above picture. The evidence raises questions whether those mental states that we use to call intentions are conscious, whether they guide or even determine actions, and which role they play for our feeling of agency. And this boils down to the question whether these states are intentions at all. We will come back to this question in the third and final section of this paper.

2. EMPIRICAL CHALLENGES

The idea that our intentions result from beliefs and desires is an important commonsense notion. As mentioned above, in the commonsense view on intentional action the agent starts with a desire and then quasi-rationally consults his beliefs about states of the world and about the effects of his actions in order to choose a particular action plan. However, there are a number of empirical findings that challenge this notion.

An extreme example that our intentions can come about in other ways than through beliefs and desires comes from neuroscience. It has long been known that electrical stimulation applied to specific regions on the surface of the brain (Penfield and Rasmussen 1950) can cause a patient to report having an intention to perform an action (Fried et al. 1991; Desmurget et al. 2009). In one study, Fried and colleagues (1991) showed that direct stimulation of the human supplementary motor area (SMA) during neurosurgery can occasionally yield an "urge to move" a limb. Subsequently, Desmurget and colleagues (2009) showed that similar urges can be elicited by stimulation to the parietal cortex. Taken together, these results show that intentions can be directly caused by stimulation to the brain, thus suggesting that intentions are *realized* by brain activity (see also Figure 12.1A) and can be caused without reference to beliefs and desires. However, direct cortical stimulation could be considered a rather crude example because one could argue that this stimulation bypasses or distorts the usual causal chain of events through which intentions come about.

However, there are many other examples suggesting that our intentions can come about in ways other than by our beliefs and desires. In a seminal paper, Nisbett and Wilson (1977) proposed that humans generally base their beliefs about why they acted in certain ways on causal theories that involve plausibility rather than immediate experience. In one experiment, conducted in a shop, passersby were asked to judge the quality of four pairs of nylon stockings arranged in a shelf. Although the subjects denied that the position of the product had any influence on their choice, they preferred the rightmost pair of stockings four times more frequently than the leftmost pair. These subjects obviously believed that a variable had no effect on their behavior, whereas in fact it did. In another example, three groups of subjects viewed an emotional film under three different conditions. One control group saw the film normally, a first experimental group saw it while a noisy power saw was heard from another room, and a second experimental group saw the film with a badly adjusted focus. Afterwards they were asked to rate how interesting they found the movie, and also state to which degree the noise had influenced their judgment. Twenty-seven percent of the poor focus subjects and 55 percent of the noise condition subjects reported that the distraction had lowered their ratings. However, compared to the ratings of control subjects their ratings were not affected. So these subjects believed a variable had an influence on their behavior whereas in fact it did not. There are numerous other demonstrations showing that our knowledge about the reasons for our behavior is highly limited, and that our behavior is often influenced by factors other than our conscious beliefs and desires (see, e.g., Custers and Aarts 2010).

Another closely related commonsense belief is that we act in certain ways because we have consciously intended to do so, and that our behavior is under constant control by our conscious intentions. There are a number of examples where even complex behavior patterns can operate automatically without requiring conscious intentions or deliberation. The famous example is that during driving of a car one might be busily engaged in a discussion with the passenger, and upon arriving one wonders who actually drove the car. Heavily automatized routines can often be performed at little or no cost to attentional resources (reviewed in Moors and de Houwer 2006). Interestingly, however, automatic processes are not completely uncontrolled (Norman and Shallice 1986). Instead control appears to have shifted from a conscious attentional supervision to background monitoring that only becomes active in cases of conflict, e.g., when a person unexpectedly appears in front of the car. So during automatic behavior it appears that the overall goals of behavior are still in operation and thus one would normally indeed consider such behavior as "intention-based"—even if the commonsense notion leaves no room for this consideration.

Another commonsense criterion is that we are conscious of our intentions. Under most circumstances we can *report* what we want to do. However, even here, there are numerous counterexamples. While we are not always aware of reflexive or automatic behavior, it is typically assumed that the self-regulation processes for complex or novel actions require awareness. However, recent research has shown that goal pursuit can occur outside of awareness, even if the details are still debated (e.g., Bargh et al. 2001; Custers and Aarts 2010; Fourneret and Jeannerod 1998). For example, in one experiment subjects were asked to draw straight lines with their hand (Fourneret and Jeannerod 1998). The hand was hidden and they saw the movement only via a computer projection. When a distortion was added so that the movement was deflected from the true path, subjects automatically corrected for this deflection but were not aware of this. In a series of related experiments Bargh and colleagues (2001) reported that even complex cognitive actions can be subject to unconscious influences. For example, in one experiment psychology students had to solve word puzzles. The experimental group first solved a puzzle with solutions that related to the topic of achievement. The control group began with a puzzle with neutral words. Then both groups performed three more puzzles with neutral solution words. The experimental group that had been exposed to (or "primed" with) achievement words, performed better on the three neutral puzzles than the control group, even though subjects stated in debriefing sessions that they were not aware of any link between the first and the following puzzles. Thus, subjects were not aware that the achievement-related prime words had subsequently motivated them to work harder. Recently this work has been extended to show that even unconscious prime stimuli can activate high-level cognitive control systems (Lau and Passingham 2007).

In line with this, several studies have shown that conscious intentions are preceded by unconscious brain activity (Libet et al. 1983; Haggard and Eimer 1999; Soon et al. 2008; Bode et al. 2010). One study from our lab used the novel technique of multivariate classification of intentions from brain activity (Haynes et al. 2007; figure 12.1A) to investigate how early before a conscious decision to act the outcome of the choice could be predicted from brain activity (Soon et al. 2008; figure 12.1B). Subjects were lying in a scanner and had two response buttons, one in their left and one in their right hand. They were instructed to relax and at some time that they could choose themselves to spontaneously decide whether to press the left or right button. At the same time a rapidly changing stream of letters appeared on the screen and subjects were asked to remember which letter was on the screen when they made up their mind for the left or right button. As expected, the subjects reported to be deciding up to a second before moving. However, it was possible to predict their choices from brain activity in medial prefrontal and parietal cortex up to 7 seconds before they made up their mind (Figure 12.1B). There are a number of conceptual aspects raised by this study that have been discussed elsewhere (Haynes 2011a). The key message for the current purposes is that the brain starts to prepare an upcoming decision long before consciousness is involved. Interestingly, the same region of medial prefrontal cortex stores prospective intentions even while they are laying dormant and a subject is busy performing other tasks (figure 12.1C; Momennejad and Haynes 2012).

Finally, even our commonsense intuition of intentional agency has been challenged (e.g., Wegner 2003). One way to investigate the feeling that we are in control of our actions is with tasks where subjects believe to be in control but that in fact have random outcomes (e.g., Langer and Roth 1975; see also Wegner 2003). In one example (Langer and Roth 1975), subjects were exposed to sequences of coin tossing. When the coin was in the air subjects were required to judge whether it would be heads or tails. Subjects were studied under three different conditions of feedback (figure 12.2): Either random feedback, where subjects were randomly told after each trial that their guess was correct or incorrect. Under ascending feedback subjects received feedback of being wrong disproportionately often at the beginning of the experiment. Under descending feedback subjects were told they were correct more often at the beginning of the experiment. Please note that under no condition was the feedback based on the actual result of the coin toss. Afterwards, subjects reported to feel more in control of the task under the descending condition and predicted that they would be successful on future trials. This suggests that the illusory positive feedback they received at the beginning of the experiment may have given them an illusory sense of control even though in fact they were not controlling the outcomes in any way.

Similar false impressions of agency can also occur during joint action, for example when two people are jointly moving an experimental Ouija board (Wegner 2003). Interestingly, the feeling of agency can not only be present where the subject is in fact not in control of a process. It can also be absent in cases where a subject is controlling a process (Wegner 2003). Importantly, the feeling of agency can be manipulated by using stimuli to get a subject to think about an action just before it happens. It appears as if the close temporal proximity between thought and action creates the illusion of agency (Wegner 2003).

Wegner concludes that our commonsense belief that conscious will and conscious intentions guide our actions is a mere illusion. What actually drives our actions are unconscious states. Conscious acts of will and something that appears like an intention exist, but they play no role in the actual causal history of an action. But how do we come to believe that we are the originators of our actions? Wegner tries to show that processes of self-ascrip-

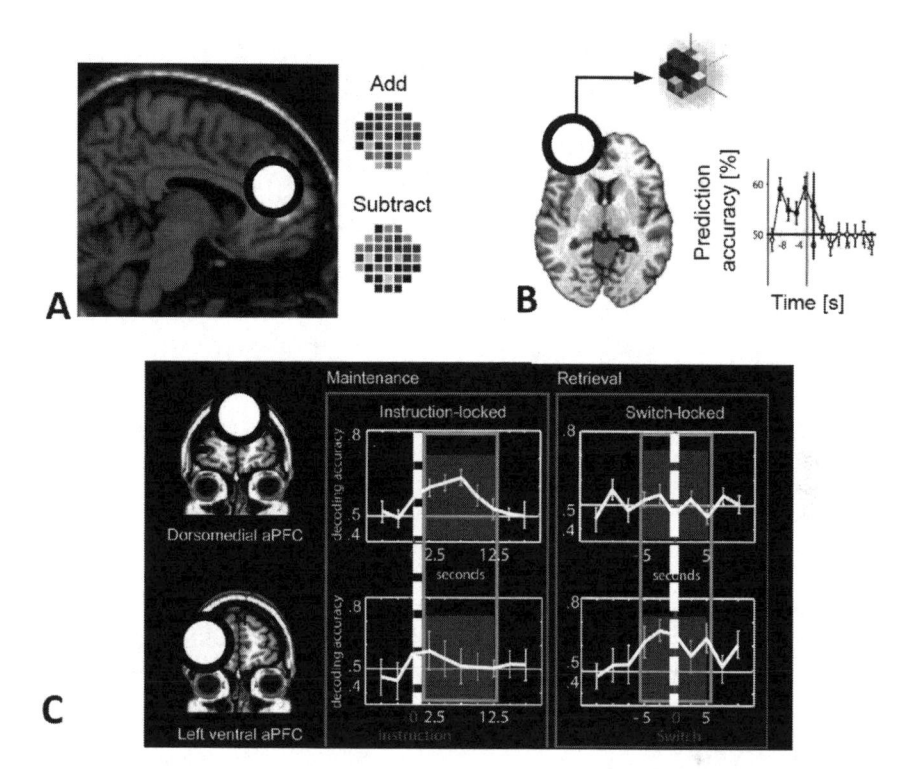

Figure 12.1. Neural encoding of intentions in the human brain. (A) A pattern classifier was trained to detect which of two intentions a subject was holding in mind. On each trial, subjects were first asked to choose whether they wanted to add or subtract two numbers. The highlighted region in anterior medial prefrontal cortex was measured with neuroimaging (fMRI). There the classifier was able to decode the intentions that subjects were holding, based on spatially distributed patterns of brain activity. From a separate region nearby it was possible to decode the intention *after* a subject had started to perform the calculation. These findings indicate that the brain encodes prospective intentions and intentions-in-action in separate brain locations (Haynes et al. 2007). (B) The modified Libet experiment. A pattern classifier was trained to predict a choice for a left or right button a subject was about to make. The classifier was able to significantly predict the choice up to seven seconds before the subject believed to be making up their mind (Soon et al. 2008). (C) This study investigated the encoding of prospective intentions while a subject was busily engaged in other tasks. Subjects were told to perform one of two possible tasks, judging the parity or magnitude of single digit numbers (after a brief delay of approximately 20s). In the meantime they were asked to do a different task (judge the color of the digits). During the maintenance period the intention could be decoded from medial prefrontal cortex (upper graph), but at the point of retrieval information switched to lateral prefrontal cortex (lower graph, Momennejad & Haynes 2012).

Descending
WWWWLWWWLLLLWWWLLWLLWWLLLLWLLLLW

Ascending
WLLLLWLLLLWWLLWLLWWWLLLWWWLWWWW

Random
WLWLLWLWLWWLLWLLWLWWWLWLWLLWLW

Figure 12.2. Illusory control over random event sequences. The example shows the sequences of feedback of win (W) or lose (L) subjects were given for their guesses of the outcome of random coin flips. In fact the feedback did not depend on the outcomes but instead was a fixed sequence with an either continuously descending, ascending or random proportion of wins.

tion exist that occur after the action has been performed. And it is these very post-hoc processes that give us the feeling of agency, including the feeling that our actions are actually guided by intention-like states that occur before the action is performed. But this is false. The idea that our actions are guided by conscious intentions is a mere delusion.

But how does Wegner arrive at this strong claim? His basic assumption is that if intentions are conscious and if they are effective—as the common-sense notion of intentions has it—then there seems to be no room for errors regarding the self-ascription of actions. Either I had the intention to leave the building—then I should identify myself as the agent of the related action—or I did not have this intention, then I should not regard myself as the agent. After all, how could I be wrong about my own beliefs and desires? But as we are sometimes wrong in self-ascribing actions, Wegner concludes that intentions, that is, conscious mental states that control our actions, do not exist. If they would, then we shouldn't be wrong about them because we can't be in error regarding our own conscious states. Given that we are in error, nothing exists that meets the folk-notion of intentionality and accordingly, we have no conscious control over our actions.

Wegner is completely right as far as the fallibility of self-ascriptions and the feeling of agency is concerned. As we will argue below, there are also serious reasons for accepting his idea of a post-hoc evaluative process that may have a decisive influence on our feeling of agency. Still, we don't think that consciousness requires infallibility regarding the contents of first-person experience. And there is even less reason to assume any infallibility regarding the causal role of intentions or intention-like states. As a consequence, we can accept that we are sometimes wrong regarding the content of our intentions and even more so as far as their causal role is concerned. So Wegner's argument does not establish that conscious will and intentional control are mere delusions.

3. A MORE ADVANCED NOTION OF INTENTION

But even if we reject Wegner's claim, the evidence reviewed above raises questions whether there are mental states that meet the commonsense notion of intention. Those states that do seem to play an important role in the control of our actions differ from the commonsense notion of intention in several respects. Most importantly they often lack consciousness, they don't seem to determine what we do, and they only play a limited role as far as our experience of agency is concerned. But does this mean that there are no intentions at all? Does it mean that conscious considerations and rational problem solving have no effect upon our actions at all? This would be highly mysterious. Normally we think that rational considerations do have an effect upon our behavior, that engineers design machines according to the ideas that they have developed, and that computer programmers are guided by their insights when they write programs. So there needs to be some connection between rational thinking and action. Intentions are among the most obvious candidates for this job.

In what follows we will present a modified view of what intentions might be and how they work. This idea is, as far as we can see, compatible with the empirical data; it differs in some important respects from the commonsense notion, but it still preserves the essential features of this notion, namely that intentions provide the connection between rational thoughts and actions. Three modifications of the commonsense view are of specific importance: First, we will argue that it makes no sense to insist that intentions need to be conscious. Specifically in cases of routine actions we do not bother to consciously think about our beliefs and desires, about our goals and the methods we might use in order to achieve them. Second, we will argue that, in contrast to the commonsense notion, intentions need not literally determine our behavior—even if they are effective. Intentions, that is, seem to work more like contributing factors. Third, it will turn out that the relation between intention and agency may be much more indirect than the commonsense account has it. Note again that in what follows we will be talking about *conceptual* requirements. So what is at issue are not empirical facts regarding human decision making processes. What is at issue is whether certain constituents of these processes count as intentions.

Consciousness

On the face of it, it seems obvious that an intention needs to be conscious in order to be effective. Saying that I actually leave the building via the staircase because I have the desire to do so and believe that taking the staircase is the best way to get out seems to imply that the related beliefs and desires are conscious. But let's see a bit more in detail why one needs to be conscious of one's own intentions. It seems that there are two reasons. First, consciousness gives us control. Apparently, we would be mere bystanders if our actions would be controlled by unconscious intentions. In this case, it would be the brain, and not ourselves, in the driver's seat. This is one of the reasons why Libet's (Libet 1985; Libet et al. 1983) experiments have been so irritating to many. They seem to show exactly this: It's the brain and not me who is in control of what "I" do. Now you might think that this is not a particularly strong argument given that the existence of the "I" or the "self" is under discussion (Dennett 1991; Minsky 1988). Maybe this is just a piece of outdated metaphysics that we have to give up anyway.

We don't think that it is sensible to give up the existence of the "I" or "self" either, but that's an issue for another paper. There is, however, still another reason why one might want to insist that consciousness is indispensable for any reasonable notion of intentionality. Even if the function and the evolutionary advantage of consciousness is still under discussion—many philosophers and scientists agree that consciousness is closely related to higher cognitive functions, that conscious cognition tends to be more flexible and creative than non-conscious cognition normally is (Kouider, 2009). The "global," or "neural workspace" account (Baars 1997b; Dehaene et al., 2006), for instance, holds that the specific character of conscious cognition is that it spreads the relevant piece of information over the entire network of an individual's higher cognitive processes, thus allowing for new solutions that would otherwise be impossible. In this respect, consciousness is a bit like the internet that connects scientists from all over the world, thus allowing them to join efforts in order to solve their problems. This goes along with the everyday experience that we have to be conscious if we look for new and relevant solutions, even if there is quite some evidence that even complex problem solving processes may in parts occur subconsciously (Nisbett and Wilson 1977).

All this shows that there are important reasons to insist on a close connection between consciousness and intention, and this goes even more so for the connection between higher cognition and intentions. As we have already said, it would be mysterious if higher cognition would not be closely connected to our actions, given the efforts that evolution has made in order to bring these abilities about. Note that this implies that there should be *always* a close connection between higher cognition and action. But does this mean that intentions have to be always *conscious* as well? In what follows, we will argue that this is not so.

The most obvious reason is that routine actions need not be guided by conscious states; still it makes good sense to say that they are intentional and they are guided by higher cognitive states. In most cases of routine actions it's quite easy to make the intention explicit: We go to the subway station every morning because we intend to go to the office, select the train that goes in the right direction, change trains, exit the train at the destination, and go from the station to the office. As long as nothing extraordinary interferes, all this may happen completely unconscious, even if this is certainly an action that is guided by the intention to go to the office.

And, of course, the action would still be under the control of higher cognitive capacities. This holds for two reasons. First, the route that you select in order to get to the office may be the result of careful considerations made earlier. So your action may be connected to higher cognitive functions even if the intention is not conscious at present. Second, as soon as something unexpected occurs, conscious problem solving processes will reappear on the scene almost immediately. So it seems that there is some kind of metacognition or monitoring involved that makes sure that consciousness and the related flexible problem-solving capacities kick in as soon as they are needed (e.g., Norman and Shallice 1986).

Conversely, imagine that your action is guided by a conscious intention but that this intention emerged out of nothing and, even worse, goes counter to some of your most important beliefs and desires: You find yourself guided by the conscious intention to smoke, say, although you are a dyed-in-the-wool non-smoker. Conversely, imagine that someone offers you a cigarette and you refuse to take it without even thinking about it—but you *did* think about all the pros and cons of smoking before you stopped it because smoking is too high a risk for your health. We bet that the latter counts as an intentional action in a much stricter sense than the former does, even if the former includes a conscious intention and the latter doesn't.

We take all this to show that consciousness is less important than commonsense holds when it comes to intentions. What *is* required is that the intentions are embedded in, or controlled by higher cognitive capacities and by those beliefs and desires that are essential for us. These requirements give us control over our actions, that is, they guarantee that our higher cognitive abilities have an effect on what we do, and that our actions are in line with what we believe and desire. This approach can also help to understand what might be irritating about Libet's results. It is not so much that these results show that volitional activities are guided and prepared by subconscious processes in the brain—what else should we expect as long as we don't believe in a Cartesian soul? Conscious states can't emerge out of nothing, so something should go on in our brain before a certain process reaches consciousness! So, what's really irritating is that the "Readiness Potential" that seems to guide our actions according to Libet is not under the control of higher cognitive functions, neither does is seem to depend on our beliefs and desires.[2]

So let's keep in mind that what is required in order to guarantee that our actions are under our control is not that our intentions are conscious. What *is* required is that these states are under the control of higher cognitive processes and that they depend upon our beliefs and desires—and this is taken care of by the requirement of embeddedness. Of course, intentions will be conscious quite frequently, but they don't need to. As a consequence, the consciousness-requirement should be dropped from the revised clarification of what an intention is.

Causation

But being embedded in higher cognitive functions, beliefs, and desires is not enough if intentions are expected to build a bridge between those states and our actions. In order to do so, they need to be causally effective. According to the commonsense notion they are: Intentions are even thought to determine or to directly guide our actions. If they do then what results is an action; if they don't then what is left counts as mere behavior. Both cases seem to boil down to a simple either/or question: Either a specific instance of behavior is determined by an intention or it isn't. And the result is either an action or it is not.

Categorical distinctions are quite handy when it comes to concepts, but in most cases, real world differences are not categorical but gradual. It is very useful to make a categorical distinction between day and night although there is a smooth transition between both and it is more or less arbitrary where, exactly, we assume the change between day and night does take place.

Something similar seems to be true for the difference between intentional action and mere behavior. A strict conceptual distinction is very useful and we should try to make it as clear and sharp as possible. This, however, can't rule out that the real difference between mere behavior and intentional action is one of degrees. Given that the present paper is not on action theory, we will not expand on this problem. What is essential, however, is that all this implies that there is also a gradual difference between paradigmatic intentions on the one hand and those mental states on the other that are not intentions but may be involved in the control of mere behavior: Even coughing or stumbling is controlled in some way or other.

There is still another reason why no clear-cut distinction between intentional action and mere behavior exists. According to the commonsense notion, intentions emerge from our beliefs and desires and they either guide our actions or they don't. But, again, this picture seems far too simple. Real world intentions emerge from an entire network of causally relevant factors, among them beliefs and desires but also emotions, memories and subconscious states. In the same vein, any intention is one of many causal factors that guide our actions. For example, your desire to stay healthy and your belief that smoking is bad for your health may not be the only motives that make you form the intention to stop smoking—TV ads showing lung cancer patients and the fact that some of your friends already stopped smoking may contribute as well. Neither does the mere intention to stop smoking guarantee that you will do so—it may well be that you do not succeed even if the intention is effective. Other factors, say your addiction and the greed for nicotine, may contribute as well and they may even be stronger. Conversely, you may succeed to stop even though your intention was not stronger than the one in the previous example: The reason why you succeeded this time is just that some additional factor came in, say one of your remote friends died of lung cancer.

This is why we follow up on a suggestion made by Goschke (Goschke 2003)[3] to treat intentions not as *determining* causes that trigger an action. Instead we see them as *contributing* causes. A contributing cause can be thought of as an insufficient but necessary part of an unnecessary but sufficient condition (Mackie 1965). Take the example of a forest fire being started by a match that was carelessly thrown away. The match is an insufficient condition, because the forest needed to be dry to catch fire. Only the combination of a drought and the match makes up a sufficient condition. However this sufficient condition is not necessary, there are other sufficient conditions that could have had the same effect, say for example an arsonist and a can of gasoline. Put differently, the idea is that single facts need to be thought of only as contributors to effects, but whether an effect comes about or not depends on many boundary or contextual conditions. Similarly, having an intention can significantly enhance or decrease the likelihood of a specific action and it may do so in different degrees; still it does not determine its occurrence just on its own.

As a consequence, an individual instance of behavior may count as an intentional action in different degrees. It may count as an action in a very strong sense if it's guided by a paradigmatic intention whose causal contribution is very strong compared to background beliefs, reflexes, instincts and other factors that may also contribute to the outcome but are difficult to control. Conversely, the behavior in question may be an action in a very weak sense if it is guided by a non-paradigmatic case of an intention whose causal contribution is very weak, say because background beliefs, instincts and sub-personal factors almost determine the action.

Again, all these are conceptual considerations. They are intended to show that it is reasonable to call mental states intentions even if they do not meet all the requirements of the commonsense notion of intention. Even if our suggestion diverges from the commonsense notion of intention, we think that it is more a clarification than a completely new and maybe controversial position, so it should be acceptable for many.

Agency

Agency is the last conceptual ingredient of the commonsense notion of intention that deserves a discussion here. It is not contested that human agents typically have a feeling of agency upon performing an action. According to the commonsense notion, this feeling is a direct effect of having an intention. So if you have the intention to leave a building and execute the related action you will end up having a feeling of agency.

This idea has been attacked by Daniel Wegner (Wegner 2002, 2003). Wegner presents evidence according to which intentions are neither a necessary nor a sufficient condition for the feeling of agency. At times, we feel as agents even if we did not perform an intentional action. Conversely, we sometimes do *not* feel as agents even if we did initiate and perform the intentional action in question. Assuming that intentions need to be conscious and effective and that we cannot be wrong regarding our own conscious states including conscious intentions, Wegner concludes that the feeling of agency is a mere post-hoc construction.

We have already made clear why we find Wegner's main argument unconvincing and why we think that intentions do exist—even if this requires a revised concept of intentions. But does this mean that the feeling or the experience of agency has to follow directly from an effective intention? Does this mean, in other words, that *post-hoc* processes that evaluate an action and decide whether or not we feel as agents cannot be part of a reasonable concept of intention? We do not think so. In order to see this, imagine a soccer player. The soccer player has the intention to score a goal, he shoots, and the ball hits the goal. On a traditional view, the player might regard himself as the originator of the action in question. He had the intention to score a goal, the intention resulted in the relevant bodily activity which in turn resulted in scoring a goal. What else could be asked for?

In order to see that there is something missing, note that other players might have intervened: One of them might have hit the ball and it may well be that it is only because of this intervention that a goal was scored. This is just a very obvious example that factors intervening after one's own action may be essential for the success—and for the evaluation—of one's action. As a consequence, the contribution of these factors and, consequently, the complementary role of one's own contribution can only be assessed *after* the intention has become effective. This may be one of the reasons why several psychological models of agency (Haggard 2005; Gollwitzer 1986) include post-hoc evaluation processes. As long as the actual intention and, therefore, the agent's actual contribution is a necessary requirement for self-attribution by a post-hoc evaluation process, we see no reason why this should not be compatible with a reasonable and empirically informed concept of intention.

CONCLUSION

So let's sum up. We started with a commonsense notion of intention which is constitutive for the distinction between action and behavior. According to this commonsense notion, intentions are conscious goal representations that permit higher cognitive states to control our actions and thus establish agency. Unfortunately, though, this notion is not supported by the empirical evidence.

According to the evidence reviewed intentions need not emerge from a rational process leading from beliefs and desires to actions. Intentions can be caused directly by external events (e.g., by direct brain stimulation) or by unconscious mechanisms that bypass our rational deliberation. Intentions might not be accessible to consciousness and our subjective feelings of control and agency might not always be correct. It would seem then that, according to the evidence reviewed, it is at least questionable whether there are any mental states that meet the requirements of the commonsense notion of intention. Thus, some scientists have concluded that there are no real intentions and even volitional action might be a mere illusion.

This is why we have asked in the third part whether a moderate revision of the commonsense concept of intention might be in place. We tried to show that such a revision is possible and that it is not just a compromise between our intuitions and the empirical evidence, rather, it makes sense in itself. Our first point was that intentions, contrary to the commonsense notion, need not be conscious but they do need to be controlled by higher cognitive states such that the agent's beliefs and desires can control her actions. Second, intentions don't need to be conceived of as triggering causes that exclusively determine a specific action. Rather we propose to understand them as contributing causes that are part of a network of factors including background beliefs, circumstances, sub-personal motives, etc. For this and other reasons, there is no categorical difference between intentions and other intention-like states and, as a consequence, between action and mere behavior. Rather, the difference is gradual in both cases, such that there may be more or less paradigmatic instances of intentions and, as a consequence, of actions. Finally, we argued that intentions do not directly constitute the experience of agency. While the existence of previous intentions seems essential for this experience, it may well be and even seems reasonable to assume that this experience includes a *post-hoc* process of evaluation.

As a consequence, we propose to define intentions as goal representations that permit higher cognitive states like beliefs and desires to participate in the control of our actions and are constitutive for the experience of agency. We think that this redefinition does justice to our conceptual intuitions as well as to the evidence available and can serve as a basis for further investigation in this field.

NOTES

Both authors contributed equally to this work.

1. This subjective notion of agency should not prevent you from endorsing an objective notion as well that is based on objective criteria, say the actual causal rather than the subjective experience of agency. As a consequence, someone can meet the subjective criteria, that is, enjoy the experience of agency although he doesn't meet the objective criteria, or vice versa.

2. This, however, might not be the entire truth. See Herrmann, Pauen, Min, Busch and Rieger, 2008.

3. Stressing that intentions merely contribute to the outcome of actions but do not determine them exclusively, Goschke describes intentions as "constraints." While we follow Goschke's main argument, we think that "constraint" is a bit misleading, given that constraints typically describe requirements or limitations that cannot be overridden. But intentions can, so we think that it's more adequate to describe them as "contributing causes."

Chapter Thirteen

Experience and Autonomy

Why Consciousness Does and Doesn't Matter

Thomas W. Clark

Consciousness seems a central requirement for responsibility and autonomy. We ordinarily don't hold each other responsible for behavior which occurs unconsciously, as when sleep walking, or which happens despite our best conscious intentions, such as an inopportune sneeze. On the other hand, conscious control—acting in light of reasons and beliefs that if asked I could articulate on the spot—generally confers responsibility. I'm held accountable as a source of action if I'm awake, aware and acting voluntarily.[1] But what's so special about consciousness that it confers responsibility? The same question arises with respect to personal autonomy: what is it about consciousness, if anything, that it makes me a genuine author of action?

Neuroscientific studies of consciousness and conscious capacities have brought these questions to the fore. Consciousness, in the sense of having phenomenal experience (paradigmatically, experiences of pain, red and other sensory qualities) is not involved in all phases of generating intentional and voluntary action. For example, the reportable experience of having made a decision may lag behind the unconscious initiation of action in certain simple choice scenarios. In more complex, real world situations, I may be unaware of significant influences on my behavior. Further, there's no clear demarcation, in terms of causal efficacy in behavior control, between brain processes correlated with conscious experience—what I will call conscious *processes*—and those not. From a neuro-behavioral standpoint, it's neurons all the way up and all the way down (or in and out, if you prefer), whether or not conscious experience is involved.

The evidence strongly suggests that neural operations correlated with having conscious experience—the neural correlates of consciousness, or

NCC—have critically important cybernetic (action guiding) functions, such as integrating multimodal information and subserving memory, learning and flexible behavior (Kanwisher 2001; Dehaene and Naccache 2001; Jack and Shallice 2001; Parvizi and Damasio 2001; Crick and Koch 2003). But phenomenal experience itself isn't needed to *explain* these functions, rather, it *accompanies* them, for reasons still obscure to the philo-scientific community; it's the functions themselves that get the behavioral job done.

Appreciating the role of unconscious processes in behavior control, the functional continuity of unconscious and conscious processes, and the fact that the brain accomplishes behavior control on its own may have some initially discomfiting implications, depending on one's pre- and post-theoretical commitments. First, it sparks a philosophical worry about mental causation: consciousness might be epiphenomenal with respect to behavior control when viewed from a third-person, neuro-behavioral perspective. Appeals to subjective experience may not be needed in scientific accounts of voluntary and intentional action. Second, it suggests that, whatever the causal role of conscious experience, conscious *processes* (the NCC) may not always be in charge of behavior to the extent we normally suppose; this threatens every day, practical notions of responsibility and autonomy. Third, it poses an existential threat to a folk dualist conception of human agency: that at the core we exist as immaterial conscious controllers separate from our brains—for instance souls—that make contra-causally free choices.

I will argue that these threats to conscious control, properly understood, need not discomfit us. Indeed, by distinguishing the possible behavior-guiding role of conscious *experience* from that of conscious *processes*, and by understanding their respective limitations, we might gain in personal autonomy, naturalistically conceived. Understanding how consciousness does, and doesn't, matter promises to give us greater real world self-efficacy and control.

Before proceeding, let me reiterate what I mean by consciousness for the purposes of this chapter. What I have in mind is *phenomenal* consciousness, that is, experienced qualitative states such as pain, the sensation of red, the "what it is like" to undergo sensations, emotions, occurent thoughts and phenomenally diffuse states such as inclinations and hunches.[2] The basic qualitative elements of experience—qualia—are notoriously resistant to assimilation by physicalist explanation precisely because subjective qualitative character isn't (yet) the obvious result, or cause, of any physical process. Moreover, while the physical processes associated with experience are all in principle observationally available, experience itself is not: phenomenal consciousness is a categorically private affair.

PART 1: DEFUSING THE THREAT OF EPIPHENOMENALISM

The problem of mental causation, or more precisely, *phenomenal* causation, can be stated as follows: How does conscious experience, as possibly distinct from the neural processes empirically found to be associated with it—conscious processes—contribute to behavior control? One solution to this problem would be to show an identity at some level, say physical or functional, between conscious experience and conscious processes. Since the central behavior controlling role of the neurally instantiated cognitive functions associated with conscious experience are not in doubt, such an identity would automatically confer on consciousness the same causal powers as those functions, solving the problem of phenomenal causation. But, despite the plethora of proposals on offer (Block, Flanagan and Guzeldere 1997; Chalmers 2010; Tononi 2012; Koch 2012; Dennett 1991; Metzinger 2003) there is no canonical theory of such an identity, and no consensus about whether it's even a live possibility.

Just as there is no accepted identity theory, there is no theory on offer to account for how, if consciousness *isn't* identical to its neuro-functional correlates, it adds its own essential contribution to behavior control beyond what those correlates accomplish. No credible dualist interactionist theory seems forthcoming, in which case, short of an identity claim, conscious experience seems simply along for the ride. Epiphenomenalists are happy to, or at least resigned to, bite this bullet: phenomenal feels are somehow produced by neural goings-on, but they don't in turn *affect* those goings-on, so are behaviorally inefficacious (Robinson 2010, 2012). In which case so much the worse for consciousness: it gets caused, but doesn't get to cause in turn.

In the absence of viable identity or interactionist theories, must we accede to epiphenomenalism? I would suggest not. First, epiphenomenalists (along with the rest of us) have precisely no story about how conscious experience is produced or generated by conscious processes. All we have are observed *dependency relations* between conscious processes—the neural correlates of consciousness, whatever they turn out to be—and conscious experience: when certain processes are active, then we're phenomenally conscious. Such relations don't necessarily entail that phenomenal states are *caused* by or *produced* by neural processes as a further effect which then, according to epiphenomenalists, fails to play any subsequent causal role in behavior control. As Dennett puts it, there's no "double transduction" by which neural activity produces something more (Dennett 1998b). Unless there's an account on offer of how conscious experience is generated as an effect, then worries about whether or not this effect could in turn be a further cause of behavior seem misplaced or premature. Consciousness may not be an effect at all, in any standard sense, and therefore not the sort of thing that could be reasonably expected to play a causal role in addition to its neural correlates.

Next, I want to suggest that although conscious experience likely can't figure in third person accounts of behavior, we shouldn't conclude from this that experience is epiphenomenal. In support of the first part of this claim, I'd propose that naturalistic explanations of a phenomenon normally require that all elements playing a role in the explanation be, in principle, observable. In particular, when explaining your behavior, we can appeal to your brain processes as they are observed to control bodily movements, and we can appeal to your intentional states, plausibly construed as being realized by those (potentially observable) processes.[3] However, we don't and can't observe your pain, your sensation of red, or any other of your experiences. Your experience only *exists for you* as an up-and-running cybernetic system; it isn't the sort of thing that can be observed at all, not even by you.[4] Consciousness is categorically, existentially private, never publicly accessible to external observers in the way its neural correlates are. Remember also from above that we can't unproblematically assume an identity between conscious experience and conscious processes, such that we can claim that in observing the neural correlates of experience we are observing experience itself. If, therefore, conscious experience is not an observable, we can't appeal to it in third person explanations of behavior, any more than we can appeal to invisible ghosts, spirits or souls. Experience doesn't appear in what we might call third person *explanatory space*: the space inhabited by observables such as brains, bodies and behavior itself.

If this is so, then, interestingly enough, it's a mistake to think that experience could be epiphenomenal with respect to behavior. To be epiphenomenal requires at least the logical possibility of exerting a causal influence, but this possibility is foreclosed by the fact that consciousness doesn't appear in third person explanatory space; it simply isn't in a position to play a causal role in observation-based explanations of behavior. By contrast, the whistle on Huxley's steam engine (Huxley 1874) *does* appear in this space, along with the engine itself, so can fairly be characterized as epiphenomenal with respect to the operation of the engine. The same applies to your appendix: it sits in physical, abdominal space but is vestigial and non-functional, hence epiphenomenal with respect to your bodily economy. Not so for experience: we don't see it sitting in the brain (or anywhere else, for that matter), so it can't be epiphenomenal with respect to the brain, the body or behavior.

My third point against epiphenomenalist worries is to note that even if, as I suggest, consciousness can't figure in third person accounts of behavior, the brain and body get the job done just fine on their own. From an external observational perspective, neural processes are *all that's going on* and are sufficient for smart cybernetics at whatever level we care to take, physical, functional or intentional. In the movie *Blade Runner*, the Tyrell Corporation bio-engineers so-called "replicants" to perform dangerous work for which it's necessary they be as cognitively and behaviorally adept as their human masters. Why, in creating the artificial neural structures necessary for human-level perception, memory and cognition should Tyrell concern itself with consciousness? Phenomenal states wouldn't appear in its design specifications for replicants, even though the specifications somehow entail the existence of such states.[5] The same is true of *our* design via evolution: we needn't suppose that conscious experience per se was selected for, only the behavior-controlling, neural-instantiated functions with which it is associated.

Since conscious processes are, in conjunction with unconscious processes, sufficient for action control, it shouldn't worry us that their associated phenomenal states aren't in a position to play a role in scientific accounts of behavior, or that they weren't directly selected for in evolution. True, we've *ended up* conscious, but from a functional, cybernetic perspective experience is neither here nor there; it doesn't matter for purposes of producing intelligent behavior. Your zombie twin, if such could exist (a question beyond the scope of this chapter), would be just as capable as you.

But there's an important caveat here. Even if consciousness doesn't matter from third person explanatory or design standpoints, it matters tremendously to you as a locus of consciousness. As the host of an ineluctable phenomenal reality, you have very strong preferences in the sorts of experiences you want to undergo. This grounds your claim to be a subject of moral concern, someone capable of suffering, and for granting (the problem of other minds aside) the same moral status to others; it's also why it matters whether future generations of AIs achieve consciousness.[6] Moreover, from the subjective standpoint of *first person* explanatory space, it strongly seems as if conscious states *do* play a causal role: it's a phenomenally given subjective fact that we wince *because* we're in pain and consume chocolate *because* it tastes so good; this will continue to be our experienced reality no matter what scientists and philosophers tell us. And since conscious experiences co-occur so reliably with behavior controlling conscious processes, citing experiences as causes of behavior is a very good explanatory proxy for the actual neuro-functional control story. Indeed, for many intra- and interpersonal purposes they are very useful, perhaps even necessary, explanatory fictions—subjective shorthand, one might say. For these reasons, we won't become skeptics about the importance of conscious experience just because it might not play a causal role in objective explanatory contexts. Subjectively and interpersonally, consciousness will continue to matter.

PART 2: EXPANDING CONSCIOUS CONTROL

Epiphenomenalism about experience aside, the practical worry about conscious processes, spurred by research in behavioral and social psychology, is that they may not be as central to behavior control as ordinarily assumed. If not, then perhaps we're not as responsible or as autonomous as we suppose. In this section I'll consider two research paradigms on threats to conscious control. One, which I will call the *precursor* paradigm, purports to show that unconscious brain processes—precursors to an experienced choice—determine that choice, so consciousness itself might be by-passed (Nahmias 2011a) or just a non-causal addendum to action. The other, what I will call the *influence* paradigm, suggests that we are unconscious of situational factors and internal biases influencing our behavior, some of which might induce us to act against our endorsed values. It's the latter paradigm, not the former, that I think should worry us.

First, in light of part 1 above, I'll reiterate that it's the role of conscious *processes*, not consciousness experience, that's at issue here. Although I'm usually accorded responsible authorship of action only when I'm awake and having experiences, it isn't experience per se that makes me responsible. As we've seen, experience is the subjective indicator of the operation of certain behavior-guiding, information-integrating functions, and it's these functions, as opposed to those associated with unconscious processes, that matter most for responsibility and autonomy, not experience. It's our neurally instantiated capacities for being behaviorally flexible, foresightful and corrigible that justify our responsibility practices as means to guide action toward the good (Morse 2004). We don't hold those without such capacities (young children, the insane) responsible, even though they are conscious. But as a matter of practical necessity we would have to hold a sufficiently sophisticated robot responsible (allocate it behavior-guiding rewards and sanctions) in order to produce acceptable behavior, whether or not we suppose it hosts phenomenal states (Clark 2006).

When acting under the control of conscious processes, we're able to behave appropriately in novel situations by simulating multiple possible courses of actions in light of memories and the anticipated consequences of those actions (Baumeister, Masicampo, and Vohs 2011). We're also in a position to state reasons and justifications for action to our peers, such that, if our reasons are considered plausible, we gain their trust, respect and cooperation in matters of moral or practical consequence. It's this process of consciously mediated reason-giving that defines our *endorsed* self, that which we would defend in public or that wins our acceptance in private deliberations. Conscious processes, therefore, are essential to what we ordinarily identify with as our most *capable* and most *justifiable* selves; they permit the formulation of consistent, publicly expressible commitments and values *and* enable action on behalf of such commitments over a wide range of possible situations. In short, they are essential to the development and actualization of personal integrity and autonomy.

Given this sketch of the importance of conscious processes, let's consider the precursor paradigm as a threat to conscious control. Besides the pioneering work of Benjamin Libet (1982), a widely cited finding is that of Soon et al. (2008). They were able to extract information from fMRI scans that was predictive, at a rate greater than chance, of subjects' simple choices (choose the left or right hand to push a button) up to ten seconds in advance of the subjects' consciously experienced decision and behavior. Imagining that this rate eventually approaches 100 percent, and that the predictive information becomes available in real time (which it was not in the reported experiments), researchers might reliably know before the subjects what their behavior will be under such conditions.

Should this worry us? I think not. Unless we suppose consciousness is something separate from brain function, for instance an immaterial contra-causal controller (the topic of part 3), it shouldn't surprise us that the experience of having decided, dependent as it is on neural processes, should be preceded by other processes contributing to the choice that *don't* give rise to that experience. We already knew that not all brain activity supporting behavior, simple or complex, constitutes conscious processing.

Second, the choices predicted in such experiments *are* simple, binary and spontaneous—they lend themselves to neural prediction precisely because the experimental situation is stripped of the subject's need to consider reasons for action and the consequences of alternative possible behaviors that are the raison d'etre of conscious processes. I don't need to, and probably can't, provide reasons for the spontaneous choosing of left over right, and of course I'm not privy to its neural determinants—that's *why* it's spontaneous. If I play by the experimenter's rules, I don't know in advance which way I'll choose, or exactly when, but the experimenter might, given enough trials. But of course this is a far cry from showing that most choices are either predictable via brain scans or solely the result of prior unconscious processing.

Third, note that conscious processes are engaged throughout the experimental situation: subjects are continuously aware of what they are being asked to do, of the apparatus, and of their behavior; without their engagement the experiment couldn't take place. All that's been shown by Libet, Soon et al. and other contributors to the precursor paradigm is that a *particular* conscious process—that associated with the experienced decision and concomitant behavior—is part of a sequence of neural operations, some of which are predictive of the conscious choice. That we aren't aware of the neural precursors of a choice in its early stages doesn't itself impugn the causal role of conscious processes, those necessary for learning and for flexible, situationally appropriate, and reasons-responsive behavior, for instance the behavior of those cooperating in a psychology experiment. It only shows that conscious processes aren't all there is to behavior control. But again, we already knew that.

Given the simplicity of the behaviors involved, the precursor paradigm doesn't cast doubt on the efficacy of the conscious capacities often deployed when making morally and practically significant choices in the real world. It is thus a minor threat to conscious control compared to the influence paradigm: the possibility that unconscious factors affecting behavior might subvert personal integrity and autonomy. Researchers such as Bargh (1997), Wilson (2002) and Wegner (2002) have documented the ubiquity and importance of unconscious influences in behavior control, some innocuous, some consequential. Some examples of the latter: Research on implicit bias (Hardin and Banaji, in press) suggests that many of us unconsciously discriminate against those not of our age, gender, ethnicity, or sexual orientation; the probability of behaving altruistically can be a function of situational factors that we don't realize are affecting us (Darley and Batson 1973; Macrae and Johnston 1998); our voting preferences might be determined in part by an unconscious assessment of a candidate's trustworthiness or competence based on physical appearance (Todorov et al. 2005; Lawson et al. 2010); and when it comes to assessing a candidate's policies, it turns out that we're often subject to confirmation bias, the sometimes unconscious tendency to systematically ignore or downplay counter-arguments and disconfirming evidence (Nickerson 1998).

These are just a few instances of how morally and practically consequential behavior can be shaped by influences outside of awareness.[7] Their net effect is that we might end up acting in ways—prejudicial, uncaring, unprincipled, uninformed—that fall short of our consciously endorsed values. Unconscious influences therefore pose a substantial threat to our becoming ideally integrated, publicly justifiable and maximally autonomous selves.

Of course, as much as I might not endorse my unconsciously driven or situationally influenced behavior, it's still *me* that's acting; I'm not *just* my endorsed self. On a naturalistic understanding, persons consist of relatively stable constellations of physically embodied traits, susceptibilities and dispositions, some of which aren't always mediated by conscious processes. I can't therefore conveniently "externalize" the less than admirable unconscious parts of me and their behavioral expression (Dennett 2003, 122). Unless I'm acting under duress or other standard excusing conditions, I have to take (reluctant) ownership of and responsibility for actions that might reflect the influence of situational factors and unconscious biases.

However, once informed of these influences—once they become objects of conscious consideration—I can take steps to reduce their effect on my behavior. If it's demonstrated to me that my voting preferences are mostly a matter of candidates' physiognomy, I can second guess my superficial initial judgments and look for more objective indicators of a candidate's competence. Knowing that advertisers and political campaigns are using every trick in the book to sway my preferences, I can monitor my behavior with a skeptical eye: to what extent am I the target of manipulation, and how can I counteract it? Knowing that situations have a material influence on my morally consequential actions, I can work to avoid or modify situations that put my integrity at risk, or if that's not possible, work on strengthening my resolve to do the right thing (Baumeister and Tierney 2011) whatever the situation.

In short, although the threat of unconscious factors to integrity and autonomy is very real, conscious processes, once engaged, have the capacity to counteract their influence. Even as the work of social psychologists increasingly reveals the role of the unconscious in controlling behavior, that very knowledge ends up expanding the scope of conscious control on behalf of our endorsed selves. The more we understand the extent to which we *are* unconsciously motivated and influenced, and understand the mechanisms of influence, the better equipped we are to become better integrated, more autonomous agents, less at risk of betraying our core values.

At the same time, however, those with commercial or ideological agendas can use expertise in situational and unconscious control to better manipulate us. We're therefore caught up in an arms race of control and counter-control, in which it behooves us—the potential unwitting marks of subliminal influence—to keep up with the latest developments in behavioral and neuro-economics and their practical applications, for instance in marketing and political persuasion. In constructing ourselves as morally and cognitively virtuous agents, and in defending against threats to our hard-won autonomy, deploying our conscious capacities in light of science is key.

Understanding the limits and vulnerabilities of conscious control also has implications for responsibility ascriptions. Responsibility for deliberately manipulated behavior is distributed between the agent who acts *and* those who consciously set out to influence the behavior in question. So although we're not absolved of responsibility when acting under such influences (we're still rationally responsive to rewards, sanctions and information), it's fair to hold others responsible as well, for instance food, alcohol and tobacco industries that are bent on inducing us to consume products that we're often better off avoiding. Understanding that an individual's conscious control capacities are targets of deliberate subversion and circumvention helps to justify regulatory polices that restrict attempts at manipulation, and it highlights the need for educational campaigns that increase awareness of our vulnerabilities and enable counter-control.

PART 3: FROM SOUL CONTROL TO NATURALIZED AUTONOMY

As much as many philosophers and psychologists might be comfortable with a neuro-behavioral view of why conscious processes matter, many lay folk might not. As possibly "natural born" dualists (Bloom 2004), and under the influence of long-standing religious beliefs in an immortal soul, they might suppose we exist as some sort of immaterial conscious controller, a categorically mental supervisor of action. This essential, non-physical self isn't bound by deterministic laws in making choices; instead, consciousness gives it libertarian, contra-causal free will, and it, not the brain, is ultimately in charge of action. But on a naturalistic understanding, such folk dualism has it wrong: consciousness can't matter in this way since it isn't independent of, and doesn't add to, what the brain does in controlling behavior.

Of course, the *experience* of being a core mental self is robust for many of us: for most waking moments, it feels as if I'm a simple, non-extended "I" located somewhere behind my eyes. If I don't take correction from the mind sciences, I might suppose that this conscious me is a non-physical substance in charge of action, e.g., a soul or mental controller, not just a phenomenal self-*model* (Metzinger 2003) that accompanies the neural processes that, from an empirical, third person perspective, are actually controlling behavior. Here's a description, gleaned from an online discussion, of what I'll colloquially call "soul control," that exerted by the immaterial conscious self, connected to but distinct from the brain:

> We have evolved consciousness which gives us the ability to make completely uncaused choices. . . . Though we are tethered to our experiences and our brains, our reasons for our choices are never the causes of our actions. Our choices and actions happen independently of our reasons, i.e., our reasons do not compel us to act in any way. Nothing compels our choices. We're always free going forward. In every moment choice is open to us. That is what consciousness has enabled—free will among living beings.[8]

It's an empirical question as to what proportion of laypersons subscribe to something along the lines of the view just quoted. Cross-cultural research suggests that beliefs in something akin to libertarian free will is widely held (Sarkissian et al. 2010), and a survey of a sample of the U.S. general population (not college students) found that majorities evinced beliefs in a non-physical soul that governs behavior (Nadelhoffer in press). A 2009 Harris poll found that 71 percent of respondents reported belief in a soul that survives death (Harris Poll 2009).

To those of dualistic persuasions, freedom, dignity and autonomy might be at risk should it turn out that the conscious self isn't the controller they suppose it to be. If the brain's action guiding capacities, even those associated with consciousness, are simply the working out of complex causes and effects, unsupervised by a self that transcends causal laws, then maybe we aren't really authors of action but just pass-throughs for impersonal causation. And if we're not personally responsible in the way contra-causal control makes possible—that is, ultimately, buck-stoppingly responsible—perhaps we're not responsible at all and can't be *held* responsible. In which case, why behave morally? The naturalistic understanding of consciousness-as-accompaniment, not independent controller, might provoke demoralization by determinism.

This possibility seems borne out by research in which subjects exposed to statements challenging free will, compared to controls not thus exposed, cheated more (Vohs and Schooler 2008) and behaved more aggressively (Baumeister, Masicampo, and DeWall 2009) in experimental situations. Such findings seem to support the recommendation, floated by philosopher Saul Smilansky (2005b), that we should conceal the truth that we're likely not exceptions to natural cause and effect. In particular, we can't responsibly let non-academics know that, because the conscious self isn't an immaterial contra-causal controller, consciousness doesn't matter in the way they suppose it does.

But of course it will be difficult to keep the science-based debunking of soul control under wraps. Indeed, the trend seems to be toward more publicly-expressed skepticism about libertarian freedom, exampled by atheist Sam Harris's monograph *Free Will* (Harris 2012), critiques from established scientists (Snyder 2012), and a spate of articles in the news and popular press (Clark 2010; Nadelhoffer 2011; Ortega 2012). Moreover, any attempt to suppress public awareness and discussion of naturalistic understandings of the self violates a cardinal value of science and the open society: the free exchange of information and opinion.

Still, as Dennett reminds us in his books on free will (1984, 2003), there are better and worse ways to let this particular cat out of the bag. What might help in addressing worries about losing soul control (not that we ever had it) is to show why an immaterial, causally exempt controller couldn't possibly contribute to making choices. This is for a very simple reason, suggested by the quote above: a controller not at the influence of *anything*, in particular one's own motives and reasons for action, isn't in a position to guide behavior. Were consciousness an uninfluenced arbiter hovering above neurally-encoded motivation, perception and cognition, it would literally have no reason to add its (immaterial) weight to any alternative under consideration. Any decision process with an unmotivated decider having the final say would of necessity fail to decide. That, and as we've seen in part 1, there's no plausible account of how an immaterial controller would get a grip on the brain and body. So not only is there no scientifically respectable evidence for the radically libertarian agent, such an agent would have neither the motives nor the means to contribute to practical decision-making. The ultimate control, authorship and responsibility conferred by the soul are not only naturalistic impossibilities, but not worth wanting, as Dennett (1984) would put it, for actual choice-making.[9]

This leads to a second, crucially important reminder to put front and center when debunking soul control: human persons, by virtue of their neurally instantiated perceptual, cognitive and behavior control capacities, are real agents that exert robust *local* control. As much as science suggests we might be fully determined in our wants, character and abilities, we're just as causally effective—more so, in many cases—as the genetic and environmental factors that shape us. Determinism isn't fatalism, the idea that our actions don't make a difference in determining our fates (Houlton in press).

What's needed for authentic authorship and autonomy is what we already are: very sensitive informavores, endowed by nature and nurture with physically embodied capacities to select between alternatives, often well in advance of action, *as determined by* our needs, desires and best guesses about the consequences of behavior. Dennett (2012) expresses this nicely:

> When the "control" by the environment runs through your well-working perceptual systems and your undeluded brain, it is nothing to dread; in fact, nothing is more desirable than being caused by the things and events around us to generate true beliefs about them that we can then use in modulating our behavior to our advantage!

In contrast to Dennett's optimistic take on determinist agency, Sam Harris says in his monograph that we are "bio-chemical puppets" (Harris 2012, 47) and the book's cover tells the same story: the letters spelling "Free Will" dangle from marionette strings. Regrettably, this suggests that without soul control we end up as passive victims—puppets—of cause and effect.[10] In comparison with the ultimate (but impossible) control exerted by an immaterial conscious decider, we might be tempted to conclude that a naturalistic understanding of agency disempowers us. But if we abandon dualism, see the impossibility of soul control, and acknowledge the causal contribution of our behavior-guiding capacities (conscious and unconscious), there's no justification for thinking of ourselves as puppets.

Getting this right is essential, since the puppet view could well prove demoralizing in just the ways suggested by the findings of Vohs and Schooler (2008) and Baumeister, Masicampo and DeWall (2009). Further, if a science-based, naturalistic view of the self is thought to imply the end of effective agency, this will impede the acceptance of science and naturalism: no one wants to be proved a puppet. In showing that consciousness doesn't matter in the way many folk might suppose, scientists and naturalists must take care not to give the impression that our conscious *capacities* don't matter, or that we cease being agents who can be held responsible, at least in the consequentialist sense of being answerable to a moral community (Nadelhoffer 2011).

On the positive side, debunking soul control, done properly, can increase our autonomy, paradoxically enough, by revealing that there's no core self that's immune to influence. Knowing that we are fully caused underscores the importance of becoming aware, as our time and energy permit, of *all* the behaviorally significant factors impinging on us, including attempts at manipulation via situational and subliminal determinants. As discussed in part 2, such awareness widens the potential scope of individual conscious control. And seeing the self as completely embedded in a causal matrix draws attention to the full range of conditions—genetic and environmental, and intentionally mediated or not—that shape the person. Although individuals are local controllers who must be held responsible in order to guide their action toward the good, the buck no longer stops with them (more precisely, it never did). Dismantling beliefs in the immaterial conscious controller and ultimate personal responsibility therefore promises to empower us, make our responsibility ascriptions more realistic, and make our responsibility practices less retributively punitive (Greene and Cohen 2004; Clark 2005; Waller 2011; Shariff et al. 2012). On the other hand, protecting these beliefs, as some recommend, keeps us in the dark about the actual causes of behavior and abets regressive criminal justice and social polices premised on the myth of the ultimately responsible self (Clark 2004).

CONCLUSION

An adequate response to folk worries about the role of the conscious self will demonstrate the reality and viability of a naturalized autonomy (Waller 1998). Such autonomy, expressed in voluntary behavior in a social context, establishes the basis for naturalized responsibility: although we are completely products of conditions we didn't choose, we are nevertheless identifiable sources of action, justifiably subject to behavior-guiding and norms-reinforcing interventions—our responsibility practices. To dethrone consciousness as a contra-causal controller is therefore not a threat to either autonomy or responsibility, suitably naturalized, and may well help to improve our responsibility practices as judged from a progressive humanistic standpoint. [11]

What *is* a threat, as we've seen in part 2, is the role of unconscious situational and motivational influences that drive behavior in opposition to our endorsed values. We are not just our conscious processes, those that play central roles in guiding complex, flexible behavior and that somehow give rise to conscious experience; we are, for better or worse, our unconscious susceptibilities and biases as well. Fortunately, the science that brings the role of unconscious processes to our (conscious) attention also makes them potential targets for intervention, potentially increasing the scope of reflective control on behalf of our endorsed values, and better integrating and strengthening the self we aspire to be. Unfortunately, the same knowledge, deployed by skillful manipulators, can be used against us, so the fulfillment of naturalized autonomy is by no means assured. Conscious vigilance, informed by science, will always be in order, and we must hold would-be manipulators responsible when their agendas conflict with our own best interests.

As we've seen, both conscious and unconscious processes matter in their respective behavior controlling roles. But so does consciousness—phenomenal experience—itself, even if it turns out not to be the contra-causal controller many folk might suppose (part 3), and even if it doesn't play a causal role in third person explanations (part 1). Whether or not naturalized conceptions of autonomy and agency ever replace the folk dualism of soul control, and whatever the ultimate impact of understanding unconscious processes might be on our autonomy, the subjective significance of phenomenal experience will stand unchallenged. And the puzzle of explaining consciousness, which matters considerably to scientists and philosophers, still stands as well. The first person reality of phenomenal experience, bringing with it the reality of moral concern, still awaits a conceptually and empirically transparent integration into a naturalized worldview.

NOTES

1. In this chapter I put aside, for the most part, questions concerning moral responsibility, credit and blame. Although I'm sympathetic with Bruce Waller (2011), Tamler Sommers (2012) and other moral responsibility skeptics, as a practical matter we can and must be *held* responsible in the consequentialist sense described by Thomas Nadelhoffer (2011).

2. Phenomenal consciousness contrasts with so-called *access* consciousness as described originally by Ned Block: information is access conscious if it's accessible for action control, whether or not there's any concurrent phenomenology (Block 1995).

3. Intentional states such as beliefs and desires are attributed on the basis of behavioral criteria, so the claim that certain behavior controlling neural processes realize these states seems unproblematic, even if their neural realizers can't be precisely specified.

4. As experiencing subjects, we *consist* of our qualitative states, including the feeling of being an experiencing subject; we're not in an observational relationship to experience itself (Clark 2005).

5. Replicants are portrayed as fully sentient beings, with a desire to live as ends in themselves, hence the poignant moral dimension of *Blade Runner*.

6. For an enlightening discussion of the ethical problems posed by creating smart AIs, see the final chapter of Metzinger (2003).

7. For reviews of literature on unconscious influences on behavior, see Baumeister, Masicampo and Vohs (2011) and Nadelhoffer (2011).

8. Posted by Rose-ellen Caminer in a discussion at the Facebook Naturalism group, http://www.facebook.com/groups/2218407727/

9. Soul control *is* worth wanting, however, if one wants to preserve strong (e.g., Kantian) desert-based conceptions of responsibility. Dropping libertarian free will may make it more

difficult to sustain such conceptions, in contrast to consequentialist conceptions (Greene and Cohen 2004; Clark 2005; Nadelhoffer 2011; Waller 2011, Shariff et al. 2012).

10. To be fair to Harris, he also says that we are puppets that can pull their own strings. So although "we are ultimately being steered" (p. 47), it seems we also have some local control on his view.

11. On improving our responsibility practices, see the references cited in note 9.

Chapter Fourteen

What Does the Brain Know and When Does It Know It?

Mark Hallett

When discussing any issue, particularly a complex one, it is crucial that the terms be defined. And since reasonable persons might disagree, I will begin with the definitions as I would like to use them. Free will, in first person form, is the sense that "I choose what I do." What does "I" mean? I will reject immediately the dualist view that "I" is my mind, separable from the brain and body. "I" is my brain. I know about "I" because I am conscious (at least some of the time, when I am awake). Consciousness I admit is a problem; its nature and physiology are unclear, and I suspect it will require a new concept in science to understand it. However, for now, I accept the relatively common view that it can be considered "awareness." So the brain is generating an awareness of "I" as a part of what it is doing. It is crucial that "I" is not separable from the brain, but an aspect of its function.

The contents of consciousness are called qualia, and "I" is a quale. Note that consciousness by this view is passive, "awareness," an observation about what is going on in the brain. Qualia are very valuable data about what the brain is doing. It is critical to recognize, however, that qualia can be deceptive.

"What I do" are generally considered movements. Movements are events that can be observed and quantified; the physiology is reasonably well known. For the purposes of investigating free will, movements are typically investigated. Thoughts are also "what I do," but these are less easy to measure, and, like consciousness, we really do not understand what thinking is. Mental events are similar to movements except there is no external manifestation. One way of assessing mental events is the study of imaginary movements. The brain activations in imagining movement are similar to those with actually making movements with the biggest difference being the lack of motor cortex activation (Hanakawa et al. 2008).

Choosing is the sense that there are various alternative movements to make, or not make, at any one time, and that "I" is actively doing that choosing. Choosing is another quale. It is undoubtedly true that at any one time, there are many different movements that a person can make. One question is how that decision happens and how it is executed. Another question is how does the quale of freely choosing arise? A third question is whether there is any relationship between the processes of decision making by the brain and the quale of free will. The quale, as commonly experienced, is that "I" chooses and then the movement happens. This would be the folk psychology view.

Another concept that is critical is that much of what goes on in the brain is unconscious. Only some of it comes into consciousness, generally only one bit at a time. When something is in consciousness, then "I" is aware of it. The relationship between the unconscious and conscious is not clear. Why do certain elements become conscious? Is there particular importance to those elements over those that stay unconscious? The answers to these questions are not clear.

Evidence for the unconscious influences on behavior is very strong, and only two brief examples are given here. The first is what I have referred to as the salted peanut problem (Hallett 2007). You sit in front of a bowl of salted peanuts, and after eating a number of them, you make a conscious decision not to eat any more. Yet, in a very short time, you find that your hand is going out to take some more. (Who is in charge?) A second example is the recent report of the parole decisions by Israeli judges (Danziger et al. 2011). Judges always seek to be fair and make objective decisions, yet parole is much more likely to be granted just after the judges have had something to eat. Apparently, hunger influences what appears to be rational decision making.

Do those quale in consciousness have any influence on outcome? Specifically, does a quale (or mechanisms in parallel to a quale) play a causal role. For something to be causal, it has to precede the effect and in some way seem to be related to it. As Daniel Wegner has pointed out, the idea has to precede the act in order for there to be a sense of free will (Wegner 2002, 2003). Hence the timing of qualia and movements are critical in understanding what is actually happening.

It is important to make one more point. Most of the time, most persons go along with their activities without specifically thinking about whether a specific movement is voluntary or not. Movement happens. If it is a pattern of behavior that is repetitive, such as the morning ritual of washing up or driving to work, the motor programs might well be run automatically with hardly any thought at all. If asked, persons would say, yes, the movements are voluntary, but it is not a common concern.

THE RELATIVE TIMING OF THE QUALE AND THE MOVEMENT

The basic experiment in regard to timing is well known. Libet et al. first tried to time the quale of willing (Libet et al. 1983). Subjects watched a clock and gave relative times for the sense of willing, W, and the sense of when the movement itself occurred, M. They also recorded the Bereitschaftspotential with EEG at the same time. Depending on the type of movement, the Bereitschaftspotential was about 1 s prior to movement while W was only about 300 ms prior to movement. M was pretty close to the movement itself. Hence the brain begins planning for the movement far in advance of the quale of willing. The facts are clear and have been reproduced many times; the issue has been the interpretation. What is to be made of the timing of the BP and W? I have often heard it said that the results appear to mean that the brain decides what to do before the person does so. This statement does not make sense. The person is his brain. Hence, the way to phrase this is that the brain decides unconsciously what will be done and consciousness is aware of this only later—but still before the movement, the timing of which is relevant to conclude that W could be a cause of M.

Libet et al. were unwilling to give up the idea that events relating to consciousness could be etiologic. Their idea was that, yes, movement might be originated unconsciously, but that the movement could be consciously vetoed before it happened, and this could be an indicator of free will. Such a veto has been called "free won't." On the face of it, this seems like nonsense. Of course, there could be brain events prior to a conscious veto just like there were demonstrated brain events prior to a movement, and an EEG potential looking like the Bereitschaftspotential precedes voluntary relaxation or decisions not to move in the first place (the no-go potential).

Soon et al. have done a similar experiment with fMRI asking subjects to freely move their right or left hand (Soon et al. 2008). Events in the fMRI signal were identified 8 s prior to movement that indicated probabilistically which hand would be chosen. The probability was low, but significant, showing very advanced brain processes in some circumstances.

We have done several experiments that also show brain events preceding the quale of willing. In one experiment, we asked patients to move "freely" while listening for tones (Matsuhashi and Hallett 2008). If they heard a tone after they had decided to move, then they should veto their movement. Hence this is formally a study of free won't. Vetoes should only be possible in the interval between the quale of willing and the movement. In this circumstance we referred to the quale of thinking about moving, and called it T, since it might be different from W. T was about 1.4 s prior to movement, much longer in advance than W, but still later than the onset of the Bereitschaftspotential measured simultaneously. We explained the difference between T and W as a difference between "probe consciousness" and "spontaneous consciousness." Probing with the tone, we could identify what the brain was doing prior to spontaneous awareness.

In yet unpublished work, we utilized sophisticated EEG methods to identify in real time when the brain was preparing to move. At such moments, we asked people what they were thinking about. Sometimes they were indeed thinking about the upcoming movement, but other times they were not. This appears to be direct proof that the brain can be preparing to move when consciousness is focused on something else.

Another important experiment that speaks to the timing of events is the work of Lau et al. who looked at the influence of transcranial magnetic stimulation on M and W (Lau et al. 2007). They stimulated the pre-supplementary motor area and the primary motor cortex both at the time of movement onset itself and 200 ms after movement onset. Almost shockingly, they found that subjects reported different times for both M and W with stimulation of the pre-supplementary motor area (and not the primary motor area). How can it be possible to influence the apparent time of M and W with stimulation after the movement, if these events occur before the movement? It turns out that there is a good answer to this question.

It takes some time from the beginning of a sensory event until the sensation gets into awareness. Libet studied this also, referred to it as the utilization time, and noted that it might be the order of several hundred ms (Libet et al. 1979). This means that what we perceive as the present is actually several hundred ms in the real world past. Actually, thinking about it carefully, this must be true. Consider watching an object touch your hand. It takes time for the visual information to get to the visual cortex and for the signals to be processed; similarly it takes time for the somatosensory information; and then there will be time needed to integrate the two sensory modalities. When all the signal processing is completed the real world event is long over, but, cleverly, the brain projects the apparent time backward in order to approximate the real world time.

Since M and W are quale and can be influenced after the movement actually begins, it is likely that they are being finally processed after the movement and projected earlier in time. Hence, from all the data, it appears that the ordinary perception of willing is happening during a period from a few hundred ms before to a few ms after the onset of movement. With probing, the intention can be identified earlier, but often other thoughts are in consciousness as the movement is being prepared.

There is another aspect to the sense of volition in addition to the sense of willing, that is the sense of agency or, in this context, self-agency. That quale is the sense that the person is responsible for having made the movement which has just occurred. Willing and agency are separable to some extent. For example, it is possible to will a movement, but it not occur (and therefore no agency)—this might happen with a patient who has had a stroke or spinal cord injury. Agency would ordinarily require two factors, one, the sense of willing the movement, and, two, the movement that occurs and can be appreciated is close to what was willed. The quale of M is related to agency, but also needs the sense of ownership. In any event, it is clear that this aspect of the sense of volition cannot be prior to the occurrence of the movement itself. The timing of the events is illustrated in figure 14.1.

NEUROLOGICAL DISORDERS SHOW THE DISSOCIATION OF VOLITION AND MOVEMENT

I have written about this before and only briefly summarize a few here (Hallett 2007, 2009; Kranick and Hallett 2013). Patients with psychogenic movement disorders (a form of conversion or somatization disorder) make movements that look voluntary, share voluntary brain executive mechanisms, but are considered involuntary by the patients. Patients with Tourette syndrome are often confused by the question as to whether their tics are voluntary or not. They may well say that the movements really are voluntary but they are compelled to make them. Patients who have the passivity phenomena in association with schizophrenia may have movements that look voluntary, but the patient will say that he is completely externally controlled. Patients with Huntington disease may say their typical choreic movement is voluntary. Conversely, patients with anosognosia claim to have made a movement, when they have not. Hence, it is clear that all goal directed movements are not necessarily linked to the sense of volition, and volition can be attached to movements that do not appear to be voluntarily generated as we ordinarily understand them.

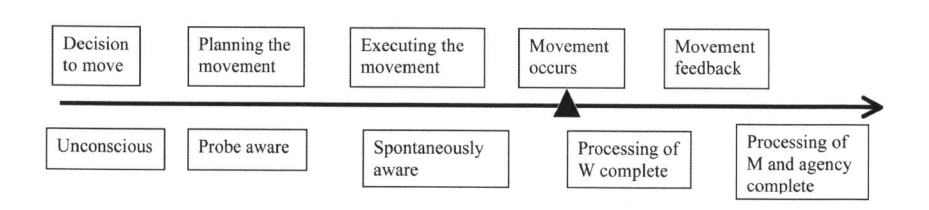

Figure 14.1. Events in the generation of a movement and the conscious correlates. The arrow is the flow of time, and the real world events are above the arrow and conscious correlates are below.

THE PHYSIOLOGY OF MOVEMENT

A good deal is known about how movements are made. The movement executive is mainly the primary motor cortex, which can be thought of as being in the center of the brain—at least it is on the anterior bank of the central sulcus. Movements can arise after external triggering or internal generation. External triggering comes in response to sensory stimuli, which generally are processed in the back half of the brain. Internal influences come from the front half of the brain and include emotion, homeostasis, cognitive processes and reward. These four factors arise from the limbic system, the hypothalamus, the prefrontal cortex and the dopaminergic midbrain nuclei, respectively (See Figure 14.2). External and internal influences are all constantly varying in strength, and there is also noise in the system. The movement that is made at any one moment reflects the strongest signals. Because the influences are largely independent of each other, the outcome can only be predicted in probabilistic terms.

As a movement is generated, the rest of the brain is alerted to this occurrence with a feedforward signal. An important region to be alerted is the temporo-parietal junction region which also receives feedback from movements that have occurred (Nahab et al. 2011). The feedforward signal is likely associated with the quale of willing. The parietal area may well be an important target for the feedforward signal since a lesion in this area delays

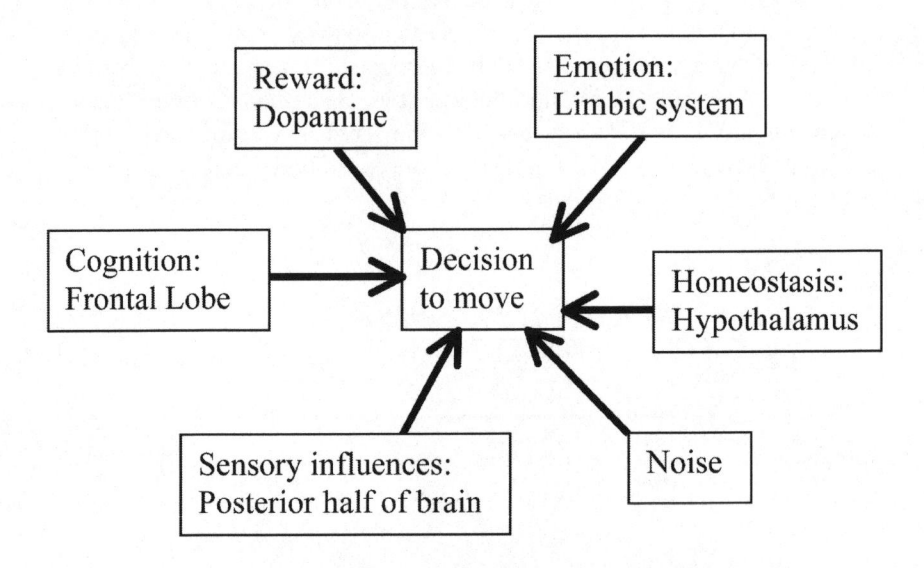

Figure 14.2. Various factors influencing the decision of which movement to make.

W (Sirigu et al. 2004) and stimulation of this area (at time of brain surgery) produces an illusion of willing (Desmurget et al. 2009). The successful concordance of the feedforward signal and feedback signal in the temporo-parietal junction region is likely associated with the quale of self-agency (Nahab et al. 2011).

Let's go back to movement generation. The physiology of this generation is clearly complex with a large number of factors. Most of this appears to be unconscious although any of the factors might be conscious at any one time. Does consciousness do any work to help select the movement or is it purely passive awareness of what's going on? If a factor is in consciousness does it have extra weight, or is it that because it has extra weight it comes into consciousness? Or, is it that the idea that it has a special influence is just one of the brain's deceptions? Certainly by timing arguments alone, it does not appear that the consciousness of willing has any influence, since it comes relatively late in the movement generation process.

One argument in relation to timing that is sometimes made by critics of this conclusion is that the events just before movement are not really the critical issue (Mele 2007). They may just play out as designed long before. This is the argument that distinguishes between proximal and distal intentions. What I have been describing is the proximal intention, the event just before an individual movement. The distal intention in the case of a Libet-like experiment would be the decision to participate in the experiments in the first place and to decide to go along with the instructions of the experimenter. According to some, it is the distal intention that manifests free will and not the proximal intention (Mele 2007). It is a thought, a thought that stays in the brain until the right moment where the planned act will be finally done. But as mentioned earlier, the physiology of thinking is still obscure. And as noted, my current view is that a thought, such as the distal intention, is an event with analogy to a movement itself and the physiology of its generation might be very similar to what I have described for a movement. Hence, I do not consider this argument very strong.

IMPLICATIONS FOR RESPONSIBILITY

The argument that I have made about free will and movement can be summarized as follows. The brain makes movements based on a large number of factors that summate and compete at any one moment for a particular outcome. Most of what the brain is doing is unconscious and that, on some occasions, the qualia of willing and agency are in consciousness. It is these qualia that the brain interprets as free will, and because the quale of willing occurs before the quale of movement, causality is inferred. However, there is no evidence that because a factor is in consciousness that it is more important than unconscious factors. Consciousness appears to be passive awareness of some (not all) of the goings on in the brain. And most of the time, there is no overt consideration of whether a movement is truly "voluntary."

Does free will then exist despite the fact that there is no support for the idea that the quale of willing has anything to do with the movement made? Since "I" am my brain, it is not necessary to ask this question only in relation to what is conscious. It is possible to say that a brain is free if the brain can function without external constraint. Ordinarily brains seem to do that. There are circumstances where brains are constrained and there are circumstances that raise interesting questions about "freedom." Starting from an easy issue, if the brain is having a seizure then it is being constrained. An overtly external constraint would be if someone is holding a gun to someone's head or being tortured; subsequent behavior would not be considered free. Brainwashing would also be considered, I would think, to take away a brain's freedom. When Patty Hearst joined the Symbionese Liberation Army and robbed a bank, she was likely brainwashed by her kidnappers. But the judicial system must have thought she acted freely since she was sentenced to prison.

What about being under the influence of drugs or being addicted? How about in a hypnotic state?

A more difficult consideration would be education in school. Of course, children have many things to learn, but some are facts and some are opinions. Math seems pretty straightforward, but how about evolution versus intelligent design? If a school only teaches intelligent design and a person acts on that basis, is that person free? Another approach (which fortunately for me most of my influential teachers took) is to make clear that you should not believe anything you are told or read. You should come to your own understanding from your own interaction with the world. That attitude seems to allow more freedom for the brain.

To be provocative, what about religion and religious education? If a child is taught weekly for many years that he will burn in hell if he does not believe in a certain way, it is not surprising that he does believe in that way. Is the brain then free to decide about religious belief? When 907 members of the Peoples Temple died from "revolutionary suicide" in Jonestown, were they acting freely?

In most circumstances, brains appear free to function, but they cannot easily escape their past histories which certainly influence outcome, just as current limbic and hypothalamic factors do. Perhaps it would be most fair to say that even in the absence of apparent external constraints, the range of outcomes that a brain could generate is always limited in some ways by past and present circumstances. The freedom from external constraints is never more than relative.

ASSIGNMENT OF RESPONSIBILITY

Google has developed a self-driving car, and California has just passed regulations allowing such a car to be used on its roads. The cars are very safe, likely safer than with human drivers. However, it is possible that such a car might get into an accident when you are sitting behind the wheel. Who is responsible? You pushed the button to go to the nearby McDonald's restaurant. Is it you or Google? Likely most would conclude that it is Google. Even though you are in the driver's seat, it is the programming external to you that was flawed. However, you still might get the ticket.

Jean Valjean of *Les Miserables* was a poor man who stole a loaf of bread to feed his starving sister and her seven children. He eventually served 19 years in prison and then was branded as a criminal. Still poor without opportunity, he continued to behave as a criminal. Upon learning a life lesson from Bishop Myriel of Digne, he changed his ways and became an "honorable" man. Yes, he was always "doing" the criminal acts, but the reason, at least to some extent, was the nature of the society in which he was living and his personal circumstances. A brief lesson from the Bishop produced a better outcome than many years (and lots of expense) of prison.

Whether a person is responsible or not for a particular action is usually judged on what was in their consciousness just before that action. Such information is only partial and may even be an inaccurate picture of brain activity. However, it is fair to say that a person's brain is always responsible for what its attached body does. The real question should be why did the person (or his brain) do that. Focusing on "why" rather than "whether" should produce a more rational consequence. Should it be incarceration, education or even medical therapy? Likely our jails are filled with many persons who would be better served given more education and job opportunities, and this might well be better for society too.

Chapter Fifteen

If Free Will Did Not Exist, It Would Be Necessary to Invent It

Susan Pockett

Back in the good (or depending on your point of view, the bad) old days, philosophy was a perilous profession. When Socrates was executed for corrupting the youth of Athens, or the Paris parliament decreed in 1624 that any person teaching a doctrine contrary to Aristotle would be put to death, people really took their philosophy seriously. Nowadays, an academic philosopher might well perceive that the worst potential consequence of espousing one idea over another could be denial of tenure. But in this, I think they would be selling their profession short.

Even in the age of junk food and reality TV, ideas matter. In fact, they arguably matter more than ever, because the internet spreads them more rapidly and effectively than ever and ordinary people have a greater capacity than ever before to act on them. Take democracy, for example—how much blood has been and still is being shed in the name of that idea? Or liberty, equality, fraternity—all are nothing more than ideas. One might argue that these are big ideas, with big ramifications. Although it would be perfectly possible to make good logical arguments against any of them, one wouldn't want to do that, because if people were to take those arguments seriously and hence stop believing in the desirability or even the existence of liberty, equality and fraternity, the world would change for the worse.

Does this also apply to the idea of free will? Would a general disbelief in the idea of free will make any difference? *A priori* there are (at least) two possible answers:

    a. No, free will doesn't really have much in the way of consequences or ramifications. All that would happen if people stopped believing in it would be that they would be forced to adopt a little seemly humility, which would be no bad thing. Evidence against this claim is discussed in Section 1.

b. Yes, it would make a difference—but never mind the consequences, the truth is always better than a comfortable lie. There is much to be said for this somewhat puritanical approach, and for that reason Sections 2 and 3 are devoted to discovering what science has to say about "the truth" of this matter. If the currently standard arguments that free will is illusory were to turn out to be overblown or inconclusive, we might legitimately avoid finding out what would happen if everyone stopped believing in free will.

1. BENEFITS OF BELIEVING IN FREE WILL

The scientific evidence on this matter takes the form of experimental results showing that if people are induced to disbelieve (at least temporarily) in the existence of free will, their behavior becomes more antisocial. In one study (Vohs and Schooler 2008), reading a passage in which Francis Crick claims that scientists now believe free will to be illusory caused participants to (a) report a weaker belief in free will and (b) cheat more on subsequent tests than subjects who had read a similar passage about something neutral. No difference between the two groups was observed in mood, or in beliefs about fate, chance and scientific causation—the cheating was specifically contingent on a disbelief in free will. In another set of experiments (Baumeister et al. 2009), subjects were assigned to read material that either did or did not support free will and were then presented with scenarios in which they had the opportunity to help other people. The clear result was that those who had read the material claiming free will is illusory were significantly more aggressive and less likely to say they would help others. Interestingly, a control group who read free-will-neutral material produced helpfulness scores indistinguishable from those of the pro-free-will group. This was taken by the authors to indicate that the default position for subjects in this experiment was to believe in free will. Again there was no significant difference between any of the three groups on tests of mood valence or arousal.

Of course, "free will" was not actually defined in either of these sets of experiments, so it is not clear whether the subjects' default position was to believe in

1. a compatibilist form of free will (which basically says that if nobody is holding a gun to your head, you're free to do as you will)
2. a stronger, incompatibilist form of free will (which could only exist if causal determinism were an illusion) or

3. a libertarian form of free will (which demands the production of truly originated acts: acts that have no physical antecedents at all).

Perhaps these alternatives were never clearly thought out by either experimenters or subjects, but one possible scenario is that the subjects' default setting was a belief in option (1), while the version explicitly contradicted by the anti-free will material supplied to them was option (2). The question of what different varieties of "folk" actually do mean when they talk about free will is currently being explored by the new discipline of experimental philosophy (Nichols 2011). But whatever the eventual outcome of these welcome philosophical experiments, the results described above (Vohs and Schooler 2008; Baumeister et al. 2009) show fairly conclusively that authoritative statements to the effect that "free will is illusory" do have the effect of increasing antisocial behavior.

Apparently there always was a good sociological reason for the Christian church's insistence on the reality of free will and one's ability to use it to mitigate original sin and increase one's chances of getting into heaven. In more secular terms, it now behooves us academics, as the authority figures of the scientific age, to be quite careful about making firm statements to the effect that free will is illusory.

But hold on, we have to tell the truth as we see it, don't we? Well yes, we probably do. But what actually is the truth in this matter? Are we really sure that free will IS illusory? The next two sections investigate this question from a scientific point of view.

2. THE NEUROSCIENCE OF FREE WILL

Has neuroscience killed free will? The answer depends entirely on one's definition of free will—and in this case it does not matter whether we are talking about the compatibilist, incompatibilist or libertarian variety. If any of these definitions of free will requires the *conscious initiation* of one action rather than another, then the answer is yes, neuroscience has killed that kind of free will. There is now an abundance of evidence that voluntary actions are not initiated consciously.

The pioneer in the matter of bringing the idea of conscious free will into the arena of experimental science was Benjamin Libet. His original experiments (Libet et al. 1982, 1983) are now well known: they show that the event-related potential coupled to a spontaneous action (the readiness potential or RP) starts off the order of 350 ms before the subject reports having consciously willed the action. For many years this highly repeatable and methodologically robust result was taken to mean that voluntary acts are initiated pre-consciously. More recently, Pockett and Purdy (2010) showed that when the same action is made not spontaneously but as the result of a specific decision, the RP preceding the action becomes so much shorter that it starts at about the same time as the reported conscious decision to make the action. This is probably explained by the fact that the earlier-onset parts of the RP relate more to expectation or readiness than to the initiation of a specific act: in the decision condition, the subject is so occupied with actually making the required (fairly complicated) decision that they have no processing capacity to spare for getting ready to move. On the face of it, this result restores the possibility that consciousness does directly cause actions.

However, numerous experiments by others show that the time at which the subject reports having willed an action is affected both by events that take place after the action (Lau et al. 2007) and by manipulation of feedback to the subject about the time at which the action occurs (Banks and Isham 2009). For example, if the subject is misled to believe that their individual actions happened progressively later than they actually did, the time at which these acts were willed is also reported as being progressively later. These and other experiments (Wegner 2002; Pockett 2004; Aarts et al. 2005; Pockett et al. 2006; Kühn and Brass 2009; Rigoni et al. 2010) strongly suggest that the *initiation* of voluntary actions is not consciously experienced at all. The subject simply infers after the event that they must have initiated their movement shortly before they made it.

This being said, however, there are at least two arguments in favor of the position that whether or not actions are consciously initiated is not of major importance to the question of whether or not an individual enjoys one of the three major flavors of free will.

1. It is a reasonable position that an individual—"you"—consist(s) of both your consciousness and the unconscious operations of your brain. If that were not so, all the unconscious processing that underpins your conscious experiences (your vision, for example) would not count as part of "you." This seems a highly dubious proposition, especially considering that the autobiographical memories generally regarded as making you uniquely "you" are unconscious most of the time.
2. Even if position (1) were rejected, the initiation and control of voluntary (i.e. non-reflex) actions is only part of the equation. The detail of any specific act is relatively unimportant in the larger scheme of things, in that it inevitably depends at least in part on environmental conditions at the time. Arguably more important to the notion of free will in general is the *decision* to carry out an act aimed at a particular outcome, at some loosely specified time in the future. Such decisions are generally made consciously.

I therefore argue that, although neuroscience has indeed demonstrated that specific voluntary (willed) acts are not initiated consciously, this does not constitute the delivery of a *coup de grace* to the whole idea of free will. In fact neuroscience goes even further than this: it also shows that apparently voluntary acts are not controlled (Jeannerod 2006) or often *even recognized* consciously (Pockett 2009). But the conclusion can still not be drawn from this that the human individual *in toto* does not have some meaningful version of free will.

3. THE PHYSICS OF FREE WILL

In section 1 three kinds of free will are defined: compatibilist, incompatibilist and libertarian. What does physics have to say about each of these?

Compatibilism is simply a definitional choice, and as such cannot be either proved or disproved by any variety of science. Libertarianism, which involves the continued production of acts with no physical antecedents whatsoever, is observably wrong for most of the population. Acts with no physical antecedents whatsoever would be completely random in relation to the outside world and so unpredictable that anyone who consistently produced them would rapidly find themselves in a psychiatric institution at best, or an early grave at worst.

So the only kind of free will the reality of which can reasonably be investigated by physics is the incompatibilist sort. On an incompatibilist definition of free will, free will does not exist if causal determinism is a fact. Much confusion and angst about free will results from the common assumption that causal determinism *is* a scientific fact. The next few paragraphs explore that proposition.

We should start with a definition. The *Stanford Encyclopedia of Philosophy* defines causal determinism (hereafter referred to simply as determinism) as "the idea that every event is necessitated by antecedent events and conditions together with the laws of nature." This definition immediately suggests that no answer is actually possible to the question of whether or not determinism is a scientific fact.

A number of problems arise:

1. We clearly do not know at present (and may never know) what all of "the laws of nature" are. Perhaps free will *is* a law of nature. This latter idea may or may not be dismissed as semantics, but the former statement is undeniably correct.
2. We also do not know (and possibly can never know, in sufficient detail) what all of the relevant antecedent events and conditions are. This means we can never reproduce exactly the same set of antecedent

events and conditions twice. This in turn means we can never run the critical experiment that might falsify determinism, which is to see whether the same antecedent events and conditions (together with the same, presumably immutable, laws of nature) produce the same outcome twice. If they did, determinism would be supported (although not, thanks to the Problem of Induction, proved). If they didn't, determinism would be falsified: but we would have to be very sure that we really had reproduced exactly the same antecedent events and conditions.
3. Apart from these general arguments, physics is undoubtedly the science which should have the most to say about whether determinism is true or false. In fact though, there is not much help to be had from that direction, for the following reasons:

   a. The deterministic, mathematical equations of physics are pretty good at describing the way the world works. At first blush, this might suggest that determinism is true. However, there is one area in which these equations are not so successful. They are all time-symmetric, which means they assume that deterministic causality can operate backwards in time as well as forwards. But all experimental observations of the world suggest that backwards causation does not occur. Weights never fall upwards. Broken vases never spontaneously reassemble themselves. The predictions of quantum mechanical models that do require backwards causation (e.g. Wheeler's model to explain the experimental results of his delayed choice experiment) are precisely matched by the predictions of similar models that do not require backwards causation (Bohm's model to explain the same experimental results).
   b. Schröedinger's equation, which accurately describes the evolution of events at the quantum size scale, is certainly deterministic. But Schröedinger's equation never delivers any certainty about the outcome of a particular set of antecedent events and conditions—it only supplies statistical probabilities. The definition of determinism requires that "every event is necessitated by antecedent events and conditions," not that "the statistical probability of every event is necessitated by antecedent events and conditions."

Hence I claim that causal determinism is *not* an established scientific fact—and perhaps never can be.

So the truth we were looking for at the end of Section 1 turns out to be that neither neuroscience nor physics has yet killed a form of incompatibilist free will which does not require the conscious initiation of actions.

And of course nothing can kill compatibilist free will. Therefore I suggest that it is probably sensible to stop saying that science now definitively shows free will to be illusory. Not only is such a statement sociologically dangerous—it is also untrue.

Chapter Sixteen

Free Will, an Illusion?

An Answer from a Pragmatic Sentimentalist Point of View

Maureen Sie

According to some people, diverse findings in the cognitive and neurosciences suggest that free will is an illusion: We experience ourselves as agents, but in fact our brains decide, initiate, and judge before "we" do (Soon, Brass, Heinze, and Haynes 2008; Libet and Gleason 1983). Others have replied that the distinction between "us" and "our brains" makes no sense (e.g., Dennett 2003)[1] or that scientists misperceive the conceptual relations that hold between free will and responsibility (Roskies 2006). Many others regard the neuro-scientific findings as irrelevant to their views on free will. They do not believe that determinist processes are incompatible with free will to begin with, hence, do not understand why deterministic processes in our brain would be (see Sie and Wouters 2008, 2010). That latter response should be understood against the background of the philosophical free will discussion. In philosophy, free will is tradionally approached as a metaphysical problem, one that needs to be dealt with in order to discuss the legitimacy of our practices of responsibility. The emergence of our moral practices is seen as a result of the assumption that we possess free will (or some capacity associated with it) and the main question discussed is whether that assumption is compatible with determinism.[2] In this chapter we want to steer clear from this "metaphysical" discussion.

The question we are interested in in this chapter is whether the above mentioned scientific findings are relevant to our use of the concept of free will when that concept is approached from a different angle. We call this different angle the "pragmatic sentimentalist" approach to free will (hereafter the PS-approach).[3] This approach can be traced back to Peter F. Strawson's influential essay "Freedom and Resentment" (Strawson 1962).[4] Contrary to the metaphysical approach, the PS-approach does not understand free will as a concept that somehow precedes our moral practices. Rather it is assumed that everyday talk of free will naturally arises in a practice that is characterized by certain reactive attitudes that we take towards one another. This is why it is called "sentimentalist." In this approach, the practical purposes of the concept of free will are put central stage. This is why it is called "pragmatist."

The structure of the chapter is as follows. First, we explain the social function of moral responsibility that is at the core of the PS-approach. The practice of responsibility arises because we work together to reach our goals, depend on others to satisfy our needs and to reach our goals and because it is not always clear how to behave as part of that attempt. Also, we might differ in our expectations and ideas concerning how best to behave as part of that attempt. The continuous exchange of reasons and the adaptation of our behavior on the basis of that exchange are crucial to this process of coordination.

Secondly, we explain how this exchange gives rise to a so-called space of reasons. The practice of responsibility serves both to adjust our normative expectations and our behavior to what the space of reasons requires and to adjust the space of reasons in the light of the difficulties we stumble upon in our social life (such as differences in normative expectations and differences in the ability to adjust our behavior in the light of reasons). We argue that participation in this practice requires people to be able to "locate themselves in the space of reasons."[5] Given the social function of the practice, however, it only makes sense to blame people who do not conform to our normative expectations when they are able to adjust their behavior in the light of reasons, not when they are unable to do so. Therefore, we have to differentiate between cases of not responding to reasons that warrant and cases that do not warrant a response with the moral reactive attitudes of blame, resentment, and indignation. It is here, we argue, that the concept of free will finds its natural application.

Thirdly, we turn our attention to the scientific findings of recent decades that to us seem relevant to free will (understood from the PS-approach). We concentrate on those findings that show that we (1) lack agential transparency, i.e. immediate and infallible introspective access to the motivational origin of our actions and that, as a result, (2) we are sometimes 'mistaken' in our understanding of our own actions. We are mistaken in the sense that we do not always know why we acted as we did or do not know the full story. That finding, we subsequently argue, is relevant to free will when the reasons we exchange to explain ourselves and understand others (a) fail to cite the causes that the sciences suggest to be efficacious or (b) structurally cite reasons the sciences show not to be of influence. With respect to (a) research on the influence of cognitive biases, stereotypes, and prejudices is used as an example. With respect to (b) the situationist literature that denies the existence of virtues is illustrative. Another illustration of (b) is a cluster of experiments that suggest that we are primarily concerned with the wish to appear moral. When correct, so we argue, this body of research should lead to serious reconsideration of the occasions on which we claim, e.g., "to act on the basis of reasons and out of our own free will," "that our own morally wrong actions were not performed for reasons (not performed out of our own free will)," and "that other people's morally wrong actions were freely willed and performed for reasons."

We also explain why given the social function of moral responsibility ascriptions and the role of the concept of free will as understood in this paper, the claim that it is an illusion makes no sense.[6] Every society needs means to coordinate behavior. In our Western society we allow people to coordinate a great deal of their shared lives within limits set by the law. That is, we delegate large parts of the regulation of our interpersonal affairs to the moral realm: To the realm in which people come to an understanding of what should and what should not be done by exchanging reasons, in just the way set out in the first two sections of this chapter. This requires that we put great trust in people's ability to figure out what is expected from them in a variety of situations, and in their willingness and ability to do what is expected out of their own free will. The scientific findings discussed in this chapter, though practically relevant and fascinating, provide no reason to think this trust misplaced.

§ 1 THE SOCIAL FUNCTION OF MORAL RESPONSIBILITY ASCRIPTIONS

Whenever people work together to reach their goals they need a way to coordinate their behavior.[7] Many goals can be reached only by organized activity. Often, the people involved in a shared project differ in their wishes and ideas about how to carry out the project and in their capacities to contribute to it. As a consequence they need to communicate with each other during the project as well as to come to a division of the labor. If we want to build a house we need to meet several technical requirements (a stable construction, how to ensure it), and we need to reach an agreement on the design of the house and the division of duties. Different people engaged in building the house will have different capacities (one might be good at laying bricks, another at painting), but also different interests (one needs the money, another will be the owner). Hence, they will also have different expectations about what is required for a good house, how much time and energy everyone should invest, and so on.

The coordination of shared practices has two important but distinct aspects. First, we must decide what is to be done (the plan of the house and the way to build it) and what is expected from the different people involved. We shall call the expectations about how people should behave "normative expectations": expectations about what should be done by whom, why, and when (and sometimes also about what should *not* be done). Second, it must be ensured that people behave as expected, that they keep their end of the deal, so to speak. Let us call these aspects the "design-aspect" and the "process-aspect" of our shared coordinative practices.

Several practices help us to realize those two aspects (obedience to authority, tradition, voting procedures). One important way to promote that people do what is expected from them is to make clear to them what is expected of them. As we will explain in the next section, it is an important aspect of our Western society that making clear to people what is expected of them and explaining why, suffices to get them to behave accordingly. Other ways to get people to behave in ways we would like them to is through conditioning and manipulation. When people fail to do what is expected we can punish them as we can reward them for doing (or exceeding) what is expected. Both punishment and rewards function as part of conditioning processes, be it in different ways. However, typical to our Western society is that we put great trust in people's ability to figure out what is expected from them in a variety of situations, and in their willingness and ability to do what is expected out of their "own free will." That is, without taking recourse to institutional force, violence, manipulation or other measures.

This means that when people's normative expectations differ, we try to bring them into line by discussing which expectations are reasonable. Out of such discussions evolves what we might call a space of reasons: Interconnected views of what we should do (and not do) in what situations and under what conditions. The moral sentiments of blame, praise, resentment, gratitude and moral indignation function as an intermediary between the space of reasons, our normative expectations, and our actions. Let us consider an example to understand how this practice, the dynamics of responsibility, works.

> Some time ago my colleague, Arno, left his bicycle pump in the corner of the café where he had lunch. He wanted to have his hands free on his after-lunch walk and the barman of the café promised to keep an eye on the pump. When he came back, the pump was stolen. He blamed the barman for being inattentive. The barman told him that he had allowed a customer to use the pump, but she had not brought it back and he promised to call her to account at her next visit. A week later, a friendly young woman rang at Arno's door, handed over his pump and apologized for having taken it. She had assumed that the owner

of the pump had forgotten it and would not miss it. Hence, she had taken it
with her to pump up her punctured tire a second time during her way home.[8]

This example illustrates the occasions when we blame, the immediate function of blaming, and its effects. We blame people when they do not behave as we think they should. In the resulting exchange, both parties explain how they think the blamed behavior fits into a shared space of reasons and they might come to share a common view of what happened, what should have been done, and the proper response. Arno expected the barman to take care of the pump and blamed him because it seemed to him that he did not fulfill that expectation. The barman explained his behavior by giving reasons. In his view he did nothing wrong: He let someone use the pump in the expectation that she would bring it back. It is the woman who is to be blamed. Arno accepted his interpretation and his explanation and, subsequently, changed his view of what the barman should have done and accepted his offer to call the woman to account. In the exchange between the woman and the barman, it is the blamed person who changes her interpretation of what happened, agrees that she should not have taken the pump and offers to return it. Finally, in the exchange between Arno and the woman, Arno changes his view of what happened again and accepts that the woman is not to blame for theft, but for having a wrong view of what one can do with objects you have permission to use.

What happens in this example is what we regard as the proper function of "ascriptions" of responsibility. Strictly speaking "ascriptions" is not the right word to use. We do not engage in any theoretical enterprise when we are involved in such everyday interactions. What the example illustrates is what it means to interact with others as responsible individuals. We see these interactions as moral because the sentiments involved in them are of a moral nature. We believe with Strawson that these reactive attitudes are a crucial and indispensable part of our interpersonal relationships (Strawson 1962), at least in our contemporary Western society.[9] They are what constitute our everyday practices of responsibility (cf., e.g., Wallace 1994; Scanlon 1998). Now let us turn to the relation of these everyday practices, the space of reasons it gives rise to and the concept of free will.

§ 2 THE SPACE OF REASONS AND THE CONCEPT OF FREE WILL

The pump-example shows how we bring our normative expectations and actions into harmony by blaming people when they do not conform to what we expect and exchanging reasons for our interpretations of what happened and what should be done in response. The exchange is not always as harmonious as we sketched here. We sometimes disagree on what can be expected from whom and on which occasions.[10] However, even if we fail to settle upon a shared set of expectations we often find ways to deal with the situation. We might agree to disagree and each go our own way. We might even take institutional measures (hand over the case to the law authorities), and by doing so, try to force one another to accept behavior in accordance with what we believe proper. This brings us to the second aspect of our ascriptions of responsibility, the process-aspect: Sometimes we need to get others to do what we believe should be done.

To prevent recourse to institutions, force or even violence, exchanging reasons and seeking a common ground are good ways to coordinate our shared practices.[11] We see this as an important assumption of our contemporary Western society. When people do what they do "out of their own free will," because they see how it fits into a network of reasons they can identify with (that they experience as their own reasons), coordination of shared activities becomes much easier. Let us return to our mundane example to argue our case. The exchange of reasons in the harmonious scenario of the pump example profits from the fact that each participant in the exchange feels responsible for her or his actions. It is because the barman feels responsible for the loss of the pump that he proposes to call the woman to account. It is because the woman feels responsible for the shared practice that she brings the pump back. Identifying with the reasons why what is expected is expected enables people to do what is expected. When people feel responsible for a shared practice and for their contribution to it (what they do), they are better motivated to keep an eye on what is expected and to act accordingly. Hence, with respect to both aspects (design and process) of the coordination of our shared activities, the space of reasons plays a crucial role. When you can explain to others why you acted as you did and or can convince them that your reasons were adequate, this will have an impact on future interactions with those involved. Though more difficult to describe, the same seems true for more complex shared activities, involving more people, hence, more interests, individual differences, and so on, as a result leading to a multifaceted conversation.

In any case, given the social, coordinative, function of our practice of responsibility it makes no sense to take or hold people responsible for transgressing normative expectations that could not have been fulfilled. It is silly to resent or blame, for example, a mentally retarded barman for failing to watch someone's pump when he does not understand such requests. Would this barman blame himself, we would reassure him not to worry and explain that Arno should not have made his request to him. Unless of course the barman's mental capacities well equip him to understand and fulfill such requests. In that case, blame is appropriate and we would fail to do justice to the barman not to involve him in our shared 'pump-lending practices' and related conversations.

It is crucial to the dynamics of responsibility ascriptions, as explained in the previous section, that it allows for differences between individuals, differences in capacities, interests, degrees of participation. It is by way of the moral sentiments and subsequent exchange of reasons that we fine-tune our mutual normative expectations: That we figure out what can be expected when, from whom, and why (Sie 2005). Everyone able to position her- or himself in the space of reasons can participate in these moral practices.[12] The concept of free will arises naturally as part of this so-called positioning process, but does not precede it. It might make sense to claim lack of free will on the part of our mentally challenged barman, for example, when his action of lending the pump did not express "his values" or "his usual way of acting." When he lent the pump because he did not pay attention to what was being asked, telling us that he did not act out of his own free will might express that he would have done otherwise if he had paid attention.[13] Likewise, the barman might claim the opposite when a customer tells Arno of the barman's impaired mental capacities. He might say something like: "No that is not the reason why I did it! I lent the pump to that other customer out of my own free will." With that claim the barman might communicate that he does not believe that what he did was wrong and does not see the need to make excuses. Or, alternatively, he might not believe that his impaired mental capacities were the cause of his action and feel guilty. In that case he uses 'free will' to emphasize that he did something that he now considers to be stupid *and* something for which he cannot be excused. That is to say, that sometimes we summon free will by way of lamentation, to convey that we think apologies and amends *are* in order, not excuses or exemptions.

Free will in the PS-approach escapes a simple and straightforward definition. It is a concept that arises naturally when we locate ourselves and others in the space of reasons. We sometimes use it to draw attention to the reasons we have for acting, sometimes to communicate that we think our action to be wrong and unexcusable, i.e., that we feel the need to apologize and make amends. We also sometimes use it to explain that our actions should be understood against our limited range of options, as in "I do not live in this neighborhood out of my own free will" or to excuse ourselves completely as in "I did not act out of my free will." In each and every case free will functions as part of the social function of responsibility ascriptions. Now let us turn to the scientific findings that some have taken as a reason to reject the existence of metaphysical free will.

§ 3 WHAT THE SCIENCES TELL US ABOUT FREE WILL

§ 3.1 The Scientific Findings

Although we often think and talk about our choices in terms of individual considerations, cognitive science has established that we often fall prey to all kinds of cognitive biases without being aware of it. So, for example, we might explain our choice not to use a particular kind of medicine because we believe the benefits do not outweigh the risks or we may explain our choice for a pair of stockings by referring to their softness. In the past decades, cognitive scientists have shown themselves able to manipulate such choices, regardless of the individual considerations we tend to cite in everyday life (e.g., Tversky 1981, for a good overview of this literature see Kahneman 2011).[14] Also they managed to identify many situations in which these biases that serve us well in most circumstances, cause us to function sub-optimally. Closely related research in social psychology and behavioral economics suggests that our choices are often influenced by features of our surroundings or the set-up of a situation or option (for a nice overview see Thaler and Sunstein 2008). With respect to these cases too, we do not tend to cite these features when asked to explain our choices (Nisbett and Wilson 1977). Moreover, recent research even suggests that we can be misled about our choices and will provide reasons even for the choices we did not make (Hall and Strandberg 2012). Does all of this research not indicate the limits of our ability to position ourselves in the space of reasons, so central in the previous sections? And what about research in other, though related, disciplines?

Research in social science also shows that other biases, prejudices and stereotypes can be activated, triggered, without us being aware of it, and in such a way that they influence our behavior (see Wilson 2002, ch.9; Fine 2006, ch. 8; Kunda and Spencer 2003). One of the explanations of why stereotypes and prejudices remain effective even after having fallen into disfavor might be the phenomenon of implicit bias (Kelly and Roedder 2008). Extensive research has shown that almost all of us are prone to implicit biases[15] regardless of our explicit attitudes with respect to those biases.[16] I will come back to these findings below. Other, perhaps more surprising findings in moral psychology suggest that our moral judgments are co-determined by features of our surroundings that trigger feelings of disgust or their opposite, cleanliness (Schnall, Haidt, Clore, and Jordan 2008; Schnall, Benton, and Harvey 2008). We know that to look fresh and clean matters in many social situations, for example when facing trial by jury. Nevertheless, that "cleanliness and disgust-related" circumstances also impact the severity of our moral judgments in a lab-setting has taken many by surprise.[17]

Many people were also taken by surprise by findings in "experimental philosophy" or "survey-philosophy." These suggest that our judgment on whether an action was done on purpose or not is influenced by our moral evaluation of the outcome of certain actions: i.e., whether we morally like or dislike it (Nadelhoffer 2006).[18] This phenomenon might be an instantiation of the more general outcome bias from which we appear to suffer: the inclination to use information presently available to evaluate the quality of a decision made in the past (Baron and Hershey 1988). Neuro-ethical findings, furthermore, seem to establish the general influence of emotions when we judge moral dilemmas, even when abstract and highly fantastic ones such as the trolley-cases are involved (Greene 2005; Greene, Sommerville, and Nystrom 2001).[19] What is interesting about these findings for the purposes of this chapter is that they disclose something about the way in which we judge these dilemmas that was not so clear before the fMRI results. That is, that differences in our judgments can be explained by our different emotional responses to the dilemmas. For the findings showed a greater[20] activation in areas associated with emotion in one set of dilemmas (those that required the agent to engage in a personal, physical act of killing) compared to another set (those that only required a distant act of killing). When we make such judgments, though, we are not especially aware of a difference in emotional responses to them, or of what this emotional response is exactly related to.

The above is only a small sample of the vast and diverse findings that have become available in the past decades. Does all of that research taken together not indicate that our everyday exchange of reasons is a very poor attempt, indeed, to explain why we act as we do? Clearly much of our mental lives is inaccessible to introspection and that should make us wonder about our everyday success in explaining why we do what we do. To be sure, how exactly to understand and evaluate the lack of introspective access that all these experiments bring to the fore is controversial, as is the question whether this inaccessibility is a truly new discovery and/or contrary to popular belief (Kozuch and Nichols 2011; Sie 2009). What seems very hard to doubt, though, is the following twofold upshot of this research, i.e., that:

1. our first-personal interpretation of even very mundane actions occasionally fails to be fully adequate
2. without us—the interpreters—realizing this to be the case

Let us refer to the first feature as the phenomenon of "subjective misinterpretation" and to the second as the phenomenon of "agential intransparency." When asked why we did something we sometimes provide answers that are incomplete or even mistaken (subjective misinterpretation), without hesitation and/or doubt (which suggest agential intransparency). Hence, even on occasions where we are, or appear to be, confident about our answers to so-called why questions, we might nevertheless miss important aspects of what made us act as we did or fail to appreciate the reasons why. We miss important aspects of what made us act as we did when we fail to acknowledge crucial influences on our actions. We fail to appreciate the reasons why when our explanation or justification bears little or no relation to the actions explained.

According to an influential view in cognitive science the phenomena of subjective misinterpretation and agential intransparency make clear that the reasons we offer as explanations or justifications of our actions are not introspective reports on the states that caused these actions (Wegner 2002; Wegner and Wheatley 1999; Hassin, Uleman, and Bargh 2005; Wilson 2002). Rather we infer or reconstruct those reasons on the basis of so called a priori[21] causal theories originating from experience and the social environment (Bargh and Chartrand 1999; Nisbett and Wilson 1977). When asked to explain an action, we determine which of the possible causes were present at the time of the action and cite that as the reason for the action. If we cannot find a plausible reason, we confabulate one, make one up on the basis of the available information (Gazzaniga 2005). Causes that escape our attention, causes that are not easily remembered, and causes that are not within our known range of possible causes will not be cited.

This view explains elegantly how subjective misinterpretations can occasionally occur and cause distortions in the space of reasons.[22] This in itself need not interfere with the social function of our exchange of reasons as outlined in the previous sections. After all, when our a-priori causal theories are basically correct and the reasons we tend to cite more or less adequate, the overall relation between our reasons and our actions will remain more or less trustworthy. But can we truly say that this is the case? Let us start with the question whether the reasons we tend to cite are basically correct. I address the question whether our a-priori theories are basically correct at the end of § 3.2.

With respect to the reasons we tend to cite when explaining our actions, judgments and choices, we do not talk about ourselves as prone to, for example, cognitive and other biases. We do not typically refer to ourselves as risk-aversive creatures, for example, whereas our common preference for a "sure thing" over a "favorable gamble" (risk-aversion) enables us to explain many of our sub-optimal choices in all kinds of game-theoretical settings. Nor do we consider our factual judgments prone to something like the outcome bias introduced above, even though this bias might distort our view on what people do intentionally and what not. Also we do not speculate on the efficacy of implicit biases in our judgments with respect to, for example, a person's suitability for a job or specific task. Chances are, as the aforementioned Kahneman believes, that the introduction of the vocabulary of cognitive biases into our everyday conversations would make these conversations more adequate (Kahneman 2011).[23] If it would, it would also increase our overall ability to locate ourselves adequately in the space of reasons. Since that ability, as we argued in the previous sections, is closely related to our ability to coordinate shared practices such an improvement would in its turn improve these practices. With respect to the design aspect of our shared practice, for example, it would help to determine what we can and cannot expect from one another given that we are prone to certain cognitive and other biases. With respect to the process aspect we might consider it proper to take certain measures that minimize unwanted behavioral outcomes and maximize desired ones, also referred to as choice architecture (Thaler and Sunstein 2008).

Related questions can be raised with respect to other areas of research. What to think of, for example, the situationists' claims of the past decades?[24] They argue that our behavior and actions are primarily the result of the particularities of the situation, not of enduring moral traits of our individual character. Those enduring moral traits are known among philosophers as 'virtues.' Clearly we often use virtues, or virtue-like language, to explain one another's behavior. We say of people that they acted cowardly or arrogantly, that what they did was dishonest, cruel, mean or brave and kind. And even in more mundane cases, we often use virtue-like language. Take the example from the first section in which the owner of a café lends the pump that Arno left in his care to one of his other clients. In the exchange of moral sentiments that follows the café owner's action, it is easy to imagine that Arno resents the owner, e.g., for being "careless" or "eager to make a good impression on young women" (such as the one to whom he lent Arno's pump). We tend to resent behavior that is indicative of a morally bad character trait. We understand the person as being guilty of the kind of behavior one should not make oneself guilty of. According to situationism such explanations are misguided. Situationists argue that we should explain behavior in terms of the situation, not by citing traits of agents that would explain their behavior across situations. The reason for this is that according to them, empirical studies show, first of all, that it possible to get people to behave in ways we (they themselves included) consider morally bad by manipulating their situation (e.g., Zimbardo 2004; Milgram 1974). Secondly, empirical studies designed to disclose differences between individuals that could count as referring to enduring character traits all failed to establish them (Harman 2000b).[25]

Another line of research in moral psychology raises questions about our standard practice of explaining ourselves by citing behavioral standards or moral principles such as "honesty is important to me," "we need to do what is just." According to a series of experiments run by Daniel Batson et al. we often do not act at all in accordance with such standards when it is not in our advantage. A much more plausible explanation for the occasions when we do act in accordance with such standards, they argue, is our wish to "appear to be moral" (Batson 2008; Batson, Thompson, Seuferling, Whitney, and Strongman 1999). They call this phenomenon "moral hypocrisy": we only act in accordance with explicated behavioral standards when that is required to appear to act morally. We, however, so the researchers suggest, are not aware of that underlying motivation. Moreover, in the right circumstances, some of us will even deceive ourselves about our motivation to act the way we do.[26]

The phenomenon of moral hypocrisy might relate to two well-researched phenomena in psychology: the asymmetric understanding of the moral nature of our own actions and those of others (the fundamental attribution error) and the idea that our own actions and motivations are much more moral than those of the average person (Epley 2000). In cases of other people acting in morally wrong ways we tend to explain those wrongdoings in terms of the agent's lack of virtue or morally bad character traits. We focus on those elements that allow us to blame agents for their moral wrongdoings. On the other hand, in cases where we ourselves act in morally reprehensible ways we tend to focus on exceptional elements of our situation, emphasizing the lack of room to do otherwise. This, finally, brings us to the concept of free will. After all, when we believe that we, or others, lacked the room to act otherwise, we might typically claim that "we/they did not act out of our/their own free will." On the other hand, when responding to morally blameworthy behavior we tend to assume that the behavior was freely willed. In the next section let us explain in what way the scientific research hitheto discussed is relevant to the space of reasons and our understanding of free will.

§ 3.2 Free Will, an Illusion?

When the social and moral psychologists presented in the previous sections are right, we tend to overestimate free will in the case of other people's wrongdoings and underestimate it in the case of ourselves. The wish to appear moral and our general tendency to feel holier than thou can be expected to aggravate that error: Both will incline us to take a favorable view of our own motives, reasons, and actions. That means that we will tend to explain our moral wrongdoings by appealing to excusing and exonerating circumstances or giving an overtly sympathetic reading to the reasons and motives for which we acted. Also we will tend to cast our own actions more easily as moral than those of other people. On the other hand we will tend to explain other people's moral wrongdoings as the result of bad character-traits rather than circumstances. In terms of free will:

1. in the case of wrongdoings we will tend to overestimate other people's free will and underestimate our own;
2. in the case of exemplary and good actions we will tend to overestimate our own free will and underestimate that of other people.

Would we be keeping this in mind that would surely change how we locate ourselves in the space of reasons. *Grosso modo*, we claim to act out of our own free will, e.g., when we (believe to) have good reasons to act as we did.[27] Or we claim the opposite, that we did not act out of our own free will, when we did not act for reasons and were caused by exceptional circumstances to act as we did. In the latter case we will offer excuses and/or apologies. On the basis of the social and moral psychology findings we need to be more modest with respect to the role of behavioral and moral principles and virtues in the explanation of our own morally adequate functioning. That is, whenever we explain our actions in terms of moral reasons (citing behavioral or moral principles or virtues) we might be alert to whether that story is all there is to it. For example, when I explain the fact that I did not lie about some embarrasing fact about my past behavior I should not neglect the features of the situation that enable me to confess. By the same token I should be suspicious whenever I readily look for excuses when explaining my own morally wrongful behavior. It just might be the case that I am able to improve myself by focussing on what I could have done differently in exactly the same situation.

Analoguosly, we need to tune down our explanations of others in terms of their moral vices and failure to observe moral standards. When people lie and we resent them for it we should not neglect the features of the situation that made it hard for them to confess. By the same token, when we explain away the morally praiseworthy behavior of other people we should keep an open mind as to whether or not they actually did something that deserves praise.

As far as the cognitive and other biases, stereotypes and prejudices are concerned, we might seriously investigate their role and impact on our functioning and introduce their possible distorting effects into our everyday conversations (Sie and Van Voorst Vader-Bours WiP). Critically scrutinizing our own and one another's professed reasons might enable us to gain more grip on ourselves and improve our shared practices.

To be sure, we might have learned the general lessons that can be abstracted from the above—know thyself, who is without sin . . . , and so on— also by reading the great classics in philosophy and literature, the bible or careful attention to common sense's wisdom. But the scientific findings of the past decades have disclosed not only general lessons but many details on our social and cognitive functioning that we can use to improve it, as well as many fascinating and surprising facts about what influences us and what barely does so. Why would we not consider how to adjust and improve our self-understanding on particular occasions and with respect to certain domains of action in light of this huge amount of scientific work? As argued, a good way to do so would be to reconsider how we locate ourselves in the space of reasons.

To conclude, let us shortly address the idea that our a-priori theories about how our reasons relate to our actions as such are mistaken. Is it conceivable that the whole idea that we can locate ourselves in the space of reasons is misplaced and that, in that sense, whatever we have to say about our free will or our reasons is misplaced? Partly on the basis of research discussed in the previous section, Jonathan Haidt and colleagues infamously argued that we should not take our reason-giving practices at face value (Haidt 2001; Haidt and Bjorklund 2008). Although we act and talk as if our reasons and judgments are the result of deliberation that is not what is actually the case. Rather, the reasons we exchange are post-hoc constructions devised primarily with an eye to influencing the judgments made by other people. We seek their approval and do not aim to provide true reports on the causal antecedents of our judgments.[28] According to Haidt the actual antecedents of our moral judgments are gut-feelings (which Haidt also calls intuitions), not deliberative processes. These gut-feelings and intuitions are "sudden flashes of evaluation" which are susceptible to all kinds of influences that escape our attention. According to him traditional rational models wrongly claim that our moral judgments originate from individual rational deliberations. In doing so they distort our view on the role and nature of moral evaluation in everyday life, mainly its social role and non-deliberative ("emotional") nature.

In the Western world we leave a large part of the regulation of our interpersonal affairs to our everyday moral practices, in much the way set out in the second section of this chapter. Being able to position ourselves in the space of reasons constitutes an important part of this moral practice. The space of reasons comes into existence by our shared enterprise of bringing our normative expectations into mutual harmony. Obviously this would not work if the reasons we exchange collectively missed all relation to the shared practices regulated by them. Even if we discover that all reasons are constructed post-hoc, this would not matter, as long as reasons that we exchange in general relate to our practices in trustworthy ways. In this sense reasons are the 'currency' of our shared coordinative practices: What holds true for the real currency, money, holds true for reasons. That is, it is not obvious or easy to determine what it represents exactly, it is sometimes counterfeited, it is often worth more or less depending on the situation, it sometimes buys us more than it should, sometimes less, in addition it is used in, and possibly even crucial to, all kinds of immoral and criminal enterprises. However, money, like reasons, would no longer be exchanged if it lost all value. That being said, the research listed in this section and the findings on which SIM relies leave little room to doubt the phenomena of subjective misinterpretation and agential intransparency. Hence there is reason to question whether the concept of free will that arises as part of this process has the application we think it has.

CONCLUSION

Every society needs means to coordinate behavior, but there are several ways to accomplish this. In our Western society the value of autonomy plays an important role: we think it is important for people to act in accordance with what they themselves think is right. Hence, we allow people to coordinate a great deal of their shared lives within limits set by the law. That is, we delegate large parts of the regulation of our interpersonal affairs to the moral realm: To the realm in which people come to an understanding of what should and what should not be done by exchanging reasons, in just the way explained in the first two sections of this paper. As we have seen, in this process individual agents take responsibility for their actions and exchange reasons when those actions transgress other people's normative expectations. Hence, we put great trust in people's ability to figure out what is expected from them in a variety of situations, and in their willingness and ability to do what is expected out of their own free will. In this paper we argued that certain scientific findings of recent decades could throw new light on those ocassions at which we (do not) act out of our own free will, in this sense. We also concluded that the view that we are unable to locate ourselves in the space of reasons makes no sense from the approach to free will endorsed in this paper.[29]

NOTES

1. See, for example, his excellent criticism on the Libet-experiments in chapter 8.

2. The debate that subsequently unravels is that between so called incompatibilists and compatibilists. The first group does not believe free will is compatible with the thesis of determinism (Van Inwagen 1975) and investigates the possibility and actuality of indeterminist free will (see, for example, Kane 1996). Others within that group discuss whether free will is required for moral responsibility and investigate what the answer implies for our current moral practices (see, for example, Honderich 2002; Pereboom 2001). For many philosophers the kind of free will worth wanting is a free will that makes us morally responsible (Dennett 1998a). The second, by far the largest, group believes that determinism and free will are compatible or that, at least, the kind of free will worth wanting is compatible with determinism. Their work explains why this is the case and/or how people are misled into thinking it is not. There are too many compatibilists of either sort to function as representative of the whole group, see, e.g., the excellent collection of Watson (1982) for a nice overview.

3. We will not discuss the relation between the pragmatic and metaphysical approach, but see, Wolf (1990), introduction, and Nagel (1979) who both argue that the metaphysical issue of free will derives from conditions we use to determine moral responsibility in our everyday practices. Albeit not in these terms, I address this issue in Sie (1998).

4. This is not to claim that Strawson himself defended a PS-approach to free will. Strawson claims not even to understand what "the thesis of determinism" is supposed to mean (Strawson 1962, 59).

5. Although the phrase "locating oneself in the space of reasons" might not sound familiar, the idea is much in line with views such as originated by Peter F. Strawson, and elaborated on by, among others, Gary Watson, Susan Wolf, Jay Wallace, Michael Smith, and Philip Pettitt. They all focus our attention on our ability to act for and exchange reasons. However, these

latter authors present themselves explicitly as compatibilists (Pettit 1996; Wallace 1994; Wolf 1990), hence, as contributing to the metaphysical discussion on free will. I explain why that is unfortunate in Sie (2005).

6. Given a different understanding of the concept of "free will" the claim that it is an illusion might still make sense.

7. This first section and part of the second was originally written together with my postdoc Arno Wouters for a workshop-paper on responsibility in 2010. Unfortunately, due to personal circumstances we failed to finish a joint version of that paper, but the ideas put forward here bear the marks of our joint enterprise to do so.

8. This example can also be found in Wouters (2011).

9. For the purposes of our claim in this paper we treat Strawson's view as a descriptive view. We are fully aware that it is possible to argue over the exact nature of the claims regarding the "indispensable nature" of the reactive attitudes made in his paper. See, for example, Russell (1992).

10. Elsewhere I argue that the need to allow for such normative disagreements is what justifies blame, not the compatibility of determinism and free will (Sie 2005).

11. There could be several ways in which this practice can be defended as a "good" one: more efficient, most pleasant for all involved, and so on. I take it that most people involved in the moral practices described in this paper agree with this point, although I also see room to argue against it.

12. When philosophers claim that it is reasons-responsiveness, rather than counterfactual freedom (the freedom to do otherwise than one actually did) that matters to moral responsibility they might very well have something in mind along the lines of this ability to "locate ourselves in the space of reasons." See the aforementioned works of Wolf, Wallace, Pettit and Smith. As said, the primary interest of these philosophers, however, still is the metaphysical discussion on free will which is why a lot of energy is devoted to working on the details of how to exactly understand this reason responsiveness (see, e.g., Fischer 1994; Fischer and Ravizza 1992, 1998).

13. Cf. Harry Frankfurt who argued extensively against the metaphysical interpretation of the vocabulary of free will and in favor of an interpretation that links free will to the things we do because we want to do them (it is our will that we do them) (see Frankfurt 1969, 1973). For his positive account of what we do mean when we say that we did something out of free will see his influential paper (Frankfurt 1971).

14. Other books often cited in this respect are: Ariely (2008); Baron (2007).

15. Introduced in the literature by Greenwald et. al. (1998). See for the test itself: (29/10/2012) https://implicit.harvard.edu/implicit/demo/.

16. Cordelia Fine discusses several findings that suggest that we can correct for these implicit biases (Fine 2006b).

17. Although controversial (e.g., Huebner 2011), this cluster of research has led to serious reflection on the ethical role and status of disgust. See, for example, Kelly (2011).

18. It is the work of Joshua Knobe that set off the discussion on the "moral slot" in our judgments on intentionality. See Knobe (2003, 2004).

19. These dilemmas were introduced in moral philosophy by Thomson and Foot (Foot 1967/1978; Thomson 1976).

20. One could also argue that the correct interpretation of the fMRI results is not "greater" activation but a "different" one. See, e.g., Prinz (2007, 1.2.2).

21. The phrase "a-priori causal theories" derives from Nisbett and Wilson (1977). We will stick to that use although the label "a-priori" is a bit confusing since the theories are based upon experience.

22. The originators of this line of thought actually believe that our a priori causal theories usually give us quite reliable estimates about the origin of our actions and why they were performed (see Nisbett and Wilson 1977; Wegner 2002).

23. Daniel Kahneman lists "spreading information about our cognitive biases to the wider audience" as his main reason for popularizing his work.

24. See Doris (2002); Harman (2000b).

25. The situationist position is of course controversial and many so-called virtue ethicists have argued against the situationist claims, especially its normative implications (Sabini and Silver 2005; Annas 2005). Note, however, that our point here focuses not on the normative implications of situationism but on the descriptive claims. If the situationist literature is right we often *misdescribe* the motives of our actions.

26. I argue that this label might be misleading in Sie (2012).

27. *Grosso modo*, as explained in the previous section in particular situations we might use "free will" differently.

28. Many philosophers have objected to the Social Intuitionist Model Haidt proposed as a replacement for rationalist models of moral judgments (e.g., Narvaez 2008; Jacobson 2008; Fine 2006a).

29. Thanks are due to Philip Robichaud, Filippo Santoni De Sio, Katrien Schaubroeck, Nicole van Voorst Vader Bours, Arno Wouters and the editor of this volume, Gregg Caruso, for lively discussion and helpful comments. I also thank Myrthe van Nus, Michiel Wielema and Gregg Caruso for their editorial work on this chapter.

References

Aarts, Henk, Ruud Custers, and Daniel M. Wegner. 2005. On the inference of personal authorship: Enhancing experienced agency by priming effect information. *Consciousness and Cognition* 14:439–58.
Adler, Mortimer. 1958. *The idea of freedom: A dialectical examination of the conceptions of freedom.* Garden City, NY: Doubleday.
Ady, Thomas. 1656. *A candle in the dark.* London: Robert Ibbitson.
Altemeyer, Robert A. 1981. *Right-wing authoritarianism.* Manitoba: University of Manitoba Press.
———. 1996. *The authoritarian specter.* Cambridge, MA: Harvard University Press.
Andreasen, Robin O. 2000. Race: Biological reality or social construct? *Philosophy of Science* 67:S653–S666.
Annas, Julia. 2005. Comments on John Doris's "Lack of character." *Philosophy and Phenomenological Research* 71 (3): 636–42.
Appiah, Anthony. 1995. The uncompleted argument: Du Bois and the illusion of race. In *Overcoming racism and sexism,* ed. Linda A. Bell and David Blumenfeld, 59–78. Lanham, MD: Rowman and Littlefield.
Ariely, Dan. 2008. *Predictably irrational: The hidden forces that shape our decisions.* New York: HarperCollins.
Atmanspacher, Harald, and Stafan Rotter. 2011. On determinacy or its absence in the brain. In *Free will and modern science,* ed. Richard Swinburne, 84–101. Oxford: Oxford University Press.
Ayer, A. J. 1936. *Language, truth and logic.* London: Victor Gollancz.
Baars, Bernard J. 1997a. Contrastive phenomenology: A thoroughly empirical approach to consciousness. In *The nature of consciousness: Philosophical debates,* ed. Ned Block, Owen Flanagan, and Guven Guzeldere, 187–202. Cambridge: MIT Press/Bradford Books.
———. 1997b. In the theatre of consciousness. Global workspace theory, a rigorous scientific theory of consciousness. *Journal of Consciousness Studies* 4:292–309.
Balaguer, Mark. 2009. *Free will as an open scientific problem.* Cambridge, MA: MIT Press.
Bandura, Albert. 1997. *Self-efficacy: The exercise of control.* New York: W. H. Freeman.
Banks, William P., and Eve A. Isham. 2009. We infer rather than perceive the moment we decided to act. *Psychological Science* 20:17–21.
Bargh, John A. 1997. The automaticity of everyday life. In *The automaticity of everyday life: Advances in social cognition,* Vol.10, ed. Robert S. Wyer, Jr., 1–61. Mahwah, NJ: Erlbaum.
———. 2008. Free will is un-natural. In *Are we free? Psychology and free will,* ed. John Baer, James C. Kaufman, and Roy F. Baumeister, 128–54. New York: Oxford University Press.

Bargh, John A., and Tanya L. Chartrand. 1999. The unbearable automaticity of being. *American Psychologist* 54 (7): 462–79.

Bargh, John A., and Brian Earp. 2009. The will is caused, not "free." http://www.psychologytoday.com/blog/the-natural-unconscious/200906/the-will-is-caused-not-free (accessed August 27, 2010).

Bargh, John A., and Melissa J. Ferguson. 2000. Beyond behaviorism: On the automaticity of higher mental processes. *Psychological Bulletin* 126 (6): 925–45.

Bargh, John A., Peter M. Gollwitzer, Annette Lee-Chai, Kimberley Barndollar, and Roman Trötschel. 2001. The automated will: Nonconscious activation and pursuit of behavioral goals. *Journal of Personality and Social Psychology* 81 (6): 1014–27.

Baron, Jonathan. 2007. *Thinking and deciding*. New York: Cambridge University Press.

Baron, Jonathan, and John C. Hershey. 1988. Outcome bias in decision evaluation. *Journal of Personality and Social Psychology* 54:569–79.

Batson, C. Daniel. 2008. Moral masquerades: Experimental exploration of the nature of moral motivation. *Phenomenology and the Cognitive Sciences* 7(1): 51–66. doi: 10.1007/s11097-007-9058-y.

Batson, C. Daniel, Elizabeth R. Thompson, Greg Seuferling, Heather Whitney, and Jon A. Strongman. 1999. Moral hypocrisy: Appearing moral to oneself without being so. *Journal of Personality and Social Psychology* 77 (3): 525–37.

Baumeister, Roy F. 2008a. Free will, consciousness, and cultural animals. In *Are we free? Psychology and free will*, ed. John Baer, James C. Kaufman, and Roy F. Baumeister, 65–85. New York: Oxford University Press.

———. 2008b. Free will in scientific psychology. *Perspectives of Psychological Science* 3 (1): 14–19.

Baumeister, Roy F., Ellen Bratslavsky, Mark Muraven, and Dianne M. Tice. 1998. Ego depletion: Is the active self a limited resource? *Journal of Personality and Social Psychology* 74:1252–65.

Baumeister, Roy F., A. William Crescioni, and Jessica L. Alquist. 2011. Free will as advanced action control for human social life and culture. *Neuroethics* 4:1–11.

Baumeister, Roy F., E. J. Masicampo, and C. Nathan DeWall. 2009. Prosocial benefits of feeling free: Disbelief in free will increases aggression and reduces helpfulness. *Personality and Social Psychology Bulletin* 35 (2): 260–68.

Baumeister, Roy F., E. J. Masicampo, and Kathleen D. Vohs. 2011. Do conscious thoughts cause behavior? *Annual Review of Psychology* 62:331–61.

Baumeister, Roy F., Erin A. Sparks, Tyler F. Stillman, and Kathleen D. Vohs. 2008. Free will in consumer behavior: Self-control, ego depletion, and choice. *Journal of Consumer Psychology* 18:4–13.

Baumeister, Roy F., and John Tierney. 2011. *Willpower: Rediscovering the greatest human strength*. New York: Penguin Press.

Bishop, Michael. 1999. Semantic flexibility in scientific practice: A study of Newton's optics. *Philosophy & Rhetoric* 32 (3): 210–32.

Bishop, Michael A., and Stephen P. Stich. 1998. The flight to reference, or how not to make progress in the philosophy of science. *Philosophy of Science* 65 (1): 33–49.

Bishop, Robert C. 2002. Chaos, indeterminism, and free will. In *The Oxford handbook of free will*, ed. Robert Kane, 111–24. Oxford: Oxford University Press.

Blackburn, Simon. 1985. Errors and the phenomenology of value. In *Morality and objectivity*, ed. Ted Honderich, 1–22. London: Routledge & Kegan Paul.

Blackmore, Susan. 1999. *The meme machine*. New York: Oxford University Press.

———. 2000. Memes and the malign user illusion (abstract). *Consciousness and Cognition* 9: S49.

———. 2002. There is no stream of consciousness. *Journal of Consciousness Studies* 9:17–28.

———. 2005. *Conversations on consciousness: What the best minds think about the brain, free will, and what it means to be human*. New York: Oxford University Press.

———. 2010. *Consciousness: An introduction*. 2nd ed. London: Hodder Education.

———. 2011. *Zen and the art of consciousness*. Oxford: Oneworld Publications.

Block, Ned. 1995. On a confusion about a function of consciousness. *Behavioral and Brain Sciences* 18:227–87.

———. 2007. *Consciousness, function, and representation: Collected papers*, Vol. 1. Cambridge, MA: MIT Press.

Block, Ned, Owen J. Flanagan, and Guven Guzeldere, eds. 1997. *The nature of consciousness: Philosophical debates*. Cambridge, MA: MIT Press/Bradford Books.

Bloom, Paul. 2004. *Descartes' baby*. New York: Basic Books.

Bode, Stefan, Anna Hanxi He, Chun Siong Soon, Robert Trampel, Robert Turner, and John-Dylan Haynes. 2011. Tracking the unconscious generation of free decisions using ultra-high field fMRI. *PLoS ONE* 6 (6): e21612.

Bok, Hilary. 1998. *Freedom and responsibility*. Princeton: Princeton University Press.

Boulton, Richard. 1715. *Complete history of magick, sorcery, and witchcraft*. London: E. Curll, J. Pemberton and W. Taylor.

Boyd, Richard. 1983. On the current status of the issue of scientific realism. *Erkenntnis* 19:45–90.

———. 2002. Scientific realism. In The Stanford encyclopedia of philosophy (Summer 2002 ed.), ed. Edward N. Zalta. http://plato.stanford.edu/archives/sum2002/entries/scientific-realism/.

Burge, Tyler. 2007. *Foundations of mind*. New York: Oxford University Press.

Cacioppo, John T., and Richard E. Petty. 1982. The need for cognition. *Journal of Personality and Social Psychology* 42:116–31.

Campbell, C. A. 1957. *On selfhood and Godhood*. London: George Allen & Unwin, Ltd.

———. 1957. Has the self "free will"? In *On selfhood and godhood*, C. A. Campbell. London: George Allen & Unwin, Ltd.

Carey, Jasmine M., and Delroy L. Paulhus. In press. Worldview implications of believing in free will and/or determinism: Politics, morality, and punitiveness. *Journal of Personality*.

Carnap, Rudolph. 1967. *The logical structure of the world*. Trans. R. A. George. Berkeley, CA: University of California Press.

Carr, Edward H. 1961. *What is history?* London: Macmillan.

Caruso, Gregg D. 2012. *Free will and consciousness: A determinist account of the illusion of free will*. Lanham, MD: Lexington Books.

Casaubon, Meric. 1670. *Of credulity and incredulity in things divine and spiritual*. London: S. Lownds.

Cashmore, Anthony R. 2010. The Lucretian swerve: The biological basis of human behavior and the criminal justice system. *Proceedings of the National Academy of Sciences of the United States of America* 107 (10): 4459–4504.

Chalmers, David J. 2010. *The character of consciousness*. Oxford: Oxford University Press.

———. 2011. Verbal disputes. *Philosophical Review* 120 (4): 515–66.

Chisholm, Roderick. 1964. Human freedom and the self. The Lindley Lecture, University of Kansas. Reprinted in *Free will*, ed. Gary Watson, 24–35. New York: Oxford University Press, 1982.

———. 1976. *Person and object*. La Salle, IL: Open Court.

Clark, Andy. 2011. *Supersizing the mind: Embodiment, action and cognitive science*. Oxford: Oxford University Press.

Clark, Thomas W. 2004. Facing facts: Policy implications of the humanist commitment to science. In *Toward a new political humanism*, ed. Barry F. Seidman and Neil J. Murphy, 343–54. Amherst, NY: Prometheus Press.

———. 2005a. Killing the observer. *Journal of Consciousness Studies* 12 (4–5): 38–59.

———. 2005b. Crime and causality: Do killers deserve to die? *Free Inquiry* 25 (2): 34–37.

———. 2006. Holding mechanisms responsible. *Lahey Clinic Medical Ethics Journal* 13 (3): 10–11.

———. 2010. Free will roundup. http://www.naturalism.org/roundup.htm (accessed October 26, 2012).

———. 2012. Singling out the agent: Review of Against Moral Responsibility *by* Bruce Waller. Naturalism.org: http://www.naturalism.org/Wallerreview.htm.

Clarke, Randolph. 2003. *Libertarian accounts of free will*. New York: Oxford University Press.

———. 2005. On an argument for the impossibility of moral responsibility. *Midwest Studies in Philosophy* 29:13–24.
Claxton, Guy. 1986. The light's on but there's nobody home: The psychology of no-self. In *Beyond therapy: The impact of eastern religions on psychological theory and practice*, ed. G. Claxton, 49–70. Dorset: Prism Press.
Coyne, Jerry A. 2012. Why you don't really have free will. *USA Today*, January 1.
Crick, Francis, and Christof Koch. 2003. A framework for consciousness. *Nature Neuroscience* 6 (2): 119–26.
Custers, Ruud, and Henk Aarts. 2010. The unconscious will: How the pursuit of goals operates outside of conscious awareness. *Science* 329 (5987): 47–50.
Dalbert, Claudia, and Lois Yamauchi. 1994. Belief in a just world and attitudes toward immigrants and foreign workers: A cultural comparison between Hawaii and Germany. *Journal of Applied Social Psychology* 24:1612–26.
Danziger, Shai, Jonathan Levav, and Liora Avnaim-Pesso. 2011. Extraneous factors in judicial decisions. *Proceedings of the National Academy of Science of the United States of America* 108 (17): 6889–92.
Darley, John M., and Daniel C. Batson. 1973. From Jerusalem to Jericho: A study of situational and dispositional variables in helping behavior. *Journal of Personality and Social Psychology* 27 (1): 100–108.
Darwall, Stephen L. 1977. Two kinds of respect. *Ethics* 88 (1): 36–49.
Darwin, Charles. 1838/1987. *Charles Darwin's notebooks, 1836–44*. Cambridge: Cambridge University Press.
Davies, Paul Sheldon. 2009. *Subjects of the world: Darwin's rhetoric and the study of agency in nature*. Chicago: University of Chicago Press.
Deery, Oisin, Matt Bedke, and Shaun Nichols. Forthcoming. Phenomenal abilities: Incompatibilism and the experience of agency. In *Oxford studies in agency and responsibility*, ed. D. Shoemaker.
Dehaene, Stanislas, Jean-Pierre Changeux, Lionel Naccache, Jerome Sackur, and Claire Sergent. 2006. Conscious, preconscious, and subliminal processing: A testable taxonomy. *Trends in Cognitive Science* 10 (5): 204–11.
Dehaene, Stanislas, and Lionel Naccache. 2001. Towards a cognitive neuroscience of consciousness: Basic evidence and a workspace framework. *Cognition* 79:1–37.
Dennett, Daniel. 1984. *Elbow room: The varieties of free will worth wanting*. Cambridge, MA: MIT Press.
———. 1991. *Consciousness explained*. Boston: Little, Brown and Company.
———. 1998a. *Brainchildren: Essays on designing minds*. Cambridge, MA: MIT Press.
———. 1998b. The myth of double transduction. In *Toward a science of consciousness II, The second Tucson discussions and debates*, ed. Stuart R. Hameroff, Alfred W. Kaszniak, and Alwyn C. Scott, 97–107. Cambridge, MA: MIT Press.
———. 2001. The fantasy of first person science. Debate with D. Chalmers, Northwestern University, Evanston, IL, Feb 2001. http://ase.tufts.edu/cogstud/papers/chalmers-deb3dft.htm.
———. 2003. *Freedom evolves*. New York: Viking Press.
———. 2012. *Erasmus: Sometimes a spin doctor is right*. Amsterdam: Erasmus Prize Institution. Desmurget, Michel, Karen T. Reilly, Nathalie Richard, Alexandru Szathmari, Carmine Mottolese, and Angela Sirigu. 2009. Movement intention after parietal cortex stimulation in humans. *Science* 324 (5928): 811–13.
Devitt, Michael, and Kim Sterelny . 1999. *Language and reality: An introduction to the philosophy of language* . Cambridge, MA: MIT Press.
d'Holbach, Baron Paul Henri. 1770. *The system of nature*. Amsterdam.
Doris, John M. 2002. *Lack of character: Personality and moral behavior*. Cambridge: Cambridge University Press.
———. Forthcoming. Talking to ourselves: Reflection, skepticism, and agency. New York: Oxford University Press.
Doris, John, and Dominic Murphy. 2007. From My Lai to Abu Ghraib: The moral psychology of atrocity. *Midwest Studies in Philosophy* 31:25–55.

Double, Richard. 1991. *The non-reality of free will*. Oxford: Oxford University Press.
———. 2002. The moral hardness of libertarianism. *Philo* 5:226–34.
Dretske, Fred. 1995. *Naturalizing the mind*. Cambridge, MA: MIT Press.
Earman, John. 1986. *A primer on determinism*. Dordrecht, Holland: Reidel.
Ekstrom, Laura W. 2000. *Free will: A philosophical study*. Boulder, Co: Westview Press.
Elster, Jon. 1990. Norms of revenge. *Ethics* 100:862–85.
Epley, Nicholas, and David Dunning. 2000. Feeling "holier than thou": Are self-serving assessments produced by errors in self or social prediction? *Journal of Personality and Social Psychology* 79:861–75.
Evatt, Cris. 2010. *The myth of free will*. Rev. and exp. ed. Sausalito, CA: Cafe Essays.
Farrell, Daniel M. 1985. The justification of general deterrence. *Philosophical Review* 104:367–94.
Feinberg, Joel. 1970. Justice and personal desert. In *Doing and deserving: Essays in the theory of responsibility*, ed. Joel Feinberg. Princeton: Princeton University Press.
Feldman, Fred. 1995. Desert: Reconsideration of some received wisdom. *Mind* 104 (413): 63–77.
———. 1996. Responsibility as a condition for desert. *Mind* 105 (417): 165–68.
Feltz, Adam. 2013. Pereboom and premises: Asking the right questions in the experimental philosophy of free will. *Consciousness and Cognition* 22 (1): 53–63.
Feyerabend, P. K. 1962. Explanation, reduction and empiricism. In *Minnesota studies in the philosophy of science, Vol. 3: Scientific explanation, space, and time*, ed. H. Feigl and G. Maxwell, 28–97. Minneapolis: University of Minnesota Press.
Fine, Cordelia. 2006a. Is the emotional dog wagging its rational tail or chasing it? *Philosophical Explorations* 9 (1): 83–98.
———. 2006b. *A mind of its own: How your brain distorts and deceives*. 1st ed. New York: W.W. Norton & Co.
Fischer, John Martin. 1994. *The metaphysics of free will: A study of control*. Malden, MA: Blackwell Publishing.
———. 1995. *The metaphysics of free will* (Aristotelian Society Series v. 14). Malden, MA: Blackwell Publishing.
———. 2002. Frankfurt-type examples and semi-compatibilism. In *The Oxford handbook of free will*, ed. Robert Kane, 281–308. New York: Oxford University Press.
———. 2004. Responsibility and manipulation. *The Journal of Ethics* 8 (2): 145–77.
———. 2006a. *My way*. New York: Oxford University Press.
———. 2006b. The cards that are dealt you. *The Journal of Ethics* 10:107–29.
———. 2012. Semicompatibilism and its rivals. *The Journal of Ethics* 16:117–43.
Fischer, John Martin, Robert Kane, Derk Pereboom, and Manuel Vargas. 2007. *Four views on free will*. Oxford: Blackwell Publishing.
Fischer, John Martin, and Mark Ravizza. 1992. Responsibility, freedom, and reason. *Ethics* 102 (2): 368–89.
———. 1998. *Responsibility and control: A theory of moral responsibility*. Cambridge: Cambridge University Press.
Foot, Philippa. 1967/1978. The problem of abortion and the doctrine of the double effect in virtues and vices. In *Virtues and Vices*, Foot, 19–32. doi: 10.1093/0199252866.003.0002.
Fourneret, Pierre, and Marc Jeannerod. 1998. Limited conscious monitoring of motor performance in normal subjects. *Neuropsychologia* 36 (11): 1133–40.
Frank, Robert H. 1988. *Passions within reason: The strategic role of the emotions*. New York: Norton.
Frankfurt, Harry G. 1969. Alternative possibilities and moral responsibility. *Journal of Philosophy* 66 (23): 829–39.
———. 1971. Freedom of the will and the concept of a person. *Journal of Philosophy* 68 (1): 5–20.
———. 1973. Coercion and moral responsibility. In *Essays on freedom and action*, ed. Ted Honderich. London: Routledge & Kegan Paul. Reprinted in *The importance of what we care about*, Frankfurt (1988), 26–46.

———. 1976. Identification and externality. In *The identities of persons*, ed. A. Rorty. Berkley: University of California Press.

———. 1987. Identification and wholeheartedness. In *Responsibility, character, and the emotions*, ed. F. D. Schoeman. New York: Cambridge University Press.

Franklin, Christopher. 2011. Farewell to the luck (and mind argument). *Philosophical Studies*, forthcoming.

Freeman, Anthony, ed. 2006. *Radical externalism: Honderich's theory of consciousness discussed*. Imprint Academic.

French, Peter. 2001. *The virtues of vengeance*. Lawrence, KS: University of Kansas Press.

Fried, Itzhak, Amiram Katz, Gregory McCarthy, Kimberlee J. Sass, Peter Williamson, Susan S. Spencer, and Dennis D. Spencer. 1991. Functional organization of human supplementary motor cortex studied by electrical stimulation. *Journal of Neuroscience* 11 (11): 3656–66.

Furnham, Adrian. 2003. Belief in a just world: Research progress over the past decade. *Personality and Individual Differences* 34:795–817.

Furnham, Adrian, and B. Gunter. 1984. Just world beliefs and attitudes towards the poor. *British Journal of Social Psychology* 15:265–69.

Gagarin, Michael. 1974. Dike in archaic Greek thought. *Classical Philology* 69:186–97.

Gardner, Eileen M. 1984. The education crisis: Washington shares the blame. *Heritage Foundation* (Washington, D.C.)/Policy Archives.

Gazzaniga, Michael S. 2005. *The ethical brain*. New York: Dana Press.

Ginet, Carl. 1990. *On action*. Cambridge: Cambridge University Press.

Godfrey-Smith, Peter. 2003. *Theory and reality: An introduction to the philosophy of science*. Chicago: University of Chicago Press.

Goetz, Stewart. 2008. *Freedom, teleology, and evil*. London: Continuum.

Greene, Joshua D. 2005. Emotion and cognition in moral judgment: Evidence from neuroimaging. In *Neurobiology of human values*, ed. J. P. Changeux, A. R. Damasio, W. Singer, and Y. Christen. Berlin: Springer-Verlag.

Greene, Joshua D., and Jonathan Cohen. 2004. For the law, neuroscience changes nothing, and everything. *Philosophical Transactions of the Royal Society of London, B* 359:1775–85. doi:10.1098/rstb.2004.1546 (accessed October 26, 2012).

Greene, Joshua D., R. Brian Sommerville, Leigh E. Nystrom, John M. Darley, and Jonathan Cohen. 2001. An fmri investigation of emotional engagement in moral judgment. *Science* 293 (14): 2105–8.

Greenwald, Anthony G., Debbie E. McGhee, and Jordan K. L. Schwartz. 1998. Measuring individual differences in implicit cognition: The implicit association test. *Journal of Personality and Social Psychology* 74:1464–80.

Griffiths, Meghan. 2010. Why agent-caused actions are not lucky. *American Philosophical Quarterly* 47:43–56.

Hafer, Carolyn L., and Laurent Bègue. 2005. Experimental research on just-world theory: Problems, developments, and future challenges. *Psychological Bulletin* 131:128-67.

Haggard, Patrick. 2008. Human volition: Towards a neuroscience of will. *Nature Reviews Neuroscience* 9:934–46.

———. 2011. Does brain science change our view of free will? In *Free will and modern science*, ed. Richard Swinburne, 7–24. New York: Oxford University Press.

Haggard, Patrick, and Martin Eimer. 1999. On the relation between brain potentials and the awareness of voluntary movements. *Experimental Brain Research* 126:128–33.

Haidt, Jonathan. 2001. The emotional dog and its rational tail: A social intuitionist approach to moral judgment. *Psychological Review* 108:814–34.

Haidt, Jonathan, and Fredrik Bjorklund. 2008. Social intuitionists answer six questions about moral psychology. In *Moral psychology*, Vol. 2, ed. W. Sinnott-Armstrong, 181–218. Cambridge, MA: MIT Press.

Haji, Ishtiyaque. 1998. *Moral accountability*. New York: Oxford University Press.

Hall, Lars, Petter Johansson, and Thomas Strandberg. 2012. Lifting the veil of morality: Choice blindness and attitude reversals on a self-transforming survey. *PLoS ONE* 7 (9): e45457. doi: 10.1371/journal.pone.0045457.

Hallett, Mark. 2007. Volitional control of movement: The physiology of free will. *Clinical Neurophysiology* 118 (6): 1179–92.

———. 2009. Physiology of volition. In *Downward causation and the neurobiology of free will*, ed. N. Murphy, G. F. R. Ellis, and T. O'Connor, 127–43. Berlin: Springer.

Hanakawa, Takashi, Michael A. Dimyan, and Mark Hallett. 2008. Motor planning, imagery, and execution in the distributed motor network: A time-course study with functional MRI. *Cerebral Cortex* 18 (12): 2775–88.

Hardin, Curtis D., and Mahzarin R. Banaji. In press. The nature of implicit prejudice: Implications for personal and public policy. In *The behavioral foundations of policy*, ed. Eldar Shafir, 13–31. Princeton: Princeton University Press.

Harman, Gilbert. 1999. Moral philosophy meets social psychology: Virtue ethics and the fundamental attribution error. *Proceedings of the Aristotelian Society* 99:315–31.

———. 2000a. The nonexistence of character traits. *Proceedings of the Aristotelian Society* 100:223–26.

———. 2000b. Moral philosophy meets social psychology. In *Explaining value: And other essays in moral philosophy*, Harman, 165–80. Oxford: Oxford University Press.

Harper, David, and Paul Manasse. 1992. The just world and the third world: British explanations for poverty abroad. *Journal of Social Psychology* 132:783–85.

Harris, Sam. 2012. *Free will*. New York: Free Press.

Harris Poll. 2009. What people do and do not believe in. New York: Harris Interactive, Inc. http://www.harrisinteractive.com/vault/Harris_Poll_2009_12_15.pdf (accessed October 26, 2012).

Hart, H. L. A. 1970. *Punishment and responsibility*. Oxford: Clarendon Press.

Hassin, Ran R., James S. Uleman, and John A. Bargh, eds. 2005. *The new unconscious*. New York: Oxford University Press.

Haynes, John-Dylan. 2011a. Decoding and predicting intentions. *Annals of the New York Academy of Sciences* 1224:9–21.

———. 2011b. Beyond Libet: Long-term prediction of free choices from neuroimaging signals. In *Conscious will and responsibility*, ed. W. Sinnott-Armstrong and L. Nadel, 85–96. Oxford: Oxford University Press.

Haynes, John-Dylan, Katsuyuki Sakai, Geriant Rees, Sam Gilbert, Chris Frith, and Richard E. Passingham. 2007. Reading hidden intentions in the human brain. *Current Biology* 17 (4): 323–28.

Herrmann, Christoph S., Michael Pauen, Byoung Kyong Min, Niko A. Busch, and Jochem Rieger. 2008. Analysis of a choice-reaction task yields a new interpretation of Libet's experiments. *International Journal of Psychophysiology* 67 (2): 151–57.

Hieronymi, Pamela. 2001. Articulating an uncompromising forgiveness. *Philosophy and Phenomenological Research* 62:529–54.

Hodgson, David. 2002. Quantum physics, consciousness, and free will. In *The Oxford handbook of free will*, ed. Robert Kane, 85–110. New York: Oxford University Press.

Hoefer, Carl. 2010. Causal determinism. In The Stanford encyclopaedia of philosophy (Spring 2010 Edition) , ed. Edward N. Zalta. http://plato.stanford.edu/archives/spr2010/entries/determinism-causal/.

Honderich, Ted. 1988. *A Theory of determinism: The mind, neuroscience, and life-hopes*. Oxford: Oxford University Press. Republished in two volumes: *Mind and brain* and *The consequences of determinism*,1990.

———. 2002. *How free are you?: The determinism problem*. 2nd ed. Oxford: Oxford University Press.

———. 2003. *Terrorism for humanity: Inquiries in political philosophy*. London: Pluto Press.

———. 2004a. *On determinism and freedom*. Edinburgh, UK: Edinburgh University Press.

———. 2004b. Is the mind ahead of the brain? Behind it? In Honderich 2004a.

———. 2005. *Conservatism: Burke, Nozick, Bush, Blair?* London: Pluto Press.

———. 2006a. *Punishment: The supposed justifications revisited*. London: Pluto Press.

———. 2006b. *Right and wrong, and Palestine, 9–11, Iraq, 7–7* . . . New York: Seven Stories Press. [British edition *Humanity, terrorism, terrorist war: Palestine, 9/11, Iraq, 7/7* . . . London: Continuum.]

———. 2013. *Actual consciousness*. Forthcoming.
Hood, Bruce. 2012. *The self illusion*. New York: Oxford University Press.
Houlton, Richard. In press. From determinism to resignation and how to stop it. In *Decomposing the will*, ed. Andy Clark, Julian Kiverstein, and Tillman Vierkant. Cambridge: Oxford University Press.
Huebner, Bryce. 2011. Critiquing moral psychology from the inside. *Philosophy of the Social Sciences* 41:50–83.
Hume, David. 1739/1978. *A treatise of human nature*. Oxford: Oxford University Press.
———. 1748/1963. *An enquiry concerning human understanding*, ed. L. A. Selby-Bigge. New York: Oxford University Press.
Hurley, Susan. 2000. Is responsibility essentially impossible? *Philosophical Studies* 99:229–68.
Hutchinson, Francis. 1718. *An historical essay concerning witchcraft*. London: Knaplock and Midwinter.
Huxley, Thomas. 1874. On the hypothesis that animals are automata, and its history. *The Fortnightly Review* n.s. 16:555–80.
Jack, Anthony I., and Tim Shallice. 2001. Introspective physicalism as an approach to the science of consciousness. *Cognition* 79:161–96.
Jacobson, Daniel. 2008. Does social intuitionism flatter morality or challenge it? In *Moral psychology*, Vol. 2, ed. W. Sinnott-Armstrong, 219–32. Cambridge, MA: MIT Press.
James I, King of England. 1597. *Daemonology*. Edinburgh: Printed by Robert Walde-graue. Printer to the Kings Majestie. Cum Privilegio Regio.
James, William. 1890. *The principles of psychology*. 2 vols. London: MacMillan.
Jeannerod, Marc. 2006. Consciousness of action as an embodied consciousness. In *Does consciousness cause behavior?*, ed. S. Pockett, W. P. Banks, and S. Gallagher, 25–38. Cambridge, MA: MIT Press.
Jost, John T., Sally Blount, Jeffrey Pfeffer, and Gyorgy Hunyady. 2003. Fair market ideology: Its cognitive-motivational underpinnings. *Research in Organizational Behavior* 25:53–91.
Jost, John T., J. Glaser, A. W. Kruglanski, and F. Sulloway. 2003b. Exceptions that prove the rule: Using a theory of motivated social cognition to account for ideological incongruities and political anomalies. *Psychological Bulletin* 129:383–93.
Jost, John T., and Erik P. Thompson. 2000. Group-based dominance and opposition to equality as independent predictors of self-esteem, ethnocentrism, and social policy attitudes among African Americans and European Americans. *Journal of Experimental Social Psychology* 36 (3): 209–32.
Joyce, Richard. 2006. *The evolution of morality*. Cambridge, MA: The MIT Press.
Kahneman, Daniel. 2011. *Thinking, fast and slow*. New York: Farrar, Strauss and Giroux.
Kane, Robert. 1989. Two kinds of incompatibilism. *Philosophy and Phenomenological Research* 50:219–54.
———. 1996. *The significance of free will*. New York: Oxford University Press.
———. 2000. Free will and responsibility: Ancient dispute, new themes. *The Journal of Ethics* 4:315–22.
———. 2002. Introduction: The contours of contemporary free will debates. In *The Oxford handbook of free will*, ed. Kane, 3–41. New York: Oxford University Press.
———. ed. 2002. *The Oxford handbook of free will*. New York: Oxford University Press.
———. ed. 2011. *The Oxford handbook of free will*, 2nd ed. New York: Oxford University Press.
Kant, Immanuel. 1788/1956. *Critique of practical reason*. Trans. L. W. Beck. Indianapolis: Bobbs-Merrill.
———. 1793/1960. *Religion within the limits of reason alone*. Trans. T. M. Greene and H. H. Hudson. New York: Harper & Row.
———. 1800/1993. *Opus postumum*. Trans. E. Förster and M. Rosen. Cambridge: Cambridge University Press.
———. 1996. *Metaphysics of moral*. Trans. and ed. Mary Gregor. New York: Cambridge University Press.

———. 1998. *Religion within the boundaries of mere reason*. Trans. and ed. Allen Wood and George di Giovanni. New York: Cambridge University Press.
Kanwisher, Nancy. 2001. Neural events and perceptual awareness. *Cognition* 79:89–113.
Kawamura, S. 1967. Aggression as studied in troops of Japanese monkeys. In *Aggression and defense, brain function*, ed. C. Clemente and D. Lindsley, 195–224. Berkeley: University of California Press.
Kelly, Daniel. 2011. *Yuck!: The nature and moral significance of disgust (Life and mind: Philosophical issues in biology and psychology)*. Cambridge, MA: MIT.
Kelly, Daniel, and Erica Roedder. 2008. Racial cognition and the ethics of implicit bias. *Philosophy Compass* 3 (3): 522–40. doi: 10.1111/j.1747-9991.2008.00138.x.
Kim, Jaegwon. 2005. *Physicalism, or something near enough*. Princeton: Princeton University Press.
King, Matt, and Peter Carruthers. 2012. Moral responsibility and consciousness. *Journal of Moral Philosophy* 9:200–228.
Kitcher, Philip. 1993. *The advancement of science: Science without legend, objectivity without illusions*. New York: Oxford University Press.
Knobe, Joshua. 2003. Intentional action in folk psychology: An experimental investigation. *Philosophical Psychology* 16:309–24.
———. 2004. Intention, intentional action and moral considerations. *Analysis* 64 (2): 181–87.
Knobe, Joshua, and John M. Doris. 2010. Responsibility. In *The moral psychology handbook*, ed. John M. Doris, 321–54. New York: Oxford University Press.
Knobe, Joshua, and Shaun Nichols. 2008. *Experimental philosophy*. New York: Oxford University Press.
Koch, Christof. 2012. *Consciousness: Confessions of a romantic reductionist*. Cambridge, MA: MIT Press.
Korsgaard, Christine. 2009. *Self-constitution: Agency, identity, and integrity*. Oxford: Oxford University Press.
Kouider, Sid. 2009. Neurobiological theories of consciousness. In *Encyclopedia of consciousness*, ed. W. P. Banks. Oxford: Elsevier.
Kozuch, Benjamin, and Shaun Nichols. 2011. Awareness of unawareness. Folk psychology and introspective transparency. *Journal of Consciousness Studies* 18 (11–12): 135–60.
Kranick, Sarah M., and Mark Hallett. In press. Neurology of Volition. *Experimental Brain Re search*.
Kühn, Simone, and Marcel Brass. 2009. Retrospective construction of the judgment of free choice. *Consciousness and Cognition* 18:12–21.
Kuhn, Thomas. 1962. *The structure of scientific revolutions*. Chicago: Chicago University Press.
Kunda, Ziva, and Steven J. Spencer. 2003. Do stereotypes come to mind and when do they color judgment? A goal-based theoretical framework for stereotype activation and application. *Psychological Bulletin* 129 (4): 522–44. doi: 10.1037/0033-2909.129.4.522.
Lane, Kristin, Mahzarin Banaji, Brian Nosek, and Anthony Greenwald. 2007. Understanding and using the implicit association test: IV. In *Implicit measures of attitude*, ed. Bernd Wittenbrink and Norbert Schwarz, 59–101. New York: The Guilford Press.
Langer, Ellen J., and Jane Roth. 1975. Heads I win, tails it's chance: The illusion of control as a function of the sequence of outcomes in a purely chance task. *Journal of Personality and Social Psychology* 32 (6): 951–55.
Laplace, Pierre Simon. 1814. *A philosophical essay on probabilities*. Trans. from the 6th French ed. by Frederick Wilson Truscott and Frederick Lincoln Emory. New York: Dover Publications, 1951.
Lau, Hakwan C., and Richard E. Passingham. 2007. Unconscious activation of the cognitive control system in the human prefrontal cortex. *Journal of Neuroscience* 27 (21): 5805–11.
Lau, Hakwan C., Robert D. Rogers, and Richard E. Passingham. 2007. Manipulating the experienced onset of intention after action execution. *Journal of Cognitive Neuroscience* 19 (1): 81–90.
Laudan, Larry. 1984. *Science and values*. Vol. 66. Berkeley: University of California Press.

Lawson, Chappell, Gabriel S. Lenz, Michael Myers, and Andy Baker. 2010. Candidate appearance, electability, and political institutions: Findings from two studies of candidate appearance. *World Politics* 62 (4): 561–93.
Lee, Victoria K., and Lasana T. Harris. Forthcoming. A social perspective on debates about free will. In *Moral psychology, Vol. 4: Free will and moral responsibility*, ed. Walter Sinnott-Armstrong. Cambridge, MA: MIT Press.
Lerner, Melvin J. 1965. Evaluation of performance as a function of performer's reward and attractiveness. *Journal of Personality and Social Psychology* 1:355–60.
———. 1980. *The belief in a just world: A fundamental delusion*. New York: Plenum Press.
Lerner, Melvin J., and Dale T. Miller. 1978. Just world research and the attribution process: Looking back and ahead. *Psychological Bulletin* 85:1030–51.
Lerner, Melvin J., and Carolyn H. Simmons. 1966. Observer's reaction to the "innocent victim": Compassion or rejection? *Journal of Personality and Social Psychology* 4:203–10.
Levy, Neil. 2011. *Hard luck: How luck undermines free will and moral responsibility*. Oxford: Oxford University Press.
———. 2012. Skepticism and sanction. *Law and Philosophy* 31:477–93.
Lewis, David. 1972. Psychophysical and theoretical identifications. *Australasian Journal of Philosophy* 50 (3): 249–58.
Libet, Benjamin. 1985. Unconscious cerebral initiative and the role of conscious will in voluntary action. *Behavioral and Brain Science* 8:529–66.
———. 1999. Do we have free will? *Journal of Consciousness Studies* 6 (8–9): 47–57. Reprinted in *The Oxford handbook of free will*, ed. Robert Kane, 551–64. New York: Oxford University Press, 2002.
Libet, Benjamin, Curtis A. Gleason, Elwood W. Wright, and Dennis K. Pearl. 1983. Time of conscious intention to act in relation to onset of cerebral activity (readiness-potential): The unconscious initiation of a freely voluntary act. *Brain* 106:623–42.
Libet, Benjamin, Elwood W. Wright, B. Feinstein, and Dennis Pearl. 1979. Subjective referral of the timing for a conscious sensory experience: A functional role for the somatosensory specific projection system in man. *Brain* 102 (1): 193–224.
Libet, Benjamin, Elwood W. Wright, and Curtis A. Gleason. 1982. Readiness potentials preceding unrestricted 'spontaneous' vs. pre-planned voluntary acts. *Electroencephalography and Clinical Neurophysiology* 54:322–35.
Luhrmann, T. M. 1991. *Persuasions of the witch's craft: Ritual magic in contemporary England*. Cambridge, MA: Harvard University Press.
Lycan, William G. 1988. *Judgement and justification*. New York: Cambridge University Press.
———. 1997. *Consciousness*. Cambridge, MA: MIT Press.
Machery, E., C. Olivola, H. Cheon, I. Kurniawan, I. Mauro, N. Struchiner, H. Susianto. Forthcoming. Is folk essentialism a fundamental feature of human cognition? A cross-cultural study.
MacKay, D. M. 1960. On the logical indeterminacy of free choice. *Mind* 69:31–40.
Mackie, J. L. 1990. *Ethics: Inventing right and wrong*. London: Penguin Books Ltd.
Macrae, C. Neil, and Lucy Johnston. 1998. Help, I need somebody: Automatic action and inaction. *Social Cognition* 16:400–17.
Mallon, Ron. 2006. Race: Normative, not metaphysical or semantic. *Ethics* 116 (3): 525–51.
Matsuhashi, Masao, and Mark Hallett. 2008. The timing of the conscious intention to move. *European Journal of Neuroscience* 28 (11): 2344–51.
McCann, Hugh. 1998. *The works of agency*. Ithaca: Cornell University Press.
McKenna, Michael. 2008a. Ultimacy and sweet jane. In *Essays on free will and moral responsibility*, ed. Nick Trakakis and Daniel Cohen. Cambridge: Scholars Publishing.
———. 2008b. A hard-line reply to Pereboom's four-case argument. *Philosophy and Phenomenological Research* 77:142–59.
———. 2009. Compatibilism and desert: Critical comments on four views on free will. *Philosophical Studies* 144:3–13.
Mele, Alfred R. 1995. *Autonomous agents*. New York: Oxford University Press.
———. 2005. A critique of Pereboom's "four-case argument" for incompatibilism. *Analysis* 65:75–80.

———. 2006. *Free will and luck.* New York: Oxford University Press.

———. 2007. Decision, intentions, urges and free will: Why Libet has not shown what he says he has. In *Explanation and causation: Topics in contemporary philosophy*, ed. J. Campbell, M. O'Rourke, and D. Shier. Boston: MIT Press.

———. 2008. Recent work on free will and science. *American Philosophical Quarterly* 45 (2): 107–30.

———. 2009. *Effective intentions: The power of the conscious will.* New York: Oxford University Press.

———. 2010a. Scientific skepticism about free will. In *Moral psychology: Classical and contemporary readings*, ed. Thomas Nadelhoffer, Eddy Nahmias, and Shaun Nichols, 295–305. Oxford: Wiley-Blackwell.

———. 2010b. Testing free will. *Neuroethics* 3 (2): 161–72.

———. 2010c. Conscious deciding and the science of free will. In *Free will and consciousness: How might they work?*, ed. Roy F. Baumeister, Alfred R. Mele, and Kathleen D. Vohs, 43–65. New York: Oxford University Press.

———. 2011. Free will and science. In *Oxford handbook of free will*, 2nd ed., ed. Robert Kane, 499–514. New York: Oxford University Press.

———. 2012a. Autonomy and neuroscience. In *Autonomy and mental disorder*, ed. Lubomira Radoilska, 26–43. New York: Oxford University Press.

———. 2012b. Another scientific threat to free will? *The Monist* 95 (3): 423–41.

———. Forthcoming. Free will and substance dualism: The real scientific threat to free will? In *Moral psychology, Vol. 4: Free will and moral responsibility*, ed. Walter Sinnott-Armstrong. Cambridge, MA: MIT Press.

Metzinger, Thomas. 2003. *Being no one.* Cambridge, MA: MIT Press/Bradford Books.

———. 2009. *The ego tunnel: The science of the mind and the myth of the self.* New York: Basic Books.

Milgram, Stanley. 1974. *Obedience to authority: An experimental view.* New York: Harper & Row.

Mill, John Stuart. 1859/1985. *On liberty.* London: Penguin Books.

Mills, Eugene. 2004. Scheffler on Rawls, justice, and desert. *Law and Philosophy* 23:261–72.

Minsky, Marvin. 1988. *The society of mind.* New York: Touchstone Books.

Mischel, Walter, Yuichi Shoda, and Philip K. Peake. 1988. The nature of adolescent competencies predicted by preschool delay of gratification. *Journal of Personality and Social Psychology* 54:687–96.

Momennejad, Ida, and John-Dylan Haynes. 2012. Human anterior prefrontal cortex encodes the "what" and "when" of future intentions. *Neuroimage* 61 (1): 139–48.

Montada, Leo. 1998. Belief in a just world: A hybrid of justice motive and self-interest. In *Responses to victimizations and belief in the just world*, ed. Leo Montada and Melvin Lerner, 217–45. New York: Plenum.

Montague, P. Read. 2008. Free will. *Current Biology* 18 (14): R584–R585.

Moore, Michael S. 1997. *Placing blame: A general theory of the criminal law.* Oxford: Oxford University Press.

Moors, Agnes, and Jan De Houwer. 2006. Automaticity: A theoretical and conceptual analysis. *Psychol Bull* 132 (2): 297–326.

Moriarity, Jeffrey. 2003. Against the asymmetry of desert. *Noûs* 37 (3): 518–36.

Morris, Stephen. 2009. The impact of neuroscience on the free will debate. *Florida Philosophical Review* 9:56–78.

Morse, Stephen J. 2004. Reason, results, and criminal responsibility. *University of Illinois Law Review* 2:363–444.

Nadelhoffer, Thomas. 2006. Bad acts, blameworthy agents, and intentional actions. Some problems for juror impartiality. *Philosophical Explorations* 9 (2): 203–219.

———. 2011. The threat of shrinking agency and free will disillusionism. In *Conscious will and responsibility: A tribute to Benjamin Libet*, ed. L. Nadel and W. Sinnott-Armstrong, 173–88. New York: Oxford University Press.

———. In press. Dualism, libertarianism, and scientific skepticism about free will. In *Moral psychology: Neuroscience, free will, and responsibility*, Vol. 4, ed. Walter Sinnott-Armstrong. Cambridge, MA: MIT Press.

Nadelhoffer, Thomas, and Galen Baril. In preparation. The moral and political psychology of believing in free will. Manuscript in preparation at the College of Charleston.

Nadelhoffer, Thomas, and Adam Feltz. 2007. Folk intuitions, slippery slopes, and necessary fictions: An essay on Smilansky's free will illusionism. *Midwest Studies in Philosophy* 13 (1): 202–13.

Nadelhoffer, Thomas, and Tatyana Matveeva. 2009. Positive illusions, perceived control, and the free will debate. *Mind & Language* 24:495–522.

Nadelhoffer, Thomas, Eddy Nahmias, L. Ross, J. Shepard, and Chandra Sripada. In preparation. The free will inventory: Measuring beliefs about agency and responsibility. Manuscript in preparation at the College of Charleston.

Nagel, Thomas. 1979. Moral luck. In *Mortal questions*, 24–38. New York: Cambridge University Press.

Nahab, F. B., P. Kundu, C. Gallea, J. Kakareka, R. Pursley, T. Pohida, N. Miletta, J. Friedman, and M. Hallett. 2011. The neural processes underlying self-agency. *Cerebral Cortex* 21 (1): 48–55.

Nahmias, Eddy. 2007. Autonomous agency and social psychology. In *Cartographies of the mind: Philosophy and psychology in intersection*, ed. Massimo Marraffa, Mario De Caro, and Francesco Ferretti, 169–85. Dordrecht: Springer.

———. 2010. Scientific challenges to free will. In *A companion to the philosophy of action*, ed. Timothy O'Connor and Constantine Sandis, 345–56. Malden, MA: Wiley-Blackwell.

———. 2011a. Intuitions about free will, determinism, and bypassing. In *The Oxford handbook of free will*, 2nd ed., ed. Robert Kane, 555–76. Oxford: Oxford University Press.

———. 2011b. Why "willusionism" leads to "bad results": Comments on Baumeister, Crescioni, and Alquist. *Neuroethics* 4 (1): 17–24.

———. Forthcoming-a. *Rediscovering free will*. New York: Oxford University Press.

———. Forthcoming-b. Is free will an illusion? Confronting challenges from the modern mind sciences. In *Reconsidering scientific threats to free will*, ed. Walter Sinnott-Armstrong, Cambridge, MA: MIT Press.

Nahmias, Eddy, D. Justin Coates, and Trevor Kvaran. 2007. Free will, moral responsibility, and mechanism: Experiments on folk intuitions. *Midwest Studies in Philosophy* 31:214–41.

Nahmias, Eddy, Stephen Morris, Thomas Nadelhoffer, and Jason Turner. 2005. Surveying freedom: Folk intuitions about free will and moral responsibility. *Philosophical Psychology* 18:561–84.

———. 2006. Is incompatibilism intuitive? *Philosophy and Phenomenological Research* 73:28–53.

Nahmias, Eddy, and Dylan Murray. 2010. Experimental philosophy on free will: An error theory for incompatibilist intuitions. In *New waves in philosophy of action*, ed. J. Aguilar, A. Buckareff, and K. Frankish, 189–215. New York: Palgrave-Macmillan.

Narvaez, Darcia. 2008. The social intuitionist model: Some counter-intuitions. In *Moral psychology*, Vol. 2, ed. W. Sinnott-Armstrong, 233–40. Cambridge, MA: MIT Press.

Nelkin, Dana. 2005. Freedom, responsibility, and the challenge of situationism. *Midwest Studies in Philosophy* 29 (1): 181–206.

———. 2011. *Making sense of freedom and responsibility*. Oxford: Oxford University Press.

Nichols, Shaun. 2007. After incompatibilism: A naturalistic defense of the reactive attitudes. *Philosophical Perspectives* 21:405–28.

———. 2011. Experimental philosophy and the problem of free will. *Science* 331:1401–3.

Nichols, Shaun, and Joshua Knobe. 2007. Moral responsibility and determinism: The cognitive science of folk intuitions. *Nous* 41:663–85.

Nichols, Shaun, A. Pinillos, and R. Mallon. Forthcoming. Ambiguous Reference.

Nickerson, Raymond S. 1998. Confirmation bias: An ubiquitous phenomenon in many guises. *Review of General Psychology* 2 (2): 175–220.

Nietzsche, Friedrich. 1886/1966. *Beyond good and evil*. Trans. Walter Kaufmann. New York: Random House.

———. 1992. Beyond good and evil. In *The basic writings of Nietzsche*, ed. Walter Kaufmann. New York: Modern Library.
Nisbett, Richard E., and Timothy D. Wilson. 1977. Telling more than we can know: Verbal reports on mental processes. *Psychological Review* 84:231–59.
Noe, Alva. 2009. *Out of our heads: Why you are not your brain, and other lessons from the biology of consciousness*. New York: Hill and Wang.
Norman, Donald A., and Tim Shallice. 1986. Attention to action: Willed and automatic control of behavior. In *Consciousness and self-regulation: Advances in research and theory IV*, ed. Richard J. Davidson, Gary E. Schwartz, and David Shapiro, 1–14. New York: Plenum Press.
Notestein, Wallace. 1911. *A history of witchcraft in England from 1558 to 1718*. Washington: The American Historical Association.
Nussbaum, Martha. 2004. Discussing disgust: On the folly of gross-out public policy: An interview with Martha Nussbaum. *Reason*, July 15, 2004.
O'Connor, Timothy. 2000. *Persons and causes*. New York: Oxford University Press.
———. 2003. Review of *Living without free will*. *Philosophical Quarterly* 53:308–10.
———. 2008. Agent-causal power. In *Dispositions and causes*, ed. Toby Handfield, 189–214. Oxford: Clarendon Press.
Oerton, Richard. 2012. *The nonsense of free will: Facing up to a false belief*. Leicestershire: Troubador Publishing.
Ortega, George. 2012. Free will refuted in the news: An explosion of coverage since 2010. http://causalconsciousness.com/free%20will%20in%20the%20news.htm (accessed October 26, 2012).
Overbye, Dennis. 2007. Free will: Now you have it, now you don't. *The New York Times*, January 2.
Pagels, Heinz R. 1983. *The cosmic code: Quantum physics as the language of nature*. New York: Simon & Schuster.
Parvizi, Josef, and Antonio Damasio. 2001. Consciousness and the brainstem. *Cognition* 79 (1–2): 135–59.
Patten, J. 1992. Article in *The Spectator*, April 16.
Paulhus, Delroy L. 1991. Measurement and control of response bias. In *Measures of personality and social psychological attitudes*, ed. J. P. Robinson, P. R. Shaver, and L. S. Wrightsman, 17–59. San Diego, CA: Academic Press.
Paulhus, Delroy L., and Jasmine M. Carey. 2011. The FAD-Plus: Measuring lay beliefs regarding free will and related constructs. *Journal of Personality Assessment* 93:96–104.
Pearce, Jonathan M. S. 2010. *Free will?: An investigation into whether we have free will, or whether I was always going to write this book*. Ginger Prince Publications.
Penfield, Wilder, and Theodore Rasmussen. 1950. *The cerebral cortex of man: A clinical study of localization of function*. Macmillan: New York.
Pereboom, Derk. 1995. Determinism al dente. *Noûs* 29:21–45.
———. 2001. *Living without free will*. New York: Cambridge University Press.
———. 2004. Is our conception of agent causation incoherent? *Philosophical Topics* 32:275–86.
———. 2005. Defending hard incompatibilism. *Midwest Studies in Philosophy* 29:228–47.
———. 2006. Is our conception of agent-causation coherent? *Philosophical Topics* 32:275–86.
———. 2007. Hard incompatibilism, and responses to Kane, Fischer, and Vargas. In *Four views on free will*, Robert Kane, John Martin Fischer, Derk Pereboom, and Manuel Vargas, 85–125, 191–203. Oxford: Blackwell.
———. 2008a. A hard-line reply to the multiple-case manipulation argument. *Philosophy and Phenomenological Research* 77:160–70.
———. 2008b. Defending hard incompatibilism again. In Essays on free will and moral responsibility, ed. Nick Trakakis and Daniel Cohen, 1–33. Newcastle, UK: Cambridge Scholars Press.
———. 2009. Free will, love, and anger. *Ideas y Valores: Revista de Colombiana de Filosofía* 141:5–25.
———. 2009b. Hard incompatibilism and its rivals. *Philosophical Studies* 144:21–33.

———. 2013a. Optimistic skepticism about free will. In *The philosophy of free will: Selected contemporary readings*, ed. Paul Russell and Oisin Deery, 421–49. New York: Oxford University Press.

———. 2013b. Free will skepticism, blame, and obligation. In *Blame: Its nature and norms*, ed. Neal Tognazzini and D. Justin Coates, 189–206. New York: Oxford University Press.

———. Forthcoming. *Free will, agency, and meaning in life*. Oxford: Oxford University Press.

Pettit, Philip, and Michael Smith. 1996. Freedom in belief and desire. *Journal of Philosophy* 93 (9): 429–49.

Pico della Mirandola, Giovanni. 1486/1948. Oration on the dignity of man, trans. Paul O. Kristeller. In *The Renaissance philosophy of man*, ed. Ernst Cassirer, Paul O. Kristeller, and John H. Randall, 223–54. Chicago: University of Chicago Press.

Pockett, Susan. 2004. Does consciousness cause behaviour? *Journal of Consciousness Studies* 11 (2): 23–40.

———. 2006. The neuroscience of movement. In *Does consciousness cause behavior?*, ed. S. Pockett, W. P. Banks, and S. Gallagher, 9–24. Cambridge, MA: MIT Press.

———. 2007. The concept of free will: Philosophy neuroscience, and the law. *Behavioral Sciences and the Law* 25:281–93.

———. 2009. Brain basis of voluntary control. In *Encyclopedia of consciousness*, Vol. 1, ed. W. P. Banks, 123–33. Oxford: Elsevier.

———. 2013. If free will did not exist, it would be necessary to invent it. In *Exploring the illusion of free will and moral responsibility*, ed. Gregg Caruso. Lanham, MD: Lexington Books.

Pockett, Susan, and Suzanne C. Purdy. 2010. Are voluntary movements initiated preconsciously? The relationships between readiness potentials, urges and decisions. In *Conscious will and responsibility: A tribute to Benjamin Libet*, ed. W. Sinnott-Armstrong and L. Nadel, 34–46. New York; Oxford University Press.

Popper, Karl, and John Eccles. 1977. *The self and its brain*. Berlin: Springer Verlag.

Pratto, Felicia, James Sidanius, Lisa M. Stallworth, and Bertram F. Malle. 1994. Social dominance orientation: A personality variable predicting social and political attitudes. *Journal of Personality and Social Psychology* 67 (4): 741–63.

Priestley, Joseph. 1775. *Experiments and observations on different kinds of air*. Vol. 2. London: J. Johnson.

———. 1788/1963. *A free discussion of the doctrines of materialism and philosophical necessity, in a correspondence between Dr. Price and Dr. Priestley*. 1788, Part III, 147–52. Reprinted in Joseph Priestley, *Priestley's Writings on Philosophy, Science, and Politics*, ed. John Passmore. New York: Collie.

Prinz, Jesse J. 2007. *The emotional construction of morals*. Oxford: Oxford University Press.

Putnam, Hilary. 1975. *Mind, language and reality: Philosophical papers*, Vol. 2. Cambridge: Cambridge University Press.

Quillian, Lincoln. 2008. Does unconscious racism exist? *Social Psychology Quarterly* 71:6–11.

Rachels, James. 1978. What people deserve. In *Justice and economic distribution*, ed. J. Arthur and W. H. Shaw. Englewood Cliffs, NJ: Prentice-Hall.

———. 1995. *The elements of moral philosophy*. New York: McGraw-Hill.

Rakos, Richard, Kimberly Laurene, Sarah Skala, and Stephen Slane. 2008. Belief in free will: Measurement and conceptualization innovations. *Behavior and Social Issues* 17:20–39.

Rawls, John. 1999. *A theory of justice*. Rev. ed. Cambridge, MA: Harvard Belknap.

Rigoni Davide, Marcel Brass, and Giuseppe Sartori. 2010. Post-action determinants of the reported time of conscious intentions. *Frontiers in Human Neuroscience* 4:38. doi: 10.3389/fnhum.2010.00038.

Rigoni, Davide, Simone Kuhn, Giuseppe Sartori, and Marcel Brass. 2011. Inducing disbelief in free will alters brain correlates of preconscious motor preparation: The brain minds whether we believe in free will or not. *Psychological Science* 22 (5): 613–18.

Robertson, Donald. 2010. *The philosophy of cognitive behavioural therapy: Stoic philosophy as rational and cognitive psychotherapy*. London: Karnac Books.

Robinson, William S. 2010. Epiphenomenalism. *Wiley Interdisciplinary Reviews: Cognitive Science* 1 (4): 539–47.

References

———. 2012. Epiphenomenalism. In *The Stanford encyclopedia of philosophy, Summer 2012 ed.*, ed. Edward N. Zalta. http://plato.stanford.edu/archives/sum2012/entries/epiphenomenalism/ (accessed October 26, 2012).

Rose, D., and Shaun Nichols. Forthcoming. The lesson of bypassing.

Rosenthal, David. 2005. *Consciousness and mind*. New York: Oxford University Press.

Roskies, Adina. 2006. Neuroscientific challenges to free will and responsibility. *Trends in Cognitive Sciences* 10 (9): 419–23.

———. 2008. Response to Sie and Wouters: A neuroscientific challenge to free will and responsibility? *Trends in Cognitive Sciences* 12 (1): 4.

———. 2010. How does neuroscience affect our conception of volition. *Annual Review of Neuroscience* 33:109–30.

Roskies, Adina, and Shaun Nichols. 2008. Bringing moral responsibility down to Earth. *Journal of Philosophy* 105 (7): 371–88.

Rotter, Julian B. 1966. Generalized expectancies for internal versus external control of reinforcement. *Psychological Monographs* 80 (Whole No. 609).

Rubin, Zick, and Letitlia A. Peplau. 1975. Who believes in a just world? *Journal of Social Issues* 31:65–89.

Russell, Paul. 1992. Strawson's way of naturalizing responsibility. *Ethics* 102:287–302.

———. 1995. *Freedom and moral sentiment*. New York: Oxford University Press.

Sabini, John, and Maury Silver. 2005. Lack of character? Situationism critiqued. *Ethics* 115:535–62.

Sadurski, Wojciech. 1985. *Giving desert its due: Social justice and legal theory*. Dordrecht: D. Reidel.

Sarkissian, Hagop, Amita Chatterjee, Felipe De Brigard, Joshua Knobe, Shaun Nichols, and Smita Sirker. 2010. Is belief in free will a cultural universal? *Mind and Language* 25 (3): 346–58.

Sartre, Jean-Paul. 1943/1969. *Being and nothingness*. Trans. Hazel E. Barnes. London: Methuen.

———. 1946/1989. *Existentialism and humanism*. Trans. Philip Mairet. London: Methuen.

———. 1970. Interview in *New Left Review*, 58. Reprinted in New York Review of Books, March 26, 1970, 22.

Scanlon, Thomas. 1998. *What we owe to each other*. Cambridge, MA: Belknap Press of Harvard University Press.

———. 2008. *Moral dimensions*. Cambridge, MA: Harvard University Press.

———. 2013. Giving desert its due. *Philosophical Explorations*, forthcoming.

Scheffler, Samuel. 2000. Justice and desert in liberal theory. *California Law Review* 88:991–1000.

Schlick, Moritz. 1939. When is a man responsible? In *Problems of ethics*, trans. David Rynin, 143–56. New York: Prentice-Hall. Reprinted in *Free will and determinism*, ed. Bernard Berofsky, 54–63. New York: Harper & Row, 1966.

Schnall, Simone, Jennifer Benton, and Sophie Harvey. 2008. With a clean conscience: Cleanliness reduces the severity of moral judgments. *Psychological Science* 19 (12): 1219–22.

Schnall, Simone, Jonathan Haidt, Gerald L. Clore, and Alexander H. Jordan. 2008. Disgust as embodied moral judgment. *Personality and Social Psychology Bulletin* 37 (8): 1096–1109.

Schoeman, Ferdinand D. 1979. On incapacitating the dangerous. *American Philosophical Quarterly* 16:27–35.

Scot, Reginald. 1584. *The discoverie of witchcraft*. London: William Brome.

Searle, John. 1992. *The rediscovery of the mind*. Cambridge, MA: MIT Press.

———. 2004. *Mind: A brief introduction*. New York: Oxford University Press.

Seligman, Martin E. P. 1975. *Helplessness: On depression, development, and death*. New York: W. H. Freeman.

Shakespeare, William. 1610/2005. *King Lear*. In *The Oxford Shakespeare: The complete works*, 2nd ed., ed. S. Wells, G. Taylor, J. Jowett, and W. Montgomery, 1153–84. New York: Oxford University Press.

Shariff, Azim F., Johan Karremans, Joshua D. Greene, Corey Clark, Jamie Luguri, Roy F. Baumeister, Peter Ditto, Jonathan W. Schooler, and Kathleen D. Vohs. 2012. Diminished belief in free will increases forgiveness and reduces retributive punishment. Manuscript submitted for publication.

Sher, George. 1979. Effort, ability, and personal desert. *Philosophy and Public Affairs* 8:361–76.

Sherman, Steven J., Denise R. Beike, and Kenneth R. Ryalls. 1999. Dual-processing accounts of inconsistencies in responses to general versus specific cases. In *Dual-process theories in social psychology*, ed. Shelly Chaiken and Yaacov Trope, 203–27. New York: Guilford Press.

Shoda, Yuichi, Walter Mischel, and Philip K. Peake. 1990. Predicting adolescent cognitive and self-regulatory competencies from preschool delay of gratification: Identifying diagnostic conditions. *Developmental Psychology* 26:978–86.

Sie, M. M. S. K. 1998. Goodwill, determinism and justification. In *Human action, deliberation and causation*, ed. J. Bransen and S. Cuypers, 113–29. Dordrecht: Kluwer Academic Publishers.

———. 2000. Mad, bad, or disagreeing? On moral competence and responsibility. *Philosophical Explorations* 3 (3): 262–80.

Sie, Maureen. 2005. *Justifying blame. Why free will matters and why it does not.* Amsterdam/New York: Rodopi.

———. 2009. Moral agency, conscious control, and deliberative awareness. *Inquiry* 52 (5): 516–31. doi: 10.1080/00201740903302642.

———. 2012. Moral soulfulness and moral hypocrisy. Is scientific study of moral agency relevant to ethical reflection? In *Morality in times of naturalising the mind*, ed. Christoph Lumer. Heusenstamm: Ontos.

Sie, Maureen, and N. Voorst Vader Bours. Work in progress. Stereotypes and prejudices. Whose responsibility? Personal responsibility vis-à-vis implicit bias.

Sie, Maureen, and Arno Wouters. 2008. The real neuroscientific challenge to free will. *Trends in Cognitive Science* 12 (1): 3–4.

———. 2010. The BCN challenge to compatibilist free will and personal responsibility. *Neuroethics* 3 (2): 121–33.

Sinnott-Armstrong, Walter. 2008. Concrete + Abstract = Paradox. In *Experimental philosophy*, ed. J. Knobe and S. Nichols, 209–30. New York: Oxford University Press.

Sirigu, Angela, Elena Daprati, Sophie Ciancia, Pascal Giraux, Norbert Nighoghossian, Andres Posada, and Patrick Haggard. 2004. Altered awareness of voluntary action after damage to the parietal cortex. *Nature Neuroscience* 7 (1): 80–84.

Smart, J. J. C. 1961. Free will, praise, and blame. *Mind* 70:291–306.

Smilansky, Saul. 1990. Utilitarianism and the "punishment" of the innocent: The general problem. *Analysis* 50:256–61.

———. 1994. The ethical advantages of hard determinism. *Philosophy and Phenomenological Research* 54:355–63.

———. 1996. Responsibility and desert: Defending the connection. *Mind* 105 (417): 157–63.

———. 1997. Can a determinist help herself? In *Freedom and moral responsibility: General and Jewish perspectives*, ed. C. H. Manekin and M. Kellner, 85–98. College Park, MD: University of Maryland Press.

———. 2000. *Free will and illusion.* New York: Oxford University Press.

———. 2001. Free will: From nature to illusion. *Proceedings of the Aristotelian Society* 101:71–95.

———. 2002. Free will, fundamental dualism, and the centrality of illusion. In *The Oxford handbook of free will*, ed. Robert Kane, 489–505. Oxford: Oxford University Press.

———. 2003. Compatibilism: The argument from shallowness. *Philosophical Studies* 115:257–82.

———. 2005a. Free will and respect for persons. *Midwest Studies in Philosophy* 29:248–61.

———. 2005b. Free will, fundamental dualism, and the centrality of illusion. In *The Oxford handbook of free will*, 2nd ed., ed. Robert Kane, 425–41. Oxford: Oxford University Press.

———. 2006. Control, desert, and the difference between distributive and retributive justice. *Philosophical Studies* 131:511–24.

———. 2011a. Free will, fundamental dualism and the centrality of illusion. In *The Oxford handbook of free will,* 2nd ed., ed. Robert Kane. New York: Oxford University Press.
———. 2011b. Hard determinism and punishment: A practical *reductio. Law and Philosophy* 30:353–67.
———. 2012. Free will and moral responsibility: The trap, the appreciation of agency, and the bubble. *Journal of Ethics* 16:211–39.
Sniderman, Paul M., and Thomas Piazza. 1993. *The scar of race.* Cambridge, MA: Harvard University Press.
Snyder, Sam. 2012. The end of free will. http://samsnyder.com/2011/05/12/the-end-of-free-will/ (accessed October 26, 2012).
Solomon, Robert C. 2004. *In defense of sentimentality.* New York: Oxford University Press.
Sommers, Tamler. 2005. *Beyond freedom and resentment: An error theory of free will and moral responsibility.* PhD diss., Duke University.
———. 2007a. The illusion of freedom evolves. In *Distributed cognition and the will: Individual volition and social context,* ed. David Spurrett, Harold Kincaid, Don Ross, and G. Lynn Stephens, 61–75. Cambridge, MA: MIT Press.
———. 2007b. The objective attitude. *Philosophical Quarterly* 57 (228): 321–41.
———. 2010. Experimental philosophy and free will. *Philosophy Compass* 5:119–212.
———. 2012. *Relative justice: Cultural diversity, free will, and moral responsibility.* Princeton: Princeton University Press.
Soon, Chun Siong, Marcel Brass, Hans-Jochen Heinze, and John-Dylan Haynes. 2008. Unconscious determinants of free decisions in the human brain. *Nature Neuroscience* 11 (5): 543–45.
Sorrentino, Richard M., and Jack Hardy. 1974. Religiousness and derogation of an innocent victim. *Journal of Personality* 42:372–82.
Spencer, Quayshawn. 2012. What 'biological racial realism' should mean. *Philosophical Studies* 159 (2): 181–204.
———. Forthcoming. Biological theory and the metaphysics of race: A reply to Kaplan and Winther. *Biological Theory.*
Spinoza, Baruch. 1677/1985. *Ethics.* In *The collected works of Spinoza,* Vol. 1, ed. and trans. Edwin Curley. Princeton: Princeton University Press.
Stich, Stephen P. 1983. *From folk psychology to cognitive science: The case against belief.* Cambridge, MA: MIT Press.
———. 1996. *Deconstructing the mind.* New York: Oxford University Press.
Stillman, Tyler F., and Roy F. Baumeister. 2012. Guilty, free, and wise: Determinism and psychopathy diminish learning from negative emotions. *Journal of Experimental Social Psychology* 46 (6): 951–60.
Stillman, Tyler F., Roy F. Baumeister, and Alfred R. Mele. 2011. Free will in everyday life: Autobiographical accounts of free and unfree actions. *Philosophical Psychology* 24:381–94.
Stillman, Tyler F., Roy F. Baumeister, Kathleen D. Vohs, N. M. Lambert, F. D. Fincham, and L. E. Brewer. 2010. Personal philosophy and personnel achievement: Belief in free will predicts better job performance. *Social Psychological and Personality Science* 1:43–50.
Strawson, Galen. 1986. *Freedom and belief.* Oxford: Oxford University Press.
———. 1994. The impossibility of moral responsibility. *Philosophical Studies* 75 (1): 5–24.
———. 2002. The bounds of freedom. In *The Oxford handbook of free will,* 1st ed., ed. Robert Kane. New York: Oxford University Press.
———. 2010. *Freedom and belief.* Rev. ed. Oxford: Oxford University Press.
Strawson, P. F. 1950. On referring. *Mind* 59 (235): 320–44.
———. 1962. Freedom and resentment. *Proceedings of the British Academy* 48:1–25. [Page references in ch.4 as reprinted in *Free will,* ed. Gary Watson, 59–80. New York: Oxford University Press, 1982.]
———. 1997. Freedom and resentment. In *Free will,* ed. Derk Pereboom, 119–42. Indianapolis: Hackett.
———. 2003. Freedom and resentment. In *Free will,* 2nd ed., ed. Gary Watson. New York: Oxford University Press.

Street, Sharon. 2006. A Darwinian dilemma for realist theories of values. *Philosophical Studies* 127:109–66.

Stroessner, Steven, and Charles Green. 1990. Effects of belief in free will or determinism on attitudes toward punishment and locus of control. *The Journal of Social Psychology* 130 (6): 789–99.

Tangney, June P., Roy F. Baumeister, and Angie L. Boone. 2004. High self-control predicts good adjustment, less pathology, better grades, and interpersonal success. *Journal of Personality* 72:271–322.

Taylor, Richard. 1963. *Metaphysics*. Englewood Cliffs, NJ: Prentice-Hall.

———. 1966. *Action and purpose*. Englewood Cliffs, NJ: Prentice-Hall.

———. 1974. *Metaphysics*. 4th ed. Englewood Cliffs, NJ: Prentice-Hall.

Taylor, Shelley, and Jonathon Brown. 1988. Illusion and well-being: A social psychological perspective of mental health. *Psychological Bulletin* 103 (2): 193–210.

Thaler, Richard H., and Cass R. Sunstein 2008. *Nudge: Improving decisions about health, wealth, and happiness*. New Haven, CT: Yale University Press.

Thomas, Keith. 1971. *Religion and the decline of magic*. New York: MacMillan.

Thomson, Judith Jarvis. 1976. Killing, letting die, and the trolley problem. *The Monist* 59:204–217.

Todorov, Alexander, Anesu N. Mandisodza, Amir Goren, and Crystal C. Hall. 2005. Inferences of competence from faces predict election outcomes. *Science* 308 (5728): 1623–26.

Tononi, Giulio. 2012. *Phi: A voyage from the brain to the soul*. New York: Pantheon.

Tversky, Amos, and Daniel Kahneman. 1981. The framing of decisions and the psychology of choice. *Science* 211 (4481): 453–58.

Valdesolo, Pierearlo, and David DeSteno. 2007. Moral hypocrisy: Social groups and the flexibility of virtue. *Psychological Science* 18:689–90.

Van Fraassen, Bas. C. 1980. *The scientific image*. New York: Oxford University Press.

Van Inwagen, Peter. 1975. The incompatibility of free will and determinism. *Philosophical Studies* 27:185–99.

———. 1983. *An essay on free will*. Oxford: Clarendon Press.

———. 2008. How to think about the problem of free will. *Journal of Ethics* 12:327–41.

Vargas, Manuel. 2005. The revisionist's guide to responsibility. *Philosophical Studies* 125:399–429.

———. 2006. Philosophy and the folk: On some implications of experimental work for philosophical debates on free will. *Journal of Cognition and Culture* 6 (1–2): 239–54.

———. 2007. Revisionism. In *Four views on free will*, ed. J. Fischer et al. Malden, MA: Blackwell.

———. 2009. Review of *Effective intentions: The power of conscious will*, by Alfred R. Mele. *Notre Dame Philosophical Reviews*. http://ndpr.nd.edu/review.cfm?id=17385.

———. 2011a. Revisionist accounts of free will: Origins, varieties, and challenges. In *The Oxford handbook of free will*, 2nd ed., ed. Robert Kane, 457–84. New York: Oxford University Press.

———. 2011b. The revisionist turn: Reflection on the recent history of work on free will. In *New waves in the philosophy of action*, ed. Jesus Aguilar, Andrei Buckareff, and Keith Frankish, 143–72. New York: Palgrave Macmillan.

———. 2013a. *Building better beings*. Oxford: Oxford University Press.

———. 2013b. Situationism and moral responsibility: Free will in fragments. In *Decomposing the will*, ed. Till Vierkant, Julian Kiverstein, and Andy Clark, 325–49. New York: Oxford University Press.

———. Forthcoming. Reconsidering scientific threats to free will. In *Moral psychology, Vol. 4: Free will and moral responsibility*, ed. Walter Sinnott-Armstrong. Cambridge, MA: MIT Press.

Vilhauer, Benjamin. 2004a. Can we interpret Kant as a compatibilist about determinism and moral responsibility? *The British Journal for the History of Philosophy*, 12 (4): 719–30.

———. 2004b. Hard determinism, remorse, and virtue ethics. *Southern Journal of Philosophy* 42 (4): 547–64.

———. 2008. Hard determinism, Humeanism, and virtue ethics. *Southern Journal of Philosophy* 46 (1): 121–44.
———. 2009a. Free will skepticism and personhood as a desert base. *Canadian Journal of Philosophy* 39 (3): 489–511.
———. 2009b. Free will and reasonable doubt. *American Philosophical Quarterly* 46 (2): 131– 40.
———. 2010a. The scope of responsibility in Kant's theory of free will. *The British Journal for the History of Philosophy* 18 (1): 45–71.
———. 2010b. Persons, punishment, and free will skepticism. *Philosophical Studies* 'Online First.' doi: 10.1007/s11098-011-9752-z, forthcoming in print.
———. 2012. Taking free will skepticism seriously. *The Philosophical Quarterly.* doi: 10.1111/j.1467-9213.2012.00077.x, forthcoming in print.
———. Forthcoming. Free will and the asymmetrical justifiability of holding morally responsible.
Viney, Wayne, Robert McIntyre, and Donald Viney. 1984. Validity of a scale designed to measure beliefs in free will and determinism. *Psychological Reports* 54:867–72.
Viney, Wayne, Pamela Parker-Martin, and Sandra Dotten. 1988. Beliefs in free will and determinism and lack of relation to punishment rational and magnitude. *Journal of General Psychology* 115:15–23.
Viney, Wayne, David A. Waldman, and Jacqueline Barchilon. 1982. Attitudes towards punishment in relation to beliefs in free will and determinism. *Human Relations* 35:939–50.
Virgin, Charles E., and Robert Sapolsky. 1997. Styles of male social behavior and their endocrine correlates among low-ranking baboons. *American Journal of Primatology* 42:25–39.
Vohs, Kathleen D., and Jonathan W. Schooler. 2008. The value of believing in free will: Encouraging a belief in determinism increases cheating. *Psychological Science* 19:49–54.
Wagstaff, G. F. 1983. Correlates of the just world in Britain. *Journal of Social Psychology* 121:145–46.
Wagstaffe, John. 1671. *The question of witchcraft debated.* 2nd ed. London: Edw. Millington, at the Pelican in Duck-Lane.
Wallace, R. Jay. 1994. *Responsibility and the moral sentiments.* Cambridge, MA: Harvard University Press.
Waller, Bruce. 1990. *Freedom without responsibility.* Philadelphia: Temple University Press.
———. 1998. *The natural selection of autonomy* (SUNY Series in Philosophy and Biology). Albany: State University of New York Press.
———. 2011. *Against moral responsibility.* Cambridge, MA: MIT Press.
Walter, Henrik. 2001. *Neurophilosophy of free will: From libertarianism illusions to a concept of natural autonomy.* Cambridge, MA: MIT Press.
Warnock, G. J. 1989. *J. L. Austin.* London: Routledge & Kegan Paul.
Watson, Gary. ed. 1982. *Free will.* 7th ed. Oxford: Oxford University Press.
———. 1982. Free agency. In *Free will*, ed. Gary Watson, 81–95. Oxford: Oxford University Press.
———. 1987. Responsibility and the limits of evil. In *Responsibility, character, and the emotions*, ed. Ferdinand Schoeman, 256–86. Cambridge: Cambridge University Press.
Webster, John. 1677. *The displaying of supposed witchcraft.* London: J.M.
Wegner, Daniel M. 2002. *The illusion of conscious will.* Cambridge, MA: Bradford Books, MIT Press.
———. 2003. The mind's best trick: How we experience conscious will. *Trends in Cognitive Science* 7 (2): 65–69.
———. 2008. Self is magic. In *Are we free? Psychology and free will*, ed. John Baer, James C. Kaufman, and Roy F. Baumeister, 226–47. New York: Oxford University Press.
Wegner, Daniel M., and Thalia Wheatley. 1999. Apparent mental causation: Sources of the experience of will. *American Psychologist* 54:480–91.
Wei Wu Wei. 2004. *Open secret.* Hong Kong University Press.
Williams, Bernard. 1985. *Ethics and the limits of philosophy.* London: Fontana.
———. 1993. *Shame and necessity.* Berkeley: University of California Press.

Wilson, Timothy. 2002. *Strangers to ourselves: Discovering the adaptive unconscious*. Cambridge, MA: The Belknap Press of Harvard University Press.
Wolf, Susan. 1981. The importance of free will. *Mind* 90 (359): 386–405.
———. 1990. *Freedom within reason*. New York: Oxford University Press.
Wolpe, Joseph. 1990. *Practice of behavior therapy*. 4th ed. New York: Pergamon Press.
Wolpe, Joseph, and Arnold A. Lazarus. 1966. *Behavior therapy techniques: A guide to the treatment of neuroses*. Elmsford, NY: Pergamon Press.
Wood, Allen. 2010. Punishment, retribution, and the coercive enforcement of right. In Kant's metaphysics of morals: A critical guide, ed. Lara Denis, 111–29. New York: Cambridge University Press.
Wouters, Arno. 2011. Vrije wil en verantwoordelijkheid in evolutionair perspectief. In *Hoezo vrije wil?*, ed. M. Sie, 190–209. Rotterdam: Lemniscaat.
Zimbardo, Philip G. 2004. A situationist perspective on the psychology of evil: Understanding how good people are transformed into perpetrators. In *The social psychology of good and evil: Understanding our capacity for kindness and cruelty*, ed. Arthur Miller. New York: Guilford.

Index

Aarts, Henk, 226, 227, 268
ability to do otherwise, 2
"action-based" desert claims, 142, 148–149, 151, 155, 157, 158n13. *See also* moral responsibility (desert-based)
actual versus hypothetical consent, 152–156
adaptive unconscious, 4
Adler, Mortimer, 63–64
Adorno, Theodor, 131
Ady, Thomas, 213
Agamemnon, 95–96
agential transparency, 14, 274, 281–282, 286
Alquist, Jessica L., 125
Altemeyer, Robert A., 127, 131
Andreasen, Robin O., 204
Annas, Julia, 289n25
Appiah, Anthony, 204
Ariely, Dan, 288n14
Aristotle, 75
Atmanscpacher, Harald, 182
Austin, J. L., 58
automaticity, 4, 71, 201n19, 226
autonomy, 13, 239–240, 243–244, 246–247, 250–252
Ayer, A. J., 53

Baars, Bernard, 232
Balaguer, Mark, 25
Banaji, Mahzarin R., 246

Bandura, Albert, 77, 79
Banks, William P., 268
Barchilon, Jacqueline, 125
Bargh, John, 4, 16n9, 71, 121, 178, 179, 181, 200, 227, 246, 282
Baril, Galen, 138, 140n1, 140n9
Baron, Jonathan, 280, 288n14
Basic Argument, 8, 41–43, 46–51
basic desert. *See* moral responsibility
Batson, Daniel C., 246, 283
Baumeister, Roy F., 4, 5, 79, 82–83, 121, 123, 125, 202n27, 215, 244, 246, 249, 250, 252n7, 266–267
Bègue, Laurent, 70, 72
Beike, Denise, 70
Bennett, William, 74
Benton, Jennifer, 280
Bishop, Michael, 204, 205, 209, 217, 217n3
Bishop, Robert, 55
Bjorklund, Fredrik, 286
Blackburn, Simon, 204, 208
Blackmore, Susan, 6, 11, 162, 163–164, 165, 169, 171
Block, Ned, 60, 241, 252n2
Bloom, Paul, 5, 248
Blount, Sally, 131
Bode, Stefan, 227
Bok, Hilary, 36
Boone, Angie, 83
Boulton, Richard, 218n12

Index

Boyd, Richard, 204, 207
Brass, Marcel, 123, 268, 273
Brewer, E., 123
Brown, Jonathon, 123
Buddhism, 173, 175
Burge, Tyler, 61
Busch, Niko, 238n2

Cacioppo, John T., 77, 79
Calvin, John, 66
Campbell, C. A., 50, 66, 67
Carey, Jasmine, 10, 124, 125–126, 127–128, 129, 133
Carnap, Rudolph, 53, 205
Carr, Edward H., 44
Carruthers, Peter, 4
Caruso, Gregg, 3, 4, 38n1, 61, 101n6, 102n9, 119n1, 202n28, 217, 289n29
Casaubon, Meric, 218n12
Cashmore, Anthony, 121, 178, 186–187, 188, 194, 199
causa sui, 3, 8, 41, 47, 215
Chalmers, David, 184, 201n13, 241
Chartrand, Tanya, 16n9, 71, 282
Chisholm, Roderick, 26, 27, 67
choice architecture, 282
Churchland, Patricia, 164
Churchland, Paul, 166
Clark, Andy, 61
Clark, Thomas, 5, 7, 13, 244, 249, 251, 252n4, 252n9
Clarke, Randolph, 26, 27, 38n2–39n3, 52n4, 105, 201n15
Claxton, Guy, 173
Clore, Gerald L., 280
Cohen, Jonathan, 121, 178, 192–193, 199, 251, 252n9
compatibilism, 1–2, 4, 9, 19, 21–25, 49, 52n4, 57–58, 67–68, 101n2, 105, 108–117, 118, 162–163, 181, 183–185, 192, 195, 201n10, 216, 266, 269, 287n2; and "racing luck", 76–77, 80, 82; reasons-responsiveness and, 21, 81–84, 184, 186, 192, 288n12; and The Trap, 108–117
confirmation bias, 246
consciousness, 13, 60–62, 232–234, 239–243, 255; access consciousness, 60, 252n2; Actual Consciousness, 9, 61–62, 63; and free will/moral responsibility, 13, 60–62, 225–230, 239–240; functionalism and, 61; global workspace model of, 232; Higher-order theory of, 61; and intentions, 223–230, 232–234; neural correlates of, 239–242; phenomenal consciousness, 60, 239–243, 252n2; physicalism and, 60–61; representationalism and, 61; stream of, 162. *See also* conscious volition; intentions; mental causation; sense of self
conscious veto, 257
conscious volition, 5, 13–14, 161, 225–230, 233, 237, 239, 240, 243–246, 257–261, 267–269. *See also* neuroscience of volition
consequence argument, 108
consequentialism, 11, 108, 141, 144, 145–149. *See also* moral responsibility; objective attitude; "people problem"
cosmic order, 96–98, 101n4. *See also* just world belief
counter-causal free will, 5, 13, 67, 122, 129, 161, 162–163, 240, 248
Coyne, Jerry, 121
"crazy ethics", 10, 103–104, 105–106, 108, 115, 117–118
Crescioni, A. William, 125
Crick, Francis, 166, 239, 266
cultural relativism, 90, 93
Custers, Rudd, 226, 227

Dalbert, Claudia, 73
Damasio, Antonio, 239
Danziger, Shai, 256
Darley, John M., 246
Darwall, Stephen, 159n15
Darwin, Charles, 48, 52n6
Davies, Paul Sheldon, 4
death penalty, 6, 142, 156–157
Dehaene, Stanislas, 232, 252n2
de Houwer, Jan, 226
Dennett, Daniel, 60, 67, 76, 77, 80–81, 84, 162, 163, 164, 166, 168, 174, 201n16, 232, 241, 246, 249–250, 273, 287n2
desert. *See* moral responsibility
De Sio, Filippo Santoni, 289n29
Desmurget, Michel, 225, 260

DeSteno, David, 216
determinism, 1, 3, 8, 9, 12, 14, 15n4, 19, 20, 53–56, 58, 62, 65–66, 105, 109, 110, 125, 128, 134–135, 181–183, 192–193, 201n5–201n6, 203, 217n1, 269–270, 287n2; consequences of, 9, 56–57, 62–63. *See also* free will skepticism; hard determinism; manipulation argument
Devitt, Michael, 211
DeWall, C. Nathan, 5, 123, 249, 250
d'Holbach, Baron Paul Henri, 3
disappearing agent objection, 8, 26–27
disillusionism, 6, 10
Doris, John, 16n9, 52n5, 52n7, 70, 71, 201n11, 201n14, 201n19, 288n24
Dostoyevsky, Fyodor, 69
Dotten, Sandra, 125
Double, Richard, 3, 101n2
Dretske, Fred, 61
dualism, 5, 61, 122, 128–129, 134–135, 137–138, 140n7, 181, 187, 195, 199, 201n17, 240, 241, 248–250
Dupre, John, 167

Earman, John, 55
Earp, Brian, 178
Eccles, John, 55
Economic Systems Justification Scale (ESJ), 132–133, 134–135, 136–138
Eimer, Martin, 227
Einstein, Albert, 56
Ekstrom, Laura, 25, 105
eliminativism, 12, 178, 204–209, 212–217; and reference, 204–206, 212–213. *See also* free will skepticism
Elster, Jon, 98
empiricism, 53–54; reflective, 53–54, 55
epiphenomenalism, 240–243
Epley, Nicholas, 284
Evatt, Cris, 15n6

Farrell, Daniel, 31
feeling of free will, 161–162, 165, 173–174, 256; and sense of self, 162, 163–164, 167, 168, 255–256
Feinberg, Joel, 19
Feldman, Fred, 159n14
Feltz, Adam, 124, 202n25

Ferguson, Melissa, 4, 16n9
Feyerabend, P. K., 204
Finchman, F. D., 123
Fine, Cordelia, 280, 288n16, 289n28
Fisher, John Martin, 15n3, 15n5, 19, 21, 52n4, 58, 65, 81–82, 84, 114, 144, 184, 201n15, 208, 288n12
Flanagan, Owen, 241
folk psychology of free will, 125–139, 179, 202n25, 203, 267; folk compatibilism, 125–126, 129; folk error about free will, 203, 206; folk incompatibilism, 125–126, 130, 140n3, 203; folk indeterminism, 203, 206; and its relationship to other moral, political, and religious beliefs, 126–139
Fourneret, Pierre, 227
framework relativism, 90–91, 93, 99, 101n2
Frank, Robert, 97
Frankfurt, Harry, 21, 184, 288n13
Franklin, Christopher, 25, 26
Freeman, Anthony, 61
Free Will and Determinist Scale (FAD-Plus), 10, 124–130, 133, 134, 136, 138, 140n2
free will illusionism. *See* illusionism
Free Will Inventory (FWI), 10, 124, 128–130, 134, 138, 140n5
free will skepticism, 1–8, 10, 12, 15n2, 19–20, 29–38, 38n1, 87–88, 91–92, 101n6, 106–108, 121–122, 129–130, 139, 141–142, 146–147, 148, 150, 156, 161–162, 177–179, 180–190, 192, 198, 200, 200n4, 213, 273; and criminal behavior, 30–32, 106–108, 156–157, 164–165, 251; and human rights, 11, 147, 151; implications and consequences of, 5–7, 10, 20, 29–38, 106–108, 122–139, 164–165, 168, 170–173, 198, 215–216, 249, 265–267; and Kantian Deontology, 142, 148–151; and meaning in life, 20, 32–34, 38, 141–142; and morality, 29, 141–142, 149, 170; and the "people problem", 141–157; and personal relationships and emotions, 34–38, 107; and the reactive attitudes, 34–38, 107, 143–147; "scientific" skepticism, 12,

15n2, 122, 123–124, 129–130, 177–179, 181–190, 192–195, 198, 200n1, 273; versus metaskepticism, 10, 87–101. *See also* disillusionism; eliminativism; illusionism; moral responsibility; optimistic skepticism
French, Peter, 69
Freud, Sigmund, 52n7, 56, 71
Fried, Itzhak, 225
fundamental dualism, 5, 105, 115. *See also* Smilansky
"funishment", 106–108, 118
Furnham, Adrian, 72, 73

Gagarin, Michael, 101n3
Gardner, Eileen, 74
Gazzaniga, Michael, 282
Ginet, Carl, 21, 38n2
Glaser, J., 131
Gleason, Curtis A., 273
Godfrey-Smith, Peter, 56
Goetz, Stewart, 38n2
Gollwitzer, Peter, 236
Goschke, Thomas, 235
Green, Charles, 125, 127
Greene, Joshua, 121, 178, 192–193, 199, 251, 252n9, 280
Greenfield, Susan, 164
Greenwald, Anthony, 288n15
Griffiths, Meghan, 27
Gunter, B., 73
Guzeldere, Guven, 241

Hafer, Carolyn, 70, 72
Haggard, Patrick, 161, 178, 182, 227, 236
Haidt, Jonathan, 16n9, 68, 280, 286, 289n28
Haji, Ishtiyaque, 29
Hall, Lars, 280
Hallett, Mark, 13, 256, 257, 259
Hameroff, Stuart, 165
Hanakawa, Takashi, 255
hard determinism, 2–3, 20, 33, 105–108, 113, 114, 118, 208. *See also* free will skepticism
hard incompatibilism, 8, 20, 25. *See also* free will skepticism
Hardin, Curtis D., 246
Hardy, Jack, 132

Harman, Gilbert, 52n5, 283, 288n24
Harper, David, 73
Harris, Lasana, 182
Harris, Robert, 80
Harris, Sam, 15n6, 121, 249, 250, 253n10
Hart, H. L. A., 111
Harvey, Sophie, 280
Hassin, Ran R., 282
Haynes, John-Dylan, 4, 12, 121, 227, 238n1, 273
Hegel, Georg Wilhelm Friedrich, 75
Heinze, Hans-Jochen, 273
Herrmann, Christoph S., 238n2
Hershey, John C., 280
Hieronymi, Pamela, 37
Hodgson, David, 55
Hoefer, Carl, 54
Honderich, Ted, 3, 9, 32–33, 38, 39n4, 54, 55, 57, 58, 60, 61, 62, 201n7, 287n2
honor cultures, 88–89, 92, 95–99, 101n5–101n6, 102n8
Hood, Bruce, 162
Hornsby, Jennifer, 26
Houlton, Richard, 250
Huebner, Bryce, 288n17
human rights, 11, 59, 147, 154–155
Hume, David, 21, 26, 57, 66, 67
Hunyady, Gyorgy, 131
Hurley, Susan, 201n15, 206
Hutchinson, Francis, 214
Huxley, Thomas, 242
hypothetical consent. *See* actual versus hypothetical consent; rational consent without free will

identity theory, 241
illusionism, 6, 10, 33–34, 105, 116–117, 118, 121, 124, 129–131, 138–139
illusion of self, 162, 163–164, 167, 168–170, 172–173, 173–175
implicit bias, 246, 280, 288n16
incompatibilism, 2, 9, 49, 57–59, 60, 65, 113, 130, 201n12, 215, 266, 269; leeway, 2, 287n2; source, 2. *See also* The Trap
indeterminism, 3, 19–20, 25, 49, 55, 56, 105, 203, 217n1
intentions, 12, 221–238, 252n3; and agency, 223–225, 236; and causal

efficacy, 223–225, 234–235, 240; and consciousness, 223–225, 225–230, 232–234; and embeddedness, 223–224, 233–234; empirical challenges to, 225–230; folk psychological account of, 221–225, 231, 237; and goal-representation, 223; proximal and distal, 261; revisionist account of, 221, 231–237
introspective transparency. *See* agential transparency
Isham, Eve A., 268

Jack, Anthony, 239
Jacobson, Daniel, 289n28
James, William, 66, 166–167, 168, 171, 174
Jeannerod, Marc, 227, 269
Johnston, Lucy, 246
Jordan, Alexander, 280
Jost, John T., 131, 132
Joyce, Richard, 90
just world belief, 9, 70–84, 86, 126–128, 131–133, 134–138

Kahneman, Daniel, 78–79, 280, 282, 288n23
Kane, Robert, 15n3–15n4, 21, 25, 27, 44, 49, 60, 105, 217n1, 287n2
Kant, Immanuel, 11, 30, 44, 57, 66, 75–76, 141–142, 147–148, 150–151, 153, 154–155, 157, 158n1, 158n4, 158n9, 158n12
Kanwisher, Nancy, 239
Kawamura, S., 68
Kelly, Daniel, 280, 288n17
Kim, Jaegwon, 61
King James I, 218n12
King, Matt, 4
Kitcher, Philip, 209–210, 218n13
Knobe, Joshua, 52n7, 69–70, 115, 140n8, 203, 288n18
Koch, Christof, 166, 182, 239, 241
Korsgaard, Christine, 45
Kouider, Sid, 232
Kozuch, Benjamin, 281
Kranick, Sarah M., 259
Kruglanski, A. W., 131
Kuhn, Simone, 123, 268

Kuhn, Thomas, 56
Kumar, Victor, 217
Kunda, Ziva, 280

Lambert, N. M., 123
Landau, Iddo, 119n1
Lane, Kristin, 71
Langer, Ellen J., 228
Laplace, Peirre Simon, 15n4
Lau, Hakwan, 13, 227, 258, 268
Laudan, Larry, 204, 207
Laurene, Kimberly, 125
Lawson, Chappell, 246
Lazarus, Arnold, 215
Lee, Victoria K., 182
Lerner, Melvin, 71–73, 74, 127, 132
Levy, Neil, 3, 10, 38n1, 39n4, 87, 119n2, 201n11
Lewis, David, 204–205
libertarianism, 1–2, 5, 25–29, 49–50, 57, 101n2, 105–106, 112, 116, 122, 130, 134–135, 137, 140n7, 143, 183, 192, 201n8, 201n12, 203, 248, 267, 269; agent causal, 8, 20, 25–26, 27–28, 101n6, 105; event-causal, 8, 25–27, 105; non-causal, 38n2
Libet, Benjamin, 4, 13, 16n9, 161, 227, 232, 233, 245, 257, 258, 261, 267, 273, 287n1
life-hopes, 32–33, 55
living "as if" we have free will, 163–166, 171
Locke, John, 151
Lucas, J. R., 52n5
luck, 3, 7, 10, 87, 101n1, 112; constitutive, 87, 101n1; moral, 112; present, 87
Luhrmann, T. M., 213
Luther, Martin, 66
Lycan, William, 25, 204–205, 207, 215, 217n2

Machery, E., 211
MacKay, D. M., 52n2
Mackie, J. L., 204, 206, 208, 235
Macrae, C. Neil, 246
Malle, Bertram F., 132
Mallon, Ron, 204, 210, 212, 214
Manasse, Paul, 73
manifest image, 189–190, 198

manipulation argument, 8, 21–25
Masicampo, E. J., 5, 123, 244, 249, 250, 252n7
Matsuhashi, Masao, 257
Matveeva, Tatyana, 124
McCann, Hugh, 38n2
McIntyre, Robert, 125
McKenna, Michael, 22, 112, 208, 217
Mele, Alfred, 21, 25, 26, 122, 125, 183, 200n2, 201n11, 201n19, 261
mental causation, 13, 240–241. *See also* epiphenomenalism
metaskepticism about moral responsibility. *See* moral responsibility
Metzinger, Thomas, 162, 241, 248, 252n6
Milgram, Stanley, 283
Miller, Dale, 72
Mill, John Stuart, 93
Mills, Eugene, 159n16
Min, Byoung Kyong, 238n2
Minsky, Marvin, 232
Mirandola, Pico della, 66
Mischel, Walter, 83
Momennejad, Ida, 227, 238n1
Montada, Leo, 73
Montague, Read, 121, 129, 177–178, 179, 181, 199
Moore, Michael S., 30, 69
Moors, Agnes, 226
moral anger, 6, 35–36, 38, 69
moral hypocrisy, 283–284
moral realism, 90–91
moral responsibility, 3, 9, 19–20, 65–68, 70, 87–90, 91, 105, 141, 143, 153–154, 180–181, 185, 196–197, 224, 261–262; backward-looking, 148–149, 151; and the Community of Responsibility, 113, 117; compatibilist conditions on, 21–25, 57–60; and consciousness, 239–240, 244, 251; consequentialist/ utilitarian conceptions of, 13, 31, 108, 111, 119n2, 145–149, 250, 252n1; constructivism about, 91; desert-based (basic desert), 3, 6, 19–20, 27, 29–30, 32, 38, 59, 62, 70, 87, 91, 105, 105–106, 142, 148–149, 151, 155, 157, 158n13, 192; forward-looking, 29, 148; honor cultures and, 88–89, 92, 95; incompatibilist conditions on, 57–59, 60; individualistic cultures and, 92, 95; metaskepticism about, 10, 88–92, 100; plateau or threshold model of, 80–82, 83–85; skepticism about, 1, 2–3, 10, 15n6, 87–88, 90–92, 100, 106–108, 141–142, 186–187, 193–195, 252n1. *See also* free will skepticism; social function of, 14, 274–277; source of the belief in, 9, 68–86; and the space of reasons, 274, 276–280, 282, 285, 287n5, 288n12; Ultimate, 3, 8, 41–45, 46–47, 49, 50–51, 51n1
moral responsibility system, 84–86
Moriarity, Jeffrey, 159n16
Morris, Stephen, 38n1, 125
Morse, Stephen J., 244
movement disorders, 259
Murphy, Dominic, 201n14
Murray, Dylan, 125

Naccache, Lionel, 239
Nadelhoffer, Thomas, 4–5, 6, 10, 38n1, 122, 124, 125, 128–129, 138, 140n3, 140n6–140n7, 140n9, 248, 249, 250, 252n1, 252n7, 252n9, 280
Nagel, Thomas, 87, 101n1, 287n3
Nahab, F. B., 260
Nahmias, Eddy, 4, 52n7, 122, 125, 140n3, 183, 200n2, 201n11, 201n14, 201n18, 201n19, 202n20, 202n24, 202n27, 202n28, 243
Narvaez, Darcia, 289n28
Nelkin, Dana, 37, 201n11, 201n14, 201n19
neuroscience of volition, 161, 225–230, 243–246, 257–261, 267–269
Nichols, Shaun, 6, 7, 12, 16n14, 29, 36, 38n1, 52n7, 69, 70, 85, 115, 125, 140n8, 203, 210, 212, 214, 281
Nickerson, Raymond S., 246
Nietzsche, Friedrich, 3, 47
nihilism about free will. *See* eliminativism; free will skepticism
Nisbett, Richard, 16n9, 226, 232, 280, 282, 288n21, 288n22
Noe, Alva, 61
Norman, Donald A., 226, 233
normative nihilism, 88, 100
Notestein, Wallace, 213–214
Nussbaum, Martha, 52n3

Nystrom, Leigh, 280

objective attitude, 11, 34–35, 85, 143–144, 145–147
O'Connor, Timothy, 26, 27, 39n3
Oerton, Richard, 15n6, 56
optimistic skepticism, 6, 8, 11, 20
"optimists", 143, 145–146
ordinary language philosophy, 58
O'Regan, Kevin, 165
original position deliberation, 142, 153, 155–157
origination, 2, 9, 57–58, 59–60, 63–64, 187, 267
Ortega, George, 15n2, 249
Overbye, Dennis, 122, 123

Pagels, Heinz, 56
Parker-Martin, Pamela, 125
Parvizi, Heinz, 239
Passingham, Richard, 227
Patten, John, 44
Pauen, Michael, 12, 238n2
Paulhus, Delroy, 10, 124, 125–126, 127–128, 129, 133
Peake, Philip, 83
Pearce, Jonathan, 15n6
Penfield, Wilder, 225
"people problem", 11, 141–157
Peplau, Letitlia, 132
Pereboom, Derk, 3, 6, 8, 12, 15n3, 19, 20, 21, 22, 25, 26, 27, 29, 35, 38n1–39n3, 144, 158n2, 158n4, 158n11, 159n18, 206, 208, 287n2
"personhood-based" desert claims, 142, 151, 155, 157
"pessimists", 143, 146
Pettit, Philip, 287n5, 288n12
Petty, Richard E., 77, 79
Pfeffer, Jeffrey, 131
physiology of movement, 260–261
Piazza, Thomas, 132
Pinillos, Ángel, 210, 212, 214, 217
Plato, 75–76
Pockett, Susan, 14, 178, 183–184, 199, 201n10, 201n12, 267–268, 269
political conservatism and belief in free will, 126–127, 133, 134–135, 137, 140n7

Popper, Karl, 55
"pragmatic sentimentalist approach" (PS-approach), 14, 273–274, 279, 287n4
Pratto, Felicia, 132
preservationist approach to error, 204, 205–209, 212–213, 213–217, 217n4, 218n13
Priestley, Joseph, 29, 38n1, 210
Principle of Humanity, 9, 63–64
Prinz, Jesse, 288n20
punitiveness and belief in free will, 126–127, 131, 251
Purdy, Suzanne, 267
Putnam, Hilary, 61, 205

qualia, 240, 255–258
qualia of willing, 257–258, 260–262
quantum mechanics, 3, 9, 19, 28, 55, 56, 182. *See also* indeterminism
Quillian, Lincoln, 71

Rachels, James, 99, 158n13
Rakos, Richard, 125
Rasmussen, Theodore, 225
rational consent without free will, 151–156
Ravizza, Mark, 15n5, 21, 184, 288n12
Rawls, John, 142, 153, 155–156, 157
reactive attitudes, 7, 11, 14, 19, 34–38, 97, 107, 143–145, 147, 273–274, 277, 288n9
reasons-responsiveness, 21, 81–84, 184, 186, 192, 196, 288n12
reductionism, 187–189
reference, 12, 191, 204–206, 217n2, 218n8; causal-historical account of, 205–206, 207–208, 210–213, 217n2, 218n8, 218n9; descriptive account of, 204, 206, 209–213, 217n2, 218n8; and free will, 12, 191, 206–209; liberal view of, 12, 205–206, 214, 215, 217n2; pluralistic approach to, 209–213, 218n8; restrictive views of, 12
reflective equilibrium, 90, 94–95; wide, 94–95, 98
relativism, 91, 92–94, 99–100, 102n8. *See also* cultural relativism; framework relativism
religiosity and belief in free will, 126–127, 132–133, 134–135, 136–138

retributivism, 6, 30, 59, 62, 68–70,
    134–135, 137–138, 140n7, 140n10,
    142, 157, 164, 251
revisionism, 12, 179, 190–191, 192,
    193–200, 208–209, 217n4–218n5,
    218n7, 218n14
Rieger, Jochem, 238n2
right wing authoritarianism, 126–128,
    131–133, 134–139, 140n9
Rigoni, Davide, 123, 268
Robertson, Donald, 215
Robichaud, Philip, 289n29
Robinson, William S., 241
Roedder, Erica, 280
Rose, D., 203
Rosenthal, David M., 61
Roskies, Adina, 182, 201n11, 203, 273
Roth, Jane, 228
Rotter, Julian, 79
Rotter, Stafan, 182
Rubin, Zick, 132
Russell, Bertrand, 67
Russell, Paul, 217n1, 288n9
Ryalls, Kenneth, 70

Sabini, John, 289n25
Sadurski, Wojciech, 158n13
Sapolsky, Robert, 68
Sarkissian, Hagop, 202n20, 203, 248
Sartori, Giuseppe, 123
Sartre, Jean-Paul, 44
Scanlon, Thomas, 19, 277
Schaubroeck, Katrien, 289n29
Scheffler, Samuel, 159n16
schizophrenia, 259
Schlick, Moritz, 29, 59, 66
Schnall, Simone, 280
Schoeman, Ferdinand, 31
Schooler, Jonathan, 5, 123, 124, 125,
    202n27, 215, 249, 250, 266–267
Schrödinger's equation, 270
Scot, Reginald, 213, 218n11
Searle, John, 61, 165, 201n16
self. *See* sense of self
self-forming actions (SFAs), 49
Seligman, Martin, 78
semi-compatibilism, 15n5, 58, 114–115
sense of agency, 13, 163, 228–230, 236,
    238n1, 258, 260, 261. *See also* feeling
    of free will
sense of self, 162, 163–164, 167, 168–170,
    232, 248, 255–256
Seuferling, Greg, 283
Shakespeare, William, 122, 123
Shallice, Tim, 226, 233, 239
Shariff, Azim F., 251, 252n9
Sher, George, 76–77
Sherman, Steven, 70
Shoda, Yuichi, 83
Sidanius, James, 132
Sie, Maureen, 4, 14, 16n9, 273, 279, 281,
    285, 287n3, 287n5, 288n10, 289n26
Silver, Maury, 289n25
Simmons, Carolyn, 73, 132
Sinnott-Armstrong, Walter, 140n8
Sirigu, Angela, 260
situationism, 4, 52n7, 71, 201n19, 243,
    246–247, 251, 274, 283, 289n25
Skala, Sarah, 125
skepticism about free will. *See* free will
    skepticism
skepticism about moral responsibility. *See*
    free will skepticism; moral
    responsibility
Slane, Stephen, 125
Smart, J. J. C., 29
Smilansky, Saul, 3, 6, 10, 15n6, 16n12, 33,
    52n7, 105, 106, 108, 112, 113, 115,
    116, 117, 119n2, 121, 124, 158n2,
    158n13, 159n16, 249
Smith, Michael, 287n5, 288n12
Sniderman, Paul, 132
Snyder, Sam, 15n2, 249
social contract theory, 155, 157
Social Dominance Orientation Scale
    (SDO), 132–133, 134–135, 136–138
social intuitionism, 16n9, 68, 286, 289n28
Solomon, Robert, 69
Sommers, Tamler, 6, 10, 16n7, 38n1, 88,
    89–91, 92–94, 95–97, 98–100,
    101n2–101n3, 101n6–102n9, 140n3,
    146–147, 202n20, 215, 217, 252n1
Sommerville, R. Brian, 280
Soon, Chun Siong, 13, 16n9, 227, 238n1,
    245, 257, 273
Sorrentino, Richard M., 132
"soul control", 5, 13, 16n10, 248–251,
    252n9

sourcehood, 2, 186–187, 194
Sparks, Erin A., 125
Speak, Daniel, 202n28
Spencer, Quayshawn, 201n9
Spencer, Steven, 280
Spinoza, Baruch, 20, 38n1, 39n4
Stallworth, Lisa M., 132
"standing" as a human being, 9, 60
Statman, Daniel, 119n1
Sterelny, Kim, 211
Stich, Stephen, 204, 205, 213, 214, 217n3
Stillman, Tyler, 123, 125
Strandberg, Thomas, 280
Strawson, Galen, 3, 8, 12, 16n7, 19, 20, 38n1, 39n4, 52n2, 52n4, 57, 105, 186, 201n15, 206, 212, 215
Strawson, P. F., 7, 11, 19, 34–35, 52n7, 65, 85–86, 117, 142–144, 145–146, 158n6, 158n8, 211, 273, 277, 287n4, 287n5, 288n9
Street, Sharon, 90
"strike back" emotion, 9, 68–70, 86
Stroessner, Steven, 125, 127
Strongman, Jon A., 283
subjective misinterpretation, 281–282, 286
Sulloway, F., 131
Sunstein, Cass, 280, 282

Tangney, June P., 83
Taylor, Richard, 21, 26, 67
Taylor, Shelley, 123
Thaler, Richard H., 280, 282
Thomas, Judith Jarvas, 288n19
Thomas, Keith, 213–214
Thompson, Elizabeth R., 283
Thompson, Erik P., 132
threat of shrinking agency, 4–5
Tierney, John, 83, 246
Tocchetto, Daniela Goya, 10
Todorov, Alexander, 246
Tononi, Giulio, 241
Tourette syndrome, 259
The Trap, 108–117
Turner, Jason, 125
Tversky, Amos, 280

Uleman, James S., 282

Vader-Bours, Nicole Van Voorst, 285, 289n29
Valdesolo, Pierearlo, 216
Van Fraassen, Bas, 53
Van Inwagen, Peter, 9, 26, 57, 65, 68, 101n2, 108, 201n13, 287n2
Van Nus, Myrthe, 289n29
Vargas, Manuel, 12, 15n3, 178, 187, 191, 192, 197, 198, 201n8, 201n11, 201n13, 201n14, 201n15, 201n19, 202n28, 206, 208, 212, 215, 217, 217n4, 218n5, 218n7, 218n9, 218n14
Vargas, Stephanie, 202n28
veil of ignorance, 155–156. *See also* original position deliberation
Vilhauer, Benjamin, 11, 15n1, 16n8, 38n1, 158n3, 158n5, 158n9–158n11, 159n18
Viney, Donald, 125
Viney, Wayne, 125, 127
Virgin, Charles, 68
Vohs, Kathleen, 5, 123, 124, 125, 202n27, 215, 244, 249, 250, 252n7, 266–267
voluntariness, 9, 57–58, 60, 64, 111, 239

Wagstaff, G. F., 73
Wagstaffe, John, 214, 218n12
Waldman, David A., 125
Wallace, Jay, 21, 37, 184, 277, 287n5, 288n12
Waller, Bruce, 3, 6, 6–7, 9, 15n1, 15n3, 15n6, 16n13, 36, 38n1, 39n4, 251, 252n1, 252n9
Walter, Henrik, 121
Warnock, G. L., 58
Watson, Gary, 70, 184, 287n2, 287n5
Watts, Alan, 175
Webster, John, 218n12
Wegner, Daniel, 4, 16n9, 38n1, 121, 161, 163, 166, 167, 171, 179, 181, 228–231, 236, 246, 256, 268, 282, 288n22
Wei Wu Wei, 175
Wheatley, Thalia, 16n9, 282
Whitney, Heather, 283
Wielema, Michiel, 289n29
Williams, Bernard, 75, 116
Wilson, Timothy, 4, 16n9, 52n7, 226, 232, 246, 280, 282, 288n21, 288n22
Wolf, Susan, 145–146, 287n3, 287n5, 288n12

Wolpe, Joseph, 215
Wood, Allen, 159n17
Wouters, Arno, 4, 273, 288n7, 288n8, 289n29

Yamauchi, Lois, 73

Zimbardo, Philip G., 283

About the Contributors

Susan Blackmore is a psychologist and writer researching consciousness, memes, and anomalous experiences, and visiting professor at the University of Plymouth. She blogs for the *Guardian*, and often appears on radio and television. Her book *The Meme Machine* (1999) has been translated into 16 other languages; more recent books include *Conversations on Consciousness* (2005), *Zen and the Art of Consciousness* (2011), and a textbook *Consciousness: An Introduction* (2nd ed., 2010).

Gregg D. Caruso is assistant professor of philosophy and chair of the humanities department at Corning Community College, SUNY. He is the author of *Free Will and Consciousness: A Determinist Account of the Illusion of Free Will* (Lexington Books, 2012) and the editor of *Exploring the Illusion of Free Will and Moral Responsibility* (Lexington Books, 2013). He works primarily on free will, consciousness, and human agency.

Thomas W. Clark is a research associate at the Institute for Behavioral Health, Heller School for Social Policy and Management, Brandeis University. He is also founder and director of the Center for Naturalism, and hosts Naturalism.Org, among the web's most comprehensive resources on worldview naturalism, its implications and applications. He is author of *Encountering Naturalism: A Worldview and Its Uses* and writes on science, naturalism, ethics, free will, consciousness, and related philosophical and social concerns.

Daniela Goya Tocchetto teaches economics at ESPM-Sul University and Senac College while completing her PhD in philosophy at the Federal University of Rio Grande do Sul (Porto Alegre, Brazil). She specializes in the philosophy of economics, political philosophy, and public policy. The goal of her dissertation is to connect the growing empirical literature on political psychology up with traditional debates in moral and political theory about justice, fairness, and desert.

Mark Hallett is chief of the Human Motor Control Section of the National Institute of Neurological Disorders and Stroke, National Institute of Health, where his research focuses on principles of normal human movement and the pathophysiology of human movement disorders. He is a neurologist and clinical neurophysiologist. Dr. Hallett has devoted some of his attention to editing and professional organizations, and he has been, for example, a president of the Movement Disorder Society. In recent years, he has been concerned with the physiology of volition and neurological disorders of volition such as psychogenic movement disorders.

John-Dylan Haynes is director of the Berlin Center for Advanced Neuroimaging (2009), professor at the Bernstein Center for Computational Neuroscience, Berlin (2006), and group leader at the Max Planck Institute for Human Cognitive and Brain Sciences, Leipzig (2005). He was previously a postdoc at the Institute for Cognitive Neuroscience and Wellcome Department of Imaging Neuroscience, University College London (2003–2005), and a postgraduate researcher at the Universities of Plymouth, Magdeburg, and Bremen and at the Hanse-Institute for Advanced Studies (1997–2003). He received his MSc (1997) and his Dr. rer. nat. (PhD) in Psychology from Bremen University (2003).

Ted Honderich is Grote Professor Emeritus of the Philosophy of Mind and Logic at University College London and Chairman of the Royal Institute of Philosophy. He has written extensively on free will, determinism, mind and body, consciousness, and other philosophical topics. His books include *A Theory of Determinism* (1988)—subsequently published in two volumes: *Mind and Brain* and *The Consequences of Determinism* (1990)—*How Free Are You? The Determinism Problem* (2nd ed., 2002), *On Determinism and Freedom* (2004), and *Actual Consciousness* (forthcoming).

Neil Levy is an Australian research council fellow at the Florey Institute of Neuroscience and Mental Health, Australia. He is the author of six books, including, most recently, *Hard Luck* (Oxford University Press, 2011) and over one hundred articles on free will and moral responsibility, applied ethics, philosophy of mind, and other topics.

Thomas Nadelhoffer is assistant professor in the philosophy department at the College of Charleston. He specializes in the philosophy of mind and action, moral psychology, and the philosophy of law—which were the focus of his research during his time as a post-doctoral fellow with the MacArthur Foundation Law and Neuroscience Project (2009–2011). He also recently edited *The Future of Punishment* (Oxford University Press, 2013) and co-edited *Moral Psychology: Historical and Contemporary Readings* (Wiley-Blackwell, 2010).

Shaun Nichols is professor of philosophy and cognitive science at the University of Arizona. He works at the intersection of philosophy and psychology. He is the author of *Sentimental Rules*, coauthor (with Stephen Stich) of *Mindreading*, and coeditor (with Joshua Knobe) of *Experimental Philosophy*.

Michael Pauen is professor of philosophy at the Humboldt-Universität zu Berlin and academic director of the Berlin School of Mind and Brain. His research focuses on the philosophy of mind and on the relation between philosophy and neuroscience. Recent papers include: The Second-Person Perspective (*Inquiry* 2012); Materialism, Metaphysics, and the Intuition of Distinctness (*Journal of Consciousness Studies* 2011); How Privileged is First-Person Privileged Access? (*American Philosophical Quarterly* 2010); Does Free Will Arise Freely? (*Scientific American* 2003).

Derk Pereboom is professor of philosophy at Cornell University. He received his PhD from UCLA in 1985, and taught at the University of Vermont before moving to Cornell. He is the author of *Living Without Free Will* (2001), *Consciousness and the Prospects of Physicalism* (2011), *Free Will, Agency, and Meaning in Life* (forthcoming), and a coauthor of Four Views on Free Will (with Robert Kane, John Martin Fischer, and Manuel Vargas, 2007). He has published articles on free will, philosophy of mind, philosophy of religion, and history of modern philosophy.

Susan Pockett is an Odinic wanderer of the academic world. For twenty-odd years she worked as a cellular neurophysiologist in departments of physiology at the universities of Otago, Oslo, Auckland, London, New South Wales, and Manitoba. She then started openly working on consciousness, for two years in the department of psychiatry and twelve years in the department of physics at the University of Auckland. She is now affiliated with the department of psychology at the University of Auckland.

Maureen Sie is professor of philosophical anthropology, on behalf of the Socrates Foundation (Institute of Philosophy, Leiden University) and associate professor of meta-ethics and moral psychology (department of philosophy, Erasmus University in Rotterdam). Since 2009 she has been leading a small research-group funded by the Dutch Organization of Scientific Research with a prestigious personal grant, that explores the implications of the developments in the behavioral, cognitive, and neuroscience for our concept of moral agency, reasons, free will, and personal responsibility.

Saul Smilansky is professor and chair of the department of philosophy, University of Haifa, Israel. He works primarily on normative ethics and on the free will problem. He is the author of *Free Will and Illusion* (Oxford University Press 2000), *10 Moral Paradoxes* (Blackwell 2007), and numerous papers in leading philosophical journals.

Galen Strawson is professor of philosophy at Reading University and at the University of Texas at Austin. His books include *Freedom and*

Belief (Clarendon Press, 1986, 2nd ed. 2010), *Selves: An Essay in Revisionary Metaphysics* (Clarendon Press, 2009), and *Locke on Personal Identity* (Princeton University Press, 2011). He is currently working on a book about the way we experience our lives in time.

Manuel Vargas is professor of philosophy and law at the University of San Francisco. He is author of *Building Better Beings: A Theory of Moral Responsibility* (Oxford, 2013) and with John Fischer, Robert Kane, and Derk Pereboom, coauthor of *Four Views on Free Will* (Wiley-Blackwell, 2007). Apart from free will, his main research interests include moral psychology, philosophical issues in the law, and the history of Latin American philosophy.

Benjamin Vilhauer is associate professor at William Paterson University of New Jersey. He works primarily on free will theory, in Kant and in contemporary philosophy. He has published a number of articles on these topics, in journals including *The Philosophical Quarterly*, the *British Journal for the History of Philosophy*, *Philosophical Studies*, and *The Canadian Journal of Philosophy*.

Bruce N. Waller is professor of philosophy at Youngstown State University. He has published a variety of articles and several books, including *Freedom Without Responsibility* (1990), *The Natural Selection of Autonomy* (1998), and *Against Moral Responsibility* (2011).